# All Women Are Psychics

## by Diane Stein

THE CROSSING PRESS
FREEDOM, CALIFORNIA

*For my grandmother Anna Backman*
*who never told me she was psychic*

Copyright © 1988 by Diane Stein
Cover design by Victoria May
Cover art by Susan Seddon Boulet
Interior illustrations by Francene Hart
Printed in the USA

For information on bulk purchases or group discounts for this and other Crossing Press titles, please contact our Special Sales Manager at 800/777-1048.

Visit our Web site on the Internet: www.crossingpress.com

**Library of Congress Cataloging-in-Publication Data**

Stein, Diane
    [Stroking the python]
    All women are psychics / Diane Stein.
       p. cm.
    Originally published: Stroking the python. St. Paul, Minn. :
Llewellyn, 1988.
    Includes bibliographical references.
    ISBN 0-89594-979-2
    1. Parapsychology. 2. Women--Miscellanea. I. Title.
BF1045.W65S74      1999
133.8'082--dc21                    98-55280
                                      CIP

## Acknowledgments

I would like to thank all the women who wrote to me, who answered my ads and questions and contributed their psychic lives and life stories to this book. Without them, the writing would not have been possible. I would also like to thank all the women who are writing about being psychic, within and without Goddess spirituality. Their books, interviews, stories, and methods are made available for all to read and learn from , and the teaching that they bring us all is vital.

Thanks, too to the women who have helped in the writing: Antiga for her review of the crystal gazing section, Gail Fairfield for reviewing the chapter on channeling, Dawn Richards for correcting my grammar and Theosophy, Lee Lanning and Nett Hart for editorial comments, and Maggie Tongue for comments. Their help and time have been given with generosity and love, and are deeply appreciated. Thanks, also to the several publications who ran my ad gratis, asking women to send me their psychic stories. No book is written alone, and these are some of the women behind the scenes.

*All Knowledge of Fate comes from the female depths; none of the surface powers know it. Whoever wants to ask about Fate must go down to the woman.*

—Helen Diner
*Mothers and Amazons:*
*The First Feminine History of Culture*

# Contents

# Chapter One
# Other Realities:
# Altered States of Consciousness and Psychic Experience

*Because the nature of our inner dimension is qualitatively different from the material world around us, we have no framework for understanding what we experience when working with it. There's a vulnerability, an insecurity, that you feel when working with the innerconsciousness, for there is no objective world to knock up against so you can know your position and what you're dealing with . . . When you understand the dynamics of innerconsciousness you will find yourself more able to trust and work with your own inner powers.*[1]

As a young child, I had the feeling that there was more than I could see. I asked questions, too many of them for grownups' comfort sometimes, and often received no answers, or unsatisfactory ones. Lying in bed at night, I'd wonder what was real, if what I was told or saw for myself was the whole story or if there might be more. I knew that there was another reality, something beyond what I could see or find out about, but that all the answers were there. I'd imagine what that other reality was like, where it existed, and create the possibilities in my mind. At times I knew I'd been there while dreaming, and waking had answers I couldn't logically have known. My parents' reactions to this, if I talked about or let slip what I knew, were often to punish—they thought I'd been listening at closed doors.

Children are universally psychic. They know that reality is multisided, other facets existing but not showing. They know that there are multiple possible realities, each capable of manifesting in its place and circumstance. They know that "real" is a relative term. Women in women's spirituality sense glimmers of this. They use the word "wicca," meaning to shape or to bend, and say that "magick is the art of changing reality at will."[2] Grown wiccans grope for it, but children live it. Children move in and out of the women's cast circles, and the energy of the circle is not broken but follows them. Children see or sense auras, "know things," talk with invisible playmates and faeries, dream vividly and fully, astral travel, predict deaths as everyday happenings, foresee births, see elementals and spirits. All these are real and take place in a children's real world, an alternate world to outside-the circle concepts of reality. The mothers watch and learn to understand, to re-member and re-claim for themselves.

Most children submerge their psychic skills as they grow up. They are told there are no colors when they talk of auras, that no one's there when they talk with a spirit guide or nonvisible animal helper, that they must have overheard adults when they know something, that it's "only a dream," that they can't leave their physical bodies. A child forseeing a death or traumatic event is punished for talking about it or blamed for it's coming true, and so she holds the information and her questions inside, is frightened into repressing and forget-ting what she knows. A child whose unseen friend is ignored by others learns to ignore her, too. Denied the validation of her dreams she stops mentioning them, then stops remembering them. The colored auras around people and animals fade, the faeries go away, the magick stops. Assimilated into the accepted version of concrete reality, the child denies her python self and forgets it exists. A skill or sense unused goes dormant, and the doors are closed.

Entering women's spirituality as an adult, the woman who had been psychic as a child becomes psychic again. She re-opens, re-members and re-claims what she's lost, works to learn again the magick of the python Goddess within her. She becomes a child again, learning to use her inborn senses in a safer, more supportive space, dis-covering and polishing her skills. Exploring the realms of women's spirituality in ritual or divination, herb lore, Goddess cultures or crys-tals, the python of psychic ability, often unasked for, awakens. Some-times frightening at first, psychic opening awes and exhilarates, fascinates and becomes a coming-together of other skills.

Psychic opening returns to women a part of reality that they thought was lost, a part they were taught to ignore. A new sense is added to the accepted five senses, and another level of reality manifests. Women re-claim their child selves, realities and knowings not gone but long forgotten and withheld. Other magick—deeper and fuller ways of seeing, hearing, knowing and feeling—come into focus.

Stroking the python, the creation Goddess within, re-claims women's heritage and birthright.

Loren is a psychic and re-members her childhood, shares the pain and beauty of experiencing other, unaccepted, multiple realities in a one-sided world. Patriarchy has always denied women's and children's realities, offered a pat explanation not wide enough for creative minds and free-ranging perspectives. This is obvious and evident, often painful, for women who were psychic as children and are again as adults.[3]

> My childhood memories are of seeing and hearing things that were not 'real' to anyone around me. I remember being taken out of kindergarten class one day because I became so entranced with watching the swirls of color and fairy forms around the class, that I no longer responded to what was happening on a mundane level . . . I remember hearing people's thoughts, and seeing the thoughts take form . . .
> I was taken to a psychiatrist for tests when I was six . . . To be told that your experience of life is not real leaves you in a very dubious position in regards to your sanity.

Loren's experiences of seeing auras and thought-forms were and are real. She has re-opened her psychic life and has a child of her own now. She understands and validates her son Gabriel's psychic world, knowing that there are many versions of "real":

> For him, it has been a much more gentle experience, because his mother accepts and nurtures it, and because he is a gentle soul. Sharing what I know of the spirit world with him has been a healing for the little girl in me, who now has a friend.

Leonie as a child felt a oneness with other lives, a rapport with animals. She lived on a farm:

> Anytime there were deer on the property and I was out, one or more of them would come up to me out of the orchard . . . stand within a few feet of me, or even come up to nuzzle me, then turn and go back into the orchard. One summer I also had a moth that came to light on my shoulder at night for about a week or so. It didn't approach the rest of the family, nor did the deer. I also had a very close relationship with dogs and some cats, occasionally birds as well. My special affinity with larger wild animals seemed to disappear when I entered puberty, although squirrels and other small animals remain quite friendly.

She experienced the dreamworld deeply, too:

> I could start a dream, pick it up the next night where I had left it and continue that way for weeks at a time. Primarily these were dreams of situations involving feelings about people and places I had never seen, but have since met and/ or visited. Colors, sensations, and emotional elements were combined, and matched the ones I had later.

In one case she dreamed of an accident, of herself and her mother being killed by a fast-coming ambulance as they crossed the street. Leonie was about eight years old at the time:

> I had this dream repeatedly, at intervals, but was never afraid to walk along that side of the street, until one day when I was with my mother again, and was seized by intense dread about half a block from that intersection. I flatly refused to go any further, or to tell my mother why, but told her she would know later. At last she agreed to cross the street. As we finished the distance on the other side of the street, an ambulance came careening into the hospital's driveway, running a red light, just as I'd seen it in my dream. Had we been standing there, we'd most certainly have been killed.

This was a precognitive dream, a clairvoyant experience.

Diane astral projected as a child and remembers a number of experiences of doing so, as well as experiences of knowing when someone would die. Her earliest experience of foreknowing death was at two years old. She believes she teleported at an early age, and had a vivid experience with apparitions or spirits at thirteen. She has known and accepted her abilities always.

> At the age of nine I astral projected. It was during a full moon in Italy. I 'woke up' one evening and was thirsty. I wandered into my parents' room and tried to wake them up. They wouldn't wake up, so I went to wake up my brother to play (he was six) and he wouldn't wake up, either. So I think I went back to my own room and saw myself on the bed. Upon realizing that there were two of me I figured that I could go outside and play and still not get into trouble (since I would also be in bed and not get caught). I went outside and began to walk up the driveway to get into the neighbor's vineyard. I quickly realized that flying would be a lot easier. So I flew.

Flying is fun, and being psychic is fun when the acceptance is there, the acknowledgement inside her of a child's own psychic reality.

Ana was raised in the Native American tradition where her psychic abilities were re-cognized early, respected, trained and nurtured. She was taught by her grandmother, an Algonquin Indian woman raised in the old ways, and initiated into Native American healing traditions, which are matriarchal. Ana saw auras and felt a strong telepathic link between herself, her mother and her grandmother, a link that protected her as a preschool child disabled with seizures. The link now extends through the generations to her daughter and young granddaughter. Ana as an adult is a healer, psychic and medicine woman:

> My family did not ridicule me, I was respected by my cousins and sisters because my grandmother told them I was chosen and special. The family came to me when I was young and still do for questions of health both mental and physical. I was told as a child that my 'gifts' were not appreciated by all peoples and not to talk of them.

These women re-member and have claimed or re-claimed their psychic abilities. Their lives are fuller for them, though in some cases their childhoods were less easy for knowing a reality that adults around them refused. And the issue again is: what is reality? Is it more than a difference in perception or perspective? Spirituality and science, matriarchy and patriarchy have different definitions. The woman or child who is psychic experiences a reality or realities that the concrete patriarchal world denies. She has an inborn matriarchal consciousness, that way of Be-ing.

The patriarchal world view has great investment in a concrete view of reality, a linear view that says there is only one way, and that refuses any event it can't explain or test by scientific methods. Psychic phenomena have been thoroughly tested in the laboratory, yet science still ignores them totally. They present a view of reality that's too threatening. Even where provable, psychic phenomena are personal and cannot be controlled—and the issue here is control. The left-brained rational male mind is totally immersed in empirical science, a science that says prove it and learn to duplicate it at will or it isn't valid. Only what is, is possible. What is, but can't be explained, is impossible and therefore doesn't exist. (A table is a table and nothing else). This hard-line linearity gives the Western world Wall Street, the technology of computers and heart transplants. It comes with an attitude of arrogance and superiority toward everyone but other patriarchs, and with an attitude of conquer (not live with or cooperate with) the Earth. Values are materialistic and unfeeling, and often are racist, ablist, classist, sexist and misogynist.

Matriarchy, women's value structures, think differently. The emphasis here is right-brain abstraction and creativity. In a woman-oriented Goddess world all possibilities exist and can be manifested, whether they are evident and provable or not. If something is possible, it is, whether it can be duplicated and controlled or not. (A table is a table, but it is also oak wood from a living tree that can be shaped to something else. A table is an altar, or a place to eat on, or a thing for children to play under). Women are psychic, and the experiences of virtually every woman prove this. Psychic phenomena as approved in the laboratory are interesting to a point, but they were already proven outside it. That they are not understood enough to duplicate reliably under laboratory conditions is irrelevant.

The acceptance of matriarchal creative thinking, unlimited reality, has given the world such ideas as weaving, pottery, agriculture, cooking, healing, building and nurturing—all the patriarchally denigrated women's work skills without which civilization would not have developed or people survived. Matriarchal right-brained thinking has given the world religion (solely Goddess worship in the beginning), culture, the arts, every form of creativity and imagination, and the caring of one Be-ing for another. The world view is that all is a part of Goddess, all life is one. The peace and environmental movements, women's spirituality and feminism, civil rights and anti-racism are outgrowths of being one with the planet instead of trying to conquer it. There is no tight-fitting box to compress what's possible in a matriarchal world; the universe is wide open and nonlinear, and reality is individual and collective at once, for the good of all.

There is a difference in focus and perspective here. Loren as a child saw auras, colors and thought-forms. Non-Western and matriarchal thought honor her as a psychic for her ability to perceive the real but usually unseen. Western patriarchal thought sends her to a psychiatrist, questioning her sanity, her fitness to live in a linear, non-imaginative world. Matriarchal perspective honors the child, mourns the loss into adulthood/patriarchy that stops the colors and traumatizes her, without teaching her to use both realities comfortably. Patriarchal reality approves when the colors stop, ignores and devalues Loren's perceptions until they do. There is no room for colors in a linear world.

Both Loren's colors and the patriarchy's insistence on "nothing there" are real. On the plane of concrete reality, there are no "invisible" colors. On the plane of unseen realities, psychic sensitivity beyond the physical senses and matriarchal forms of Goddess consciousness, there are colors indeed, and countless other psychics see or sense them, not to mention all the children who see the colors until they are told that colors are impossible. Perception is the difference, the crucial thing here, perception and perspective, and perception and perspective are crucial keys to fostering psychic development in women.

Says Eileen Garrett, one of the great woman mediums and psychics who cooperated extensively with science to find proofs for parapsychology, the idea of perspective is all important.

> The supersensory experiences of clairvoyance, trance, telepathy and so on depends upon a fundamental shift of one's awareness. The field of stimulation is itself changed.
> I can now consciously shift my breathing when I choose and by doing so I can constantly change my activity from one phase to another.[3]

Medium Gail Fairfield, quoted earlier, expressed something similar. There are alternate forms of reality, alternate levels, and women who stroke the python learn to shift between them. They re-cognize both values, the concrete and the formless, as real, and train themselves to perceive and move between realities. Loren's colors and "a table is a table" are both at once. Entering between the worlds in ritual is a version of this, and so is the shift in concentration between the here and now and the events going on between pages when reading a good book. It begins to make sense. Says crystal ball gazer Antiga, clairvoyant divination (or being psychic in other ways):

> is a way of looking at the world and my life in that world from a different perspective. This perspective is round and whole—no part of it is split off from the rest.

Though women's and patriarchal perspectives and perceptions seem miles apart, a group of highly placed scientists, the quantum physicists, are working to combine the views—and are succeeding. They are renegades in science, children with the frogs still in their pockets, who get away with it because of ideas so complex that they only understand each other. They talk of a world of hard matter but define matter in terms of open space, the spaces between atoms and the nonstatic activities of atoms themselves. A table is a table for them, but also much more.

According to accepted scientific thought, all matter is made up of atoms, and an object's hardness or density depends on how fast the atoms are moving. In quantum physics, matter is made up of not only atoms but of the vast spaces and electrical fields between and inside them, and atoms themselves are made up of complex component parts. The grade-school model of an atom looking like a solar system, electrons and protons whirling around a solid nucleus, has given way to other things that are almost beyond definition.

Arthur Koestler, in his book *The Roots of Coincidence*, presents a chapter titled "The Perversity of Physics," in which all of scientific theory of reality becomes a comedy of the impossible, improbable and unreal. The point of the discussion is this:

> When we get down to the atomic level, the objective world in space and time no longer exists, and the mathematical symbols of theoretical physics refer merely to possibilities, not to facts.[5]

A table is a table, on one hand, but on the other it is "sheer nothingness," comprised mainly of the empty spaces and energy fields between the small amounts of actual atomic matter that comprise it.

"The interior of the atom is empty," and the atoms themselves, of which all matter is supposedly comprised, "turn out to be not things but processes."[6] Since science in all its linear glory cannot define reality, the quantum physicists proceed to blithely and happily go about proving what psychics, healers, mystics and non-Western cultures have known for thousands of years: that reality is multiple and creative, and the world consists of not one linear way but of limitless possibilities. The physicists think they discovered it, but women have always lived and experienced it. To quote another of the physicists:

> If we choose to regard our existence within the framework of quantum physics, then every time we look at an object, we are to some extent making a construction of reality: the universe changes each time we alter our method of observation![7]

Or to put it in a woman's terms, that of Christian mystic Evelyn Underhill:

> It is a paradox of human life, often observed by the most concrete and unimaginative philosophers, that (wo)man seems to be poised between two contradictory orders of reality. Two phases of existence—or perhaps, two ways of apprehending existence.[8]

These two ways of apprehending existence, two orders, Lawrence LeShan calls the difference between sensory and clairvoyant realities. They can also be defined as the difference between linear and psychic realities, or the difference between patriarchal and matriarchal consciousness. They are the difference between "a table is a table" and Loren's colors.

Women who stroke the python are aware of and live in both realities, and learn to shift from one reality to the other. The perspective in stroking the python (or what LeShan calls the clairvoyant reality) is one of going beyond the linear. It's an addition of perspective and perception that mirrors the difference between patriarchal and matriarchal emphasis. While sensory/linear reality is necessary for survival in the concrete world, this form of perception is a limited and incomplete way of experience. Women's matriarchal reality, clairvoyant reality, sees the world in terms of oneness and wholeness (Antiga's quote), and perceives the possibilities of the unseen and implicate along with the linear parts. Going even beyond the clairvoyant reality is yet another reality mode, what LeShan calls transpsychic awareness,[9] Gay Bonner calls the God As You, and women in women's spirituality calls Goddess.

In Marion Weinstein's terms:

> We live in two worlds: the World of Form and the Invisible World. In this case, the World of Form is manifest as our planet, Earth. The Invisible World includes 'Everywhere' else. But our goal is to move and to *live* perfectly and easily between the Worlds—always.[10]

Her world of manifest form is the linear world, while the invisible world and "everywhere else" includes the matriarchal, Goddess and python-within perspective.

Along with the concept of multiple realities and the world of possibilities is the concept of nonlinear time or the idea that all time is one. In women's shift of perspective from the linear to the multi-possible, from patriarchal to matriarchal realities, time is an important factor. Though seeming to be a fixed concept, a procession of minutes, hours, days and years following in a row, time is subject to the laws of wicca and can be shaped at will.

There are spontaneous examples of this, familiar ones: a work day in the office lasts forever, but the same length of time on a beach flies. A day moves far more slowly in a child's life than in an elder's. A psychic healing can take a few moments or an hour, but the healer and healee lose all conception of time in the process; time seems to stop entirely. A woman experiencing a precognitive dream or incident sees events before they manifest on the physical plane. Psychic awareness defies the linearity of time, and psychic events happen without regard to what the clock measures. In women's matriarchal, nonlinear thinking, time is simultaneous, a concept known in spirituality circles and rituals as being between the worlds, and an idea known always to Native American, Indian, African and other non-Western peoples.

Science has its version of it.[11] If it takes a beam of light eight minutes to travel the distance between the Earth and the Sun, there is always a time lag on Earth as to what is happening on the Sun itself. If a woman is standing on the Sun and a woman is standing on the Earth, and both are witnessing an event, which woman is seeing the event "now"? "Now" occurs at a different moment for each, and so which of the "nows" is the real one? In quantum physics, Einstein gave a concept of space-time, in which time and space are inseparable from one another. Psychic reality places "now" within a multitude of possibilities, as it does the concept of the "real."

Eileen Garrett puts it this way:

> Everything that was, is, and if you are a sensitive you stumble on it.
> On clairvoyant levels there exists simultaneity of time, and the clairvoyant message may concern future events and future relationships which today seem impossible, or meaningless to the person to whom they are revealed.

> Since at clairvoyant levels time is undivided and whole, one often perceives the object or event in its past, present and/or future phases in abruptly swift successions.[12]

Jane Roberts, channeling an entity called Seth, discusses extensively the concepts of time and perception. Her conclusions, ones very close to the concept of time in wiccan ritual, are that all time is now and all space is here. Along with this is the idea of multiple possible realities, multiple dimensions, and multiple simultaneous lives.

> Time as you experience it is an illusion caused by your own physical senses . . . The physical senses can only perceive reality a little bit at a time, and so it seems to you that one moment exists and is gone forever, and the next moment comes and like the one before also disappears.
>
> But everything in the universe exists at one time, simultaneously. The first words ever spoken still ring through the universe, and in your terms, the last words ever spoken have already been said, for there is no beginning. It is only your perception that is limited.
>
> There is no past, present and future.[13]

Time as a simultaneous or now concept is relevant in understanding and using a number of psychic skills. All forms of clairvoyance and precognition operate in this open time frame. Incidents of astral projection where the woman is seen in two places at once (dopplegangers) involve it. The concept of manifesting and movement of matter uses it. Past lives and reincarnation work are especially based on the idea of simultaneous time. *The Seth Material* discusses multiple concurrent lives and multiple possibilities, where all choices are experienced instead of only the one put into action. Much of this is advanced stuff, but going back to the examples of the Sun and the day at the beach, it's not so far-fetched at all.

In Lawrence LeShan's model of the clairvoyant reality, time is linear only on the sensory level. On the psychic level, "all events *are*" and past, present and future are meaningless limits. Past, present and future are all happening at once, and it's only the linear perspective that creates a narrow window on the present, that makes the present seem to happen in the now.[14] This theory, derived from interviews with Eileen Garrett, is reinforced by classical mysticism, (particularly Hindu and Zen thought), and reinforced again by the gurus of quantum physics:

> According to modern mechanics (field theory) each individual particle of the system, in a certain sense, at any one time, exists simultaneously in every part of the space occupied by the system.

and

> The world thus appears as a complicated tissue of events, into which connec-

tions of different kinds alternate or overlap or combine and thereby determine the texture of the whole.[15]

In the psychic perspective of reality, time is eternal, and all time is now; time and space are one. Leonie dreamed of the runaway ambulance before it threatened her, and also knew on which day to cross the street away from it. Diane knew when someone in her family would die. These are cases of precognition, of knowing before it happens. A clairvoyant may look at the future as if remembering it, though she has not experienced it yet.[16] The matriarchal python concept of time and space, of what is real and when is now, includes a perspective of merging all time into one time, simultaneous time. Time so merged becomes something that can be tapped into and manipulated, used as a tool. Through this awareness comes the skill of manifesting, from creating convenient parking spots to sequences of life changing events. Yet linear time still exists, too, and linear reality denies and defies the concept. Both linear and psychic/clairvoyant realities exist.

Gay Bonner, the entity channeled through Sheila Reynolds, puts it this way:

> As you are beginning to become aware, all is now. Cause and effect don't exist. Now is all. You can see how important now is. It means your control of past and future is now. Right now.[17]

According to Sheila and Gay, reality does not include linear cause and effect on the psychic plane, and does not include past, present or future here. Reality is all possibility and without time constraints. With these ideas in mind and the concept that "magick is changing reality at will," the woman psychic is in the position of the Fool card in the tarot: everything is possible.

Time and realities are simultaneous, and so are women's lives. Women have had experiences showing them realities beyond the linear "now," times when two "nows" merge. Bonnie describes this incident, occurring when she was very ill, of slipping in and out of two realities. She was in her room, and in another room at once:

> It was nearly noon and I couldn't wake up for keeps. I kept slipping back into another room. The ceiling was high, at least twelve feet, the room large, ceiling cream with a six-inch fancy wood moulding around the edge. There was a narrow door to the left of the bed, a thick white door, standing open. An outer screen door led to a small outside landing and wooden steps. It was late afternoon by the light and tree leaf shadows were on the walls. I could hear the wind in the trees.
>
> I was lying on a bed, head to the screen door wall, on starched white sheets with wrinkles. A male attendant with a clipboard went in and out. I knew he was

not a doctor. It was quiet. The floor was white, 'cast iron' plants were in a wicker window box stand to my right. I was old. (I assume male, by the attendant).

Every time I woke up, I was confused that it was still morning here, and shocked to see the small room. Though I tried to break free, it was impossible to shake the image. Every time my concentration faltered, I was back in that other room.

I managed to go to the bathroom, and as I sat down, a second bathroom was superimposed over it, seeing both at the same time. The other had a big space to the right and left of the toilet, which now had an oak seat, the toilet bowl deeper, with a pull chain. Brass fittings were on a metal sink. White, small tiles were on the floor. A fern stood in a wicker stand to the left front of the toilet. There was lots of light-windows. I was half here and half there. I struggled back to bed. Mom asked if I was ever getting up. I said, 'No, I have to die before I come back.' And I have no idea why I said that.

I went to bed, and instead of flipping to that other room, it stayed mine. But now there was a sense of a tightly enclosed space around me. Suddenly, it felt as if my feet flipped down and my body slid. I thought, 'Apricot satin, how decadent . . .' Then I was fine, the room never returned.

I believe I was that closely meshed with a previous existence (or *someone's* anyway), and that only that person's death and realization of it could snap me back. I think that last flip upright was the coffin being slid off a wagon for burial—and that thought an aesthetic caustic comment on the coffin liner. By then I was in my own bed and body, and the last was only *feeling*, not visual . . .

I have flipped before into a past, but only for a second and never before to that extent, or that difficult to get out of.

Gloria's present life also slipped into an alternate reality. Jane Roberts and Marion Weinstein, whose work is discussed more fully throughout this book, state that women live many lives, and live them simultaneously. Bonnie and Gloria describe touching upon other existences. Here is Gloria's other reality:

We had driven up an old narrow, winding road. Pine and aspen grew thick beside a small stream which the road follows. We were in no hurry, enjoying the scenery, when I heard a sound I couldn't identify at first. So I turned the radio down and listened. It sounded like horse hooves and a constant other sound.

My friend inquired what was wrong, and I told him I heard something. About then I saw a horse drawn buggy in front of us. The other sound was the buggy wheels. We were travelling faster than the buggy, so I braced myself with an arm on the dash for the collision.

We drove through the carriage and I turned around quickly to examine what I saw. The carriage driver was very ugly with hard set features. He had pale skin and wore a tall hat. The carriage and horse were black. There was a woman passenger with a black veil. Their clothing was black.

I told my friend to stop. I was trembling with excitement and fear, and curiosity all at the same time. We sat there in the road as the carriage caught up with us. It passed through and was once again ahead. This time I examined it more closely. My senses told me I was seeing the same road but another time. The driver worked for an undertaker, and he was driving this woman home.

She was numb. I could feel as she felt. She heard the horse hooves and the wagon wheels as I did.

I told my friend to drive slowly but to follow what I was describing. My friend could see nothing unusual. It was like I was seeing two roads, a movie film running. Along with regular time there was another time. These bits of film are like holograms. I could examine all sides if there is time to. I can feel the emotions and learn what is being felt, even her memories, if it lasts long enough. 'He is gone' was the only other impression I could feel from her. She was sobbing inside, though there was no sound.

About a quarter of a mile down the road the carriage slowed and turned left across a long bridge crossing the stream. The bridge was there in both times, but there was a chain across it now and tall grass and young trees in what was a road continuing on out of sight.

We stopped the car and I watched as the carriage went down the lane back into the woods. She was going home, back to an empty house. Her numbness was the strongest feeling I could feel.

There was nothing I could do for her. There were 'no trespassing' signs on the old bridge. I didn't feel there was any message for me or any reason why I should invade on her sorrow anymore. These things don't have to have reasons. It was a strong emotional moment that we shared across time, so we went on.

Gloria's experience took place in 1975, off Highway 34, between Drake and Glen Haven, Colorado. Her experience and Bonnie's illustrate graphically the idea of other realities, simultaneous realities, and the concept that all time is now. More stories from both women follow in this book.

Women aware of space-time reality, and simultaneity of time, find themselves drawing what they need into their lives. The events occur at the right time by "coincidence" or "synchronicity," a tapping-in consciously or not to the limitlessness of the universe. Examples happen again and again, and are less dramatic than Bonnie's and Gloria's experiences. In a typical one, a woman walks up to another one in women's space, one she barely knows, and asks her, "Do you know anyone who's looking for an apartment?" The woman she asks is looking for an apartment. In another example, looking for a quote from Sandra Stevens for this chapter, I opened the book at random and found my quote on the open page. Women developing psychically experience these all the time, and later learn to manifest them at will.

The science-accepted theories of synchronicity were developed by C.G. Jung, Wolfgang Pauli and Paul Kammerer, a psychologist and two scientists, in another example of giving patriarchal approval to an idea women have always been aware of. Kammerer developed the idea first, offering the model of a "world mosaic," the wholeness and unity of experience that Antiga and other Goddess women speak of.

He re-cognized the existence of a world unifying force, an "acausal coincidental principle ... (that) brings together objects or events with some affinity for each other."[18] Women call this force Goddess or Goddess within.

Jung and Pauli developed the concept, which Jung named synchronicity, and other psychics and mystics who have always used it have carried it further. Marion Weinstein works with it in interesting ways. What it comes down to is that "coincidences may result from our ability to control the form of events by the very way in which we think."[19] They are operative in every aspect of psychic reality, and controlled by the process of manifesting or visualization (discussed in Chapter Six). They are another form of the space-time psychic reality that differs from linear versions of space and time, and also are a function of this nonlinear reality.

Rigidly defining things in terms of space, time and individual (unrelated) events is a Western and probably Christian concept. The matriarchal/wiccan/women's spirituality world view is wholistic and cyclical. There is a unity in all things, known as Goddess, and Goddess exists in all that lives. Events in a Goddess universe are cycles rather than isolated. When the Wheel of the Year ends at Hallows, the new year and new Wheel rebegins. There is a pattern of flowing, of waxing and waning and waxing again in a circle. Where Christianity sets a beginning and ending date for the birth and death of its God, [19] women's spirituality includes the Goddess' emergence at Yule as implicit in her underworld descent at Hallows. Time is a continuance, and Goddess does not live or die, start or end; she simply and inclusively *is*. Goddess time is not linear time or patriarchal time, but psychic, matriarchal and circular.

In a system of wholeness, coincidences are regarded with an "of course" attitude, and the nature of both reality and time are very different from the linear patriarchal mode. What exists or could exist, is. A woman who sees herself as Goddess within, sees all others as Goddess and all the parts of the universe as parts of her life. She is tapped into the source, the abundance, that gives her what she needs, when she needs it, without harm or deprivation to anyone else. There is a basic harmony of Be-ing in the Goddess universe, and the woman psychic operates in cooperation with that basic harmony or natural law. Where all things are related and reality is a series of possibilities, nothing is coincidence. Everything is part of the pattern and plan, and women very definitely self-determine, within natural law, what the plan for them is to be. There is free choice and free will over a multiple of possible realities.

These ways of perceiving are very different from the concreteness of the patriarchal world. Since perception is nonlinear, the ways of gaining meaningful information about other reality and time models is also nonlinear. Put more simply, in the concrete world there is one way of seeing and one set of meaningful data, but in the matriarchal psychic world there are different ways. Sensory perception is not enough and does not provide clairvoyant information. Psychic information, like psychic perception, goes beyond the senses.

In the patriarchal linear reality, information is gained only by the senses, by cause and effect, by scientific method. Any information not gained in these ways is ignored. Establishment medical doctors ask a patient what's wrong, but they won't take her word for it until enough tests, numbers and mechanics say the same thing the patient did. In matriarchal psychic reality, the reality of stroking the python, information is gained beyond the senses, by women's knowing. A healer asks the woman being healed what the problem or issue is, and together they work on releasing that issue. The woman seeking healing knows what's wrong, and her knowing is not denied. The woman experiencing a psychic incident knows that the information she's received is real, and she acts accordingly. She is able to determine for herself where truth is, and when it is. Leonie knew there would be a careening ambulance, and she knew when to cross the street.

How that information comes, that knowing comes, is seen as a manifestation of Goddess reality. If Goddess is something within everyone, and all life is a part of her, there is a oneness and unity of all the universe. Information is shared, is a part of what Jung calls the collective unconscious, to be tapped into by anyone open to it. This tapping-in is a woman's work skill thoroughly derided and denigrated by the patriarchal system that is both afraid of it and envious of it, a system that says since it can't reliably duplicate it, it has to ignore it. The skill is women's intuition, her stroking the python, creation Goddess, matriarchal consciousness that has access to more than sensory knowing.

Women's intuition is an entrance into the unity of creation or into Goddess within. It's a way of knowing that goes beyond explanation into a state of heightened awareness. The awareness can be an instantaneous flash or a slower inner certainty. It can be accredited to coming from Goddess or Goddess within, from the higher or inner self, from discarnate spirits, helpers or guides. Different women define it differently, but wherever it comes from, it's a way of gaining accurate information to the psychic or clairvoyant reality, a way of becoming part of the timeless and whereless space-time/Goddess continuum.

Every act of psychic knowing is an act of women's intuition, and a major part of using it is the ability to shift back and forth between linear and psychic reality at will. Spontaneously, the shift occurs at times of deep relaxation or times of intense emotional involvement. Every non-Western culture has teachable methods for inducing the relaxation state and/or focusing the emotional one, causing the shift in perception to happen. Emotional desire is discussed more fully later, under visualization and manifesting. The most commonly known name for the relaxation process, the basic process of shifting perceptions and realities to intuitive levels, is meditation.

Meditation is the ability to shift from sensory to intuitive information, from isolated concrete aloneness to Goddess unity and the collective matriarchal consciousness. Every psychic experience occurs in the state of concentrated awareness that is more than sensory and concrete, whether that state has been induced consciously or not. The meditative state is chosen and controlled, evoked at will, learned and teachable to others. Its method is available to everyone, able or disabled, and the basic root of women's psychic development begins with it.

Quoting Eileen Garrett again:

> There are certain concentrations of consciousness in which awareness is withdrawn as far as possible from the impact of all sensory perceptions . . . Such withdrawals of consciousness from the outer world are common to all of us in some measure, in the practice of prayer, meditation, and abstract thought.
> What happens at these times is that, as we withdraw from the environing world, we relegate the activities of the five senses to the field of the subconscious, and seek to focus *awareness* (to the best of our ability) in the field of the super-conscious—the timeless field of the as-yet-unknown . . .
> In such types of consciousness-activity all our illusions of present time, or situation in space, and differentiations in consciousness (individuality) are transcended.[21]

Meditation is the key to shifting realities from the daily patriarchal and linear to the between the worlds of intuitive awareness of Goddess and psychic reality. Entering this state, which is not a loss of control or consciousness in the everyday world, opens the perceptions to other worlds. It's the place where knowing beyond the rational happens, where biofeedback and psychic healing take place, where visualization manifestation is induced, where the matriarchal consciousness is opened to experiences of clairvoyance, precognition, seeing auras, and knowing spirit guides. It's a skill that is learned and is beneficial to use, with such bonus side effects as inducing grounded-ness, better health, greater mental awareness, heightened creativity, and reducing stress. It begins with full physical relaxation and with clearing the conscious mind of tensions and worries.

In meditation, the brain enters what is called an alpha state, something measurable scientifically on an EEG (electro-encephalograph), a machine that measures and charts brain wave activity. The human brain works on four levels, all EEG measurable, that reflect the type of thinking and consciousness occurring at the time. Linear reality, the everyday form of concrete patriarchal awareness, occurs at beta brain wave consciousness.[22] This is the activity of the rational mind, using linear time and concrete space, as well as sensory perception reality. Beta waves measure from twenty-two to fourteen cycles per second on the EEG.

The next slower level is the alpha state, the level of meditation, from thirteen to eight cycles per second. This is the starting place of matriarchal reality, nonlinear and timeless thinking. The world is unified and flowing at this level, and this is the place of daydreaming and creativity. Rhythmic activities, when the conscious mind dis-engages as in running, occur at the faster end of this level. At the mid-dle and slower end of the scale occur sudden inspirations, intuitions and creative ideas, psychic healing, and most forms of psychic recep-tivity. The meditative mind, disengaged from rational thought, is opened to other, nonsensory information and other realities. Rationality is not lost, just set aside. This is the level reached in meditation work, and is the beginning level of stroking the python, experiencing and using psychic reality.

Theta and delta states are the other two brain wave levels, slower than beta or alpha. The theta level is deeper, seven to four cycles per second, and is marked by a one-pointed consciousness that is a com-plete stepping aside from the linear. The level occurs in brief waking periods of intense emotional consciousness or concentration, the emotional intensity times when many psychic experiences occur, and in sleep.

The threshold between alpha and theta consciousness is the threshold of psychic experience, and this is the time of hypnogogic states of lucid dreaming, astral projection, and the feeling in near death experiences of one's life passing by like a movie. There is complete focus of awareness on the activity going on—emotional state, dream, creativity state or projection—with a total unawareness of other possible realities. Gaps in time that occur while writing or in other forms of creativity are time spent in theta. Some esoteric traditions use drugs in controlled ways to induce this level, such as peyote in Native America. Things are experienced without the ability to rationalize or judge; there is no good or evil, only what is, at this state. Slower than theta are delta waves, which happen in deep sleep beyond dreaming, and are not a part of waking consciousness.

Work by Dr. Lutsia Pavlova, an electrophysiologist at the University of Leningrad in Russia, uses EEG measured brain wave states to register psychic phenomena. She asks her subjects to enter the meditative state of relaxed awareness. When this alpha level is reached on the brain wave charts after about half an hour, the doctor has a telepathic transmission sent to her subject. The subject's brain waves, as shown on the electro-encephalograph, change drastically as the telepathy message is received.[23] Outside of the United States and particularly in Russia, science is aware of psychic development and phenomena, seeking to prove it on a scientific method basis. They are succeeding. Work similar to Pavlova's is also being done in England.[24]

Other scientific work connects psychic phenomena to the brain's temporal lobe, particularly the hippocampus and amygdala portions. The temporal lobe seems to be evolving, changing in shape to asymmetry, and some researchers connect this evolution with increasing numbers of people developing psychically.[25] Scientific knowledge and re-cognition is far behind actual occurrences in psychic reality.

Whatever science has determined, meditation is the simple method for leaving concrete reality and entering the matriarchal, intuitive, stroking the python consciousness level. It's a cumulative skill and a pleasant one, but like tennis or typing does not reach pro-status on the first try.[26] Set aside some quiet, unhurried time every day to do it, either first thing in the morning or last thing at night. Doing it daily, the skill develops and grows without forcing the process. With practice, the alpha to theta state is entered easily and quickly at will, where it can be used for psychic information and for healing work, as well as for biofeedback, problem solving, and physical/mental relaxation.

To begin, find a quiet place to meditate, an uninterrupted spot that feels safe and comfortable. Disconnect the phone. The room should be neither too warm nor too cold, and with a straight-backed chair to sit in or a soft rug for sitting on the floor. This is a private place, alone. Work in loose comfortable clothing or skyclad, and not for several hours after a meal. Light a candle to focus on, and a crystal held in the left hand or both hands is optional. Keep arms and legs uncrossed, unless using the lotus position. Sitting instead of lying down prevents falling asleep, but relaxation is often deeper lying down. Shut off the electric lights, and get comfortable.

Once seated and ready, focus concentration on the candle flame, until with eyes closed the image of the flame remains. Take several full deep breaths to slow and calm the body, and clear your mind intentionally of all outside cares. Emptying the mind of all thoughts is the goal of some forms of meditation, but takes practice and time and may not happen early on. Let go of worries one at a time, acknowledging and releasing each and letting it fade. Cast a surrounding circle of protection and invoke the four quarters to reach a between-the-worlds state, the state of psychic reality. Use rhythmic breathing and a full process of physical relaxation to deepen the meditative state.

Relax each part of the body, step by step. Tense and release each part, from toes to crown, continuing rhythmic breathing. Tense the toes, then relax them, then the feet and relax, the calves, knees, thighs, abdomen, etc. Tense each part of the body from feet to head in turn, repeating it in any part where tension remains. Pay special attention to the muscles of the face, mouth, eyes and head. When every part is tensed and released, check for any left over tension areas, breathing into them or tensing and releasing them again until they relax. The whole body, physically and mentally, is fully relaxed at the end of this. The process is slow, deliberate and quiet.

Margot Adair suggests creating a symbol that represents body relaxation as you go through this process, and using the symbol every time you meditate as a key to reaching relaxation and invoking it at will.[27] She then suggests noticing your mental state, one of physical and mental relaxation with heightened awareness, and creating a symbol to return to that means that state. Create a symbol that represents your psychic center, psychic reality and knowing, also to return to at will. Then:

> Imagine yourelf to be a leaf upon a tree on a warm sunny afternoon. Imagine that a gentle breeze comes along and lifts you up . . . Imagine floating through the air as long as you like and when you're ready slowly fluttering down upon the ground, feeling that you're becoming increasingly aware of yourself with each descending layer of movement, toward the ground. Upon landing on the ground you'll discover yourself at a much more enhanced level of inner

awareness—your inner experience will have become much more vivid . . . and if
you like you can land in a brook and softly, easily float through your inner
dimensions, feeling yourself gently bobbing up and down as you safely rest
upon the surface of the water, and being carried ashore whenever you
wish.[28]

Savor the feeling, experiencing the relaxation in other ways.
Notice your quiet breathing and body, or take yourself on a journey to
a favorite place, imaginary or real. Visit a Goddess or a foremother
and speak with her. Ask her for a piece of information, and feel it float
into your mind. Ask to connect with another woman, and sense her
there in images of sight, sound and touch. Ask her something you
wish to know from her, offer her something from you in exchange,
then wish her well, and the Goddess well, as they leave. Notice how
the woman looks and what she says and does, to ask her about it later
in the linear world. Enjoy the peace and well-being of the process.

When ready to return to now, allow the images to fade, count
from one to five, then open your eyes slowly. Sit or lie still for a few
moments, noticing surroundings and the present without moving yet.
Notice what changes there have been since starting the meditation,
how you feel, and how much time has past, your rate of breathing.
Stretch a bit, then change physical position slowly. You may be pleasantly
spacey, dizzy or feel like you're floating, but this passes soon. Enjoy
the feeling of relaxed and refreshed awareness. Open the cast circle,
then ground yourself by placing palms to the floor, feeling the excess
energy leaving. Get up slowly, and do meditation work again the next
day at the same time and place. Make it a daily habit.

Ability to enter and leave the alpha state grows with practice and
happens more quickly with experience. Duplicate the time and physical conditions daily. Full breathing routines and full body relaxation
are needed at first, but gradually become a shorter process. Eventually
the concentrating keys of the candle flame, the place, time, quiet and
surroundings are enough by themselves to will entrance to the psychic reality through meditation. Eventually the state is triggered with
a few deep breaths or with invoking the symbols created for mental
and physical relaxing, the symbol chosen for psychic reality. This is
called centering and deepening, becoming still inside at any time, and
brings psychic information to the forefront at any chosen time or
place. Enter into the psychic meditative state and ask for information,
and it's there.

A number of books and tapes are available to guide women
through relaxation and meditation processes and how to use them.

Two I recommend highly are Margot Adair's *Working Inside Out*, (Berkeley, CA, Wingbow Press, 1984), and Diane Mariechild's *Mother Wit: A Feminist Guide to Psychic Development*, (Trumansburg, NY, The Crossing Press, 1981).[29] For the woman who meditates regularly, psychic development begins and progresses in steady ways. She may start seeing auras, having precognitive flashes or "coincidences," or realizing her awareness levels have heightened into more creative realities. The changes happen slowly and often imperceptibly, and they become a way of life.

Meditation work is the most major route into stroking the python, the most positive and sure. Once the process is established, it can be used for divination, for psychic linking and telepathy, for manifesting, contacting spirit guides, healing, inducing astral projections, and for just about every other controlled use of psychic experience. Meditation is the key entrance into matriarchal nonlinear realities, the way of shifting at will from linear to nonlinear states, the way to open women's intuition and oneness with the Goddess universe. All the theory of the clairvoyant reality becomes clear with practice and everyday use, beginning with meditation.

Pam writes in a letter from New York State about her place to meditate:

> Although the alpha state comes uncalled at times, most often I get the best results by 'setting the stage.' In the Fall-winter, it's easier to meditate or get into a trance state . . . for me, anyway. I have two special spots in the house where it's most comfortable and works best.
>
> Years ago, when I was a single parent and had very little money to spend, I went to an auction and bought an easy chair and ottoman. It's in one corner of my living room still, and has become my 'spot.' The house is an old Victorian and we supplement heating it with our wood stove. In the middle of Winter, with lights low and the snow falling outside, perhaps a New Age disc on the machine, the chances of having the perfect time for meditation are very high.
>
> The other place is at my desk in my workroom. I haven't spent as much time there as downstairs, but it's turning out to be a great spot. That's where I keep my tarot cards . . . Again, I set the stage with incense and music. There's also a door that I can shut, too. Can't do that down in the living room, so upstairs is a more secluded and personal place.

Shekinah Mountainwater writes about a different style of meditation work, and her entrance into Subuud, before she chose the Goddess:

> Subuud is a world-wide religious organization that most people have never heard of because its membership doesn't believe in proselytizing. I learned to go into trance there, though they didn't call it that. To them it was the 'latihan' and they interpreted it as 'god entering you.' 'Opening' was what they called your first time going into that state. First you had to be 'on probation' for three

months, which meant you sat outside the room where the women were doing the latihan twice a week and listened. The men were doing their's separately, but at the same time. Later, everyone would hang out and socialize and maybe have something to eat or drink. The sounds the women made were eerie and beautiful . . . sort of a moaning/singing kind of sound. At the end of the three months I was brought into a smaller room with a few 'helpers,' people who volunteered to 'open' newcomers, and who also got the group sessions started. They explained to me that I would be given about ten minutes to relax and empty out, then someone would say 'begin' and I was to simply surrender to whatever happened. If I was 'open' I would feel 'god enter me.'

Well, I felt it alright, a kind of floating, drifting, lifting sensation all through me. They said just surrender completely and let whatever happens happen. My arms moved around by themselves and I kind of undulated around the floor, or sometimes just drifted. At the end of half an hour someone said 'finish,' and that was it. After that I went in with the main group and did latihan with everyone twice a week for about two years. Women did all kinds of things in latihan. Everyone was different. Some slept, some danced, some moaned, some wept. And some sang these eerie, wordless, echoing songs.

Later the latihan became a part of my singing. I would find that I was floating into that same kind of trance during songs, especially the more modal and mythical ones.

Sunlight describes a moment of transcendence during meditation:

I was meditating, when I realized with the most amazing feeling, that it was my eternal Self there. It was a very powerful experience and when I had it, I became aware of having it, of knowing that and slipped into my ego-consciousness for a moment, then went back to the feeling/knowledge again for another short time. I haven't had that experience since, but it is still with me in the sense that I know She's there, that I *am* eternal, underneath this body.

The process of stroking the python is begun, of claiming or re-claiming women's intuition, reality and birthright. A lesson in psychic anatomy comes next.

## FOOTNOTES

1. Margot Adair, *Working Inside Out: Tools for Change,* (Berkeley, CA, Wingbow Press, 1984), p. 73.

2. A wiccan proverb, from Isaac Bonewitz.

3. Over the past two years, I have asked women to share their psychic lives for this book, and more than 90 women have written to me. The experiences that appear are given with first names only, unless the women have asked otherwise. This book could not have been written without them, and I thank these women deeply for their time and trust.

4. Eileen Garrett, in Lawrence LeShan, *The Medium, The Mystic, and The Physicist,* (New York, Ballantine Books, 1966), p. 29. Many of the ideas in this chapter are owed to LeShan, and I recommend this book highly.

5. Werner Heisenberg, in Arthur Koestler, *The Roots of Coincidence: An Excursion Into Parapsychology,* (New York, Vintage Books, 1972), p. 51.

6. *Ibid., p. 53-54.*

7. F.A. Wolf, in Rodney Marsden, *Psychic Experiences For You,* (Great Britain, Aquarian Press, 1983), p. 183.

8. Evelyn Underhill, in Lawrence LeShan, *The Medium, The Mystic, and The Physicist,* p. 57.

9. Lawrence LeShan, *The Medium, The Mystic, and the Physicist,* p. 156-159.

10. Marion Weinstein, *Earth Magic: A Dianic Book of Shadows,* (Custer, WA, Phoenix Publishing Co, Revised and Expanded Edition, 1986), p. 2.

11. This argument comes from Rodney Marsden, *Psychic Experience For You,* p. 181-182, but has been discussed in other sources.

12. Eileen Garrett, in Lawrence LeShan, *The Medium, The Mystic, and The Physicist,* p. 37.

13. Jane Roberts, *The Seth Material,* (New Jersey, Prentice-Hall, Inc., 1970), p. 147-148.

14. Lawrence LeShan, *The Medium, The Mystic, and The Physicist,* p. 37-38.

15. *Ibid.,* p. 65-66. Quotes are by Max Planck and Werner Heisenberg.

16. Zak Martin, *How to Develop Your ESP*, (Great Britain, Aquarian Press, 1986), p. 53.

17. Sandra J. Stevens, *Being Alive Is Being Psychic*, p. 99.

18. Rodney Marsden, *Psychic Experience For You*, p. 169. Also in Arthur Koestler, *The Roots of Coincidence*, Chapter 3.

19. Rodney Marsden, *Psychic Experiences For You*, p. 194.

20. Lawrence LeShan, *The Medium, The Mystic, and The Physicist*, p. 48.

21. Eileen Garrett, in Lawrence LeShan, *The Medium, The Mystic, and The Physicist*, p. 55-56. I am indebted to LeShan for making this woman's work available to me.

22. Margot Adair, *Working Inside Out*, p. 9-14, and Rodney Marsden, *Psychic Experience For You*, p. 48-49.

23. Sheila Ostrander and Lynn Schroeder, *Psychic Discoveries Behind the Iron Curtain*, (New Jersey, Prentice-Hall, Inc., 1970), p. 20-21.

24. Arthur Koestler, *The Roots of Coincidence*, p. 123-125.

25. Michael A. Persinger, "Psi and the Human Brain," in *Fate Magazine*, Vol. 40, no. 1, January, 1987, p. 83.

26. Material following is from Diane Stein, *The Women's Book of Healing*, St. Paul, Llewellyn Publications, 1987), Chapter Three.

27. Margot Adair, *Working Inside Out*, p. 26-38. From a superb meditation in a book full of superb meditations.

28. *Ibid.*, p. 35-36.

29. I also have meditation tapes. Try Diane Stein, *Two Meditations: The Goddess Within and The Rainbow of the Chakras*, (St. Paul, Llewellyn Publications, 1986).

## Chapter Two
# The Invisible Woman:
# Auras, Chakras and Psychic Bodies

The concept of a human aura, a radiating luminous cloud surrounding the body, goes back centuries. Pictures from early Egypt, India, Greece, Rome, showed holy figures in a luminous surround long before artists in the Christian era began to paint saints with halos. This convention may actually have been based on the observations of clairvoyants who could reportedly see the radiance surrounding saints. The famous psychic, Mrs. Eileen Garrett, reports in her book *Awareness*, 'I've always seen every plant, animal and person encircled by a misty surround.' According to people's moods, the surround changes colors and consistency.[1]

I am at Bloomer's restaurant, women's space, hearing and watching Nancy Day play piano onstage. She is a composer, pianist, singer. The restaurant is dimly lit and the night is almost over. Mellow and relaxed I listen, watching her perform, enjoying what I hear. Slowly and suddenly, a soft light appears around the woman's head and shoulders as she performs. It's like a clear mist that seems to coalesce, to take form, following the contours of her upper body. It brightens as I watch, being careful not to move and thus to lose it, trying not to blink. I take my glasses off, hold the crystal always with me in my hand, and breathe slowly. I am sitting at the end of the antique bar with my decaf, at the foot of the small stage. The mist changes from clear to an intense golden yellow color, a band of light, brighter and wider around Nancy's head and upper arms, tapering to her waist as she sits at the piano singing. At widest, the color band is about eight inches, at thinnest about four.

The song ends and Nancy leaves the stage to applause, the lights on her dimming and the colors gone with them, evaporating instantly as if a dream. I tell her as she walks down the steps to where I am, "I could see your aura. It was beautiful." There are tears in my eyes, for the beauty. She asks the color, and when I tell her she says, "Someone once told me that my aura's yellow." The experience is magickal. It happens from time to time when I'm relaxed enough, when the lighting conditions are right. It's something to treasure and to nurture. Many women see or sense these colors, and many children.

Women's bodies don't stop with their skins; their visible dense bodies are only a fraction of who they are and what their Be-ing is comprised of. There is more than the physical body: there are four bodies, and eight aura layers, and eight major (out of forty-nine or more total) chakras, dozens of meridians and thousands of nadis (nerve ending centers). Many women see or sense the auras and their colors, and most can learn to visualize in meditation to see the chakras.[2] The healing arts of reflexology and acupuncture/acupressure are based on work with the meridians.

It's important for a woman developing psychic knowing to understand these psychic unseen levels of existence, since what happens in the physical affects the aura, chakras and nadis, and what happens in the unseen levels affect the physical body. A woman who strokes the python works with her psychic levels as much as she does with her seen ones; she is not complete without all of her anatomy. And though work directly with the aura and chakras is primarily the realm of healers, an understanding of psychic anatomy is useful in understanding all forms of stroking the python.

Unseen anatomy has long been known to psychics, healers and nonpatriarchal cultures since the beginning of time. The art and science of acupuncture has been recorded in China for 5,000 years, and used successfully long before that. Western science is beginning now to notice it. The concept of prana was understood in ancient India, long before atomic theory and quantum physics. Hawaiian Huna made use of the levels of the physical/emotional/mental aura bodies thousands of years before psychiatry dis-covered them and gave them "scientific" names. The women witch-midwives and healers of Europe knew about psychic anatomy long before male medicine came along and pooh-poohed it (and destroyed the healers in the witch-burnings)—and long before more recent scientists have renamed and experiment with it now. Psychics and mystics have seen auras for thousands of years, since long before Kirlian photography. The energies of laying on of hands have been known by different names in different cultures, but known and used for countless centuries worldwide. Science is noticing and proving these ancient things, yet no medical book or health course in the patriarchal West mentions that women don't stop at their skins.

The unseen bodies and aura layers, and the vortex spirals of the chakras are comprised of energy, the "nothingness" that fills the spaces and voids of the atom. Quantum physics says that matter is mostly open space, nothingness, and for lack of a better word defines that nothingness between dense components as energy. What energy actually is hasn't been defined in the West, but in Eastern mysticism that energy is long understood. It's called Prana in India, Ki in Japan, Ch'i in China, Mana in Polynesia, Orenda in Native America, and has been given various other names in other cultures and in more recent times.[3]

Prana in India is life or light, the energy that fuels the universe and the unseen psychic bodies, the energy of thought-forms and thought-transference (telepathy). Defined by theosophists as a sun-vitalized energy globule, a collection of molecules, it is drawn into the body through the solar plexus chakra, where the globules separate, each molecule drawn to its specific chakra or energy center for distribution.[4]

As a child I could see these globules, and was laughed at when I told my mother I could see the "air." Other women have told me that they see them, too. Look toward a light-colored distance, toward the horizon especially over water, and watch for rapidly moving particles of clear or yellowish light. They move quickly in a floating motion, and the brighter the day, the more of them and the more rapidly. They are the "energy" of the life force, the Goddess universe. Theosophists have a full theory as to how and when divinity activated them. They fill the scientists' "spaces between atoms."

Prana (or Ki, Ch'i, Orenda, Mana) is separated into seven colors, seven molecules, when it enters woman's aura at the solar plexus chakra/ energy center. Each molecule energizes a different chakra, different energy vortex, and the release of this energy is what causes the aura. This is the energy that transmits thought-forms, psychic information, and is used in laying on of hands/pranic healing. Mary Coddington offers a list of properties for this aura energy, and how it can be used:

1. It can heal.
2. It penetrates everything.
3. It accompanies solar rays.
4. It has properties similar to other types of energy but is a distinct force unto itself.
5. It possesses polarity and can be reflected by mirrors.

6. It emanates from the human body and is especially detectable at the fingertips and eyes.
7. It can be conducted by such media as metal wires and silk threads.
8. It can be stored inside inanimate materials such as water, wood and stone.
9. It can fluctuate with weather conditions.
10. It can be controlled by mind.
11. It can cause things to happen at a distance, and enters into the dynamics of many paranormal phenomena.
12. It can be used for good or evil.[5]

Prana is the building block of the psychic bodies and the fuel source of Be-ing. Taken in through the chakras, it comprises and becomes woman's aura, and the media of psychic experiences.

Woman's psychic anatomy is composed of four bodies, which in turn are built by eight aura layers. The four bodies are the physical, emotional, mental and spiritual.[6] The physical and emotional aura bodies are comprised of one aura level each, one light band, the mental body of two aura levels, and the spiritual body of three levels plus one beyond physical coordinates. Each aura layer and coordinate chakra is connected to one or more psychic skills.

The first body and first aura layer, coordinate to the first chakra, the root chakra, is the *physical aura body*. This is dense physical matter, what can be touched, and also is a psychic mirror of the dense physical called the etheric double. The etheric double is the first aura band, the first layer of energy that comprises the aura and surrounds woman's body. The etheric double connects the seen and unseen woman together by a "silver cord." In astral projection, the dense physical and psychic bodies separate, sending the etheric double and consciousness "flying" while the body remains at home. The silver cord stretches infinite distances, connecting the dense physical woman to her psychic bodies. Its severence is death, when the etheric and unseen bodies return to the astral world for rest and rebirth.

The chakra, wheel or energy center that coordinates with the etheric double is the root center, whose colors are red and black, and body location is at the vagina. This is the center of survival, of incarnation and reincarnation, birth and death, and the place of functioning in the physical world on Earth. This in psychic anatomy is the place of past life experiences. Its physical counterpart is the womb, the gateway of life and death.

All of the chakras are located on the etheric double/physical aura body, but also extend downward to the dense material body and outward to the emotional, mental and spiritual psychic bodies. Chakras are shaped like spirals, the point of the spiral rooted in the central nervous system at the spine, and the vortex or wide part of the spiral, passing through the dense body, at the front. Each chakra has its correspondents in what body organs and attributes it affects and controls, but primarily psychic skills for each center are emphasized in this book. For going further about the chakras, look into the work of Kay Gardner or the traditional theosophists, or read my *Women's Book of Healing.*

Women can see their etheric doubles easily. Enter the meditative state, seated on a dark colored rug floor, the room lit by candlelight from above on a dresser or altar. Choosing a bare portion of skin, arm or leg is easiest, start at the edges of the body, the rug in the background of seeing. Hold your eyes still, but blink when you need to. If you wear eyeglasses take them off, this is not physical sight, and allow your eyes to unfocus. After a few moments, a thin line of light becomes visible, knife-edge thin, running along the contours of the arm or leg. Above that is a red/black ribbon, striped in texture like grosgrain, about a quarter to a half inch thick. Beyond that line is another band of light, from half an inch to a few inches wide. The image is elusive, shifts when you blink, but remains as long as you hold your vision steady on one spot. Lighting conditions are important here—the dark background of the rug, dim room and candlelight from above—and being centered and grounded. The more relaxed the wider the outer band, and the easier the etheric double ribbon is to perceive.

To sense this level nonvisually, rub hands together briskly for a moment, then hold them apart, palms facing but not touching a few inches away. Feel the energy build over a few minutes' time, then slowly fade. The sensation is of warmth, tingling, coolness, magnetism or electricity, and is in fact what causes a dog or cat to spark when you touch her fur in winter. With practice this energy grows, and is the basis for pranic healing, laying on of hands.

The second body of woman's psychic anatomy is the *emotional body*, comprised of the second aura layer and second chakra, the belly chakra. This is the emotional aura, the place of shifting colors or clear misty light that women who sense or see auras are aware of. While everyone has a predominating color or two colors in her psychic emotional body makeup, the colors shift and change with women's

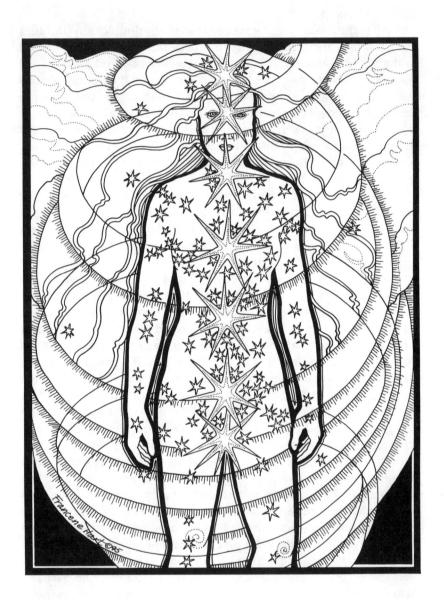

emotional feelings. When you see an aura this is what is visible, and the colors are a universal key to reading emotions.

Clear colors in the aura are clear emotions, unclouded by negativity. Muddied colors are less positive aspects, and grey with a color denotes fear. Darker, deeper colors are more intense emotional states than lighter ones. Red is the life force, and clear tones of red reflect life vitality, deeper tones sexuality. Orange is pride, leadership and certainty; yellow, intelligence and mental activity; green, sympathy and adaptability; rose, loving trust; light blue is clarity and spirituality; indigo blue is devotional; and violet is idealism and union with Goddess.[7] The beginning stage of seeing or sensing these colors is the clear mist, a combination of all the colors together as light. Black is the Earth, associated with the etheric double and root center, rather than the emotional body, and is the combination of all the colors together as matter. This combination is seen in the red/black ribbon of the etheric double aura. Clear and black are the two ends of the color/aura scale.

Psychic development is often marked by the growing ability of women to sense or see the emotional body aura. To find out if you can see the emotional body, try this. Have a woman sit or stand still in front of a white background, light coming from in front of her. The softness of candle light is a good light source. Sit a few feet away from the woman standing, and put yourselves in a meditative state by deep breathing and body relaxation, as in observing the etheric double. Staring steadily at the forehead/third eye of the woman being seen, allow your physical eyes to unfocus and third eye to open. Remove your eyeglasses, if you wear them, for this.

The aura first appears as clear light, shimmering and moving faintly, usually a glow around the head. It appears as a dim haze, then brightens. Colors, or a personality predominating single color, appear after longer watching, and after willing them to happen or asking for them. When you blink, the colors or light waver but do not disappear, as long as both women hold the meditative state and keep still physically.[8] This is what Loren saw as a child, and what many children and women who are psychic see. Many women see the clear light, but not the colors. Seeing colors often develops later, and many women sense the colors without seeing them visually.

To feel the emotional aura nonvisually, hold your left hand above your head or the head of another woman. By the tingling sensation, find the aura, and notice where it ends or stops above your crown. Using both palms, stroke your hands along the unseen line of that aura or tingling, running from the top of the head down the body. Do not touch your or the other woman's dense body. Two hands and working with another woman are the strongest ways to feel this, but it can be done on yourself and with one hand. Use the left hand. The invisible but very much felt energy is the emotional body aura.

The chakra coordinate with the emotional body and emotional body aura is the belly center, located in women between the ovaries and in men at the spleen. Its color is orange, and this is the place of emotions, feeling, the subconscious, taste in every sense of the word, and sexual or nonsexual desires. Imagery and first impression ideas are stored here. The physical location is about two inches below the navel. Tantra yoga develops from this center, and this is the place of clairsentience, the psychic skill of clear feeling, as well as astral travel.[9]

A woman enters a room and suddenly becomes depressed, realizing only later that someone else in the room is depressed. She may not know what happened, but she responds to another's emotions. If she is a healer, she sometimes or always absorbs the symptoms she is working to heal. If a friend is in trouble, this woman knows about it, she doesn't have to be told; the friend could be a thousand miles away. A woman who is clairsentient has a "feeling" and follows it; she is sensitive to situations and to moods of women she is close to. To prevent trauma derived from others' feelings, she learns to protect herself when in a crowd, doing healing work, or when listening to someone in need. Use a circle of light for this protection, clear or blue, or a visualized grounding cord into the Earth to channel off the emotions from this chakra. Wear protective gemstones. Visualize slightly closing down (never shut any chakra completely) the belly center when a clairsentient situation is too intense. Work to develop the heart center instead, for empathy that is less emotional. Astral travel is also associated with the emotional (astral) body, emotional aura and belly chakra. This is women's ability to leave the physical body, and "fly" to other places.

The *mental body* is comprised of two aura bands and two corresponding chakras, usually known as the higher and lower mental bodies. The lower mental level is the rational, conscious mind, the place of patriarchal reality. This level is also the place of thought-forms, and the seat of what the Hindus call the kama-manas, or desire-mind, significant in all psychic work in visualization and manifesting. The higher mental body is the inspirational, imaginative superconscious level of the mind, the place of limitlessness and matriarchal consciousness, the heart.

The lower mental body and lower mental aura is coordinate to the solar plexus chakra, located just above the navel. This center is the psychic energy pump for the physical and nonphysical bodies, the place where prana and nutrition are brought into the system and distributed, and where ideas and psychic impressions are also brought in and distributed. The color of this center is golden yellow, the color of the sun-based pranic energy. Emotional and psychic balance are located at this center, and thought-forms are produced here.

Thought-forms are the energy patterns of desires generated in the emotional body. They are mental constructs seen by psychics in the emotional aura as flashes of rapidly moving light, or as patches of color within the emotional body aura. From the place of the physical, the vibration rates of the psychic unseen bodies increases with distance from dense matter. The etheric double level moves more rapidly in vibration than does the dense material body; the emotional body moves more rapidly than the etheric double level, and the mental body, with its thought-forms, moves more rapidly than does the emotional body. Fewer women see thought-forms visually than see the emotional aura, and fewer see the emotional level than see the etheric double.

In the work of Annie Besant and the theosophists, "thoughts are things" and have impact on the concrete world of form.[10] They are transmitted from the psychic/aura bodies to the "real" world through the mental body and the emotional level, in a merging of the two bodies called kama-manas, the desire-mind. Nothing manifests, according to this concept, without the production of a thought-form or idea and without the emotional desire for the idea to become real. Emotions are powerful things, as any woman in love knows, and emotions are directed and controlled by the mind. Energy from the mind travels by way of the emotions to the etheric double and from there to the dense physical body or world of form. This is the principle of creative visualization and the psychic skill of manifesting. The images of dreams are also created this way, dreams in conjunction with the third eye/brow center and middle spiritual body. Some researchers place astral travel at this level, rather than at the emotional body/belly chakra.

Annie Besant and C.W. Leadbeater describe thought-forms in terms of color and pranic energy. They are created in the mind, which is not the physical brain, and transmitted by way of the energy that is the "spaces between atoms" (or prana) of atomic theory. Psychics see them as whirling objects in the emotional aura, and the ability to see or sense them is developed by working to see or sense the emotional aura. Moving at a more rapid vibration rate, these are visually available to fewer women but the skill is there and can develop in time. A personal experience of watching rose and golden projectiles of light moving through Kay Gardner's aura at a workshop is one I'll never forget, and my only experience so far of seeing thought-forms visually.

The higher mental body is the place of empathy and compassion, of oneness with others, and the place of nonrational thinking, imagination, intuition, the superconscious, and matriarchal consciousness. The linear world expands from the lower mental body's concrete form into the limitless potentials of formlessness and multiple realities. Native Americans call this body and chakra center the place of Be-ing, woman's connection between the physical and spiritual, the Earth and universe as Goddess within.

This fourth aura band is coordinate with the heart chakra, located at the breastbone and between the breasts. Its color is green, though some women working with it perceive it as rose. The crucial skills of love and self-love, of knowing Goddess within, are located here, and the psychic skill for this center is healing. The woman healer uses her knowledge of all the previous levels in her healing work: the rational mind, ability to visualize, ability to sense and to feel, ability to survive physically and help others to survive, and her knowing of the cycle of birth, death and rebirth. She combines these knowings with imagination and intuitive thinking, and with the spirituality levels of hearing, expression, knowing, the nonphysical senses, and connection with Goddess. Healing is a tuning in to all the processes of stroking the python, and is something that can be learned by most women who choose to do it. Healing has a chapter of its own in this book, and a full book as *The Women's Book of Healing*.

The fourth psychic body is the *spiritual body*, comprised of three physical and one beyond-the-physical aura layers with their coordinate chakras. This is the most rapidly moving in vibration of the unseen psychic bodies and the one furthest away from the physical/material world of the dense body. These levels can be experienced, and are operative in most psychic phenomena, but are usually too fast moving to be visually seen. Theosophists connect them to the Three Monads, the three waves of activating life force, and women in women's spirituality translate that to the Maiden, Mother and Crone roles of Goddess. Described from lower to higher, as the lower, middle and higher spiritual bodies, they are not in fact hierarchies, but are compatible, inseparable and overlapping processes.

The lower spiritual body, coordinate with the throat chakra, is the place of communications sent and received. Its color is light blue, in gemstones often aqua, and this is the center of receiving others into yourself and expressing yourself to others. Clairaudience, clear hearing, where the woman who is psychic hears voices giving her information from the nonlinear world, is located here. Such voices are interpreted by many as spirit guides, transmitting from the crown center but received and heard at the throat. All forms of telepathy, receiving information from others nonverbally, are located here, including psychic links and group telepathy. It's believed that telepathy messages are received through the throat center and sent through the middle spiritual level, the third eye. In the spiritual body, skills overlap. Communication on the earth plane is also from this center, as are all forms and expressions of creativity. If you are creative in any way, if you hear information as voices within, if you listen to your "inner self" or "higher self," you participate in lower spiritual level psychic ability. All of us do.

In the middle spiritual body, aura band and chakra, are located the skills that are considered classic psychic phenomena, the skills of knowing, precognition, clairvoyance and clairvoyant divination. This is the legendary third eye center, its color azure or indigo, dark blue, located behind and between the physical eyes. From this level comes the ability to shift between realities, to navigate between the rational patriarchal world and matriarchal limitlessness, to do meditation work and visualization that leads to manifesting. Vizualizations originate in the third eye, then are brought to the concrete world, manifested at the solar plexus center, with the help of the emotions/belly chakra. Dreams are a working together of the solar plexus and third eye centers, the lower mental and middle spiritual bodies.

What is conceived of on this level is brought into the world of form through the mental and emotional bodies, the kama-manas, then into the etheric double before it reaches concrete reality. Seeing or sensing auras and auras' colors happens at this third eye/middle spiritual center, as does receiving psychic information by pictures in the mind. This form of seeing is not physical seeing, but beyond the physical, and being physically disabled by blindness does not prevent its development, or the development of other psychic skills, including visualization. Clairvoyance means clear seeing and is the ability to know information not perceivable through sensory reality or awareness. This is women's intuition, and all women experience this on some level, all women are psychic.

The fastest vibrating of the spiritual body levels that are within physical coordinates is the higher spiritual aura level and crown center chakra. This is the top of the head center, called by the Hopi the *kopavi*, and is the place of women's connection with Goddess, her knowing this connection in everything she does. The color for this center is violet, a color traditionally connected with transcendence. Being a clear channel is the psychic development skill of this higher spiritual body. Women who are mediums and channelers, who connect with spirit guides, are spiritists or automatic writers, work through the knowledge of this center and aura level. Healers work to become a clear channel for the prana/healing energy that comes through them, and some artists and performers are aware of this connection and channeling when they create or perform. A connection with Goddess is an opening of all psychic skills and psychic development, and all psychic development comes from that level of knowing and being a channel.

There is one more aura band, beyond physical body coordinates, that is listed among the major (most easily perceptible) chakras and aura levels. This is known as the transpersonal aura or chakra point, as designated in the work of Kay Gardner.[11] The color here is clear light, all the colors of light merged together, and its attribute is Goddess herself. Feel it by holding your left palm high above your crown center (top of head) and noticing the energy. In discussing psychic skills and psychic phenomena, I place near-death experiences here, and a discussion of what is beyond and after physical existence. There is another reality, or realities, beyond the physical linear world of incarnation on the earth plane.

These are the major energy bodies, with their comprising aura bands and corresponding chakra centers. Other less talked about chakras are those in the palms of the hands that pranic/laying on of hands healers use, the soles of the feet, the lips and in the eyes. There are chakras at the tips of each finger. All of these are developed by recognizing and using them in meditation work, in healing, and in daily awareness and sensitivity.

Petey Stevens, in her aura work, discusses twelve major chakra and aura layers, the seven major physical ones given here, plus five levels beyond the body (and one in each hand and foot):[12]

1. Root chakra, survival chakra (etheric double).
2. Clairsentient chakra (emotional body, belly chakra).

3. Solar plexus chakra (lower mental body).
4. Heart chakra (higher mental body).
5. Throat chakra (lower spiritual body).
6. Third eye, spirit eye (middle spiritual body).
7. Crown chakra (higher spiritual body).
8. Cosmic energy regulator and earth energy regulator (out of body, above and below crown and feet).
9. Probable universe (also chakras above and below the feet, out of body).
10. Possible universe (above and below the body, out of body).
11. Universal chakra (above and below, out of body).
12. All That Is (Goddess and Goddess within).

The five beyond-the-body levels occur above and below the physical body, Stevens' eighth chakra corresponding to the transpersonal point. Each chakra and aura level also contains twelve levels of consciousness within it. Women truly do not stop at their skins.

Along with the four bodies, eight major aura layers and twelve major chakras, there are the meridians and nadis, the radiating channels for prana flow, that are the basis of reflexology and acupuncture. These are connected to the nerve endings on a more than physical level. They have been mapped for 5,000 years and there are thousands of them. Like the rest of unseen, psychic anatomy, the meridians are known to psychics, healers and mystics worldwide, but ignored by anatomical and medical science. All of these are the builders of non-visible anatomy, and the transmitters of energy, prana, psychic information, and thought-forms. They are the rest of woman's body, her emotional, mental and spiritual components as well as her energy/etheric double. Matriarchal consciousness includes awareness of women's full psychic makeup, along with her concrete physical reality.

Many women see auras, know psychic anatomy as more than theory, and learning to see or sense them frequently occurs for women developing psychically. Along with aura awareness comes the awareness of processes, of the transmission of energy in psychic ways, the distances possible in psychic healing, astral projection and telepathy, the nonlinear ways of communication, information and perception that are outgrowths of nonphysical psychic anatomy. The matriarchal feeling of wholeness, of all life being connected and all actions and abilities being important, is a part of this awareness.

Sunlight writes about seeing auras:

> I was at a Friends' Meeting for worship at a women's encampment where we were practicing nonviolent ways of resolving community conflict. Some of the women in the meeting house were glowing around their heads and shoulders. It was beautiful and fascinating to me and I realized then it was their auras I was seeing. After that, I began seeing auras from time to time at AA meetings when someone was talking about her life. Since then, I've seen them in various times and places when I've been sitting quietly listening to someone speak. Most often, they appear to me as white light or tinged with pastel colors, especially green or lavender or golden. Usually they come as a glow, but sometimes they are like colorless flames moving up from the head, like heat waves from the desert or the patterns of different density when a concentrated solution is mixing with water.

The colorless flames are thought-forms, while the glow, beginning as clear light and later becoming pastel colors, is the emotional body aura.

The changes in color and thought-form have meaning enough for some psychic women to do "readings" from them, interpretations of what they see in someone else's aura. Irene experienced such a reading, given by a woman teaching a class in psychic phenomena.

> When it came to me—she said the whole background was blue, a deep blue. She saw a crescent on one side and a pentagon on the other. She said she felt that in a past life I was affiliated with some group or temple—maybe even a priestess. She saw a bright yellow-white light going from the top of my head straight up. She said this was meant I was channeling energy and could be good at it. Then she looked for my guides. . .

The background color is the emotional aura, and the forms of crescent and pentagon are thought-form images. These images can also be carried over from other lives, as the woman doing the reading indicated. Energy being channeled is an important concept, visible in Irene's aura, and everyone has spirit guides, known or not, that this psychic was able to read.

In a similar reading done for me by Ida Shaw, Ida noted from watching my aura both health and emotional traces, and defined them accurately. Watching my friend Sue from across the room, Ida who had not met her, asked me, "Is something wrong with her back? I can only see her aura from the front." Sue indeed has an injured back. A few women see auras continually, and see deeply into them. They use them for healing work and for understanding others, use them as an added sense.

Irene was asked to:

Put my arms straight out and to draw the energy from the guide on my left, visualize it as a healing ball of fire, and send it through my body and out of my right arm to someone I felt needed it.

It was amazing! I could really feel it and the group said they could see it happen.

This is psychic energy, prana, in action.

Ana saw auras as a child, and still sees them, uses them in her work as a healer:

As to auras, I can turn them on or off. But yes, I still use them and see them generally when a healing or reading is requested. I scan the aura for clues to the real nature of the problem since people do not always state their real problem and symptoms do not always mean one particular disease. There are many connections to the inner mind which manifest disease.

When she was a child, she drew people like "giant colored eggs," much to the amusement of adults watching her do it. Her Algonquin grandmother taught her healing and nurtured, trained and respected her psychic abilities.

Eileen Garrett writes of seeing auras as a child, a skill that continued throughout her life. She called them surrounds, and saw them "encircling every living plant, animal and person":

As a child, I knew that the character of people depended on their 'surrounds.' By the quality of the light and colour they gave forth, I could judge their personality . . . By their colour and their tone, I knew whether people were sick or well. This was equally true for me of plants and of animals . . . It was difficult for me to understand what other people meant by personality; for to me personality was a blending of the light nimbus, which surrounds each form, with its physical body. It was the colour and movement of these 'surrounds' of living things, and not the physical body, which gave me complete understanding of their being.[13]

In this passage, excerpted from her 1939 book, *My Life As a Search for the Meaning of Mediumship*, she also writes about prana, the light energy of the psychic bodies:

I first became aware of movement in light and colour before I was five years old. I grew conscious of it by lying still on my own bed and looking into the shadows. I began then, to see globules of light bursting at intervals within the beams of sunlight. When I knew them better, I discovered them moving in any kind of light, they swirled around each other, enlarging and bursting as bubbles do, when they give way one to the other; and just as bubbles reflect colour, so also did the bursting globules have colour within them. These light balls presented themselves in so many shapes and sizes that my head ached from trying to see them all moving simultaneously in many directions. They were always egg-shaped and not quite round. Their movements were like the steps of a dance, weaving in a well-regulated pattern as they swirled.[14]

When seeing auras is a new experience, it can be a startling one.

Present-day psychic Diane saw auras during lovemaking:

> An electric blue light that came from me and surrounded us. . . It didn't mean
> that we were meant for each other or anything other than 1) we were raising an
> awful lot of power, and 2) for awhile we were greater than ourselves.

Her first reaction to seeing the aura color was to scream, and she comments, "I don't normally see auras, especially in color." Intensity of emotion can trigger various forms of psychic experiences; aura colors come through the emotional body.

Pam from Idaho, a different Pam from the last chapter, sees auras regularly:

> Ever since I can remember I have been able to see other's auric fields and subtle
> energies, and know what the energies, colors, disturbances, etc. relate to—
> whether health or personality. Also, I can feel many things, even at distances,
> with or without a mental image. With my left hand I can feel even very minute
> physical imbalances and/or energy pulses. I also have very good hearing and
> can hear many things at distances, and know usually when someone, a friend,
> relative or stranger, is going to say or do something. Many times, just being
> exposed to other people, places, events, or even written material, I can extrapo-
> late upon it and come up with many things that can be later verified.

A psychic skills teacher, she sends this material on learning to see auras:

> There are several things one should keep in mind. The first is, of course, to
> keep one's thoughts of the highest order—that is, thinking good positive
> thoughts, knowing that you have the innate ability to do this, and to know that
> you are protected at all times. (Some people forget and/or do not know to
> remind themselves that they are protected by god/goddess/all that I am, when
> expanding their awareness and inadvertantly absorb any energy imbalance
> from the other person).
>
> Also, the term 'aura' is confusing to some, but the aura is actually one of the
> subtle bodies and the auric field is the color/energy combination of all or any of
> these subtle energy bodies and their related colors . . . Certain people can see
> one particular color or energy pattern and someone else will see some other
> color/s or energies. It also depends on how much the person being viewed is
> willing to open up and/or concentrate on feeling expansive to allow another to
> see their energies.
>
> However, if everyone feels comfortable, relaxed, etc. the process is quite simple
> and a lot of fun, and with practice can lead to more awareness on many
> levels.

Pam's process for seeing the emotional aura is one I've already given, and she adds this method. I've described it to two other women, who tell me it works:

> There have been a few instances when the first process has not worked for
> certain people, so this other technique has been used. Sit in a totally darkened
> room, with or without a partner and stare intently at where you know the per-
> son is (or at your hand) for several minutes, and the color/energy patterns
> will appear . . .

Each person is different, so I suggest practicing on different people or have them view you, as it is interesting to note the differences with others and/or times of day, and so forth.

With practice, one can simply and automatically look at another and note the colors, energy patterns, meridians, and etc. Sometimes a novice will be overwhelmed by all they see and/or drained, disrupted by others' energies, so I gently remind them to not only continue practicing but to know they really are protected, and it is generally wise to not blurt out what one sees, but to see and learn from what they are experiencing.

Pam has had much experience with aura work, and her advice is valuable. Judy, who also sees auras, had a typical child's experience with them:

As a child, I thought my eyes were bad because I saw 'rainbows' around people. Now I know the truth. Some of my experiences have frightened me and some have no doubt saved lives. My family shares these powers.

Aura work is the basis for women's healing, and for many aspects of psychic information.

For one more experience, a somber one, Chris describes the aura of a man who committed suicide, shortly before it happened. The experience was another reflection of emotional states, or was it a precognition?

I was playing with the little kids in the lake when I looked up and saw him coming towards us. The kids tensed up, figuring he was about to spoil their fun, but all he did was tell them to get out of the water. The odd thing was that I saw him as a tremendously dark presence. At the time I figured it was a trick of the light, as if the sun were behind him. But I realized that it was afternoon and the sun was shining behind me, on him. But instead of being a positive presence, it was as if he was blacking out the light or absorbing it in some strange way. Maybe all I saw was a very disturbed aura. The thing is, I don't see auras usually. I don't know what it was except that it stuck in my visual memory. Later, when he killed himself, the image came back to me and made sense somehow. I wonder if this is like Scottish 'second sight.' I've never seen anything else like that.

When my dog, Tiger, was dying, I was unable to find her aura, either visually or by touch; it seemed totally absent, a light gone out. Auras are a key to states of emotion and Be-ing in human, animal or plant. Chris had seen the light gone out also, in a Be-ing near death.

Science has investigated auras from time to time, proving their existence in terms science asks for, then often rejecting the evidence. British physician Walter Kilner worked with the human aura just after the turn of the century. He dis-covered a system for seeing auras through chemical dye screens that made them visible to anyone. A scientist and not a psychic, he worked with children and adults, but most of his subjects were women. He learned to read the aura through his screens, and to use what he saw to diagnose various illnesses and conditions, emotional and physical. He traced changes in the healthy aura from childhood to adolescence and adulthood, and observed the differences between boys and girls, men and women, in these normal changes. He could see in the aura whether a woman was in good health or not, whether she was menstruating or about to menstruate, and could diagnose very early pregnancies. He observed pregnancy with his screens, the aura changes in the mother and fetus. That women's auras are more highly developed than men's was one of his conclusions.

Kilner also worked with thought-forms, seeing them in his screens, and dis-covering that women can make changes in their auras, can transmit auric energy, by willing it to happen.

> Before commencing any experiment we showed her how the Aura emanating from the tip of one finger could be extended or diminished at will, and asked her to try and influence hers in the same manner. This, she almost immediately succeeded in doing, so we endeavored to perform the same in different parts of her body, to which she agreed.
> After about half a minute from the commencement of *willing*, the Inner Aura looked brighter and gradually extended outwards and upwards as far as the Outer Aura. When the ray thus formed had reached this point, she stopped willing and the ray rapidly receded.[15]

What Kilner terms the Inner Aura is the light band beyond the etheric double; his Outer Aura is the emotional body aura. The energy emanating as a streak from the woman's finger and controlled by will is a thought-form. The energy of laying on of hands is willed transmission of psychic/aura energy. The willed energy effects changes in the aura of the woman being healed. This energy can also be transmitted telepathically.

Kilner's chemical screens are a way of seeing auras that is easily repeatable and the instructions are in his book. One theory of why viewing the aura through a glass coated with dyes brings them to sight is the concept of perceptions again. Scientists know that there are sounds beyond human hearing range, dogs hear things humans cannot, and there are color waves beyond the recording ability of human eyesight. It's possible that the Kilner screens bring imperceptible light waves into the range of normal viewing. It is also possible that women who see auras without mechanical aids have developed their vision, physical or psychic, to include this light wave range. To induce the seeing psychically, the key is the meditative alpha brainwave state, as it is for all psychic enhancement. The woman opens her third eye, her nonphysical sight, activated by the pituitary gland, that master gland in the skull behind the forehead whose full functions are unknown. She opens a way of seeing that is not concrete or of the linear world.

*The Human Atmosphere*, Kilner's book, was first published in 1911 in London, to the worst of reviews. He was discredited and disgraced in the medical profession, forced to resign his hospital post and close his practice because of his unorthodox views. World War I halted his work, since his dicyanin dyes came from Germany. When the book was reissued to better notice in 1920, he had already died. Psychics have adopted, verified, and continued his work, while science still ignores it, and Kilner's book remains in print as *The Aura* today. He was never writing for a psychic audience, but it is the psychics who have honored him.

The next scientific breakthrough came in 1939, in Russia, with the work of Valentina and Semyon Kirlian. The wife and husband team of Valentina, a teacher and journalist and Semyon, an electrician and photographer, discovered and developed the use of high frequency live photography to record and photograph the human aura. Still-life work grew into moving photography, so that auras could be observed directly, living plants or living, moving body parts under the generator lens. A hand held under the lens

> looked like the Milky Way in a starry sky. Against the background of blue and gold, something was taking place in the hand that looked like a fireworks display. Multicolored flares lit up, then sparks, twinkles, flashes. Some lights glowed steadily like Roman candles, others flashed out then dimmed. Still others sparked at intervals.
>
> The Kirlians placed a fresh leaf under the lens of a microscope connected to the high frequency generator. They saw a picture similar to that of the human hand. Next they tried a half-withered leaf. There were almost no flares and the sparks and 'clouds' scarcely moved.[16]

What the Kirlians saw in a living hand compares to what Irene, Ana or Eileen Garrett describe when they see living auras psychically, or what Loren described. Their description of the dying leaf sounds very much like what Chris saw. Women and psychics have described these things since the beginning of time, and now concrete science sees it but still discredits it. Kirlian photography records states of health or ill health, and states of positive or negative emotions and mental Be-ing. When someone is tired "energy appears to pour out of the body."[17]

The Soviets named the energy in the Kirlians' photographs bioplasmic energy, and it took them over twenty years to accept and validate their work. Bioplasmic energy is what the Hindus call prana, vitality or the life force. Scientific definitions run like this:

> it's the oxygen we breathe that converts some of its surplus electrons and a certain quantum of energy into the energy body.[18]

The description sounds very much like what Eileen Garrett described seeing as a child, globules of light that she compared to bubbles, and very much like what I called "seeing air" and was laughed at for. Kilner's chemical screens and Kirlian photography have made the aura provable and controllable in the laboratory.

Kilner's description of the woman willing energy to appear in one part or another of her aura is described scientifically again in experiments with psychic healer Olga Worrall. An atomic cloud chamber was used.

> Mrs. Worrall . . . agreed to experiment. Placing her hands at the side of the chamber without touching the glass, she mentally 'treated' the contents as she would a patient. A wave pattern developed in the mist, paralleling her hands. When she shifted the position of her hands 90 degrees the waves also shifted to right angles of their former motion. Similar results were obtained in experiments with (other healers).[19]

When Olga Worrall attempted to transmit laying on of hands/pranic/psychic healing energy to a cloud chamber six hundred miles away from her, the results happened, too. Other work with Olga Worrall, based on her healing but useful for other psychic phenomena, brought the following conclusions:

1. An energy associated with healing does exist and it can be measured with suitable instruments.

2. Water which has been treated by a healer changes . . . solution color, surface tension, hydrogen bonding, and electrical properties.

3. A healer is most effective when in an alpha relaxed state of consciousness.[20]

Brainwave changes can be measured with this transmission of psychic/pranic energy, as other physiological changes in blood pressure, hemoglobin volume, heart rate, and enzyme activity. Women like Delores Krieger, Shafica Karagulla and Sister Justa Smith continue seeking, and finding, scientific proofs for what psychics, healers and mystics have always seen and known. Hiroshi Motoyama, a research doctor in Japan, has developed electronic instrumentation that mirrors the work of acupuncture and charts the meridians. The conclusions are that:

Psi-energy is ejected from the chakra and the points on the acupuncture meridians . . . Through the chakras, prana, a higher dimensional vital energy force, is received from the universe and converted into a kind of physical energy. Through this energy psi-phenomena are produced.[21]

Psychokinesis, mind over matter, occurs by bursts of pranic or thought-form energy, and the same energy effects physical changes at a distance in psychic healing or telepathy. In laying on of hands, direct transmission of prana takes place, while telepathy is the transmission of thought-forms and energy in the same manner as in psychic distance healing. This energy is controlled and concentrated by the mind in the alpha or alpha to theta state.

Mind or will, kama-manas thought-form energy, creates physical concrete world changes by transmitting prana through the psychic bodies. If "thoughts are things"—and they seem so—they are things that move through the aura bodies, accumulating energy/prana as they travel. A mental idea moves through the mental to the emotional body, then makes changes in the etheric double before changes in the dense physical happen. Ideas/thought-forms originating in the spiritual bodies, move from spiritual to mental, then through the emotional body to the etheric double, and finally into physical manifestation, the world of form. The progression can move in the opposite direction, from the physical outward, as well. These changes are physical ones, as in healing work, or can be psychic phenomena of any sort.

Each type of psychic phenomena is correspondent with a chakra, along with an aura body and aura layer. Developing a particular chakra develops that chakra's psychic skill, and all of the chakras are developed in positive ways by meditation work. The skill for the root chakra is past life regression, for the belly center astral travel, for the solar plexus dreams and mind over matter manifesting, for the heart healing, for the throat telepathy, for the third eye divination and clairvoyance, for the crown center, channeling, mediumship and spirit guides, and for the transpersonal point after-death speculations and experiences. These are the chapters that follow. A knowledge of psychic anatomy gives women the basis for understanding the various types of psychic phenomena, and the mechanism for transmission of energy and thoughts in seemingly impossible ways. Patriarchal science, despite lots of proof on its own terms, says that psychic phenomena are impossible, but matriarchal consciousness is aware of women's psychic bodies.

# THE INVISIBLE WOMAN*

| Aura Layer | Body | Chakra | Psychic Skill | Healing Area | Attribute |
|---|---|---|---|---|---|
| 1. Dense Body & Physical Aura/ Etheric Double | Physical | Root/ Red and Black | Past Lives/ Reincarnation | Laying On Of Hands | Life/ Physical Survival |
| 2. Emotional/Astral | Emotional | Belly/ Orange | Clairsentience/ Astral Projection | Color Work | Feeling/Desire (The Subconscious) |
| 3. Lower Mental | Mental | Solar Plexus/ Yellow | Manifesting/ Psychokinesis Dreamwork | Creative Visualization | Intellect (The Conscious) Linear Reality |
| 4. Higher Mental | Mental | Heart/ Green or Rose | Healing/ Rapport with Animals and All That Lives | Creative Visualization | Intuition (The Superconscious) Matriarchal Reality |
| 5. Lower Spiritual | Spiritual | Throat/ Light Blue or Aqua | Clairaudience/ Telepathy Animal Telepathy | Psychic Healing | Communication/ Will The Crone |
| 6. Middle Spiritual | Spiritual | Brow or Third Eye/ Indigo | Clairvoyance/ Precognition/ Divination | Meditation | Realities/Knowing The Mother |
| 7. Higher Spiritual | Spiritual | Crown/ Violet | Spirit Guides/ Mediumship/ Spiritism | Meditation | Connection with Goddess/ The Maiden |
| 8. Transpersonal | Beyond the Physical/ Spiritual | Transpersonal Point/ Clear | Astral Planes/ Beyond Death/ Near Death Experiences | Meditation/ Transcendence | Goddess Within |

* A.E. Powell, *The Mental Body*, (Wheaton, IL, Quest/Theosophical Publishing House, 1984, original 1927), p. 221; S.G.J. Ouseley, *The Science of the Aura*, (Essex, England, L.N. Fowler and Co., Inc., 1982, original 1949), p. 17-18; C.W. Leadbeater, *Man Visible and Invisible*, (Wheaton, IL, Quest/Theosophical Publishing House, 1980, original, 1925), p. 21-27; and A.E. Powell, *The Causal Body and the Ego*, (Wheaton, IL, Theosophical Publishing House, 1978, original, 1928), p. 70-71; and Amy Wallace and Bill Henkin, *The Psychic Healing Book*, (Berkeley, CA. Wingbow Press, 1978), p. 27-31.

# FOOTNOTES

1. Sheila Ostrander and Lynn Schroeder, *Psychic Discoveries Behind the Iron Curtain*, p. 197.

2. See Diane Stein, *The Women's Book of Healing*, (St. Paul, Llewellyn Publications, 1987), Chapter Two. Also on tape, *Two Meditations: The Rainbow of the Chakras*.

3. Mary Coddington, *In Search of the Healing Energy*, (New York, Destiny Books, 1978), p. 16.

4. C.W. Leadbeater, *The Chakras*, (Wheaton, IL, Quest/Theosophical Publishing House, 1927), p. 42-54. Much of Leadbeater's work comes from Helen Blavatsky and Annie Besant. He was also clairvoyant.

5. Mary Coddington, *In Search of the Healing Energy*, p. 16-17.

6. For more detailed material on the bodies, aura and chakras, see Diane Stein, *The Women's Book of Healing*, Chapters One, Two and throughout.

7. Based loosely on the work of Annie Besant and C.W. Leadbeater, *Thought-Forms*, (Wheaton, IL, Quest/Theosophical Publishing House, 1980, original 1925), p. 22-23.

8. Diane Mariechild, *Mother Wit: A Feminist Guide to Psychic Development*, p. 38-39. Also in Diane Stein, *The Women's Book of Healing*, Chapter One.

9. Psychic skills for the centers are referenced to Amy Wallace and Bill Henkin, *The Psychic Healing Book*, (Berkeley, CA, Wingbow Press, 1978), p. 27-31. Highly recommended, especially for healers.

10. Annie Besant and C.W. Leadbeater, *Thought-Forms*, p. 6.

11. Kay Gardner, *A Rainbow Path*, audio tape, (Durham, Ladyslipper, Inc., 1984).

12. Petey Stevens, *Opening Up to Your Psychic Self: A Primer of Psychic Development*, (Berkeley, CA Nevertheless Press, 1982), p. 47-78. Material in parentheses are added.

13. Eileen Garrett, "My Life As A Search For the Meaning of Mediumship," in David C. Knight, Editor, *The ESP Reader*, (New York, Grosset and Dunlap, Inc., 1969), p. 197-198.

14. *Ibid.*, p. 199.

15. W.J. Kilner, *The Aura*, (York Beach, ME, Samuel Weiser, Inc., 1984, published originally in 1911 as *The Human Atmosphere*), p. 308-309.

16. Sheila Ostrander and Lynn Schroeder, *Psychic Discoveries Behind the Iron Curtain*, p. 199.

17. *Ibid.*, p. 205.

18. *Ibid.*, p. 214.

19. George C. Meek, Editor, *Healers and the Healing Process*, (Wheaton, IL, Quest/Theosophical Publishing House, 1977), p. 137.

20. *Ibid.*, p. 139. Material is condensed.

21. *Ibid.*, p. 150-151.

## Chapter Three

# The Root Chakra: Reincarnation
# How Many Lives?

*When I was under six years old, I had strong and recurrent memories of other times and places. I now understand that these memories came from previous lives. However, the result of these powerful feelings as a child was that I had great difficulty handling reality. The present life is all that really matters, I was quite sure that whatever was the matter was not my parents' fault, that it was deep within myself. But, this insistent memory-voice inside caused me to be more attuned to it, than to the real people around myself. Frequently I experienced deja vu, feeling like I'd been in a place before, but that was merely a matter of idle curiosity. It was the urgency and power of the inner voices that moved me to take action. As I got closer to being forty, I began to fear that the inner voices would shatter me into pieces. I feared psychological chaos. So, I decided to get to know them, to ask them to tell me what I seemed to need to hear.[1]*

I am a tourist at Mesa Verde, Pueblo Indian ruins, an abandoned city in Colorado. As I walk down the trail, I quickly become enthralled, charmed by the place, knowing my way where I have never been before. The signs say stay on the trail, but at one turning of the concrete path, I walk off it, onto a path that I know. The day is hot and dry, the altitude exhilarating, and the yellow clay of the land is welcoming and beautiful.

The path I know is a streambed, dry now and narrow, but it will fill and run rapidly in springtime. There is some amount of brush, but it doesn't bother me, and doesn't bother a usually obedient tourist to defy the signs. I go where I know to go. A hundred yards or so from the walkway a small tree trunk, dusty and dead, is lying across the path and behind is an overhanging cliff face, not deep enough to be a cave. I sit down on the tree trunk, drinking in the atmosphere of this place, abandoned but alive with spirits. I idly run my hand through the sand of the stream bed, and find an object. I don't know what it is, but should know. The piece is about an inch on each side and not quite square. It's a deep red color, smooth on one side, and the other side looks like weaving. I look at the object, hold it, and instantly am in another time.

A woman is walking by the stream, which has water in it. She is barefoot, and wears a coarse grey-white skirt that comes to midcalf, and a top to the skirt that is not quite a blouse of the same material. She is a Pueblo woman of strong hands and middle age, wide bones but not tall, red skin, and black hair in shoulder-length braids tied with leather cord. She wears a string of turquoise beads. The woman walks to a place at the side of the stream, this place near the overhang, and begins scooping clay, mixing it with straw she pulls from around her, and dishing enough water with her hands from the stream. She shapes the yellowish material into thin ropes, twirling them between her palms. There is no waste of time or motions as she works. She winds the rope of clay into a circle, pressing the coils flat, then winds ropes of clay to form the sides of a jar.

I watch her shape the pottery, make it into a tall rough pot with a fairly wide mouth. The jar bows outward near the top, then in again to the mouth. As she works, she takes a stick with a smoothed end she has brought and smoothes the inside of the jar. I see the jar later, dried in the sun, when she comes back to find it. She then places it near a large communal (?) fire, digging a hole in the soft ashes near the edge, ashes cool enough to touch. She buries the pot then brings pinewood and flame to burn over it as she cooks there. I see her digging the pot up again with the fire cooled, and the pot is reddish and hard, a thing of use, not of beauty. I know who this woman is, she is the widowed village midwife who needs a new water jar. She is also me.

Suddenly the scene shifts and I see the woman again. She is older now, her hair white, her face all knobs and wrinkles, her hands gnarled but still strong. She comes to the stream with her water jar, bending over to fill it, and the jar slips from her hands and breaks.

With a jolt I am back in the present, sitting on a thin fallen tree trunk over the now-dry stream. I know what I hold is a piece of the water jar. I know I have seen myself. The silence and aliveness of the spot bewilders me, disturbs me. I pocket the shard and return to the concrete path to be a tourist again. The piece of pottery stays with me, and I show it to a store owner back in Durango, who verifies it as a pottery shard, probably from a cooking pot or water jar. She tells me that Mesa Verde was abandoned in 1298 A.D., no one knows why.

I had never heard the word "reincarnation" but I knew I had lived at Mesa Verde as a midwife and healer, and had made the pot. The shard is a treasure that I feared to touch for many years, since every time I hold it I see the woman, watch her make and break the jar. Reading about Native American crafts, I learn how the pot was made, but I had already seen it. Ten years later I heard about women's spirituality and in five more I understand. I had seen a past life vision of myself, a spontaneous past life regression.

Until the Western patriarchy, every culture globally knew and accepted the concept of reincarnation, the idea that people are born many times and live many lives, that the soul outlives the physical dense body. The concept is implicit in the wiccan Wheel, where death is followed by rest and rebirth, for the purpose of growing and learning again and again. African-descended women who follow voudoun and macumbe speak of ancestors that after death help the living, become spirit guides for their children and grandchildren until they themselves are reborn. A similar concept exists in China, where ancestors are worshipped. In Egypt, a system of embalming and preserving the body after death was developed for the soul to have a place to live until it reincarnated. In India, some religious groups do not eat beef, on the chance that a human soul has experienced rebirth in the cow, which is a sacred animal and a Goddess symbol. This idea of transmigration of souls was also held by the Greeks. The Eskimos say that the Goddess of Animals controls reincarnation, since she doesn't like to see too many of her animals and people killed.[2] In Native America and in ancient Scandinavia, in South America, China and in India, the cycle of birth, death and renewal is central to religious thought, and this is also the cycle of women's spirituality and wicca.

Theosophist and psychic Annie Besant traces the development of human ethics to belief in reincarnation, to the idea that life continues beyond the body and has an accounting in other lives, that deeds have consequences in this life and in future incarnations. This is the meaning of karma. She writes about reincarnation and karma as tenets of all Eastern pre-Christian religions, of the Pharisee Jews and the Kaballah, and of the earliest days of Christianity. The doctrine was submerged in both religions during the Dark Ages, and Besant comments that world ethics have deteriorated ever since.[3] Belief in reincarnation is a universal thing outside the West, a part of matriarchal traditions everywhere, and major in women's spirituality.

In the theory of reincarnation, everyone has been born many times, entering the world in each life for a specific process of learning. There are tasks assigned and voluntarily chosen for each lifetime, and the reincarnating soul chooses the circumstances of her rebirth carefully for best ways to meet these tasks. Women choose their physical and mental attributes, their bodies, races, physical and mental ableness or disabilities, illnesses, and the families, friends, lovers, places and circumstances of their births and lives. A soul chooses to be female in some incarnations, but can choose to be male in others. Some souls change sexes frequently, while others seem to remain female (or male) for many cycles. A woman who is white in this lifetime may have been (and probably has been) Black, Asian, Indian or Native American in other lifetimes. A woman able now may have been disabled in the past, and vice versa. The directions and learning skills of a given life are chosen, as are some actual events. Other events are choices, and karma can be changed by will and awareness.

The object of reincarnation is learning, and each soul passes through a myriad of experiences that the cycle of lifetimes is meant to fill. It would be impossible to experience all of Be-ing in one lifetime, and reincarnation expands the possibilities, makes the realities limitless. Every soul lives the gamut of emotions and lifestyles, life experiences, and works on specific learning tasks. The end purpose is wholeness and oneness with Goddess within and a union with Goddess and all life. The keyword is universal love.

In India, reincarnation is explained as the desire for action and understanding on the part of the soul.[4] Hindus and Buddhists define divinity as the impulse to manifest (the creative Goddess), and the impulse of the individual soul or creative individual ego (Goddess within) to manifest as well. This impulse in Goddess is to create all life, and in the soul to become incarnate (flesh-born). When that impulse (kama or mind) and desire (manas or emotion) to manifest are fulfilled, the soul no longer seeks reincarnation into the world of form. She has reached the goal of being freed from the wheel of karma. The way to do this is not to withdraw from the world while living in it, but to expand desire into universal love. What is desired for the self is desired for all, and for the good of all.

In women's spirituality and wicca, the emphasis is not on withdrawing from the need to manifest. The goal for women is more present in the here and now, to experience, learn and grow. The focus on ethics and karma is to inspire higher spiritual development in this life and the lives to come, without setbacks in future lives created by negative actions in this one. Some choices of incarnation are to manifest on behalf of the whole at the sacrifice of the individual, and this is always voluntary. "Cleaning up your act," as far as karma goes, is the goal, along with the desire to learn and achieve as much as possible in the present lifetime. Each woman has chosen this particular time and place for reincarnation, and she has reasons for being here. She makes the best use of her time and reasons to fulfill her life in the most positive ways and to learn what she's come here to learn.

What reincarnates is the causal or spiritual body, the fastest vibrating of the aura body levels:

> When the death hour comes the subtler bodies free themselves from the physical, the etheric double disintegrating gradually with the dense frame. The thought-body resulting from the past life persists for a considerable time and goes through various processes of consolidation of experience .... As the period for reincarnation approaches, the causal body or reincarnating Ego, builds a new mental and a new astral (emotional) body, .... and after this the etheric double is built.[5]

The etheric double passes its impressions of the past life onto the emotional and mental bodies (kama-manas), which in turn pass them onto the spiritual body (reincarnating ego or Goddess within) before disintegrating. The reincarnating spiritual body then recreates new mental, emotional and physical bodies (etheric double) to enter a new dense physical Be-ing. The reflections of each past life are locked in the spiritual body, but are passed on to the nearer-to-dense-physical levels. They remain in the soul's desire mind (kama-manas), which is not the physical brain, and the information becomes available spontaneously, by progressive psychic development, or by past life regression work. The woman who works to develop her psychic abilities gains contact with her unseen psychic bodies, and the information comes within reach.[6]

The concept of karma is the vehicle and reason for rebirth into a series of lifetimes. Barbara Walker, in *The Woman's Encyclopedia of Myths and Secrets*, defines it as Fate, derived from the Hindu Goddess Kauri-Ma or Kali Ma.

> The Goddess' law was that any individual evolution must be worked out by a series of reincarnations through the turnings of the great wheel of time. Evil actions resulted in rebirth to a more evil life; good actions brought lives of increasing virtue and happiness.[7]

This is the Hindu stance, but in women's spirituality karma is seen somewhat differently. It is not viewed as a punishment for every wrongdoing or mistake ("God will get you for this"), but as a process of learning and growth, of increasing women's abilities, knowledge, experience and power. Natural law or balance is achieved by it, and the goal is spiritual evolution. When this evolution is completed, the soul returns to Goddess and the urge to manifest physically on Earth is ended.

In Diane Mariechild's work:

> Reincarnation is the path the soul takes as it moves to rediscover the knowledge that we are all one. There is no within and without.... We were all created simultaneously by a universal creative energy force, and once created, we become creators.[8]

This sounds very much like what Annie Besant said. On the idea of karma, Mariechild defines it this way:

> Karma is a complex dynamic involving the molding of past, present and future. We should never reduce it to a simplistic concept of reward and punishment.... Karma is the law of action, of change. We can create, and are creating, ourselves at every moment. Our power is in the present. We are not trapped by a difficult past life and more than we are by a difficult childhood.... Fate is simply the result of our thoughts, feelings and beliefs, and as we change them our fate also changes.[9]

The idea that if someone does evil, that evil must be paid for, is the basis of popular views of karma: that if someone commits murder in one life, she will in turn be murdered in the next. This could possibly be the case, but "an eye for an eye" is too simple. First of all, whatever karmic retribution happens to a soul is chosen voluntarily by that soul, and can be chosen disproportionately in one lifetime, and secondly retribution is not the goal, but learning, growth and awareness are. Punishment and paying back are not the issues; a return to oneness with all life and with Goddess is.

An increase in suffering anywhere is not a resolution and serves no purpose. Two wrongs don't make a right, or a return to karmic balance. If a woman's actions caused suffering in one life, why not have her work to alleviate others' suffering in this one? Suffering experienced in this life can be chosen to show a woman how to overcome it. Karma is cause and effect, not vengeance.

> The law of cause and effect is a Universal Law. For every action or cause there is a reaction or effect that is unchanging and beyond our control. What is within our control is the action or cause we set into motion and the attitude with which we deal with the effect. It is our attitude which makes karma into a negative or positive influence in our lives. Karma, of itself, is neither good nor bad. Karma just is.[10]

All of the accumulations in wisdom, experience and learning gained by living many lives is karma also.

> We have, in our eons of living, gained an incredible amount of knowledge and expertise in a vast number of areas. Some fields of endeavor we have pursued to the fullest. Others we have abandoned for one reason or another. But that knowledge is still a part of us, and if we so choose, it can be retrieved for use in our present lives.[11]

The process of growth and development, of understanding mistakes and wrongdoings is the process of karma, but so is an accumulation of rewards and wisdoms. Women live lives created by choice, by cause and effect, and causes can carry effects over into other lifetimes: this is karma. Problems are there to be solved by present action, and are chosen, not put there arbitrarily. They are not punishments, but challenges.

Choice is crucial in present actions. Every action is a choice and every choice has consequences. If the consequences are to be positive, then the choice and actions must be. If chocolate gives a woman migraines and she chooses to eat chocolate, then the migraines are chosen as consequences. The woman has a choice. All of the simple ethics of women's spirituality are based on the idea of choice, cause and effect, and are "rules" designed to bring positive consequences, positive karma. The first law of women's spirituality and wicca is "harm none," and the second is that "what you send out comes back to you." If good is chosen and generated (the cause), then good returns to the sender as consequence (the effect). The same is true for karma. Annie Besant's comment that karma is the underlying cause of human ethics makes sense, as do her reincarnation principles of desire to manifest/create and take action.

Says Jane Roberts,

> We live as many physical existences as we feel we must in order to develop our abilities and prepare ourselves to enter other dimensions of reality.[12]

We choose the circumstances and every detail of our rebirths for what issues need to be resolved, what karma "burned," in that lifetime. Each rebirth is a series of choices, made to balance causes and effects. Karma is the problem solving of the issues, and solutions come from the experiences gained along the way in living the lifetimes. If there is one direct route to the resolution of karmic issues, that route is through love, love of self and others in universal ways, love of Goddess and the Goddess within all that lives.[13]

That everyone has lived many lives is accepted in women's

spirituality and in most matriarchal traditions. Only in patriarchy and the West is reincarnation denied. Knowledge of past lives comes in a variety of ways, spontaneously and with intention, and knowledge comes either whole cloth or in tantalizing fragments. You enter a place you have never been before, yet know every turning and where to find things there. You dis-cover a skill you've never been taught. Meeting someone, it's as if you've known her always, and you like and trust her immediately not knowing why. Meeting someone else, there's a dislike that's inexplicable and irrational. Scenes in a dream are real ones and the place is real, but waking you've not been there in this life.

In therapy, an age regression trance to find the cause of a phobia takes the woman not to another age but to another existence. Phobias and irrational fears can be past life carry-overs. So can an attraction or aversion to a particular place or culture, an intense love that is or is not problematic, or a complex relationship with someone not a lover.[14] The feeling of deja vu, of having been somewhere or experienced something before that you know you've never seen or experienced in this life can be a past life memory. Past life experiences happen spontaneously or can be induced in the meditative state.

Souls tend to incarnate in groups for the purpose of working out issues, relationships and affinities with each other, and for being supportive to each other. Relationships vary. Many past life experiences are of people meeting each other again in several lives, re-cognizing their connection. One aspect of this is the idea of soul mates or essence twins. The relationships are not necessarily of lovers, though that idea is popular, and they aren't necessarily a story of soul mate meets soul mate and both lives happily together ever after.

There are two theories of soul mates.[15] One is that the two meet and re-cognize each other, are drawn together by an intense attachment that is total and may last a lifetime. They become lovers, mates throughout this existence, as they have been in other lives. They may also become close friends, sharing each other's lives in nonsexual ways, but in primary relationship with each other. The other theory is more difficult, that one re-cognizes the connection while the other does not, or both re-cognize it but one refuses it. Their meeting is painful and ends in separation, leaving one or both of them longing. One is ready for the relationship, but the other is not at the time it becomes available. Says psychic Susan Sheppard,

> You have felt the yearning to complete yourself through the love of another

who is at one with you, yet she refuses to recognize this. Therefore, the time is not right for either of you . . . The soul becomes quite sad when it recognizes its own essence and then is not allowed to blend and interact with the 'twin.' Or maybe more appropriately, 'the other' . . . But remember, there are many casts of 'essence twins.' We can be essence twins with more than one.

Ruth Montgomery, in *Here and Hereafter*,[16] writes about families, soul mates and friends reincarnating together in life after life. Each soul has her support system on earth and between lives, her guides, mentors, "twins" and family members that incarnate with her. Plato wrote of double souls, in bodies that attached together, until they were separated by angry gods and spend their lives searching for their "other half." Some soul mates appear in one's life only for short periods of time. Others, like Dee and Jim who met at five years old and at sixty are still together, are lifelong experiences. Some refuse the connection, but for others the magick happens.

Here are some women's experiences with soul mates and reincarnation. Maggie's story has elements of both. Her experience began at a farm community, where she was visiting, and where she had not yet met one of the community members. The group experienced a past life regression tape, a guided meditation and journey:

> The first side of the tape was a typical relaxation and visualization; the second side was a guided past-life regression. Both sides took me to the same image and the same place, a narrow beach, facing a western sunset. Behind me rose green hills of close-cropped grass, a net of stone walls lacing the hillside. I looked down at my bare feet, my rolled-up pants, my coarse shirt. Mine, but not mine. A young man's feet, a young man's legs. In the distance I could see the figure of a woman. As she drew closer I could make out her face, familiar, beloved.
>
> I had never thought about reincarnation except as theory. I certainly didn't believe in it. What I had 'seen' and felt during the tape I supposed was fantasy, my imagination at work. Still, the details surprised me. I could see how the shirt was stitched. No one else who had done the tape had seen anything, I discovered, had had no such experience. I said nothing about mine.
>
> The next afternoon the missing person (from the farm) came back . . . I could hear the car door slam, knew that she was walking towards us, and suddenly I was afraid to look. But I did, finally. There she was, *the woman walking towards me on the beach*. She was a little older, her hair a little darker, but there was no mistaking. Not only that, she was totally, in every way, familiar to me and totally loved. I couldn't speak. There she was—my—what was her name—I knew her name. But her name, when she introduced herself was foreign to me. It was Cheryl. It means 'the loved one.'
>
> During the next week I entered as much as I could into the life of the community . . . . Each night I repeated the tape with those who seemed interested in it. Each night the familiar scene unfolded in more and more detail. Soon I knew what I was—a fisherman—as was my brother. I lived, it seemed, with my brother and his wife in a white-washed stone hut just above the beach. They had a child, a little girl. I knew what the family was like, how we felt about one

another, what we ate and what our work was like: I knew how our boats were made . . . I knew that I loved the woman who sometimes walked and sometimes road horseback on the beach, on the hills. We were both young. It seemed that she was 'beyond' me in the sense that nothing was easy; she had wealth (or so it seemed to me) and I was poor; . . . she was educated and I was not. Yet, we spent time together, talked, laughed, kissed. She liked to tease me but was always kind. I knew that. What I didn't know was whether she loved me.

There was finally, some confrontation with her father . . . I think that we had talked, at least, abut running away together, had spun those fantasies, but how serious she was I can't guess. In the tape a curious thing began to happen. I would be sitting in early morning fog on the hill at our meeting place, waiting for her to come. She was going to tell me something, coming to say whether she would run away with me? To say *some* kind of yes to me that meant 'I love you, I am serious, I make this commitment to you.' I see her coming on horseback, riding too fast, being reckless. And then I see her fall and I run down the hill towards her and see the horse standing and the white dress on the ground and I fling myself down beside her, kneeling—and at that point, night after night, the scene would cut off and switch to a dusty country road with trees to one side and a ditch and beer cans in the ditch: Schlitz and Coors and something else I can't read.

During the next week, Maggie had a precognitive experience, a "feeling" that an accident was pending for Cheryl. She and another woman cast protection around her, and included Cheryl in the awareness and need to protect herself. Maggie knew the day it would happen, and though not present knew when it was happening and when it was over. It was a car accident. She had a moment of transcendence and knew that Cheryl was unharmed. Cheryl's car had been totaled, but Cheryl was unhurt, and asked Maggie to take her back to the scene of the accident the next day.

The country road—I'd never seen it before—became more and more familiar. We parked where the accident had happened. There was glass on the road, pieces of metal. I got out, stood in the sandy road, in the dust, trees to one side, and looked at the ditch. There were the beer cans, just as I had seen them. Schlitz, Coors and one so rusted I couldn't read its name.

That's the end of the story, at least for that summer, but it was not the end of what it meant . . . the purpose of our meeting again continues to unfold for both of us. We now know that it was for our growth, for consciousness, and that it was about love.

More about Maggie's precognitive experience in Chapter Nine.

Susan Sheppard describes a past life connection, a soul mate, of my own life:

I feel you were sisters in a past life as well as lovers in a different life. I feel she was a man and you were a woman in either Wales or Northern England around 1100 A.D. It was at this time you were lovers but she was married to someone else. I feel she worked as a stone mason but was into the realm of spirit and created great monuments as worship centers . . . You were a weaver at this time from a poor family . . . I know very little about the caste system of

England and Wales, except I believe that you worked for her family since you were a very small girl and often watched her riding by on horseback . . . I pick up a name like 'Wyndal' or 'Wendal' or 'Wyndl.' This was her name. Your name was 'Guin' or 'Gwuinn' or 'Gwen' . . . You looked very much like you do now except you had very fiery red hair which hung almost to your ankles. You had exactly the same eyes and expression. Yet you had an arthritic condition which left you partially crippled in your spine and your feet. Despite your handicap, you created wonderful masterpieces in tapestry and weaving which now hang in museums today . . . The relationship was ill-fated because you were not in this world very long, only until you were about twenty-seven when you died, . . possibly of appendicitis. Wyndal was devastated, although lived to be about eighty years of age . . . She built your monument with her own hands. No one understood why she did this, as your relationship was not known to anyone but both of you . . . Possibly she fears a relationship in this life, because she lost you once before.

In this life, I have long hair below my waist, though it is dark brown, and a curvature of the spine. I embroider. The woman I feel to be a soul mate is also an artist, though not a sculptor. She was not able to accept the connection between us.

Meg writes about her past lives:

I know that I had a very special daughter in a past life. I was a young single mother in Pompeii with a four month old daughter—Sarah. I had gone into the market to get some food and left her home. All I remember is what felt like an earthquake and bells sounding an alarm. I tried running home to Sarah but the ground just opened up around me. I fell and suffocated.

This came to me over a period of months. It was triggered by a piece of music. Every time I heard this piece, I would cry. It was like a lullaby.

Then one day, my best friend in Indiana . . . called to say that my daughter had visited her. She said she knew she wasn't awake, and wasn't dreaming. But that a two-three year old little girl ran out to her from nowhere. Georgia asked her who she was. She answered, 'Meg and John's little girl.' Georgia asked why she hadn't met her before. She said it was because she hadn't been born yet. Georgia asked her name. She answered, 'Sarah Louise.' Then she was gone.

At this time, I'm still waiting for my daughter to return to me.

Perhaps because of the intensity of the experience, women often remember their deaths in past lives. This is Joanne's experience:

I was looking into the blazes of a log fire when I saw the vision of a woman, a young woman, surrounded by fire. Her hands look to have been bound behind her. There was a woman throwing small branches onto the fire and as she did, she screamed at the girl, 'Burn witch burn!' It wasn't until much later that I realized the woman being burned was me.

Several woman have traced phobias for fire or water to deaths in other lives by burning or drowning. My own phobia is of water, and I believe I was drowned as a witch in another life.

There are cases of small children having memories of other lives, making connections that are verified by curious adults. Florence McClain's small daughter spoke her first words in German, though she had never heard German spoken since her birth. And this before she was three:

'Such garbage I vud not feed you ven you was kind (child),' she said, eyeing the french fries. 'Gut boiled potatoes I feed you. Come, I teach you to cook gut deutsch food.' I stood in shocked silence as she continued, 'Mommy, why are you the mother this time and I am the child? I don't want to be a child again.'[17]

Perhaps the most famous case of this sort is the 1937 case of Shanti Devi in India. At the age of four, she talked of her life as a woman of another village, and her parents wrote to the people she named. Taken to the village, she identified people and places, knew the streets and how to get to the house she had once lived in. She identified her former husband and former parents, and the room where she had buried some money under a floorboard. She knew her way around and where things were in houses she had not been in in this life.[18]

In another typical story, people find themselves in bodies of other races when they experience past life regression. Mimi, doing regression work for two women who are friends, found that they were sisters in several other lives. One was Black in two of her past lives and is Black in this one. The other woman is now white. Says Mimi, "They were always associated somehow." The lives of the two women were varied and their reincarnations mostly female. They lived in Asia, the South Pacific and East India, as well as in France and Italy. Ruth Montgomery relates the story of a woman she regressed, white in this life, who was a Chinese woman and footbound in one past life, and a Black woman slave in another.[19]

Sunlight describes the past life visions of a birthing mother:

The baby called to me in a different voice. Then she came into my mind in the form of a Black woman and I saw us together by another river, another tree. I knew we were in Africa, that she was my mother and I was her small son . . . We changed again and the river changed. We were slave women drying papyrus by the Nile, plotting our revolt. We were secret lovers in an attic room above a busy market place where people were shouting in French . . . We were Pomo Indians somewhere in these hills—I was the medicine woman, helping her give birth.[20]

Maggie remembers a past life as a man, a soldier in sixteenth century France. During the witch burnings she helped another man, a witch, escape:

I can still feel in my body and my spirit how it was to be that soldier. He limped, left leg, had done too much, seen too much, was much disillusioned. The compassion that moved him, suddenly, to save the fugitive probably saved him as well.

Incidently, when I am very tired or feel overwhelmed by the culture's darkness, I find I walk with a very slight limp in my left leg. I remember him, then, and his kindness, and am kinder myself.

## Linda also experienced the witch persecutions, but in Salem:

Oftentimes during my daily meditation, I have memories of a past life. The name that I keep coming up with is the name of Cassandra Allenby. She may have lived during the time of the Salem persecutions or during the time of the English Church persecutions (which would put it around the seventeenth century). During that time, she was (or rather, I was), the High Priestess of a coven located in the Scottish Highlands around Ross and Cromarty County.

Somehow I abused the power that I was given, and I was forced out of my coven leadership. I repented of my wrong-doing and left for the New World, which was a very rough crossing to say the least. I settled in or around Salem, MA and I began to practice my Craft in secret. My father was a wealthy silk merchant, but we were not allowed to wear silks, because our father told us that it would be frowned upon by the village elders.

So, we wore the simple Puritan clothes that everyone else wore at that time. I was the oldest of seven children, four girls and three boys. My father and mother were also coven leaders, but they relinquished their leadership when they emigrated to America. I led and organized a new coven for a while, but I finally decided to return to solitary practice.

A close friend or a beau of mine, I'm not sure which, thought that it would be great fun if he turned me in to the elders of the town. One elder in particular was already after me in a very ungentlemanly way, and he was delighted when I was taken in for trial. My last memory was being placed on the Ducking Stool and being lowered into the water. This may explain why I cannot swim in this incarnation and why I have trouble in my relationships with the opposite sex.

## Linda has had past life flashbacks since childhood:

When I was a Baptist, this would bother me a great deal. I still have trouble accepting the reality of past lives in this incarnation, but I'm learning to keep an open mind. I now practice as a solitary, as I did those many centuries ago, and I'm re-learning my lost talents. Perhaps I will be able to verify my existence as Cassandra Allenby through a hypnotist who does past life regressions.

## Bonnie, whose experience with simultaneous lives is recorded in Chapter One, had this past life flashback:

A *very* brief flash, odd in that 'I' seemed to have been looking down, and so only had a glimpse of legs and horse's legs. I was standing on a grassy hill, with lowland in between a second hill, no trees. I had on rough leggins with tied up legs, like straps. It was before a battle. I could smell the horse, and hear the leather creak on it. The horse snorted, lifted its back hoof and thudded it down. I heard the real *weight* of that. Then back. This one only lasted as long as it took for the horse to lift and drop its leg.

## Gloria's story from Chapter One also continues. She stopped for a picnic in the Colorado canyon:

There were wild strawberries growing everywhere along the bank. I started

62

busying myself picking berries. I heard a woman's laughter and smiled at the thought of others up here enjoying the day. When I turned around and looked, there she was, young, her hair down, a white dress with puffed sleeves and high topped shoes. She was balancing on a big rock at the side of the stream. 'Oh, No,' I thought, 'here it goes again.' The film was running.

She was tall, maybe 5'8", and here came a man, maybe 6'2". He had on a uniform, very nice and orderly, though I had never seen one quite like it. Everything reflected the late 1800's. This may have been a Navy uniform.

He came up the path beside the stream and he smiled and held out his hand to help her from the rock. She took it and I could feel the joy in her heart. She was playing, running ahead of him on their walk. They stood and looked at each other for a moment and she turned and went on up the trail ahead of him. He followed and they were soon out of sight.

I was feeling pretty good by the time we left and started back to the city.

Was this an earlier view of the woman in mourning, and was that woman an alternate or past life of Gloria's? She isn't sure.

Sheila met Paul on a blind date, after her ouija board told her that she would marry a man named Paul. She met him several years later and found a soul mate.

We were sitting on the cushions, working a puzzle on the coffee table. That's when it happened. I knew—almost like a light or a bell—not that I saw or heard anything—but I knew that this was the person I had been looking for. I can still see him, see his elbow on the table, his head in his hand, his head slightly tilted. Something clicked—there he was.

It certainly was irrational: the first time we were alone, our first single date and I make a lifetime decision. I still didn't want to get married, but he was the person for me. He wanted a wife and a family; I wanted a lover with no strings. I thought long and hard. I had never met anyone who was even close to the ambiguous 'someone right for me' and here he was—almost perfect. I had no problem with being engaged, I loved it—but married?

Marriage was never in my plans. Kathy wanted to get married, have babies, and bake brownies. Everybody had a plan. Mine was to live alone in the North Woods. In the summer I would guide canoeists. In the winter I would write—like Thoreau (I never figured out what I would write or who would buy it, just that I would live in a cabin in the woods, by a lake).

Yet, the more I looked at Paul, the less certain I was of my plans, because I knew he fit in my life. Finally, I told myself, 'Go ahead, try marriage. If it doesn't work, you can always go live in the woods. If you don't try marriage, (marriage to anyone else was unfathomable) you will always wonder if you should have.'

So we did. I know I have my soul mate. I think that is what I felt on New Year's Eve, 1971, but I didn't know what it was called.

At five years old, in kindergarten, Jim gave Dee a plastic wedding band from a Cracker-Jack box. He told her they would get married and they did right out of high school. There was never a question about it in either of their minds. They are retired now, and still together. Dee's experience and Sheila's are of soul mates.

If the purpose of reincarnation is to experience as many types of lives as possible, these women have met the definition. Barbara Hand Clow, in *Eye of the Centaur*, describes a variety of lives and occupations over many centuries. She had lived lives as male and female, of all races, social classes and statuses, in many different cultures. Reading her descriptions, the reader is drawn into the lives, invoking past lives of her own. She describes herself as Aspasia, Oracle of Delphi:

> I am tall with a big barrel-chested body and small breasts. My hair is medium-length ringlets like a bunch of grapes, and I wear a heavy decorative head band of copper and semi-precious stones in my hair. My neck is thick and strong, my whole face is large with very prominent cheekbones, and my nose is long and perfectly straight. I am beautiful, a paradigm of Minoan beauty . . . I am standing with my hand rested on one of the pillars looking out at the side of a hillside. It is very warm and breezy. The hillside is on my left, and the Aegean Sea on my right.[21]

And as Lydia, an Assyrian prostitute:

> I wear a blue robe with my face covered by a shroud. I am outdoors, and there are people around. They are behind me, talking loudly, and they whisper my name. Lydia, Lydia. I'm 22. It's not that they are talking about me, nor am I respected. I am a fallen woman. I do not like to be here when they are here. I leave because they bother me.[22]

Barbara is also aware of a female life as a Victorian lady, dead only a few years before her rebirth as Barbara in 1943. The range of her experiences is mind boggling, and I recommend the book. There is not one life, but many lives, a past eons long for women incarnate today.

Maggie comments on the idea of reincarnation and the connection of past with present lives:

> I know that psychology often treats past-life experience as if, like many dreams, it were simply a way for the unconscious to make itself known. Past life characters would then be parts of ourselves and past life situations would be a way of projecting our inner drama upon an outer screen or stage. I know from experience that it is important to consider past-life experience in just this way, to understand how it speaks to our psychology *now*, what it says about us in this life. But there is no reason, I believe, to limit the inner story being told to one lifetime or to see it as 'purely' psychological. We repeat situations in our lives until we become conscious of what we are doing and why. So too, I think we repeat situations life after life, continue to draw the same energies to ourselves, repeat the theme, over and over, until we have learned what we need to learn, and until we learn that we have ourselves chosen the necessary experience and are able to take responsibility for the choice.
>
> Perhaps one day when we understand what time and matter and energy really are, we won't make these limiting distinctions any longer. I hope I am born in that interesting time. I hope that Cheryl and I are born together in that interesting time! I believe we will be.

She touches on an idea that has become strong in reincarnation theory since Jane Robert's work, the idea that past lives are not lived in sequence, but like the rest of time, are lived simultaneously. There are other realities, running concurrently with the one we call "now," and we live other lives in them. Marion Weinstein calls this the Aspect Theory. In it, familiarly, is the idea that "all time is now."

> According to this theory, each of us has myriad lifetimes and personalities, and contrary to the more popular beliefs about reincarnation, these lifetimes are not sequential, because time itself is not sequential (i.e. moving to present, moving to future). Human perception in our culture may experience time as sequential, and therefore assume that reincarnation is linear, but this is only perception. In the Aspect Theory (and now in the New Physics also), all time is considered to be actually *simultaneous*. In other words, although most people believe that time includes past, present and future, all time is really made up of one vast present.[23]

In this theory, all of a soul's incarnations are happening at one time, "now," divided from each other by a focusing of each part of the personality on its own incarnation, to the exclusion of its other parts. Explains Jane Roberts' channeled entity, Seth:

> You live all your reincarnations at once, but you find this difficult to understand within the context of three-dimensional reality.
> The various reincarnational selves can be *superficially* regarded as portions of a crossword puzzle, for they are all portions of the whole, and yet they can exist separately.
> Because you are obsessed with the idea of past, present, and future, you are forced to think of reincarnations as strung out one before the other. But . . . only the egos involved make the time distinction.
> The whole self is aware of *all* of the experiences of *all* of the egos.
> Since all events occur at once in actuality, there is little to be gained by saying that a past event causes a present one.[24]

All of this points back to the idea of different perceptions and realities, and the concept of simultaneous time, space-time, of Chapter One. According to Jane Roberts and Seth, the experiences of all incarnations blend together, and the happenings of a past life cannot be the *cause* of happenings in this one, since all of the happenings occur at once. Maggie's comment about repeating situations until we resolve them comes clear here, a trying-out on several different levels until the problem is solved. This is the center of karma. Situations are repeated, says Maggie,

> until we have learned what we need to learn, and until we learn that we have ourselves chosen the necessary experience and are able to take responsibility for the choice.

Nothing is predestined, only directions are set before birth, directions and events that can be changed by the personality/Be-ing in action. Carrying Jane Roberts' work further, each woman has a multidimensional personality, with a self that exists in more than one dimension and reality plane. Other alternate personalities exist, in other lives, in the "now," all choosing experience by free will.

> No event is predestined. Any given event can be changed not only before and during but *after* its occurrence . . . The individual is hardly at the mercy of past events, for she changes them constantly. She is hardly at the mercy of future events, for she changes these not only before but after their happening . . . The past is as real as the future, no more or no less.[25]

Some women, like Gloria and Bonnie in Chapter One and the women of this chapter, have spontaneous access to past life/other reality experiences and use them to influence their currently focused lives. Others separate their conscious awareness more fully from other existences. Most women have clues—deja vu experiences, unexplainable phobias or knowledges, strong aversions and attractions that have no rational reason or known source, instant attractions or dis-attractions to another. No one has all the information of all her other lifes; it would prevent her from handling her this-life reality, and threaten what is called her sanity. Barbara Hand Clow writes of this, in her passage that opens this chapter.

Women who have learned to shift between linear reality and matriarchal/womb consciousness are women most likely to gain access to past life material either spontaneously or by intention. The skill of past life regression is a root center, etheric double awakening, since the root center with its red and black colors is the outside and inside of the womb. Past life experiences are stored in the spiritual body, and transmitted into the etheric double by way of the mental and emotional bodies. Root center awareness of past lives is then transmitted to the physical brain by the kama-manas mind. The connection of past, present and future lives is through the gateway of life, woman's womb and the vagina/birth canal. Through past life regression by meditation work, information about other lives is accessed. The process of this-life regression back to birth and the process of rebirthing, also access past life material. The information gained is usually material important for work ongoing in the current incarnation, and at the present time.

Begin this work on a rational reality level. Keep a notebook or journal listing incidents that could be past life connected, incidents from waking or from dreams. The things to look for are:

1. Deja vu experiences.
2. Dreams that have no basis in daily reality.
3. Places that are familiar when they shouldn't be.
4. People that are familiar when they shouldn't be.
5. Strong affinities for a person, place, object, taste, sound or fragrance.
6. Irrational fears of things, people, etc. with no reason.
7. Phobias.
8. Unreasonable aversions to a person, place, object, etc.[26]

Entering the meditative state, explore each event, one at a time, listing the impressions and images that come for each incident or entry. Go back to childhood or other events that made a strong impression, usually events of strong emotions, and in the relaxed meditative state go deeply into the event. Allow the images to go where they will, and make note of the places visited. Use one incident or event per meditation, no more. Going to bed, hold a chosen incident in the mind before sleep, and make an effort to record your dreams for that night upon waking. List the responses next to the triggering incident in the past life journal.

Information/answers come as fragments that add together later to form a whole, or in spontaneous scenes that replay full experiences. Fragmented material complies and is cumulative, and repeating a meditation on an incident already worked with can produce new material. Visualize exploring a place or another time, a dream scene that hints of being a past life connection.

The other way to access past life material is through fully guided past life regression. This is a meditation going to deep mind levels of the alpha to theta brainwave state. In that state, another woman asks questions that lead to past life recall, guides her friend into the meditative state and through one or more past life memory scenes. These meditations are available on several tapes for women working alone, but regressions are usually more effective when guided by someone who follows what's happening and responds to it. Maggie's past life as a fisherman and her connection with Cheryl were opened by repetitions of a regression tape. One such tape is Zana's *Journey to Another Life*, and LaVedi Lafferty, a Llewellyn Publications author, has a series of them.[27]

Meditation work that is guided by another woman is the most

effective way to obtain past life regression, and detailed instructions are given in several excellent books. Recommended are: Florence Wagner McClain, *A Practical Guide to Past Life Regression,* (St. Paul, Llewellyn Publications, 1986); Diane Mariechild, *Mother Wit* (Trumansburg, NY, The Crossing Press, 1981); Jane Roberts, *The Coming of Seth,* (New York, Pocket Books, 1966); and Marion Weinstein, *Earth Magic,* (Custer, WA, Phoenix Publishing Co., Expanded Edition, 1986). Here is how it works. The past life meditation is described for the woman doing the guiding, but it can also be taped for self-use.

First guide the woman into full physical and mental relaxation, invoking personal symbols, and going through the tensing and relaxing of each part of the body. Direct her through each body part a second time, asking her to become *unaware* of each part of her body in turn. The object is total relaxation and entrance into the slowest possible brainwave state.[28] Suggest to the woman that she will remember everything from the regression that is beneficial to her, leaving behind anything that is not. Direct her to be in front of the building she lives in, and to describe it. Wait for her response. Then to be in front of the building at another season, and describe that, and then another season. Wait for verbal responses. This, after the relaxation, is done only at the first regression.

Then,

*Imagine that you are standing in front of the door to your home. Imagine that you are opening the door. Imagine that the door opens into a long tunnel and that you can see a light at the end of the tunnel. I am going to count from twenty to one. With each descending number imagine that you are moving down the tunnel toward the light and moving back through time to a lifetime you lived previous to this one. At the count of one you will step from the tunnel into the light, into a lifetime which you lived previous to this one.[29]*

The guide counts backwards, and at the end says, "You are now in a lifetime which you lived previous to this one." Ask her to look down and describe her feet, what she's wearing on them, and then go through the following questions, relating them to the situation and responses that come:

*What are you wearing on your body?*
*About what age are you?*
*Are you male or female?*
*What is your name?*

*Where are you? What place or city? Describe your surroundings. What year is it?*[30]

Direct her to talk about relationships in her life, parents, sisters, lovers, children. Ask her to quickly describe a day in her life, then move her forward in time to an older age.

*Move forward in time to the point where you are approximately five years older, about the age of_____. It will only take a moment. You will feel time passing around you like currents of air or the pages flipping off a calendar. Tell me as soon as you are there.*[31]

Ask her about her life again, questioning her on important people, daily life, does she have children, what is her spiritual life, her occupation, is she happy? Ask her about high points in her experience. Repeat this again over several time jumps.

Take her to another lifetime, asking her to go back to a life previous to the one she's been describing. Pick an age for her to be, and ask her to tell you when she gets there. Do this questioning again. If there is no response to a particular question go on to another; if there is a blank, go to a different age or different life—you may have passed her lifespan in that life. To end the regression, say:

*In a moment I will count from one to five. At the count of five you will open your eyes in the here and now, feeling alert and refreshed. You will bring with you everything on every level which might be beneficial to you in any way. You will leave behind everything which might be detrimental to you in any way.*[32]

Do the counting, and bring her back to now slowly. Ask her to remain still until she is fully in the present, then to talk about her experience, noting any new details. Be supportive.

Florence McClain suggests directing regression work after the first experience to specific lifetimes, if there are memory clues to trace. Guide them by saying, "You will be in the lifetime where _____ happened," or where you lived as _____." If a particular time period is looked for, direct her to the one where she *may* have lived in _____. (She may not have had a lifetime there, so use *may*). In one regression, ask her to go to the lifetime that has the most importance to her present one.

For phobias or fears, ask a woman during past life regression to go to where the problem started, also suggesting that she will feel no fear, pain or distress in reliving that experience. Do this after some experience with regressions, not at the first time. Many women have their first experience with past lives during a psychologist's attempts to relieve a phobia by trancework regressing her to an early period in this life. If in any of these, the suggestion draws a blank, go on to another experience or suggestion.

Soul mates and other relationships can be investigated by past life regression meditation work, as can any clue or experience for which information is wanted that seems to suggest a past life. A person for which you have aversion or attraction in a seemingly inexplicable way can be a past life relationship, and can be understood by past life regression. Direct the meditation specifically for this. All of the items listed in a regression notebook, the deja vu experiences, dreams, attractions to an object, person, etc. can be investigated this way.

Always make the regression safe, the guide keeping her voice calm and continuing in control of the happenings. If the woman lands in a painful or traumatic experience, either move her from the experience, or suggest that she go through it without feeling pain or emotion. When the meditation ends, be supportive; the woman experiencing the work may feel embarrassed or feel that she's imagined all of it, made it all up—which is how it feels at first but is not the case. Do past life regression work only with others you trust, either as a guide or being guided. Know when to stop for the day, don't get too tired. Meditations can be done again. The woman guiding can switch places with the woman experiencing, so both have a chance for information and the past life regression experience. Tailor questions in the regression to the situation as it evolves.

Many women get a response on the first try at past life work, others take more than one session before they do. The deeper into the meditative state, the more relaxed before regression, the better chance there is of finding meaningful information. After doing it a few times and being in a past life, the process gets easier and fuller. The rich material of Barbara Hand Clow's *Eye of the Centaur* came from a series of past life regressions over a period of years. This work can be done gently with children, by a process of meditation and visualization, to help children with nightmares or phobias.[33] Encourage children to talk about their stories and dreams and be aware of the possibility of past life connections in them.

Helen Wambach, using this form of regression work on 750 people, took her groups to the time of birth and prebirth, and asked them questions about their incarnations in this life. She asked her subjects whether they were being born voluntarily, and who had helped them make the choices. She asked them why they were female (or male) in this life, why they were choosing this time period to be born, what purpose did they have for this lifetime? She asked them about their mothers, had they known them before in other lives, and were they being born at a time to connect with others they had known? Then she asked them about their feelings and thoughts on experiencing the birth process.

Her results, published in her book *Life Before Life*, (New York, Bantam Books, 1979), are interesting and exciting. Issues of past lives, karma, soul mates and other life relationships arose again and again in the responses. Her conclusions are that women choose to be born, choose their sex and circumstances, place of birth, purpose and parents for the pending lifetime. Birth is chosen with almost universal reluctance, and guided by "others" who help but who do not coerce the soul into a new life.

> Fully 87 percent of all subjects responding to any of the questions about the birth reported that they had known parents, lovers, relatives and friends who were known to them in past lives. Some had more detailed impressions than others, but there was little doubt that my subjects under hypnosis were aware of how they knew people in their lives now from past lives.
>
> Among the 87 percent responding 'yes' to the question about knowing parents in past lives, there was an astonishing variety in the relationships reported ... Often parents in this life were friends or distant relatives in past lives.[34]

More on Helen Wambach's work in Chapter Thirteen.

Past life regression is an entrance into the inner world of stroking the python, a journey into the womb of the creation Goddess and Goddess within. The connection with past lives, whether perceived linearly or simultaneously, is a shifting of perceptions from patriarchal reality and "now," to matriarchal universal consciousness. Evidence shows that everyone has many life experiences, and that these experiences figure into day's life realities. By accessing other realities/ other lives, the woman who is psychic opens deeper and fuller dimensions of her Goddess Be-ing.

# FOOTNOTES

1. Barbara Hand Clow, *Eye of the Centaur: A Visionary Guide Into Past Lives*, p. 23.

2. Barbara Walker, *The Woman's Encyclopedia of Myths and Secrets*, (San Francisco, Harper and Row Publishers, 1983), p. 847-849.

3. Annie Besant, *Reincarnation*, (Wheaton, IL, Quest/Theosophical Publishing House, 1985, original 1892), p. 3-4.

4. *Ibid.*, p. 52.

5. *Ibid.*, p. 38.

6. *Ibid.* This is classic theosophical thinking, probably originating with the work of Helen Blavatsky and based on Eastern tradition.

7. Barbara G. Walker, *The Woman's Encyclopedia of Myths and Secrets*, p. 495.

8. Diane Mariechild, *Mother Wit: A Feminist Guide to Psychic Development*, p. 82.

9. *Ibid.*, p. 85-86.

10. Florence Wagner McClain, *A Practical Guide to Past Life Regression*, (St. Paul, Llewellyn Publications, 1986), p. 18.

11. *Ibid.*, p. 19.

12. Jane Roberts, *The Seth Material*, p. 155.

13. Laeh Maggie Garfield and Jack Grant, *Companions in Spirit*, (Berkeley, CA, Celestial Arts, 1984) p. 23.

14. Sandra A. Bruce, "Past Lives as Metaphor," in *Circle Network News*, (Mt. Horeb, WI), Winter, 1986-87, p. 9.

15. I thank Susan Sheppard for our many discussions on this subject over several years.

16. Ruth Montgomery, *Here and Hereafter*, (New York, Coward-McCann, Inc., 1968), Chapter Nine.

17. Florence Wagner McClain, *A Practical Guide to Past Life Regression*, p. 1.

18. Ruth Montgomery, *Here and Hereafter*, p. 146.

19. *Ibid.*, p. 79-80.

20. Sunlight, *Womonseed*, p. 228.

21. Barbara Hand Clow, *Eye of the Centaur*, p. 50.

22. *Ibid.*, p. 71.

23. Marion Weinstein, *Earth Magic*, (expanded edition), p. 73.

24. Jane Roberts, *The Seth Material*, p. 148-149.

25. *Ibid.*, p. 220. Pronouns are changed to "she."

26. Ruth Montgomery, *Here and Hereafter*, p. 24-25. Also, Nadine, "Past Lives" in *Circle Network News*, (Mt. Horeb, WI), Winter, 1986-87, p. 12.

27. Zana, *Journey to Another Life*, 12150 W. Calle Seneca, Tucson, AZ 85743, $10. LaVedi Lafferty, *Past Life Memory Program*, Five Audio Tapes, Llewellyn Publications, POB 64383, St. Paul, MN 55164, Dept. DS, $10 each.

28. This regression is from Florence McClain, *A Practical Guide to Past Life Regression*, p. 37-48.

29. *Ibid.*, p. 42.

30. *Ibid.*, p. 43.

31. *Ibid.*, p. 43-44.

32. *Ibid.*, p. 45.

33. Donna Clark, "Children's Past Life Experiences," in *Circle Network News*, (Mt. Horeb, WI), Winter, 1986-87, p. 13.

34. Helen Wambach, *Life Before Life*, (New York, Bantam Books, 1979), p. 91-92.

# Chapter Four
# The Belly Chakra: Astral Projection Women Flying

*I was one day surprised and disturbed to perceive a shadowy replica of myself at some distance in front of me. After observing it for a moment, I rose and attempted to approach it; as I did so it lost outline and drew back towards me—it was my own 'surround'... What is not generally accepted by science, but which I nevertheless know to be true, is that everyone has a 'double' of finer substance than the physical body, the 'Astral' body. This is not to be confused with the 'surround' which remains in position enveloping the body, while the conscious projection (of the astral/emotional) is accomplished.*

*This projection should be more fully understood, for I am always coming into contact with numbers of people who had experienced it and have been afraid to accept its significance. I believe that projection takes place far more often than any of us realize . . .* [1]

I am in my bed and nearly asleep, missing a friend terribly. All I want is to be with her, but she is across the country, thousands of miles away. Suddenly, I feel a jolt and a blacking out, a high speed floating. There is no other way I can describe the sensations. I am in a room with white walls, and a print of flowers on the wall. There is a beige square-looking couch, a tan ginger jar lamp and windows in a row. On a Danish style coffee table is an album and another book, some pens. The room is airy, bright and clean. I see her come into the room, wearing white slacks, sandals, a summery print blouse. She stares, starts to say something, then stops again.

I get scared, and find myself moving swiftly, too swiftly. There is a seasick feeling and another jolt, and I'm back in my bed, at nighttime, in winter. The daylight, summer scene, woman and white room are gone. I am frightened and disturbed. I have seen her, I know that but I don't know how. I have never been to her home.

Almost a year later, I visit her town and she takes me to her house. She has moved since the time of my experience, but the new place is the room I saw on that strange night when I visited her. The walls are white, couch beige and square looking, the print on the wall, lamp, coffee table, album. I feel the color drain from my face for a moment, then shake it off as she starts to show me her home. I'm psychic aren't I? These things happen every day. I think I must have astral projected that night; it's happened once or twice before. I haven't the nerve to ask her what *she* saw, I only know what *I* saw, and it's this room I'm standing in. I've been here before.

Astral projection is the separation of the emotional body/belly chakra consciousness to travel through time or space. The dense physical body, surrounded by its etheric double aura, remains at point of origin. A silver cord of astral matter, stretching infinitely thin, connects the dense physical body and physical aura at home with the flying and roving consciousness. The emotional, mental and spiritual bodies travel, and as long as the silver cord remains intact and connecting them to the physical bodies, they return safely. Many women describe experiences, usually spontaneous ones, of astral travel, astral projection, or as it's also called, OBE or out of body experience. The experiences are spontaneous or induced, and some women learn to astral project at will.

This is a belly chakra/emotional body phenomena, connected with kama-manas, the desire-mind of theosophical anatomy. Some researchers place this skill at the solar plexus, the center of will, but will is not enough to induce astral travel unless the emotional need is there with it. The silver cord that connects the emotional body to the physical it leaves behind is seen in some projections to attach at the navel (solar plexus center), and in others at the belly or the crown. Entrance of the consciousness into the emotional body occurs from the belly chakra in the beginning stages of the skill. At this point, travel is limited; the silver cord is thicker and less elastic, and travel remains close to the body, usually in the same room. In cases where the cord comes from the navel or the crown, it is thinner and more flexible, and travel is unlimited. I visited my friend in California, from my bedroom in Pittsburgh. It is the synthesis of kama-manas, the emotional (belly) and lower mental (solar plexus) centers that offers wide-ranging astral projection, but without the desire emotional body there is no travel at all. Consciousness is sent out in the emotional body of the aura, the place associated with the belly chakra, that is sometimes called the astral body.

Out of body experience is a universal phenomena, known world-wide and cross-culturally, as in other psychic skills. It has been des-cribed in India, Tibet, Africa, China, Europe, North and South America, Polynesia, Native America, Australia and Siberia. In Hawaii the Huna describe a shadowy double of the lower and middle selves, as well as of the soul body. These bodies are the physical, emotional, mental and spiritual bodies, also known as the subconscious, conscious and super-conscious. The Huna's lower self is the etheric double, middle self the emotional body. In Africa, the Zulu know and accept astral projection, and call the bodies the *inyama* (physical body/etheric double), and the *isithunzi*, which means "shadow" and is the vehicle for *umoya*, the soul. It is the *isithunzi*, the emotional or astral body, which travels, leaving the *inyama* or etheric double behind with the physical body.[2]

Estimates are that as many as twenty-five percent of all people have had astral projection experiences, though the numbers vary with the source. Some researchers believe that the astral emotional body leaves the physical nightly during sleep and that this is a natural fact of women's Be-ing.[3] Astral projection is regarded as an archetypal experience, something within reach of all women, just because they exist. Worldwide, the accounts of out of body experiences are similar in nature, describing the process, the silver cord, the feeling of leaving and returning, the nature of the travel, and the circumstances under which it occurs. The thousands of descriptions of "ghosts" or appari-tions written about under psychic phenomena and manifesting are in many cases astral projections, if the "ghost" is of someone alive. Women's beginning reactions to experiencing astral travel is typically fear at first, with sometimes a conviction she has died, followed by an understanding of the process, and an exhilaration and wonder at the +imitlessness of it. Once the understanding comes, the experience is joyous. Children astral project routinely and seldom have fear. Women can fly, and be freer in time and space than even the envied birds.

The emotional body is the center of desire, emotion, sexuality, imagery storage and taste. An influx of "powerful sexual energy"[4] is reported by some people who experience astral projection. Ann Faraday, who connects out of body experience to "flying dreams," and flying dreams as a forerunner of an OBE (out of body experience), comments that, "Psychoanalysts tend to reduce all pleasant flying dreams to sexual desire, but this is at best a gross overgeneralization."[5] The connection of astral projection to dreams is a strong one, but they are two different phenomena. An out of body experience is easiest to access at a state between waking and sleeping (the theta brainwave state), but astral projection is not a dream at all. Ann Faraday, noted dream researcher, says that lucid dreams involving sexual arousal often lead first to the flying dream and then to an actual astral projection. Sexual energy pervades the whole physical body in instances that become astral projections, where in a typical erotic dream, the energy remains at the genital level.[6] The intensity of the belly chakra/emotional body energy transcends the physical, carrying consciousness beyond the body, and leaving the physical levels literally behind.

Women who see auras generally see the colors of the emotional/astral body. When that body is away from the physical and etheric double it is still visible, but as a double of that physical body. This transference of image is the source of some "ghosts" or apparitions. A child describes seeing her sister in her room at night, when her sister lives in another city. A woman sees another on the street walking, but the other did not walk there that day. There are reliable accounts of women being seen in two places at once, and even photographed there. Many "ghosts" are real-live women traveling in the astral, and seen by others sometimes thousands of miles away from their bodies. They may or may not be conscious of their projection and appearing. In a dream, there is no materialization of an astral form, nothing for oneself or others to see.

In astral projection, the woman projecting can see her own body below her on its bed or chair. She floats above it, noticing the silver cord, then travels where she wills away from it and the physical body remains behind. The usual reaction is of complete detachment, both emotionally and mentally from the physical body. Comments are of how pathetic the body looks, how fragile. The body remaining behind is not the self, consciousness has entered the psychic anatomy, rising free of limits from the physical; there is a sense of boundlessness and freedom. The woman goes anywhere she wishes just by willing herself to be there. Time and space are irrelevant. She travels with a feeling of flying that's the archetypal wish of anyone who's ever watched the freedom of a bird. Coming back to the physical is being grounded again, limited to the concrete, linear world. Once a woman has astral traveled, and accepts the experience without fear, her desire to fly again is often intense. A woman telling me of several spontaneous out of body experiences now takes flying lessons in a small plane. She wants that much to reproduce the feeling.

Yet, in the astral the advantages of physical Be-ing, of having a body, are left behind. In astral projection, a woman can go wherever she wishes, but she cannot affect dense matter by anything she does, once she has left proximity to her body. She can pass through doors and solid objects by willing herself through them, but she cannot hold a doorknob and open the door herself. She can appear to a friend in another place, but cannot touch her. She can transmit messages telepathically, but cannot speak them, since her vocal cords, throat and mouth are at home in her physical body. No matter how good the food looks where she travels, she cannot eat. If her sexual desire is aroused, she can consummate it only with another Be-ing in the astral.

Entering the astral/emotional body and projecting away from the physical happens spontaneously for women during times of great physical or emotional pain, in trauma, or at other times of total relaxation. It occurs in childbirth labor, fevers, during surgery when under anesthetics, in states of shock, seizures, at times of extreme emotion, in near death experiences, and at times of death itself.[7] It also happens, and can be induced to happen, when simply the desire to be somewhere else is strong enough and the woman in an alpha to theta brainwave state—in lucid dreaming or almost asleep—visualizes herself effectively in that other place. Like other psychic skills and psychic phenomena, out of body experiences/astral travel occur spontaneously in certain optimal conditions, or can be induced by training. Many women have OBE's spontaneously, many children do, and of women who wish to induce it, most can learn how.

There are four ways of experiencing out of body phenomena:

1. Involuntarily and without consciousness.
2. Involuntarily and with consciousness.
3. Voluntarily and without consciousness (the watcher).
4. Voluntarily and with consciousness.[8]

In the first case, involuntarily and without consciousness, the woman wakes in the morning having had "weird" dreams that she may vaguely remember, and feeling more tired than when she went to sleep. In some unusual cases, the ejected astral matter causes poltergeist effects in the woman's bedroom, noises or rappings, shakings. Astral travel that is involuntary and with consciousness is spontaneous astral projection, the kind that most women describe in their psychic experiences, and that a selection of is given in this chapter. My experience of travel to California was such an incident, not a willed astral projection, but with conscious awareness of where I had been. Diane's experience as a child in Italy, quoted in Chapter One, is another example.

Projection voluntarily and without consciousness is a tool of magickal practices, used to send the astral form out to gain impressions and return them. Denning and Phillips call this a watcher, an exteriorization of emotional body substance without the transfer of consciousness into it. The fourth category is induced astral projection, a skill that can be learned by most women. The focus of this chapter is on categories two and four, involuntary and voluntary out of body experiences with full consciousness. Women should be aware of the first category, and for those wishing to make use of the watcher, a concept in Huna, see Melita Denning and Osborne Phillips' book, *The Llewellyn Practical Guide to Astral Projection*.

Women experiencing astral travel universally describe the same process or stages. The start is of leaving the physical body, often with the sensation of a snap or a click when it happens, and often preceded by a feeling of paralysis or catalepsy just before the separation. In most cases, the woman is near sleep or thinks she is asleep when this happens. She may feel a sensation like suffocation or experiencing a high wind, or one like electric shock felt usually in the head. Some women describe a tingling moving from their feet upwards to their heads, and being freed from their bodies when the sensation reaches their heads. The woman sees her physical body on the bed below her, feels herself floating above her body. The body looks stiff and lifeless, eyes sometimes open, but the traveling consciousness consistently has no concern for the physical body left behind or its condition.

At this point, the woman becomes aware of the silver cord, connecting her to her physical body and etheric double below. The cord is seen when the woman looks down, and its thickness varies with distance from the physical. When the woman's consciousness in her emotional/astral body is close to the physical, the cord is thick, and the woman can still affect physical objects. When she travels way from her body, the cord becomes thinner, a trailing stream of light, and she can no longer affect the material world. The cord is described as ranging from a quarter of an inch to three inches thick,[9] and thinner cords give greater mobility. Within a "critical distance," solid objects are affected by the projecting woman, but not after she has left the proximity of her body:

So long as these 'doubles' were within this critical distance (fairly close to the body) they were relatively dense and (i) might be able to move physical objects, i.e., to exercise telekinesis, (ii) might be obstructed in their movements by walls, and (iii) would strongly feel the pull of the body. If and when these 'doubles' moved further away from the body and passed beyond their critical distance they were relatively tenuous and (i) were unable to move physical objects, (ii) could pass unhindered through walls and (iii) no longer felt the pull of the body—they were free.[10]

The silver cord is described as an elastic thread of light, connecting the double, usually at the crown of the head or back of the neck, to the physical body at the solar plexus. Descriptions of where the cord attaches are varied and unclear. Some women describe it as an umbilical cord, some even describe two cords, from head and solar plexus. In the work of Melita Denning, the silver cord is sent in induced astral projections from the solar plexus of the physical body/etheric double, to connect with the emotional/astral transmitted body at the chosen place that is the woman's center of consciousness. This can be her solar plexus, throat, third eye, heart—wherever she feels that her Being is.[11] The cord extends to this spot.

As the woman moves away from her physical body, the silver cord lengthens and extends to wherever she goes. The woman thinks of and visualizes a particular place and she is there. Distance is no limit, nor are physical barriers—she can pass through walls, but not affect dense matter. Others can see her, and her "apparition" can be photographed. In the process of traveling to the willed spot the woman experiences a sensation of great speed, sometimes with windiness, and usually feels she is traveling in a long dark tunnel. This experience can be a frightening sensation, even when the woman knows what's happening, but it lasts only for a short moment. At the end of the tunnel is bright light, and her destination. This description also operates in past life regression work and in the near death experiences that will be discussed later.

Thinking of her body or feeling fright while traveling returns the woman to her physical body. As long as the silver cord remains intact, the woman returns to her body without effort, but usually with a jolt. Some have the sensation of hovering horizontally above their bodies before reentering. Then there is a sudden jolt, feeling of shock, or another click, and the emotional/astral consciousness merges again with the physical body and etheric double. A distinguishing characteristic of the process is that the woman is fully aware of the happenings, knows she has projected and where she has been. Astral projection is not a dream.[12]

Here is a classical astral projection description, that of Genevieve McGarrigle in Crookall's *Casebook*:

> I lay in bed on the verge of sleep. All was quiet and I experienced a sense of complete relaxation and peace. Just before losing consciousness, I began to feel a tingling in my toes which gathered momentum as it surged through my body. As it reached the top of my head, I felt a violent pull upward.
>
> Suddenly, like the bursting of a taut elastic band, I was released. I was floating, a free agent capable of traveling with indescribable speed. I looked down and saw my body lying open-eyed on the bed, but I couldn't bother with what I had left behind on the bed.
>
> I passed through the closed door of my bedroom and rushed out through the walls.
>
> Again I was pulled far up into the heavens. In the distance I saw a white light, which became more and more dazzling as I approached. The whiteness was blinding. Afraid to face that light although it beckoned me to come, I turned back.[13]

Such descriptions are typical, and several casebooks of astral projection experiences are in print. Spontaneous projections are listed at times of accident or illness, in the death process, produced by anesthetics or drugs, produced at times of strong desire, occur during sleep or in the waking state, occur with spirit helpers involved, and occur by induction or in hypnosis.[14] Cases of "ghosts" are often astral projections of living women, and also can be prompted by the death process. At time of death, the psychic bodies leaving the physical is seen as an "escaping gas" or as an astral projection, and the legend of witches flying to sabbats or broomsticks could be astral projection phenomena.

Women describe their experiences. First is Leonie, who early projected spontaneously, and then learned to induce the experience through meditation:

> When I was about fourteen, I began to have 'serious' out of body experiences, although they scared me at that point. I would be walking down a corridor while, at the same time, I was also hovering above myself, *watching* myself walk down that hall. I thought I was going crazy and hoped, if I didn't tell anyone, no one would notice, or that it would go away. It didn't, but not until about eight years later, when I took up yoga, did I realize what had happened and recognize this for what it was.
>
> With time and practice, I have found it easy and comfortable to leave my body during meditation and trances ... I am no longer bothered by these phenomena because I realize that many people share these and other 'paranormal' experiences with me. I know I'm not crazy, only functioning on more than one level or plane at once, as opposed to people who are taught to block out other information.

Another woman, a performer, describes the same type of event when she says she watches herself singing. This most often happens when she's tired, having a headache, or under stress.

Mrs. J. Martin, the only name given her in Robert Crookall's book, describes her second astral projection experience and her delight in it. In her first experience, she had become frightened and her fright brought her back to her body immediately. This time she knew what to expect:

> My head seemed to be very tight and buzzing and I urged it on. I had an idea what was about to happen. I found myself near the ceiling, looking down toward the bed ... then I said, 'Well, now, you won't ever doubt again, will you?' and answered, 'No! This is wonderful!' I floated softly and weightlessly up and down and then I thought I had better get back. I was in my bed as suddenly as I had found myself out of it ... I was not dreaming. It was the most wonderful feeling I have ever had experienced.[15]

In the same book, Florence Brady from Australia describes astral projection:

> I was up under the ceiling and could look down upon my body on the bed ... I went right through three rooms, seeing sleeping occupants, and then came to the side of my bed. I stood there for a minute, looking, then put out a finger and tried to touch an arm—immediately, I was back in the body and 'awake' ... Sometimes I would find myself returning through a big 'tunnel.'
> On one occasion, I awoke from a short doze to see a grey-blue mist moving before me in wreathing fashion.[16]

Any thought of or contact with the physical body returns the traveling emotional double to it. The grey-blue mist she describes is what Eileen Garrett described at the opening of this chapter. Such mists are often taken for ghosts or apparitions by someone else seeing the projected woman. At other times, the body seen seems solid, and only later does the woman seeing it realize it was a projection.

Cheryl describes seeing the projection of her lover and thinking it was her physical body that she saw. They had both fallen asleep. The same thing happened to her with Brandy, a Doberman:

> One evening I lay reading in my bedroom while my lover watched TV in the living room. When I woke up, it had gotten dark and I saw a figure I thought was my lover, bending over me in the dark. I sat up in bed and said, 'Thought you could fool me, huh? Well, I'm awake!' The figure dissolved into thin air, literally—just dematerialized. My lover was still asleep on the couch.

The fine line between sleeping and waking is the time for astral projections to occur. Cheryl continues:

> One morning, after my lover had gotten up and gone to work, I slept in. Awake, briefly, I felt her dog Brandy, jump up on the waterbed and lie across my legs. The weight of a Doberman is hard to mistake. Since she wasn't allowed up on the bed, I yelled, 'Down, Branny,' and felt her get up and jump off the bed. I heard her paws and toenails hit the wood floor, and drifted back to sleep. A few

hours later, when I woke again, I discovered Brandy had been *locked out* on the front porch—ever since my lover left for work.

In another experience with animals, Lady, who really *is* a "ghost," a thought-form of a once-living Be-ing, takes the astral projections of three living dogs for a walk. Stories of animals have been some favorites of the experiences women describe. Originally wanting to make a chapter of only animal experiences, I decided instead to include them with each individual psychic skill. Animals are naturally and genuinely psychic, as are children, and as women can re-learn to be. Mimi writes about Lady, a German Shepherd:

> I looked out the window and saw Lady walking down the road with three small dogs at her side. She was much taller and her proud prance was very evident. With an attitude of authority she was teaching them how to patrol the neighborhood as she did in life . . . She was telling them to be most watchful. They stayed surveying the tall grass and wild growth. When Lady was satisfied that all was clear they all moved down the road and disappeared in the distance.
>
> My wonder was, how did Lady contact these three dogs which were all new in the neighborhood and which I knew that at this early hour were still asleep in their homes. I am happy to have a canine patrol active again even with an invisible teacher.

Theosophists call such Be-ings Invisible Helpers, and usually describe them in human terms.

A woman astral projecting and thought to be a ghost is described in this experience. The woman's name is given only as Mrs. Butler.

> In 1891, Mrs. Butler who lived in Ireland . . . 'dreamed' of finding herself in a very beautiful house furnished with all imaginable comforts. The 'dream' made a deep impression on her. It returned for many nights in succession. The next year the Butlers took up residence in London. They went to see a house in Hampshire . . . When they reached the house she recognized it in every detail, except a certain door, which, as it turned out, had been added to the place within six months. The estate being for sale at a very low price, the Butlers decided to buy it. Afterward they began to suspect that, owing to the great bargain, there must be some defect. The agent then admitted that the property was haunted. The phantom seen was Mrs. Butler.[17]

In another such case, Joanne, who described seeing herself burned as a witch in a past life, describes going to her sister astrally, while physically remaining home and unconscious. She and her sister had conversation, while her sister's husband saw nothing.

> I must have sunk into oblivion because I wasn't myself for several hours. But at the same time I was out, across town at my sister's house. She was on their couch awake, with her husband not more than three or four feet away from her, when she started having this strange conversation with someone (else) . . . When he spoke to her to get her attention, she told him that I had been there and told her I was very depressed. She couldn't figure out why he didn't know what she was talking about and why he hadn't seen me.

Loren experienced astral travel in connection with a shamanic vision. The experience occurred in deep trance, and was therefore an induced experience, if not a controlled or chosen one:

About seven years ago, a Medicine Man came to one of our midwife gatherings and did a Pipe ceremony. I enjoyed it, but didn't give it much thought afterwards. A few days later, I was lying in a 'cup' in the earth, in a grove of trees on my land, and I fell into a deep trance. I felt that I was in a Pipe bowl, being smoked. It was a very peaceful and comforting experience. As this was happening, I felt a compelling urge to go see the Medicine Man, who lived about sixty-five miles away. When I came out of the trance, I was covered with leaves and a squirrel was sitting next to my face, watching me. I felt a little like Rip Van Winkle awaking from a long magical sleep. I went to the Medicine Man and he was not surprised to see me; he said that I was to be a Pipe Carrier and teacher, and so I worked with him for a year. He immediately addressed the concerns I had about the fearful side of my psychic life. In seeing it from the shamanic view I was able to begin dealing with it.

Barbara describes this projection experience, in a letter to me:

Did I come for a visit with you on Thursday, June 25? I mean, are you aware of me having been there with you? It would have been around ten or eleven in the evening. I was in bed, getting ready for sleep, lying on my back. I don't remember falling asleep at all. Anyway, I felt the weight of a large crystal in my left hand (I wasn't holding onto anything), and could hear you having a conversation with someone. I turned around to speak with you then everything disappeared, and I was back in my bed (and body, I guess). I opened my eyes and thought that I'd been to visit you. I had been thinking of you all day, so perhaps I came to see you and said 'hi'. At any rate, did you notice if I was there?

I was aware of her presence, but didn't see her visually. Barbara described accurately what I was doing at the time.

Freya saw her mother's astral projection:

In 1934, I woke up in the middle of the night and looked out my upstairs window into very bright moonlight. I saw my mother—who was so afraid at night—walking west. I raced downstairs to go get her, and lo! she was sound asleep in her bed.

Shekinah writes about Subuud, a religious organization, and an out of body experience:

I had a wonderful out-of-body experience once. It was around the time I was 'opened' in Subuud, and I was having a lot of psychic experiences. I felt all my chakras open up, and I was completely telepathic for two weeks. I could communicate with animals and I knew what everyone in the house was thinking—even in other rooms. I felt weightless when I ran. And then one afternoon I was dozing on the couch and I started to draw myself out of my body. It took tremendous effort. I was almost all the way out when I looked down at myself and saw I was made of this shimmery silvery watery sort of stuff. Then something scared me and I woke up suddenly and was back in my body, lying there staring at the ceiling.

Here is Ann's experience with a flying dream. This type of dream connects closely with astral projection, or is astral projection:

> This is a recurrent dream that I have been having for over twenty years. I'm in St. Joseph's Catholic Church in Marinette, Wisconsin about 1948 or 1949. I can pinpoint the date as there was a fire in the church about that time which changed the interior considerably. This was our family's church. It is gothic in style and has a high dome. I am almost always able to fly in my dreams, using my arms as wings. I'm flying around the inside of the church, looking at the beautiful wall paintings, stained glass windows, colorful statues and pictures, when I slowly begin to sense that something is very, very wrong. It is not anything that I can see or hear, it is more what I feel. This feeling becomes stronger and stronger as I begin to frantically search every nook and cranny in the building for this terrible thing. I feel terribly threatened and paranoid. I know that I'm in big trouble, but I still can't identify the problem . . . Then slowly I begin to see minute details that appear wrong. It's as though someone substituted the real church for an imitation. Here is a statue with a strange smirk on his lips, a picture is hanging crooked, and the main crucifix has Jesus on it in a grotesque position. Then intense fear and horror overtake me as I realize that this place of peace and love is in reality a place of terrible evil. It is a church dedicated to the devil. I can now feel an evil presence and I attempt to get out of the church. I am flying around, and I finally make a break for the doors. I go through the doors but instead of finding myself in the outer lobby, I am now in the sanctuary. In my attempt to get away from the Evil, I have gotten in deeper. I try another door that I know to be a door to the outside. Then I find that the blue sky that is shining through the glass window is just a painted background. I'm now in the sacristy. By this time I usually wake up, drenched with sweat and screaming for help. I began to understand it when I realized that Christianity is but a perverse adaptation of the Goddess religion.

Jane Roberts describes an out of body experience, titling it, "I Pop Into a Taxi While My Body Stays at Home." It occurred during a channeling session:

> As I sat in my favorite rocker speaking as Seth, suddenly I found myself in the back seat of a cab. The next instant the cab took such a sharp turn to the right that I was shoved over into the corner of the seat. For a minute I was really frightened. I wasn't used to being comfortably seated in the living room one minute and in the back seat of a swiftly moving cab the next!
>
> While this was going on, I lost all contact with my body in the living room. My subjective sensations were those of someone suddenly thrown off-balance by the sickening swerve of the car's turn. Yet while this was happening, my physical body sat upright in the rocker, speaking without pause . . . [18]

Astral projections occur frequently at times of accident, shock, fever or trauma. The bodies' connection to physical matter is loosened at these times. On one occasion of my own, I was extremely ill with adult chickenpox and had a high fever. The dis-ease kept me home from the National Women's Music Festival, where I'd planned to be that week, and was very sorry to miss friends performing there, the women's jazz ensemble Alive!. On the night of their concert, I was in bed, thinking about them, wanting to be there. Suddenly, I was there, watching them perform and seeing each woman in her aura color, as I usually see them. Later, women from the group said they felt I was there, and a photo of the stage confirmed physically what I had seen. This was a conscious astral projection, induced by the desire to be with friends and prompted by my fever and illness. Strong desire is a major component in out of body travel, since this is a skill of the desire/emotional body and the belly chakra.

Anesthetics also cause a loosening of the psychic unseen bodies from the physical, and may be a reason why recovery from surgery is long and difficult, though the physical body heals quickly. There is disturbance in the etheric double's connection to the dense physical. In some cases, women report astral projection experiences during surgery, watching their bodies being operated on, seeing who is in the room, reporting conversations going on. The case here is listed as the Porter Case, with no name given of the woman experiencing it:

> At the age of twenty-four I underwent a surgical operation. An anesthetic was administered to me. At the instant when I would have come to myself again, it seemed to me as if I found myself free in the room, wholly myself, although without my body.
> I felt myself transformed into a spirit, and thought that by means of pain I had attained the peace for which I had yearned so earnestly.
> I beheld my body stretched out below me on the bed. In the room were both sisters of my mother-in-law, one of whom sat on the bed warming my hands, while the other, on the opposite side, stood looking at me.
> I had not the least desire to enter my body again, yet felt myself impelled against my will to return into it.[19]

In another example of illness, Eileen Garrett at a time of dis-ease seeks her medication. Confused with a dream, she astral travels, and this was her first astral projection experience:

> One evening I dreamed that I was in Amsterdam at the house of my friend's relative. I appeared to enter the house and . . . found myself upstairs. Upstairs I found everyone fast asleep—my fears for my friend were groundless. Thereupon I appeared to return to my bed. I rose again, however, to go in search of medication on the dressing table. I do not remember if my searching fingers found the medication.
> I awoke, and then I watched myself (double) get out of bed, go to the dressing table, and search among the toilet articles. I didn't seem to find what I was looking for.
> The experience confused me. I slept. When I awoke, the medication was on the bedside table, within reach of my hand. Which journey to the dressing table had found the medication?
> Since then, I have had many out-of-the-body experiences; they almost always occur when I am ill or depleted.[20]

Out of body experiences often merge with other phenomena so

that separating and defining them can become unclear. This experience is mixed with dreams, as many astral projections happen at the edge of sleep and dreaming. Loren's was coupled with a shamanic vision. Rebecca describes projecting as a child, and her experience is mixed with that of manifesting, a skill discussed in Chapter Six.

> One of my first experiences was when I was eleven, after reading a How-to on astral projection. I lay down and tried it and reached the stars. When I came back to earth I thought that was nice—but I could have been dreaming. So I went back 'up' and told whoever might have been listening that I was lonely and would they send some friends over. I hadn't even finished asking when my mother called me to answer the door. A few of my friends had 'dropped by because they were in the neighborhood'! I was astonished and humbled—my friends looked so bewildered.

Irene's astral projection experiences involve both dreams and precognition, and are similar to mine of visiting a house where my friend hadn't moved yet. She describes flying dreams, defined as either dreams or projections, or probably the forerunners of projections:

> My dreams during these years always involved flying. I would float up, sometimes with my bed, and I would be in space . . . I think I was doing a lot of astral travel at night then. If I was curious about somebody's house I would dream about it and months later it would be a deja vu type of experience. I knew it was my first trip there, yet I knew exactly how a particular room would look before I really saw it.

Ann also described flying dreams, and dreams are the subject of the next chapter.

One last type of projection is the near death experience, which begins as an astral projection but continues into a process beyond it. This type of happening is discussed more fully in the last chapter of this book. Gloria describes an early part of her near death experience. Her body was in a sleeping bag on the ground beneath a tree.

> I looked around. I was above the tree, the tree I was lying under. There was our car and the road! I calmly looked around. I knew I wasn't in my body. I could see me and the sleeping bag about twenty-five feet below.

An experience of transcendence follows, before Gloria returns to her body and the linear world. Near death experiences are often described as or with astral projection studies, and the blue escaping mist described by Eileen Garrett and Florence Brady in their astral projections is also described by women watching the process of physical death. In this case, the silver cord is withdrawn from the physical/etheric double. More on these experiences later.

Astral projection is a skill that women can learn, if their wish to achieve it is strong and their ability to visualize, to create mind imagery of objects and events, is developed. A kama-manas, emotional body skill, both the emotions and the rational mind are involved. Petey Stevens teaches women to change their center of awareness by "pulling yourself up in the corner." The purpose of this is perspective, to change the viewpoint from linear to limitless worlds, and to show an objective way of viewing oneself and the world. Use her exercises to learn astral projection.

First, enter the meditative state, or at least become quiet, grounded and centered. Notice your crown chakra, the energy center at the top of the head, slightly to the back, that is women's connection to Goddess. Transfer awareness/Be-ing to that center and be in the center of your head.

> There is a silvery blue light at the exact center of your head . . . this is the essence of your Soul . . . be that silvery blue dot of light . . . be in the center of your head.[21]

Try this a few times, moving awareness to this place and back again.

Still in the meditative state and doing deeper, visualize a cord or thread of light extending from the dot of light at the crown:

> Remind your Body of your deep desire to try something completely new. Remind your Body that you love it.
>
> With your eyes open, choose a ceiling corner in the room—close your eyes and go up in the corner . . . pull yourself entirely up in the corner. Notice the silver cord of light that is attached to you and goes from you in the corner to the crown of your Body's head . . . Notice your body sitting in the chair. Notice how you feel when you are up in the corner.[22]

Transfer awareness back to the center of your head, experience that, then return to the ceiling and experience being out of the body totally. Make the switch from ceiling to crown and back again a few times, then return to your crown and come out of the meditative state. Return to the linear world.

Some women are able to do this immediately, while others achieve it with some practice and repeated attempts. The more relaxed and the more into the meditative alpha to theta state you are when trying it, the more successful. Become very comfortable with transferring back and forth from crown to ceiling, and being out of the body at the ceiling, before projecting anywhere else. When beginning to move from the ceiling in this state of being out of the body, first fly within the room and become comfortable with that before moving further away. Do this only at times when your physical body is safe and you won't be interrupted. The body on the bed is unresponsive, and can scare someone walking in on it who would think you are in distress. What usually happens on interruption, though is a quick return to your body, usually with a jolt. Stevens also suggests using a grounding cord, an umbilical visualized from the root center, running into the Earth, while doing astral projection exercises and travel. This is a safeguard and protection for your physical body.

Once you are comfortable being in the crown of your head and pulling yourself up in the corner, use visualization—the ability to see or feel yourself in a place and thus to be there—to gain control of your travelling astral/emotional body. Enter the meditative state, and imagine a column of light moving from above your crown through all of the chakras and leaving your body through your feet. The light moves along the spinal column in a steady flow, and can be visualized in colors.[23] Use blue, gold, violet or clear light for this, and the process is called running energy. This is a major protective, energizing and clearing exercise in all meditation and healing work. Use the grounding cord. Now go to the crown of your head and be the dot of light at the center, extending it to a trail or cord of light as you transfer yourself to the ceiling.

Return to your crown, and then:

> Project yourself into another chair in the room . . . Psychically sit in that chair. Feel that chair as you sit on it . . . . Notice what your Body looks like from your view from the chair . . . Be in the center of your head . . . . Pull yourself to be in front of your Body . . . Notice what the room looks like from this view . . . Be in the center of your head . . . . This time project yourself to be behind your body . . . What does the room look like from this view . . . . Be in the center of your head.[24]

When comfortable with being at all perspectives inside the room, go out of it. Go to the roof of your house or the sidewalk in front of your door. Go there by thinking yourself there, visualizing where you want to be. Pay attention to surroundings. Go to another house on your street, or the home of a friend, but pick one where your presence won't startle someone. Don't feed into the hysteria about ghosts! If visiting a friend, tell her in advance that you've been learning astral travel, but for beginning flights keep it simple, go where no one's home.

For my first attempt at this, I went to see the bakery across the street from my apartment. It was late at night and the bakery was closed. I felt myself floating through the front door, going right through the front door, going right through the glass, and entering the bakery's front room. I saw the cases emptied and the left-over bread on the counter tops covered with white cloths. I went to the back room and saw the ovens and kitchen, white enamel and stainless steel. I left the building through the back wall then reentered it, and came back home again through the front show window. The inside of the display window had a white sheet thrown over it. I came back to my room, thinking of my bedroom and being there without seeing or feeling the means of getting there. The silver cord is visible if you turn around and look back at it, or look down at it from above. I came back to my body, unsure if I had traveled or if I had simply been meditating. The next day I went to the bakery, and as far as I could see through the swinging door between the rooms, I verified what I had seen the night before. I rarely enter this bakery and had never seen the back room until my flight.

As in any other psychic or magick work, use astral travel by intention only when feeling well and centered. Avoid it if ill or tired, and avoid it if feeling stressed or angry. Though spontaneous out of body experiences happen frequently during illness, induced projections are the most positive when the energy is controlled and directed. Be completely relaxed and in the meditative state for best success; simple grounding and centering is not usually enough to induce projection.

A significant number of women's projection experiences mention a Full Moon. Many women feel heightened psychic sensitivity on the Full Moon, and New to Full Moons are the most favorable time for many other psychic and magickal practices. Some women feel heightened psychic sensitivity on the waning Moon, particularly in the last quarter, and particularly for women who menstruate on the New Moon. Women are individuals, with personal biorhythms, and become aware of their bodies and their psychic needs. Experiment, and use what works best. One final suggestion is to use any form of meditation work only several hours after eating and not on a full stomach. Food is grounding, and the point of astral travel is to leave the ground.

When projecting with the desire to be with a particular person, and reaching her successfully, try to make contact in the astral. The skill here is telepathic, and a bit ahead of this chapter's instructions, but physical communication methods won't reach her when you astral project. Offer her a message by thinking it intently, and visualize her receiving it. Ask her later if the message was received; ask her if she felt your presence.

The most important factor in achieving astral travel is the desire to do it.[25] This is an emotional body/belly chakra skill, directed by the mind but fueled by the emotions and desire. The more intense your desire to achieve an out of body state, the more probable your success. If you want to be somewhere enough, you can be there. Once succeeding in astral projection, most women want to do it, and the desire to do it becomes a built-in part of using desire in the process. The woman whose name is given as Mrs. J. Martin said it was the most wonderful thing she had ever experienced, and this is a common reaction. Spontaneous projections can be frightening at first, but usually only at first. The desire to repeat the experience, to induce it at will, helps it happen.

The major factor in controlling an out of body experience, going where you want to go, is visualization. This is a solar plexus/rational mind skill cultivated in women's spirituality for manifesting and ritual work, healing, and in most forms of meditation and guided journeys. The ability to visualize, to create the image by sight or other senses of an object, place or person is what directs astral travel. By thinking of a place, you can be there. Seeing yourself at the ceiling, you are at the ceiling; seeing yourself in the center of your head, you are there. Though called visualization, all the senses are involved; this is not a skill limited to sight.

The two factors together, desire and visualization, are the fuel and medium for astral projection, and are examples of kama-manas/desire-mind. Astral travel is described as a belly chakra/emotional body skill, while visualization is located at the solar plexus and the lower mental body. Dreams are a related skill to out of body experience, as so many astral projections happen when the woman is in the alpha to theta state between waking and sleep. Many astral projections happen in dreams when desire is added to the formula of the visualized imagery. The next chapter discusses dreamwork, the mental imagery of the rational mind/lower mental body as it is affected by stroking the python and women's psychic realities.

In learning astral travel, women learn to fly. Some recommended books on astral projection and out of body experiences, with how to material or meditations in them are: Melita Denning and Osborne Phillips, *The Llewellyn Practical Guide to Astral Projection*, (St. Paul, Llewellyn Publications, 1986), Diane Mariechild's *Mother Wit: A Feminist Guide to Psychic Development*, (Trumansburg, NY, The Crossing Press, 1982), and Petey Stevens' *Opening Up to Your Psychic Self*, (Berkeley, CA, Nevertheless Press, 1982).

# FOOTNOTES

1. Eileen Garrett, in Robert Crookall, *Casebook of Astral Projection,* *545-746,* (New Jersey, Citadel Press, 1972), p. 99. Quote is from her books *Awareness, My Life As a Search for the Meaning of Mediumship,* and *Telepathy,* published 1939-1943.

2. Robert Crookall, *Casebook of Astral Projection, 545-746,* p. 97-98.

3. Diane Mariechild, *Mother Wit,* p. 54.

4. Sylvan Muldoon and Hereward Carrington, *The Phenomena of Astral Projection,* (London, Rider and Co., 1969), p. 157.

5. Ann Faraday, *The Dream Game,* (New York, Perennial Library, 1974), p. 72.

6. *Ibid.,* p. 340.

7. Robert Crookall, *Casebook of Astral Projection, 545-746,* p. 98-99.

8. Melita Denning and Osborne Phillips, *The Llewellyn Practical Guide to Astral Projection,* (St. Paul, Llewellyn Publications, 1986), p. 32, 36-37.

9. Robert Crookall, *Casebook of Astral Projection, 545-746,* p. 113 ff.

10. *Ibid.,* p. 120-121.

11. Melita Denning and Osborne Phillips, *The Llewellyn Practical Guide to Astral Projection,* p. 165-166.

12. Sylvan Muldoon and Hereward Carrington, *The Phenomena of Astral Projection,* p. 217.

13. Robert Crookall, *Casebook of Astral Projection, 545-746,* p. 6-7, Case No. 554.

14. Sylvan Muldoon and Hereward Carrington, *The Phenomena of Astral Projection,* is arranged by chapters on these types.

15-16. Robert Crookall, *Casebook of Astral Projection, 545-746,* p. 56, Case No. 650, and p. 54-55, Case 644.

17. *Ibid.,* p. 29, Case No. 593.

18. Jane Roberts, *The Seth Material,* p. 71-72.

19. Sylvan Muldoon and Hereward Carrington, *The Phenomena of Astral Projection,* p. 57.

20. Eileen Garrett, in Robert Crookall, *Casebook of Astral Projection,*

545-746, p. 84-85, Case No. 723.

21. Petey Stevens, *Opening Up to Your Psychic Self*, p. 15. Some women see the color as silvery violet, rather than blue.

22. *Ibid.*, p. 16.

23. For more on color work and the chakras, see Diane Stein, *The Women's Book of Healing,* also Melita Denning and Osborne Phillips, *The Llewellyn Practical Guide to Astral Projection*, Formula One, p. 73 ff.

24. Petey Stevens, *Opening Up to Your Psychic Self*, p. 230-231.

25. Anthony Martin, *The Theory and Practice of Astral Projection*, (Great Britain, Aquarian Press, 1980), p. 49.

# Chapter Five

# The Solar Plexus: Dreamwork
# Women Dreaming

*A dream brings you messages from many dimensions. Here in your dreams you can connect with your Oversoul, glimpse another incarnation and gain information about other people, places or events. Each of these occurrences must be interpreted in light of your present situation as well. Such things are being revealed to you now because there is a direct relationship to your immediate situation.* [1]

I am in Tallahassee, Florida where I lived for a few months several years ago. There is a decision pending: I want to make a trip home to Pittsburgh, and do it at a time when friends are also passing through. The trip is expensive and on short notice. There isn't the money for it and I don't like to use charge cards. Yet I want to go badly, and can't decide. Tallahassee is not going well, either. I want to go home, and stay home.

In the dream, I am at Wildsisters, before it became Bloomer's. I am sitting in a dark place with another woman, bundled up for the cold. She is one of the women passing through, the reason for the timing of the trip, and I am very glad to see her. She's wearing a maroon jacket and grey slacks, holding a white paper cup of steaming tea. I tell her about Florida, how unhappy I am, how I want to leave. She in turn is depressed and we comfort each other. "You did what you had to," she says. "Let me hug you."

I awake with her words in my mind vividly, the whole scene, and decide to make the trip. In the meantime the crisis comes, and I am going home for good. Four weeks later, I am sitting on Wildsisters' patio, in November in the cold, talking with my friend. She is wearing a maroon jacket and grey slacks, not feeling well, sipping a white paper cup of tea. I am used to Florida heat and shivering; we should be indoors. She tells me of things that are hurting her, major things, and I tell her about Florida. I am home now, back in Pittsburgh but homeless, jobless and broke. She asks me what happened, why I left, and I tell her. "Well," she says when I finish. "You did what you had to. Let me hug you," and she does. Throughout our conversation I have an intense feeling of deja vu. Despite the length of time, I remembered and still remember the dream. I appreciate this woman deeply for her encouragement, her caring and her hugs. And yet I knew these things would be there; I had seen them before in the dream.

Dreamwork is the women's psychic skill given most notice by the patriarchy. Dreams are respectable, are a gold mine of neuroses and complexes for psychiatrists and psychologists. There are dozens of books available on dreamwork, several dream dictionaries, lots of seminars, and lots of arguments on which patriarchal school of thought to follow—Freudian, Gestalt, Halls' or Jung. The EEG (electro-encephalograph) makes dreams visible and studies for the last decades use it. The hippies of the sixties used LSD for waking dreams, and the yuppies of the eighties discuss dreams with their expensive analysts. But dreams as a psychic tool and a part of women's unique consciousness are still mostly submerged, as is all that is women's reality.

In the wealth of books on dreamwork, psychic, shared and precognitive dreams are passed off with a line or two, and dreams' connection with astral projection is given much the same shrift. Only Jane Roberts, Diane Mariechild, Helen Farias of *The Beltane Papers* and a few others, women involved with spirituality, take dreams seriously as a part of stroking the python. Yet, of all the experiences women sent me in the process of collecting stories for this book, the solar plexus skills of dreams and manifesting were the two subjects with the most replies. Dreams are one of women's major psychic tools, and using them is major in women's psychic lives.

Patricia Garfield, one of the noted dream researchers, describes dreamwork as used in ancient Greece and Rome, by Native Americans of many tribes, by the Senoi of Malaysia, and by Indian and Tibetan Yogis.[2] Nowhere does she connect these peoples with the matriarchal consciousness their work derives from, and her vision of even matriarchal Greece is seen from after the takeover by male gods. Her description of a supplicant to the healing dream temples, to a place like Delphi, is of a male seeking information and healing from the gods.

This was the temple of sixth to fifth century B.C., after the loss of the matriarchy, but remnants of the Goddess are evident. The place is Epidaurus and the god is Asclepius. Apollo's murder of Pythia and his installation of himself as the Oracle is a metaphor for the loss and submergence of the Goddess and her female python wisdom.

The supplicant—I have femininized her and taken her back to Goddess times—comes to the temple with offerings, engages in fasting and abstains from sexuality. She arrives at the temple and bathes, and goes through a process of physical and mental purification. There are rituals, meditations and chanting. To enter the sanctuary, the supplicant is invited by a preliminary dream, given a sign to enter the abaton, the sacred dormitory. Once there,

> In the dim light, she watches the movement of the large yellow serpents that writhe across the floor. These are non-poisonous, she knows, but so many and so enormous. She reminds herself they were nurtured by the Goddess. She lays her head on the fluffy sheepskin, the air heavy with incense. Now the temple priestess walks through the porticos extinguishing the torches and telling the pilgrims it's time for sleep. In the quiet blackness, she hears only the echo of the chants in her mind and the soft swish-swish of the slithering snakes.[3]

The process of stroking the python, for dreams, healing and psychic information begins. Most supplicants got their dreams, and the information they were seeking. There are records of cures. Garfield connects the snakes with phallic symbolism, but they are female, symbols of the spiral and of shedding and rebirth. Despite her masculine orientation, the matriarchal roots shine through. The supplicant visits the temple of the Snake Goddess, the creative mother, to stroke the python and find dreams of healing and peace. Women continue to do this today, using other terms, and other dreams.

Early Christianity and Judaism accepted and used dreamwork, but both denied it by the time of the witchburnings from the thirteenth to seventeenth centuries. Talmudic scholars of Judaism in the Middle Ages dropped much of esoteric practice from Judaism. Dreams were connected with psychic information in Europe, and therefore with witchcraft, that too-dangerous connection of women to matriarchy. A woman could be burned at the stake for being a dreamer, and more so for being a prophetic one. Some notorious herbals of the era— poppy, morning glory, nightshade and belladonna—were dream invokers or hallucinogens.[4] Dreamwork known worldwide was used by the witches for psychic information and healing, and the skill was lost with other skills in the West because the teachers died. Dreamwork went underground with the Goddess and with the witch-midwife healers; it was not talked about in public again until Sigmund Freud.

Freud's emphasis on the illness of all minds did nothing real for women's dreamwork but brought dreams back into discussion. They were safe to talk about again, even if only as signs of mental illness and sexual repression or aberration. Carl Jung developed the idea of an archetypal consciousness in dreams that sounds very matriarchal, but often isn't. Fritz Perls developed Gestalt therapy, widely used today, if somewhat patriarchal and judgmental. Halls offered content analysis. Dreamwork is being revived in the West, though with small emphasis in the mainstream on its psychic components.

Before and outside of patriarchy there has always been dreamwork. Egypt, India, China and the early Middle Eastern countries all have or had ritual methods for dream induction. Yogis and healers in Tibet and India use deep relaxation and meditation work to induce dreams and receive psychic information from them. In Native America, there is a strong emphasis on dreamwork and dream vision that is prominent in most tribes. Dreams are taken seriously, and elaborate dreams in repetition are asked for and received as guidance. Animal and spirit helpers come to a woman dreaming, offering her information, direction and healing. One of the purposes of the vision quest is to invoke meaningful dreams. In the Ojibwa, women use dreamwork for childbirth issues, and a woman becomes a midwife by being called to it in her dreams.

> A favorable dream could bless a woman with childbirth powers. The required cultural pattern was a dream of an animal who has easy deliveries, such as a bitch, a mare or a cow. Ojibwa women believed that a she-dog has the easiest time. One popular midwife reported a dream of a she-wolf that looked like a human person, with the voice of a wolf. The dream animal told her that she would have five children (which she did). The she-wolf licked the dreamer's hand and told her she would help her in childbirth.[5]

The woman had five children, and became an honored midwife. Dreams in every part of life and life experience are taken seriously and carried over into waking issues. Favorable or informative dreams are rewarded by the society.

The Senoi of Malaysia are the classic example of a dream society, where the most important event of the day is discussing the dreams each family member had the night before. In this mostly vegetarian, peaceful society, there is no crime, no war and no fighting among individuals. They are cooperative people and seem to have equality of the sexes; women participate in the tribal councils. In dreams—which become waking reality—any hint of danger, anger or aggression is met and resolved. If the dream is of conflict with another, the dreamer goes to that other and they talk it out, resolve the issues before trouble manifests. Dreams are rewarded, are always seen as a gift to the dreamer, and in the discussions are always given positive outcomes and interpretations.[6] The material of dreams is the guiding material of lives, and dream information is looked for, taken and used seriously. The results are a creative, peaceful, cooperative people who have no concept of war or hate, and who live in respect for each other. Contrast them to the patriarchal West, which denies dreams as anything but fantasies or indications of mental disturbance.

Dreamwork is a solar plexus center skill, deriving from the lower mental body of the aura. This is the place of women's intake and process-ing of prana, distribution of pranic, nutritional, and psychic energies. All psychic impressions enter the unseen bodies through the solar plexus chakra on the etheric double, and along with prana are then distributed to their appropriate chakras and bodies. Mental ideas are received here, too.

Dreams are visualizations of events, ideas, places, people and information that are brought into the energy bodies at the solar plexus. They are assumed to be visual images, but women who are blind also dream, and if without visual context use sensory images that are meaningful to them. Dreams are solar plexus visualization images combined with the psychic knowing of the brow chakra (third eye/middle spiritual aura band). Precognition is a third eye skill that is transmitted in dream visualizations through the solar plexus. This combination of chakras is different from waking precognition, and the information in dreams often comes in symbols. Healing in dreams is from the heart, brow or crown center combined with the solar plexus, and creativity information, often transmitted in dreams, comes from the higher-mental and spiritual body centers, the heart, throat, third eye or crown combined with the lower mental body/solar plexus. Some creativity and healing dreams are attributed to spirit guides or helpers, the same helpers respected in Native American traditions. These helpers come by way of the crown center, women's connection with Goddess, and again are received by the solar plexus as visuali-zations in dreams. While dreamwork is discussed as a solar plexus/ lower mental body skill, it is a combination of chakras and aura layers that invoke it, with information transmitted through the solar plexus.

In theosophical theory, dreams are recollections in the physical brain of the emotional body's travels during sleep.[7] If this sounds like astral projection it is, and theosophical theory says that everyone travels in the astral during sleep. At this time, woman's spiritual body self withdraws from the physical and her psychic bodies are free to travel. The unseen bodies are much more receptive in sleep to psychic impressions, and travel with a consciousness that is beyond the linear. Because the spiritual bodies are disengaged from the physical, the impressions received can be confused ones. The dreaming spiritual body moves beyond time and space and enters the world of multiple realities. Impressions are transmitted to the mind and brain by way of solar plexus distribution and the lower mental body.

The spiritual body and lower mind together create dreams, and the information is transmitted in symbols.[8] Only the lower mental body understands and works in words; the other psychic levels operate on dramatization and sensory consciousness, picture visualizations instead of intellectualizing. In dreaming, women see symboled dramas of events. One dream picture is worth a thousand words, and dreamwork is learning to understand rationally (in the lower mind) what these symbols mean. The conscious lower mind is the solar plexus center. In astral travel, women's consciousness is there; dreaming is a movie replay of where the spiritual bodies have been and what in symbols they have seen on psychic planes.

Science studies dreams with an electro-encephalograph, measuring the brainwave states of the dream process. This is a fairly recent dis-covery, since 1953. Dreams occur during a period of Rapid Eye Movement, or REM, and women awakened when this is seen are virtually always dreaming. REM sleep occurs also in infants, where it was first noted, as well as in dogs, cats, and other mammals. Women without vision also dream and show Rapid Eye Movements when doing so. There are four stages or depths of sleep, and women move in and out of them, completing the whole cycle of about ninety minutes five times a night.[9]

In stage one, the body is relaxed and the woman is aware of things happening in the room, but is not actually awake, though she thinks she is. This period lasts about ten minutes, and the EEG shows the alpha brainwave state, with respiration, pulse, blood pressure and temperature lower than at waking levels. This is the place between waking and sleeping, the alpha level, when hypnogogic dreams occur.[10] These are images in the process of changing from the concrete to the abstract, the place where many visions and apparitions manifest, and creative inspirations. Women who are artists describe seeing their paintings in dreams and painting later what they saw. A poet finds the line to open a new poem here, and writes it down quickly or loses it. Answers to problems occur here, too and women who ask for problem solving in their dreams, who "sleep on it," find answers at this level. Women also see things like "people moving about the room, perhaps disembodied faces floating in the air,"[11] or hear voices clairaudiently. A feeling of falling, the body jerking, happens sometimes, and no one knows why. Senoi adults instruct children not to be afraid of these falling dreams, since going with them turns them into flying dreams (astral projections). It's easy to awaken from this level, to write down an image or idea for later use. Part of the outline for this book came in a lucid, hypnogogic dream, and I made notes then went back to sleep. This level can be used to ask for healing information.

In the second stage of sleep, the brainwaves show movement from the alpha to the theta level, and this period lasts twenty to thirty minutes. Women are functionally blind at this point, the brain no longer accepts transmitted images, and the eyes slowly move from side to side. This is still a light stage of sleep with easy awakening, and beginning dreams here are disjointed and confused ones. Sleep learning and use of subliminal tapes for changing habits are effective at this level.

Stage three descends to delta brainwaves, as slow as three cycles per second, and dreams are seldom remembered. Muscles are relaxed, and body temperature, pulse and blood pressure fall lower than before. Women turn over in their sleep, but are not easily awakened from this level. Coming back quickly to a ringing telephone is difficult. Eyes continue to move, and the period lasts from ten to twenty minutes.

Stage four is the deepest level of sleep, lasting about twenty minutes and with no dreams remembered. Sleepwalking occurs here, as does bedwetting and night terrors, where the dreamer waking cannot remember what frightened her. From this deepest place, the woman begins to rise again, taking about fifteen minutes to move back up through levels three and two. Sleep is still deep so that only a loud noise awakens her, and the mind and body become active. REM sleep begins here, at level two again, and full dreaming. As many as five dream scenes occur during one twenty minute period of Rapid Eye Movement sleep, separated by turning over or changing body position. These are the dreams and nightmares that are dramatized astral travel images. While the NREM (Non-REM) levels three and four also produce dreams, they are not remembered ones, but REM dreams at this rising stage are vivid and memorable. Here is where dreamwork begins, and REM sleep is the place of psychic dreamwork particularly of precognitive dreams.

After this phase, the dreamer returns to level one briefly then starts the cycle again. Four or five cycles happen each night, totally about ninety minutes long each. Each REM dream period contains as many as five different dream scenes. As the night progresses, the woman spends less time in stages three and four and her stage one sleep lengthens. By the end of the night, she spends most of her dream time in stages one and two, and it is these later dreams that are most easily remembered.[12] Dreams happen in the alpha to theta brainwave state, as do other psychic phenomena, and everyone dreams every night, several times a night. Dream recall is a process women learn.

Along with the sleep cycle, women's menstrual cycle and the phases of the Moon affect women's dreaming.[13] For women who ovulate at the Full Moon and bleed at the New, the correlations are strongest and most evident, but for women who don't (or who don't bleed at all), the cycle still works. In the case of women who do not menstruate, chart the pattern of dreams entirely by the moon phases. In the case of women with irregular cycles, or that ovulate and bleed at different times than the Full and New, a couple months charting of dreams with the Moon and menstrual dates shows the patterns. Try calling the first day of menstruation day one of the cycle. In prepatriarchal times, when there was no artificial lighting to confuse natural cycles, women's cycles in a community happened together, so that everyone ovulated on the Full Moon and bled on the New. Dream cycles were predictable, as was fertility.

Women's dreams follow the waxing and waning pattern of the Moon and menstruation. Days given here are moon days, matched with the days of women's ovular cycles when ovulation is at the Full Moon. In menstruation, the New Moon, days 1-6 of the cycle, women dream erotic dreams. These are sexual dreams, sometimes sexually confused, and filled with desires. In these days, heterosexual women often have lesbian dreams and lesbian women heterosexual ones. On days 7-14, when the follicule or egg is developing, the dreams are tense and also sexual, but given in the terms of the dreamer's sexuality. If she is heterosexual, the dreams are heterosexual, and if she is lesbian they are lesbian dreams.

In days 12-16, the pre-ovular and ovulation stage (the Full Moon), women dream of babies, children, eggs, round objects, pearls, breasts and moons. These are less tense and more relaxed and satisfied dreams. Where the dreams are of conflicts with lovers, men or mothers, they indicate the rejection of conception, no pregnancy for this cycle. Many women describe out of body experiences, precognitive dreams, telepathic or shared dreams, at the Full Moon. In the post-ovular days, days 15-17, there are giving and receptive dreams reflecting pregnancy, motherhood and nursing, whether pregnant or not. The Full Moon in women's spirituality is considered to be three days before and three days after the Full Moon date, which is the fourteenth day of the cycle.

From here the waning phases begin. In the luteal phase of the womb cycle, from the 18-25th day, there are confused and excited dream images. Change, sexuality and anger are common themes. Helen Farias suggests asking for dreams of a spirit guide or animal helper as a way of relieving PMS (premenstrual syndrome).[14] Is this the time of greatest receptivity for spirit guides in dreams? Many women have heightened psychic experiences and psychic dreams at this time.

The premenstrual days 24-29 of the moon cycle are days when women have dreams with highly sexual, often violent overtones. The woman would like to forget these dreams, but the violence in them seldom manifests and they may be a means of safe release for women's anger and rage. Some women experience heightened psychic sensitivity at this time, waking or sleeping, and this is a good time to ask for a past life dream. Dreams on these days have a strong emotional charge.

Most women writing their experiences for this book said that their psychic levels are highest on the Full Moon. My own psychic dreams occur primarily on the luteal days, days 18-25, and often in the premenstrual phase. The precognitive dream that happened to me in Florida occurred on the eighteenth day of the moon cycle, and came true on the Full Moon almost four weeks later. Leslie writes that premenstrual times are her most powerful times psychically, and Ana indicates that Full Moon or past Full Moon dreams are significant for her:

> As to whether or not there is a link in my experience to my menstrual cycle, yes there is. During waxing moons prior to my flow (at the waning moon between last quarter and dark) my experiences are heightened. I communicate in various ways to other planes at these times. There is no dread, I seek these

experiences. I was able to tell people where 'lost' things were, what illnesses they have and what would 'cure' it. I only got upset when I 'saw' injury or death—until I was old enough to fathom karma and rebirth. There is no dread now.

Her dreams of healing, clairvoyance, other planes and precognition are examples of psychic information found in dreams. Diane in Chapter One astral projected on the Full Moon, as did other women in the last chapter, and Helen Farias suggests that dream recall is strongest at the Full Moon phase. Since individual cycles vary, women interested in this can chart their dreams in regard to moon and menstrual cycles.

This chart by Migene Gonzales-Wippler also helps. In it she records dreams' chances for coming true (being precognitive) on each day of the lunar cycle. Her sources are Eastern.

### New Moon:
1. Dreams generally cheerful.
2. Beneficent day. Bad dreams have little effect.
3. Useless dreams. Take no notice.
4. Good dreams come true.
5. Fateful day. Dreams doubtful.
6. Good day. Do not tell your dreams.

### First Quarter: (Waxing)
7. Dreams generally come true.
8. Dreams of travel come true.
9. Dreams quickly come true.
10. Vain dreams, for your day must have been good.
11. Vain dreams. Your day was anyhow.
12. True dreams. Your day was bad.
13. Dreams quickly come true.

### Second Quarter: (Full Moon)
14. Very lucky day. Dreams doubtful.
15. True dreams following on a bad day.
16. True dreams following on a happy day.
17. Dreams come true within three days.
18. True dreams following on uneasiness.
19. Coming true soon.
20. True dreams after an interesting day.

### Last Quarter: (Waning)
21. Day of rejoicing. Vain dreams.

22. Maleficent day. True dreams.
23. Day of ill humour. False dreams.
24. Indifferent day. Vain dreams.
25. Malificent day. Indifferent dreams.
26. Malificent day. True dreams.
27. Day of enterprise. Doubtful dreams.
28. Indifferent day. Vain dreams.[15]

Gonzalez-Wippler's list supports Helen Farias' work. Most pre-cognitive dreams occur at the Full Moon, and she lists these days (three days before and three days after the Full, which is the four-teenth day) as being true dreams except for the eleventh day. On the fifteenth to seventeenth days, the days of spirit or animal helpers, Gonzalez-Wippler lists true dreams. Her last quarter designation of "maleficent days" with "indifferent" or "doubtful" dreams possibly reflects the nature of premenstrual dreaming that many women choose to deny. An old style value system is at work here. In the beginning of the cycle; the first six days of the New Moon, which are menstruation, Gonzalez-Wippler lists positive dreams coming true.

Women have active and varied dream lives and find information for waking life in their dreams. Dream messages are symbolic, are visualizations and dramatizations of the message, and take some rational thought to comprehend. Symbols in dreams are personal ones, and though there are several dream dictionaries, everyone's symbolism is finally her own. Gestaltists say that every character, object and place in a dream is the self offering a subconscious (emotional body) message. Dreams also come from the mental body, with ideas, warnings and encouragements, or from the higher mental body of inspirations and creative solutions. They can come from spiritual body levels with spirit guides and psychic phenomena: precognition, retrocognition, telepathy and shared dreams, clairvoyance, healing and past lives.

In interpreting dreams, women look first to the real world, and to issues shown in dreams that can be concrete ones. If for example, the dream was about falling over a railing, she might in waking check to see that the real railing is safe. Beyond that are symbols to be individually interpreted, and after that logical solar plexus process are the psychic events. Danger or death in a precognitive dream can sometimes be averted as in Leonie's dream as a child of the careening ambulance. Karma is often changeable by choice and action. In other instances, the woman sees her dream come true, knowing that she has not caused a traumatic event, only witnessed it. Because of the emotional content, traumatic precognitions occur often. In creativity or healing dreams, the woman acts on the information and inspirations given her. In shared dreams, the two sharing it exchange information and acknowledge the telepathy link between them. Retrocognition is when a woman dreams in full drama of an event that known to her or not has already taken place. Past life dreams are investigated more fully by regression work.

Women write about their dreams, beginning with Maggie, whose dreams are precognitive, past lives, and spirit guides/shamanic journeys.

> This last year I had a series of dreams which, after they happened, I was able to identify as shamanistic initiation rituals and experiences. These included the use of a ceremonial 'world tree" to travel through the worlds; descent into the underworld (burial) followed by dismemberment, restoration to wholeness and return to the world of ordinary reality; dancing among bison-like animals to lead them over a cliff, thus providing food for the tribe; and the experience of tumbling, of flying through the air.
>
> Some of my dreams are very clearly past life experiences, factual and extremely detailed. They are different in feel and quality from other dreams, and usually focus on some turning point or moment of great intensity in a previous life . . . Occasionally I have a precognitive dream in which a scene or event will present itself. Usually within a day or two the event happens or I see the scene as it appeared in the dream. None of these have ever been important or useful events/dreams in themselves. Perhaps they serve only to remind me that this is another way of seeing.

Jane Roberts suggests that dreams are so often precognitive, and so routinely so, that women can miss their significance unless the precognition comes true almost immediately. She says that precognitive dreams are so frequent that they are intrinsic to daily life, so frequent that they tend to almost go unnoticed.[16] Dreams of coming deaths or traumatic events to loved ones are re-cognized more often and noticed, as are recurring dreams, because of their emotional content. Most precognitive dreams are not traumatic, but are everyday happenings that come and go. Maggie's shamanic dream resonates strongly with Loren's of the pipe, her experience of the last chapter that ran the fine line between dreaming and astral projection.

Leslie defines her psychic experiences as "really more telepathic and dream oriented":

> I will dream of someone I haven't thought of in years and the next day get a letter, or run into their mother. . . I have had occasions where friends and I dream about each other the same night. One bizarre item . . . one night I went into our

bathroom for a drink about three AM. We had a drop ceiling, with those panels. Well, I heard a noise and looked up and the panel over me was sagging down considerably because of water leaking from the floor above us. I jumped away seconds before it came crashing down. The next night we were at friends' and related the story. Their mouths dropped open and they told us that one of them had dreamed that our bathroom ceiling had collapsed on us.

Carol's dreams, connected with her pregnancy and children, are precognitive dreams. She mentions a link between herself and her daughter.

I was pregnant with my first child, due March 20th. I dreamt three times during the pregnancy that the child would be born April 5th. First borns are usually late, but April 4th at 6:30 AM, I went to the hospital with pains two minutes apart. I recall saying to my husband, 'I missed by one day.' I ended up in labor over twenty hours and my son was born April 5th at 4:05 AM.

Four weeks after the birth, one night I woke screaming about my baby suffocating. There were three nightmares in a row, three nights. The following evening I woke without the nightmare and went directly to the crib and found my son suffocating under blankets. He had wormed his way under and caught his head on the way out. He was almost blue.

My second child was born March 20th. She is now seventeen and her whole life has been flashes of what may or may not happen to her. One of these was when she was two and I had three nightmares in a row seeing her falling out a window. I never knew if I was to catch her or not because I would wake up screaming. It was summer and it was hot but I locked all the windows and doors in the house. . . One day I was bringing magazines to a neighbor's a few streets away; I took my daughter with me for the ride . . . As I was walking up her walk, the flash hit—I dropped the magazines and swung myself around to see my daughter falling out the (car) window. I caught her.

Leonie has had precognitive dreams since childhood:

I've been having predictive and cautionary dreams since about the age of 10 and out of body experiences since about the same age. My predictions have about an 85% accuracy rate, but it has only been within the last two years that I've become seriously interested in getting further involved with this facet of myself. I can tell my 'predictive' dreams from my 'regular' dreams in that they're usually repetitive and tend to become *more* vivid with the passage of time rather than fading . . .

Her ambulance dream, occurring at about eight years old, is in Chapter One, and this dream happened about two years later.

I was standing in a room totally unfamiliar to me, but I knew it was in Great Neck, a neighboring town. I was playing the violin, a piece which at the time of the dream I had never heard before, let alone played. (I had begun to play the violin at the age of three). The room was papered with a floral print, and had heavy drapes. The accompanist was someone unknown to me. I knew I was having an audition, but felt no anxiety or tension. Instead, I experienced a great sense of elation and the knowledge that this was an extremely important occasion, that it would change my life. This dream too I had repeatedly. Three years later, I did have that audition. It did change my life because I won it and decided to attend Julliard, which altered the entire course of my future.

A traumatic dream can be a warning, with information of how to avoid disaster. Nett had this dream and it saved her life:

> When I was thirteen, I had a vivid dream about being caught in the basement with a baby and the house was on fire, blocking my approach to the steps. I ran around looking for ways out, covering the baby's and my face to prevent smoke inhalation. We found a window that would open from the inside. I pulled a table under it, laid the baby outside and crawled out, too. I woke from the dream exhausted, but not disturbed.
>
> Two weeks later I was in the basement with my infant brother and the furnace exploded, blocking the way between us and the stairs. I covered our noses, went directly to the window I had used in the dream and we both escaped completely unharmed in exactly the way I had dreamed.

Precognition of a disaster doesn't necessarily come true, either. Nett had this experience:

> I dreamed I was delivering a funeral sermon for a small child, using a biblical text one would never think of as funereal. As the sermon ended I looked in the casket and it was my friend's four year old daughter.
>
> A month later I picked her up for school and she was white. Her daughter had awakened unable to move her legs . . . The girl had spinal meningitis. The doctor's prognosis was not good. She lost all motor control and speech. I began to feel I should have told her the dream, but I didn't want to now. For a week we took turns, my friend and I staying with the girl . . . She began to respond to the medication she had been given and began to heal. She was released and gradually regained speech and movement. *Then* I could tell my friend the dream. She assured me that even if the girl had died I was not responsible, even though I had the dream. I began to accept my psychic awareness as information. It was possibility, not fate, and I was not controlling it.

The text that was not for a funeral could have been a clue here of the happy ending. Women who have precognitive experiences are not the cause, only witnesses, if the events occur. Taking blame, or fearing that they've caused it, is a common reaction.

Loren is a midwife, with experience of this. Her dreams are one form of healing dreams:

> Often I would dream or have a vision of what was going to happen at a birth, and sometimes it was a frightening picture, but I found that I could use that foreknowledge, both as a way of averting a complication and as a way of handling it safely. Most midwives develop or have psychic gifts; it is a part of working in harmony with the powerful creative forces surrounding birth (and death). The midwife stands between the worlds, to aid the soul in passage, and to help the birthing mother stay on her course. It was a great blessing to my life to do this work for eight years.

Bonnie had this recurring nightmare, of a bridge collapsing under her car. One day she was confronted with the place of her dream:

One recurring nightmare from teenhood was to be driving down a road, and top a hill where I couldn't see over the top. In a deep dip below was a huge body of water. The road went across a low-railed bridge almost at water level. When I'd get halfway out, the bridge ahead would sink and my car would go into the water. This dream occurred for years.

Then in 1971, I had to go to Maryland for a job interview. Following the map, I was deep in the country, when I topped a hill and *there it was*, the same bridge over the same water (it was a reservoir). I braked the car and stayed frozen at the top of the hill.

This was the only road this way; going back (*way* back!) onto an alternate route would mean hours. I had to cross it. I put the car in the middle of the road and drove across in blind terror. Had there been another car coming toward me, I'd never have been able to move off that center painted line. I crossed the bridge, and the dream never recurred.

## Bonnie comments on the incident:

Warnings tend to be overdone. For example, once I had the strongest urge not to go down an alley. Well, I did, and met a fundamentalist who tried to convert me on the hoof!

While Bonnie's dream warnings didn't manifest as disasters, Ginny's bridge dream did. Her precognitive dream of the collapse of the Florida Sunshine Bridge after a boat rammed it in 1980 was a traumatic one. Ginny's dream happened probably at the time of the accident's occurrence, and since she told others about it before newscasts verified it, it was written up as a scientifically verified psychic precognition. The transcript is recorded fully in Chapter Nine, under clairvoyance, but here are Ginny's reactions to the incident, and to her ability to pre-dream major disasters:

My reaction to the 'bridge' dream was to just 'acknowledge it.' I didn't read any newspaper articles about it, though—I really wanted to avoid hearing about the details—and it wasn't until four years later that I actually sat down with my psychologist friend to describe the dream. I can still flash the dream in my mind like I had the dream yesterday. I have yet to this day to read anything about the incident.

## After other disaster precognition dreams,

I really wondered if I was going crazy and I really wanted this to stop. The experiences changed in the sense that they became more 'personal' experiences...

I think my strongest feelings about all of this is what I do with these experiences to help myself and others. I am feeling more and more the need to express my experiences in the hope of helping.

Ginny has also had clairvoyant dreams that were not traumatic. This one was a personal event:

Two weeks after the Cincinnati Community Women's Choir, Muse, began (of which I am an original member), I had a dream. I dreamt that my Aunt Betty was visiting my mom. She had a book she had kept for many years, which belonged to my Grandma Wuestefeld who passed on in 1974. The book was about some women Grandma knew. The book had a picture of these women. I had the feeling that Grandma was real proud of these women.

When I woke up from the dream, I rolled over and fumbled for my pen and dream journal. I wrote the dream down and rolled back to sleep. A few days later, I called my Mom just to bullshit and I just happened to tell her about the dream. She thought it was 'funny' that I had the dream because my Uncle Don (Aunt Betty's husband) came over a few days before and gave my Mom an old box that had belonged to Grandma. Excited about finding more roots, I went to my Mom's a few days later.

Picking through the box, I found a small book entitled, 'Mothersingers of Cincinnati.' With the book was a little pamphlet with a picture of the Mothersingers saying that they were a community women's choir.

In the book, Ginny found several connections between her current women's choir and its women, and the early women's choir that began in 1925.

This was the first psychic experience I received in the process of beginning this book, and major in my decision to write it. Dozens of women have sent me accounts of precognitive dreams, of dreams that were visionary, shared or clairvoyant, dreams that affected their lives. There isn't room for all of them in this chapter, and I regret that deeply. A few more are given here though, and further dreams are recorded in Chapter Nine.

An example of a creativity dream is one of my own. In the days before beginning *The Kwan Yin Book of Changes*, I wondered if "tampering" with a psychic/magickal tool was a good idea, if it was something that could be done, or even should be. The night before starting the book, I decided to pick one hexagram and work on it the next day, and let the results of that tell me if doing this book was possible. That night I dreamed of a large, bright cauldron over a fire. The fire was scarcely brighter than the pot, which was steaming and bubbling over. In the steam rising from the cauldron was a Chinese letter, which I couldn't read. A dream remains vivid for me only occasionally, and when it does, I accept the image as important. I looked in the index of the Wilhelm/Baynes *I Ching* the next day, looking for a hexagram to experiment with, and found Hexagram 50, *The Cauldron*. The Chinese character for that hexagram's title was the image I had seen in the steam. I began *Kwan Yin* that day with translating Hexagram 50.

Sunlight and her lover had a shared or telepathic dream. In this case, Sunlight dreamed what Judy was imagining before sleep. In other cases, two women have the same dream. They don't need to be sleeping in the same room, but are usually emotionally involved with each other for such experiences to happen:

> I was lovers with a woman I'll call Judy. One morning when we were sharing our dreams, I told her the dream I'd had where I was making an eloquent speech in Japan about saving the whales, about what beautiful and wonderful animals they are.
>
> Judy asked me, 'Were you thinking about whales before you went to sleep?'
> 'No.'
> 'I was. When I can't get to sleep, I pretend I'm a whale and go down to the bottom of the ocean and swim around there.'

Psychic closeness offers women knowledge of each other, and that knowledge often comes in dreams. Pam dreamed this one and had the news before her sister-in-law did:

> Several years ago I dreamed that my sister-in-law was pregnant. She had tried for about five years with no success. One day when she came to visit, I met her at the door and told her about the dream, to which she replied that she had just found out about thirty minutes ago from the doctor.

While women's dreamwork is focused on the psychic events relayed in dreams, women's stroking the python skills manifesting through dream visions, traditional dreamwork uses the subconscious. The emphasis is on knowledge of self coming through from deeper levels in dreams. Dreams offer inner knowledge, with a rich symbolism unique to each individual. Some of these dreams are visionary, rites of passage or dis-covery as was Maggie's. This one is Ann's:

> This is more of a vision. It only occurred once and that was a few weeks ago. I don't remember much of it, but I know that most of it had to do with fear, and my fears specifically. I'm told to examine them closely and then reexamine them. I see them and suddenly realize where they come from. It's an 'Aha' experience. I suddenly know. I see that they come from me as I give them power to be . . . Then I say, 'Now I understand.' Suddenly fireworks go off everywhere. There is shouting and cheering as though I'm at a great celebration . . . I know that I have done something right and I feel good.
>
> Then I see this beautiful Black woman. This part is very clear. She is smiling and pointing to her neck. There is a huge dark red arrow on her neck. The point is pointing downward. It seems to be painted on her. She is gesturing to me to take the arrow. Her lips don't move but I hear her voice saying, 'It is yours. Congratulations.' Then I see just the arrow. It is painted on paper or wood. I see it in detail. It is a blood red, not a fire red. There seems to be a drop of blood at the tip. I know it is freshly painted. I know it is a power symbol and that it is important. At that moment I wake up.
>
> I drew a picture of the Black woman and the arrow on a pad I keep by the bed. It was given to me as a reward for learning my lesson about fear. It took me awhile to figure it out but later I understood the meaning of the symbol. The blood red arrow pointing downward from her neck indicates bleeding down below . . . menstruation. She is an African Black woman and in her culture the rite of passage from childhood into womanhood occurs when the menses

begin. It is a time of celebration. I was given the symbol of womanhood. My childhood is over.

On one level this whole vision or dream made me laugh. I am a grandmother and have just recently stopped menstruating. Now I'm being told symbolically that it is just beginning. This Black woman is one of my teachers, guides, etc. She comes to me in dreams and is always very patient. As you can see, she has to be. I'm what you would call a slow learner.

I wonder what moon phase Ann's dream happened in! In learning about fear, she takes control of her life and is given her womanhood, her acceptance of woman's blood power, as a gift. Such gifts and rites of passage come when each is ready and are never too late. Dreams of this nature are also examples of spirit guides and helpers, to be discussed more fully later, or of manifestings. Here is one more, a dream of Patti's that is also a dis-covery or rite of passage:

In this dream I was walking on a path through a forest, at night, with a full moon luminated my way. The path was slightly uphill but easy walking. I stopped in my progress and turned to my left. Before me was a clearing. Immediately a woman appeared before me saying, 'You are here for your initiation.' She escorted me into the clearing. When we reached the center we turned to our right and walked to the end of the clearing where a small hillock rose slightly from the ground. My escort vanished. On the hillock was a woman that I knew was the Goddess, and she was busy with incense tripods and bowls of ingredients. As I waited for her to speak to me, I realized that though I couldn't see them, the clearing was full of my peers in knowledge. I felt very comfortable, as though I had 'come home.' The Goddess then came toward me holding in her hand a medallion. She said, 'Each of us here represents a god. This is the god that you are to represent. His name is Thoth.' She placed the medallion around my neck. It weighted heavily on my upper chest/base of throat. In meditations since then I have often felt the medallion on my chest. The medallion was a gold filigree five-pointed star. The center was solid and on the solid metal was an etching of Thoth, in an Ibis-headed representation.

Patti found Goddess as self and as god in her dream, and used its knowledge to see further into her own potential. Her children grown, she has gone through divorce and started over on her own and in college. She attributes her courage in making major changes to this dream. Thoth is (quoting Patti), the "God of Learning, Lord of the Moon, Lord of Magic." He is also herself.

Women's dreams run the circle from precognition to rites of passage symbolism. Everyone dreams and everyone dreams every night, but not everyone remembers her dreaming. When a dream has important information, it often recurs or is too vivid to forget. When a dream is of past life or precognitive material, it remains vivid over years, something that ordinary dreams seldom do. One of the biggest factors in learning dream recall is the desire to remember. Going to bed with that thought in mind is the strongest stimulant to starting dreamwork.

Other stimulants to begin the process can be holding a crystal in the left hand while sleeping, or putting one under the pillow. Program the crystal for dreaming and remembering dreams, and an amethyst or moonstone are also dreaming tools. Make a dream pillow of fresh mugwort with rose petals. Place a notebook and pen next to the bed, opened and ready to write with, or have a tape recorder set and ready within reach.

Dream recall is a habit, and like other new habits it has to be established and "programmed" in the subconscious (emotional body) mind. Each night before sleep, tell yourself out loud that you will wake with remembered dreams and will write them down. Say it several times, and particularly when relaxed and as close to sleep as possible. Make this statement a habit, and the writing down of dreams immediately on waking a habit. Within days it becomes one.

On waking, follow these instructions from Jane Roberts exactly:

> In the morning, lie with your eyes still closed. The dreams will still be in your memory. Write them down at once. Do not get out of bed. Do not have a cup of coffee first. As you write down your first remembered dream, you may recall others. Date your dreams. This is extremely important. Write down those details that are in your mind, but make sure that you do not consciously add to your dreams.[17]

On getting up or even the night before, make note of the day of the Moon, the Moon phase, and the day in your menstrual cycle. The next step is to compare your dreams to waking reality, and this simply means going over the dream notebook frequently. Even written down, most dreams are quickly forgotten. Where a known person figures in a dream, check with her on the dream events, where possible, to see if events in and out of the dream match. Some tact may be involved in this, and time can pass before a dream manifests. Go back to the dream notebook and record any event in it that proved precognitive or clairvoyant. Leave space under each dream for doing this. Take as much note of everyday happenings as traumatic or emotional ones; these are more easily forgotten but prove more frequent. The unknown person of last night's dream could be someone met tonight at a women's dance. Keeping records of these experiences becomes exciting. Match the occurrence of psychic dreams with your menstrual cycle and with the phases of the Moon. The information is revealing. Notice Migene Gonzalez-Wippler's Days of the Moon Chart, also. See which dreams come true and how long it takes. In time you will develop a sense for knowing immediately which dreams are pre-cognitive, know they are before the proof manifests.

Dreams remembered on waking are usually those of the last dream cycle of the night. For more dreams, women can set an alarm clock at two-hour intervals and catch dreams through the night. Waking from a period of REM sleep, easily visible to someone watching you sleep, always results in dream recall, if the dream is written down immediately. Emotionally intense dreams have more chance of being remembered than less emotionally charged ones, and these dreams are more vivid. Theory says that sudden awakening usually offers more recall than slower awakenings. (I personally find the opposite). Self-aware women, women working on psychic and spiritual development, are more likely to remember their dreams, and women who ask for dream recall usually receive it, even if they have not remembered their dreams before.[18]

Ann Faraday's suggestions:

1. Keep pen and paper or tape recorder always ready by your bedside.
2. Have a dim light or flashlight ready near the bed.
3. Make the suggestion several times before sleeping that you will dream and remember it.
4. Use the alarm clock for chronic nonrecallers who wish to catch dreams. The clock should go off softly.
5. On awakening, sit up gently and switch on the dim light. Move slowly.
6. Write down or tape the dream immediately in as much detail as possible. Do not fall asleep again before doing this or you will lose the dream.
7. Add as many comments or associations as you can after writing down the dream. Do this before going back to sleep or getting up for the day.
8. If you awaken in the morning with a dream, write it down or record it before getting up.
9. As soon as possible that day, work on the dream noticing:
   a. objective facts in real life, the day's events.
   b. events that could be past life or precognitive.
   c. symbols that are important within your life.
   d. act it out on Gestalt lines making every object, fact, person, place speak as itself and as a facet of you.[19]
   e. note lunar and menstrual cycle days.

To work on a dream for symbolism, go back to your dream

notebook. On the opposite side of the notebook page from where the dream is related and where space is left for precognition follow-up, list every noun of the dream. Find your own associations for each word, in or out of the dream, brainstorming on it. Be aware of possible puns, and of the qualities of an object. (A ball is round, what else is round, how does this fit in the dream?). People in dreams can be themselves or yourself, or symbolic qualities. In Gestalt work, every person and thing in a dream, including inanimate objects, is the dreamer and has a message for the dreamer's understanding. The collection of words and associations of these nouns become the dreamer's own personal dream dictionary, something that grows and becomes more valuable as time goes on.[20] Try to see the symbolism in a dream for how it operates in your own life and personal reality.

Dreaming dictionaries are available, but dreams are personal symbols. The dictionary can offer ideas, but unless a meaning really resonates, keep looking. When a meaning for a symbol is reached, you know it. It feels right. Also go with instant impressions or gut feelings that happen at the time of the dream or after. Remember to note these down when recording the dream.

In looking for meaning in a dream, pay special attention first to what happened in real life the day before it. Dream events, people and symbols often refer to things that happened recently in real life. Once those are understood, go further. Every symbol in a dream has meaning, every event and character. If the meaning isn't clear immediately, it could become so on later reading. The person seen in the dream turns up or phones, or the event of the dream happens. Understanding the symbols gives the dream a deeper meaning, usually a personal rather than clairvoyant one.

The more dreams recalled and recorded, the more the pattern of psychic phenomena comes through. The first step in doing dreamwork is to make it a habit to autosuggest dream recall and to record or write down every dream you can. Next note the patterns, reading back often to see what dreams have come real on the earthplane. The more complex part of the process is learning dream symbolism, but major messages come through and come through clearly for everyone. As in any other skill, dreamwork takes practice.

Jane Roberts began doing dreamwork in November, 1963. In the year 1964, she recorded 104 dreams, 13 (about 10%) of which were precognitive, and 13 more held important psychic information for her. Five were healing dreams. From January to May, 1965, she recorded a total of 174 dreams, more in five months than in the whole past year, and often several dreams a night. Thirty of these had later-proven psychic information.[21] While 104 dreams in a year is major, 174 in five months is yet more. The increase came with practice in dream recall, and in interpreting the dreams for precognitions that were verified later. Begin the process and watch it grow in frequency and meaning.

Dreams can also be programmed to give needed information, the old idea of "sleeping on it" to find answers to a problem. Before going to sleep, state the affirmation of having a dream that tells you what you need to know. "I have a dream tonight that answers my problem, and I remember it." Problem solving, healing, creativity suggestions can be accessed in this way. You can also ask to dream about a particular person, to "check in with her" and use the dream to tell you how she is. Remember to record the dream you wake up with, or you will lose it. I have often used this in solving writing problems, separating ideas into outlines.

Women can also learn to enter their dreams and create them as they happen, change their directions if they choose, create an ongoing scenario. Leonie talked of continuing dreams as a child, and I had such a dream fantasy of my own that continued for long periods. These are lucid dreams, and in Native American traditions are considered very powerful. They occur in the hypnogogic state of stage one dreams, and on an EEG show the alpha to theta brainwave state that is evident in every form of psychic phenomena. The dreamer at first isn't sure she is dreaming, may think she is awake then decides otherwise, and from that point enters her dreams as her own creative Goddess. Some of these dreams become flying dreams, as when the Senoi children learn not to be afraid of falling dreams that happen in the early sleep stages, and thereafter astral projections. Some of these dreams open other realities for the dreamer, alternate worlds and higher consciousness.

When the dreamer takes control of her dream, Ann Faraday calls the process a High Lucid dream. The connection with astral travel is a strong one, and inseparable from this form of dreaming. The dreamer begins by knowing she is dreaming, but not being able to control her dream, or realizing that she can control it. From there she learns to take charge, and Faraday sees that as a reflection of taking charge of her waking life as well. She uses an exercise from Carlos Castaneda for learning to control lucid dreaming:

> Don Juan suggests that we tell ourselves before falling asleep that we shall look at our hands in a dream and become aware that we are dreaming. We are then

gently to shift our gaze to some object in the environment, and after a minute or two, bring the gaze back to our hands. This exercise should be repeated until the dreamscape is stabilized. 'Every time you look at anything in your dreams, it changes shape,' he told Carlos. 'The trick in learning to *set up dreaming* is obviously not just to look at things but to sustain the sight of them. Dreaming is real when one has succeeded in bringing everything into focus. Then there is no difference between what you do when you sleep and what you do when you are not sleeping' . . . Don Juan's technique proved valuable *after* I had achieved some measure of lucidity in dreams through dream work in waking life.[22]

The process is one of changing realities, changing planes of realities, from concrete daily life to matriarchal, stroking the python consciousness. For Ann Faraday, not a believer in the psychic world, the High Lucid dream becomes astral projection:

> I had become lucid in a dream and had been flying around when I suddenly felt myself on the shoulders of a giant. All I could feel was the pressure on my legs as I struggled to free myself from his grasp. Suddenly there was a kind of click and I twisted free of my dream body in some way, to find myself in an even lighter body in a dreamscape of brilliant white light looking down on the Eternal City. (I don't really know what the Eternal City is, but that's what it was in the dream.) I wondered whether to fly over and explore but feared the light might burn me, so I continued my explorations in the new world of even more brilliant colors and strange shapes . . . [23]

We are back in the world of astral projection, the world of limitless realities of time and space. With practice and experience at this type of conscious dreaming, lucid dreams can be preplanned, and become astral projections that are chosen and controlled. This in clairvoyance is one use of women's dreams, and the possibilities are limitless. Lucid dreaming is an advanced form of dreamwork.

Dreamwork can be used with or stimulated by meditation. Use the meditation process to reenter a completed dream and direct or change it—make it lucid.[24] It can also be used to work on a particular symbol for understanding, or to ask for information or problem solving. Work out anger or fear issues, relationship issues, by asking for a specific dream that helps with solving these. Ask for dreams to clarify an emotion: "Why am I feeling this way?" or, "What am I really feeling?" Phrase the suggestion/question carefully before sleep, and repeat it over several nights if needed. Diane Mariechild's *Mother Wit* offers several dreamwork meditations, all good ones.

The world of women's dreams is an opening on psychic worlds of other realities and altered states of consciousness. Psychic phenomena happen here, without the resistance and interference intrinsic in concrete daily life, and in a relaxed state more receptive to psychic happenings and information. Dreams are a valuable wellspring of women's psychic experiences, and an endless source of knowledge and meaning. By opening to the symbols and dramatizations by which the psychic bodies transmit information to the conscious/linear mind, women learn another form of shifting between realities and of stroking the python.

Some recommended books on dreamwork are: Ann Faraday, *The Dream Game*, (New York, Perennial Library, 1974) and *Dream Power*, (New York, Berkeley Books, 1972); Patricia Garfield, *Creative Dreaming*, (New York, Ballantine Books, 1974); and the chapter on dreaming in Jane Roberts, *The Coming of Seth*, (New York, Pocket Books 1966). *The Coming of Seth* is also published under the title of *How to Develop Your ESP*.

The next chapter discusses manifesting, another solar plexus skill involving images and how to use them. As in every chapter of *Stroking the Python: Women's Psychic Lives*, the women in Chapter Six have stories to tell.

# FOOTNOTES

1. Diane Mariechild, *Mother Wit: A Feminist Guide to Psychic Development*, p. 102.

2. Patricia Garfield, Ph.D., *Creative Dreaming*, (New York, Ballantine Books, 1974). Highly recommended, along with Ann Faraday's books.

3. *Ibid.*, p. 20, feminized and adapted.

4. Adrienne Quinn, *Dreams, Secret Messages From Your Mind*, (Takoma, WA, Dream Research, 1981), p. 11.

5. Patricia Garfield, *Creative Dreaming*, p 76.

6. *Ibid.*, 80-86.

7. A.E. Powell, *The Astral Body*, (Wheaton, IL, Quest/Theosophical Publishing House, 1982, original 1927), p. 99. Material on dreams comes from Annie Besant and C.W. Leadbeater.

8. *Ibid.*, p. 97-101.

9. Adrienne Quinn, *Dreams, Secret Messages From Your Mind*, p. 38-47. The stages of sleep are from her work.

10. Patricia Garfield, *Creative Dreaming*, p. 182-183.

11. Adrienne Quinn, *Dreams, Secret Messages From Your Mind*, p. 39.

12. Ann Faraday, *Dream Power*, (New York, Berkeley Books, 1972), p. 21.

13. Ovulation and dream material comes from Helen Farias, "The College of Hera: The Beginning Lesson of the Pool," in *The Beltane Papers*, (Clear Lake, WA), Vol. I, no. 8, Eostre, 1985, p. 21.

14. *Ibid.*

15. Migene Gonzalez-Wippler, *The Complete Book of Spells, Ceremonies, and Magic*, (St. Paul, Llewellyn Publications, 1988), p. 228.

16. Jane Roberts, *The Coming of Seth*, p. 49.

17. *Ibid.* p. 52-53.

18. Ann Faraday, *Dream Power*, p. 64.

19. *Ibid.*, p. 306-307. Condensed and slightly adapted.

20. Constance Mead, "My Dreaming Self (Part 2)," in *The Beltane Papers*, Eostre, 1985, p. 15.

21. Jane Roberts, *The Coming of Seth*, p. 60-61.

22. Ann Faraday, *The Dream Game*, p. 336-341.

23. *Ibid.*, p 342.

24. Diane Mariechild, *Mother Wit*, p. 102-103.

# Chapter Six
# The Solar Plexus: Manifesting Mind Over Matter

*We are always manifesting our reality. Everything in our lives is there because we put it there. Every person in our lives is there because we drew them there. Most of the time, we are completely unaware of when and how we do this. This unawareness leaves us at the mercy of emotions, beliefs and thoughts that give us what we may not consciously wish in our lives. Once we become aware of this process, however, we can put the 'laws' of manifestation to conscious use in our lives and be active participants in the forming of our personal reality . . . Recognize the intricacy of how everything 'fits' and set aside the logical, expected have-tos and how-tos of conventional reality, and soon the playful freedom of creativity begins to drop whatever is appropriately desired into our laps.[1]*

I lost my job the day before starting *The Kwan Yin Book of Changes*. I had $1800 in savings and thought I could get unemployment compensation. I thought it would be okay to give myself a vacation, three months to write a book, it would be finished by then. I knew I had enough until I finished the book. Always in my life I'd been a hoarder—of food, books to read, writing supplies, money. Always I'd been afraid of being hungry, and have been hungry at times. This time I could allow myself to be nourished, to live on what was there, instead of scrounging for nourishment and being afraid. I began the book, not letting go of my survival fears fully, but determined to finish at least the first draft before I found another job.

A week later at a picnic, I lay down in a quiet grassy place under a tree, my belly to the Earth. I had just begun to meditate and was in the stage of trying too hard, of "practicing" and missing the point because I hadn't learned to relax and let go. This time I had an intense mystical experience based on the Tree of Life meditation in Starhawk.[2] Instead of trying to visualize a tree, I became it, felt my roots going deep into the nourishment of the Earth and my branches touching the stars. I became the tree, and understood for the first time that the Earth nourishes everyone. All I had to do was extend my roots and accept the gifts. I didn't have to be afraid for survival, I would survive. I saw myself drawing safety and nourishment in through the roots of the world, and felt my book out there in the stars, my branches touching and holding it. I knew I could draw it in. I relaxed.

*The Kwan Yin Book of Changes* took not three months, but thirteen months to write and I worked on it every day, all day. My $1800 got me through. Every time an expense beyond rent came along, the money came, too. A woman brought me her typing to do for $1 a page. I babysat, and put ads in the paper to sell unwanted objects. I bathed dogs and toward the end had food stamps. I lost the unemployment compensation case, but didn't need it. I tapped into the roots of the Goddess universe and there was always enough.

$1800 lasted me to live on for more than a year. *Kwan Yin* took five drafts, and in the very last one I worked in a factory for a few weeks, then started waitressing part time at night. I had a billing job part time from home. I wasn't hungry and I always had enough. Of hundreds of job resumes I sent out in those thirteen months, I never got one interview—I was supposed to write full time and had enough to live on, that was my job. The week I mailed *Kwan Yin* in to her publisher I had a job offer, and I took it. My whole life changed.

Women tell me I live a charmed life, and I probably do. I have felt extremely taken care of since the day of becoming the Tree, of tapping into the nourishment of the universe. If I need something, it is there. It has been there all along. Having learned the secrets of manifesting, to trust in the universe and be clear in what to ask for, I have what I need and always will. Only when I forget this do times get tough.

Women have immense power to create their own realities, to ask for what they need and to have it. This is probably the best-kept secret of the patriarchy, and its re-claiming is matriarchy's re-turn. We are told from childhood, "You can't do that," "You can't have that," "You have to live in the real world," "If you don't do it well enough, someone else will get it," "You aren't good enough." None of it's true; in fact the opposites are true. Women can do anything and have anything they need or want. The real world is there for the creating, and women are creators of what's real. There is enough for everyone and no one is deprived by someone else's "luck." Women are good, and are good enough, and are able and capable. Just extend the roots. It's all right there. Just ask for it.

Affirmation and manifesting are one of the things that women's spirituality is based on, the knowledge that women can have anything they want. Self-determination is a women's movement skill, and manifesting in women's spirituality takes it deeper and further. Women create their own realities, make their own choices, direct their own lives. The psychic skill of manifesting is learning to understand the process and use it as a tool for better living, for comfort, joy and positivity. The skill is available to women in several ways, in the understanding of coincidence, in the use of affirmations/visualization, in mind over matter skills of psychokinesis, and in the understanding of apparitions, poltergeists and ghosts. Once understood and used, women have a tool for creating reality, for making what starts as idea become manifest in the concrete linear world, and for preventing negative ideas—what you *don't* want—from coming into Be-ing.

The solar plexus skill of manifesting is a function of the lower mental body, the conscious mind as influenced by kama-manas, the desire-mind. This is rational consciousness, used to create chosen realities, and its vehicle is controlled thought. The most powerful element in the universe, thought is a form of energy expressing the limitlessness of the aura and the spaces between atoms. Energy is the life force, the prana that comprises the universe, and thought is a part of that energy. Mary Coddington's list of characteristics for prana or aura energy in Chapter Two also applies to the energy of thought.

Thought penetrates anything, including what is called dense matter. It can heal, be conducted and stored, is transmittable across distance and time, causes things to happen and can be used for good or evil.[3] Thought is directed and controlled by women's minds, emotions and wills. By controlling and using thought, women have the power of mind over matter, over an energy force that directs universal creation. The solar plexus chakra and lower mental body are the places of women's will, thought and mental attributes, and their transmission to and through the other psychic unseen bodies.

In theosophical theory, "thoughts are things"[4] created by the lower mental body. Each thought has vibration, and causes a ripple-in-a-pool effect on the lower mental body of the aura. Under this impulse, the mental body throws off vibrations that reflect the thought, and these are thought-forms. Women who see rapidly changing colors in auras, sometimes as shooting projectiles of light and color, are seeing these vibrations or thought-forms. These vibrations or energy forms become powerful when directed by will.[5] What transmits these thought-forms from the mental body to bring them from idea into manifest reality on the earth plane is the emotional body or kama-manas. An idea with desire behind it is transmitted and takes effect, one without it does not. If a woman wants something badly and thinks of it, she creates it. It has a better chance of manifesting than an idea of something she has no real desire or caring about. When thought is combined with desire, kama-manas, the idea is duplicated in the etheric body to manifest in the physical concrete world. This is the principle of directing affirmation, manifesting, psychokinesis and more. This process as psychic healing is discussed in Chapter Seven.

A thought created once has power, but a thought created repeatedly has greater power. What a woman thinks and desires becomes part of her and is visible in her aura. A thought repeated becomes habit, and positive thoughts become positive habits. Think repeatedly and often, "I have enough for all my needs," and you do. Woman's power and will create her thought-forms and creates her images of herself and others.

> If a woman's thought is about herself, it hovers around her astral body and is always ready to act upon her when she is in a passive condition. Thoughts of impurity cloud the aura. Each woman travels through space enclosed by a case of her own making, surrounded by forms created by her habitual thoughts. She sees the world through this cloud of thought-forms.
>
> If a woman's thought or feeling is directly connected with someone else, the resultant thought-form moves toward that person and discharges itself upon her astral and mental bodies.[6]

What Annie Besant is saying here is that women's thoughts create who they are, and women's thoughts of others affect others, carrying her image of herself to what someone else sees. A woman thinking of another is actually there in the traveling astral (emotional body, thought transmitted by emotion), and the other woman sees or senses her thought-forms. This is a distant use of thought-form, called telepathy. What a woman thinks about is who she is, and causes what manifests in her life. Thoughts originate in the mental body, but become real on the concrete linear—woman's thought-forms become her real world.

If that much power is involved, then the issue here is how to use this power to get what you want and need in the here and now. Things happen by "coincidence," seemingly random, that drop goodies into women's laps, but how to control that process is the question. And if women's thoughts create their realities, then maybe coincidence isn't so random after all. The how-to is affirmation and visualization, manifesting work, known to most women consciously or not, and described in this chapter.

Coincidence, according to the dictionary, is "the striking occurrence of two or more events at one time, apparently by chance." But what are time and chance? They are different things in women's psychic consciousness than in concrete reality. Time and chance are irrelevant concepts in matriarchal reality, things to be used as tools. The components of a coincidence, the things that come together spontaneously at the right time and place, can each happen separately in time and space, and can happen anytime or anywhere. Here is Rodney Marsden's explanation of what it is that happens:

> My own explanation for coincidences centers on the proposition that it is the human mind which causes such events . . . We can picture this as a process with many components. At one level, the clairvoyant and precognitive faculties of mind obtain information which is then passed on to the subconscious, which in turn directs the individual to a certain place and time where events with some particular relevance for her will happen. At another level, some telepathic process can alter the attitudes and behavior of other people in the world, as a result of which favorable circumstances and events are set up. PK (psychokinesis, mind over matter) may also have a role to play in this, but there is no way of being sure.[7]

In other terms, Annie Besant's terms, the mental body receives information via the solar plexus chakra and prana, energy or thought-form that it passes on to the emotional body (subconscious). The emotional body passes the information to the etheric double, and from there to manifesting by directing the woman to the right time and place. When other people are involved, the thought-forms of the woman affect others' behaviors, creating favorable circumstances and events for her. What she needs or wants happens, in ways that seem spontaneous and unexplainable, but she creates these fulfillments herself.

Coincidences happen in several styles. In what Marsden calls the "Small World Syndrome," you camp next to a woman at the Michigan Women's Music Festival and dis-cover you went to grade school together. In another, and this one has happened to me frequently, you are looking for a particular reference and open the book at "random" to the right page. In another case, a name or idea catches your attention and suddenly that name or idea comes up every time you turn around. Totally unconnected people are talking about her or it, and there's an article in the newspaper. It's an idea or name that was foreign to you yesterday. A doctor notes that if someone comes into her treatment with a broken leg today, she'll see ten of them that week, even out of skiing season and when she hasn't seen a broken leg in months.

Sandra Stevens describes another type of coincidence, set up for her and Sheila by their channeled entity/teacher Gay Bonner:

> Each day as they returned . . . before lunch, before dinner, or during the mid-afternoon break (of a conference they were attending), they would see a family of quail scurrying across their path near their room. Neither woman had ever been that close to these cute, little birds before. They found them adorable . . . Gay had spoken to them that afternoon urging them to set aside their learning and problems and have some fun . . . Afterwards they talked to Gay again:
> 'They are quite a family and sight. They go across the same time you come to your room, and if you notice, it is not always the same time, according to your concepts, that you walk to your room; but the quail run across for you, and you are here for them!'[8]

The quail were a "cosmic gift" from a spirit guide, but more, were an introduction to the women of the idea that all things have meaning, and manifest for a reason and a purpose. The concrete world reflects the woman's inner realities, something she creates herself. Had Sheila and Sandra not been open to a fun experience, the quail would not have been there. Had they not been able to resonate to and appreciate them, they would not have even noticed them, and the quail likely would not have manifested for them. The quail co-created this reality, too. Reality and coincidence happen in a woman's own terms, with cooperation of the coincidence's components.

How many times have you thought of something in particular for dinner, and been invited to a friend's house who was making it? How many times have you said out loud or to yourself, "I need _____," and had it come to you? Have you ever in a game asked for a two of clubs or a two on the dice, and had them happen? Have you ever needed $30, and then had $30 come in the mail? These are all "coincidences" that have happened because you've asked for them, visualized them happening, want them, are open to and have created the thought-forms to make them manifest. The question of cosmic helpers or spirit guides is a further issue, and a corresponding one.

All the possible realities exist, and all exist at once, and women choose and create the reality they want now. Says Jane Roberts:

> In a very real manner, events or objects are actually focal points where highly charged psychic impulses are transformed into something that can be physically perceived: a breakthrough into matter. When such highly charged im-

impulses intersect or coincide, matter is formed. The reality behind such an explosion into matter is independent of the matter itself. An identical or nearly identical pattern may reemerge 'at any time' again and again, if the proper coordinates exist for activation.

In your system of reality you are learning what mental energy is, and how to use it. You do this by constantly transforming your thoughts and emotions into physical form . . . What seems to be a perception, an objective concrete event independent from you, is instead the materialization of your own inner emotions, energy and mental environment.[9]

The ability to visualize, conceptualize a happening, object or person is the key to making them manifest. That and the knowing that this is another reality, a reality and limitless possibility open to women and there for women to use.

A slightly different emphasis of this and of coincidence is psychokinesis (PK) or telekinesis, the ability of women's minds to affect dense matter. Not only can women draw to them what they create in thought-forms, but can use thought-forms to affect what is already present on the material linear plane. Physics is dis-covering that dense matter is not so dense at all, that there are spaces between atoms filled with energy. Thought is also energy, and with the power to move objects. Most women never try it, since linear reality says it's impossible, but many who do learn otherwise.

Stories circulate of the lucky gambler who asks for the numbers she wants on the wheel or dice and has them come up again and again. The gambler has learned to ask for her needs in a relaxed way, visualizing her intent and knowing the outcome is possible. If she can't accept it as possible, she doesn't get it. Children watching Uri Geller on a talk show try bending spoons themselves and the spoons bend. No one has told an eleven-year-old girl that bending spoons just by willing it is impossible.[10]

Ninel (Nelya) Mikhailova has been studied and filmed in Russia for her ability to move solid objects with her mind. The work of doing this intentionally is a serious physical strain for her but she has worked extensively with scientists:

Nelya held her long fingers parallel to the table about six inches above the compass and began to move her hands in a circular motion. The strain etched the dimples deep in her cheeks. Twenty minutes passed. Her pulse raced to 250 beats a minute. She moved her head from side to side gazing intently at the compass needle. Her hands moved as though she were conducting some unseen orchestra. And then as if the atoms in the compass needle were tuned in to her, the needle shivered. Slowly it began to spin counterclockwise, turning like the second hand of a clock. Then the entire compass, plastic case, leather strap, and all, began to whirl.[11]

She is able to select among objects on a table and move one while leaving the others stationary. The weather affects her psychokinetic ability, in storms it lessens, and gold is more easily and quickly moved than other types of matter. In physiological testing, where the norms are for three-four times the electrical activity from the back of the brain than from the front, for Mikhailova it is fifty times as much.[12] EEG measurements indicate increased activity in the part of the brain controlling sight. (There are chakras in the eyes, and in the third eye).

The Soviets have machinery for measuring the body's magnetic fields (aura), and when objects move for Nelya Mikhailova her aura begins to pulse in rhythm with brain waves and heart beat.

> It was as if she'd caused a wave of energy to vibrate through the invisible energy-envelope around her . . . Not only was her entire force field pulsing, the detectors showed that this pulsing force field had *focused* in the direction of her gaze.[13]

The theory is that these vibrations are magnetic, and act to magnetize what she is focusing on, causing the object to move. Solar plexus ability to will and direct energy is the medium for moving solid objects with the mind. This is the first scientific investigation of PK and the power of woman's aura to affect dense matter and reality.

Nelya Mikhailova dis-covered her psychokinetic ability by accident, turning spontaneous happenings into an understanding and use of a psychic ability.

> I was very upset and angry that day. I was walking toward a cupboard in my apartment when suddenly a pitcher in the cupboard moved to the edge of the shelf, fell and smashed to bits.
> After that, all kinds of changes began to take place in my apartment.[14]

The falling, following and breaking of things as she walked past them were a manifestation of her energy and anger, were what is called a poltergeist. She one day realized that she could control this energy and that it was coming from her. She experimented with it, learned about it, and learned how to use it. Mikhailova believes she inherited the ability from her mother.

Poltergeists are uncontrolled manifestings of psychokinetic ability, and usually happen around teenagers. Things fall, shake, break, fly across rooms, spill when the youth is there, and things seem to follow her. The activity is the subconscious result of repressed anger, confusion and hostility, emotions common in the difficult teenage years. The young woman causing the effects usually has no knowledge that they come from her, and therefore takes no control of them. Poltergeists more often follow girls than boys, suggestive of the anger that all women internalize living in patriarchal societies. Helping a daughter understand and safely channel her rage is a way of stopping them, as is teaching her how to control and use her PK ability. She is not to be blamed and punished, but supported, loved and made aware. Experimenting with intentional psychokinesis, mind over matter, as Nelya Mikhailova did, is a way of transforming the poltergeist phenomena.

When Alla Vinogradova, another Russian woman, dis-covered her telekinetic ability, she decided that it was natural energy that should not cause physical stress. Using relaxation and meditation techniques, she learned to move objects psychokinetically without Nelya Mikhailova's strain. Unlike Mikhailova, she can move objects blindfolded and does not need to use her hands. She traces the energy for doing so from her solar plexus center, as amplified by her third eye/brow.[15] Intensified desire makes moving objects easier for her, and Kirlian photography of her aura during PK work shows the intensification of focus and vibration that was dis-covered with Nelya Mikhailova. Alla Vinogradova's use of her hands strongly suggests the energy and motions used in laying on of hands work in healing.

> The next object placed before her was a ping-pong ball. In this instance, Vinogradova moved her hand in a circular motion a few inches above the object. The ball obediently followed her hands. It was noted that she rubbed her hands briskly before attempting this feat and that she directed the ball's motion with a few fingers rather than with her hand. For the two (cigar) tubes, however, Vinogradova appeared to be utilizing her entire hand for the movement.[16]

Remember that there are chakras also at the tips of the fingers and in the palms of the hands. The thought-form solar plexus energy used to move objects is directed through these chakras, or in Nelya Mikhailova's case, through the chakras of the eyes. New objects are more difficult for Alla Vinogradova to move than ones she has already worked with, and when an object can be rolled like the cigar tubes or ball, she can move up to 100 grams in weight. She teaches others to move objects also, and with success.

Along with moving objects and causing ideas to become reality, PK or manifesting is involved in healing, where the "object" moved or changed is the state of a woman's health, and in divination, where the card or hexagram that comes up on a tarot or I Ching reading is the answer to a question. These are examples of ideas/thought-forms making physical changes or bringing ideas to concrete reality. In telepathy, thought-forms travel between two people, one who creates them and another who receives the creation. The levitations, rappings and table tippings of seances are also psychokinetic, manifestation phenomena. In the case of apparitions, another form of manifesting, what manifests on the physical plane is the thought-form idea of a person or Be-ing from another plane of reality.

Apparitions are common psychic phenomena, probably the most common experience of the many women wrote to me about. They are the much fabled and much maligned "ghosts," the appearances of people or animals no longer alive. They most often occur at night, and usually when the woman perceiving them is near sleep, awakening from sleep, or is otherwise fully relaxed. If there are two women in a room, one may see the apparition while the other sees nothing. In Rodney Marsden's analysis, ghosts are mental perceptions or thought-forms, the manifesting of a state of "historical clairvoyance—a precognition in reverse"[17] or the retrocognition thought-form of a past presence. The Be-ing seen is no longer on the earth plane, but it once was, and it usually lived in the place it is being seen.

Manifestings of this type are seldom negative, and never anything to fear. They can be or can come from spirit guides or helpers, appearing in the form of what the woman seeing them would expect. Her expectations create their way of appearing. They can be figures from past lives, or figures of people who lived there that were once alive. They can be the thought-forms of deceased relatives, bringing information and help. Apparitions or visions or manifestings are not the result of insanity, as patriarchy insists. They are real appearances from a different-than-linear reality.

Here is a manifesting described by Sandra Stevens:

> The room was filled with a light so bright she felt as if day had instantly returned. She thought, 'But I've turned out the light—' She looked around the room. Over to her left, floating mid-air in front of her bookcase, she saw a miniature figure—an angel without wings or halo, feminine, cherubic, dressed in white. It was smiling. Sandy's eyes widened in disbelief. The figure then began sending what looked like large balls or rings of fire—brightly colored light—toward her head. The balls pulsated from the figure and entered her head in a steady rhythmic pattern. Frightened, she squeezed her eyes closed and mentally yelled, 'Help!' One more ball of light entered her head through her closed eyes; then everything became quiet. Sandy felt quite wide awake. She opened her eyes and the room was perfectly normal . . .

Gay Bonner's explanation:

> The vision you experienced was energy being sent to help you learn. Often energy is sent, but of course, many don't actually see this happening to them. It involves a transfer of thoughts to you. You will be hit with some very creative

thoughts in the next few weeks. They will seem as if they simply hit you.[18]

The creativity happened, spontaneously it seemed, and the vision or apparition was a positive experience. This is a form of manifesting women experience frequently, particularly women who are psychically sensitive or involved in psychic development. These happenings often occur in ritual; women invoke them.

Women write about their experiences with manifesting—apparitions, coincidences, psychokinesis and poltergeists. These were the most frequent of all the psychic experiences women described. In tapping into the limitless abundance of the Goddess universe, women dis-cover nurturing from the cosmos, the appearance of needed and asked for material objects and prosperity, of ideas and synchronicities, and of material or nonmaterial apparitions and events. Learning that thought creates reality, they understand the happenings and take control of them, for their good and the good of all.

This is Gloria's story of a series of "coincidences" that changed her life, begun by her visualization of prosperity. At the start, she is homeless, fully down and out, choosing to accept this and not interfere until she knew it was time. She felt her misfortunes were the fulfilling of a lesson, that she had manipulated others and so lost what she had. Rule one is, "What you send out comes back to you": thought-forms have power.

> Psychic experiences and manifestations are daily puzzles and pleasures. They are also painful lessons of unintended or well-meaning manipulation which backfired as always. After experiencing such a backfire last year I turned my back on spells and manifestations through visualization.
>
> I lived the life placed before me. I had lost every financially valuable item I owned. I was isolated from my friends and family. All I knew I could count on was change. I had vowed to myself not to ask for anything ... Tarot told me it was because of my misuse of power, karmic justice.
>
> I waited and reflected a year. It was a few weeks before Christmas when I Ching said the time for my withdrawal was over. I was unemployed, living on the street along with many homeless. I had found an old friend who had an extra bedroom I was welcome to. My youngest daughter and I were all that was left of my family still at home or with me.
>
> I didn't have a dime. I ran into a gal I knew one day and she persuaded me to go shoot a game of pool with her. While we were playing, a couple of guys asked if we would like to play doubles for $1 a game. We played and won $5 that afternoon. When we left I had $3 in my pocket.
>
> Next door to where we were shooting was a secondhand store. We went in and looked around. I smiled with fond tempting memories upon finding a very nice large green candle for 50¢. With some tender loving care it would have many hours of pleasure left in it. I bought it.
>
> That night, I carved most carefully to find the right degree to insure proper wax pool to wick ratios. Before lighting, I went ahead out of old habits of never

burning a candle without it having a clear purpose, and dedicated it. A rhyme came to mind that Marion Weinstein had taught me years ago, short and sweet:

> Money, money come to me,
> Money come right away,
> As I will, so mote it be.

So I added this to the carvings I placed on the candle.

This was on a Wednesday. That night the candle burned brightly beside my bed. I enjoyed its light. Remembering its purpose of drawing money to me, I clarified that I called for this knowing I was depriving no one else and in turn didn't believe I should be deprived myself. I visualized myself counting money. I visualized what I'd spend it on. I'd give my friend a month's rent in advance. I'd buy my daughter a coat and some warm shoes. I visualized a coat for me. I fell asleep.

Thursday I relit the big green candle . . . I could feel the warmth of my envisioned coat. I could see the smiles on my daughter's face. I could hear my friend thanking me for the financial help. I fell asleep.

Friday I received a check for $250, payment on a debt over two years old. There had been no hint of it coming. The money ordered was dated Thursday. That night I lit the candle again, this time envisioning my sincere thanks to the Powers That Are—for listening to my needs.

Saturday morning an old ex-boss of mine, I hadn't seen her in four years, came to the house. She asked if I'd consider working for her again. I accepted. That evening I was so happy I invited my friend back for another evening of pool—this time on me.

We left about 9:30 and I decided to walk home, so we went our separate ways. About halfway home, I noticed a small zippered bag lying on the curb . . . I walked several blocks before even opening it. As I crossed under a streetlight I unzipped the bag and pulled out $346. I watched the papers for any mention of the bag, none appeared. I'd received $596 in four days, plus the job I still hold. I lit the green candle again and added to my thanks that this was enough to get me on my feet. I'm still very cautious of what I ask for and why.

So much has Gloria's life changed that her next visualization was for a microwave oven!

My roomate and I had decided we needed a microwave. Neither could figure any ordinary way we could budget one . . . Each time I would go to the kitchen I expressed out loud how nice it would be if we had a microwave. Every time I cooked on our conventional stove, I read aloud the microwave cooking instructions. I verbalized how much easier our cooking chores would be. Finally, I cleared a spot for the microwave, placing a white towel on the counter where it would sit.

The next time I went to our neighborhood store, I noticed a contest box, First Prize a microwave. I knew we would win . . . The drawing came and we didn't win. I came home disillusioned. It had seemed so perfect.

A few days later my boss at work started talking about how she was going to sell her motor home, and since it would sell for the same price with it or without it, would I be interested in a small but near-new microwave.

She thought me very appreciative with smiles, hugs and almost tears, more for the fact that my visualizations still worked than for the microwave. She said it was just a thought she had had. I agreed, yes, just a thought. Now the little Litton sits on a white towel in our kitchen, loved by all. And my roommate thinks we really could use a vacuum cleaner.

Nan also describes an empty wallet, filled by visualization and "coincidence." Such cosmic gifts have happened to me, also.

> We were walking home from a friend's house feeling low because we were flat broke. We decided to risk bouncing a check at the store with our next money expected in over a week. We were that depressed. We got home and found a five dollar bill from my mother in the mail. P decided to search through his wallet, turning it literally inside out, and he found another five in it. We carefully looked through it again, while I pocketed the ten we had. Nothing else. We went to the store, spent the ten, wrote the check for five more anyway, and as P was opening his wallet to put that five in, we found another five in his wallet! It had appeared out of thin air.

Like Sandra and Sheila's baby quail, such happenings are there to be enjoyed. Twice now I have reached into my pocket for what I thought was my last dollar, and it turned out to be a five or a ten.

Sarah Rheam Harris visualized a new car and a cleaned up garage. They were spontaneous visualizations that could have been precognitive experiences. This is a great example of thought-forms manifesting in the material world.

> Last April I walked into our utility room where I was doing the laundry. Through a closed door leading from this room is our garage, then holding two cars and quite a cluttered, disorganized mess. But as I entered the utility room this one morning, I saw through the door into a clean and straightened garage with an ivory station wagon (new car) sitting in one of the places, and the other two cars were gone.
>
> This scene took approximately one split second. I gave it no more thought and proceeded to wash clothes. Two other times that same week, the same visual appeared unconsciously as I entered the utility room; and each time I gave it no conscious thought and forgot about it.
>
> A month later, I found myself selling my car, and my husband and I thought we would trade the other car in on a new one . . . Since we had some cleared space in the garage, we spontaneously set to cleaning and hanging things up in the garage . . . (No mention or recollection of the visual at the time on my part).
>
> Within a few weeks, we had selected a car and worked on our trade . . . But as we were ordering our new car, the interior colors we wanted only came in the ivory exterior. So there we were buying an ivory car.
>
> The morning after we ordered the car, I awoke quite early remembering the visual that had happened just two months before and was truly amazed.[19]

Cindy and Norma bought an amethyst to put on their dog Molly's collar, in hopes of calming wild Molly down. Gemstones and crystals have a way of re-turning to their owners, if they are needed by them, and of dis-appearing, seemingly dematerializing when the time comes for them to leave. In this case, the stone reappeared, but Molly lost it again later—and I replaced it for her.

> We put the amethyst on Molly's collar the same day we bought it. We were both a little worried she'd lose it because the ring was flimsy and she is so hyper. Sure enough, 24 hours later it was gone. We both combed the backyard two or three times, wishing she had just lost it on the porch where it would be easy to find. I kept asking Molly where she had put her stone, didn't she know she needed it to help her calm down, and didn't she know it cost us $10!! Well, it was gone for about a week, and we had given up hope of finding it, because the grass is about a foot high and the lawn is partially covered with fallen leaves. But a couple of days ago, when Norma was on the porch feeding her birds, she found the amethyst! It was right in front of the birdcage, where Norma feeds the birds daily, and where there is no way it could have been missed had it been there before. Our theory is that Molly found it and put it on the porch. It appears that what you said about crystals finding someone if they need them is true!

Maybe Molly found it and maybe not, but the amethyst appeared.

Women get what they ask for in visualization/manifesting, so "Be careful what you ask for" has become another adage in women's spirituality. Rebecca in her astral projection experience of Chapter Four asked for friends to stop over and they did. Gloria got the money she needed for a new start and a microwave besides. Amy made this wish, and it was tragic:

> I was a sophomore or junior in high school. There was a boy who always flirted with the girls even though he had a girlfriend, and being quite shy and romantic this both thrilled and exasperated me. One spring night I was riding in a car with my girlfriend and her sister. I said that I wished this boy would have an accident with his car, to total the car but not to hurt him . . . That same night after midnight, he had been coming home from a bar outside of town and started to race with another car. His car went off the road, hit a post or tree and then flipped over. The boy who was riding with him was killed but he was not hurt except for a sprained back. The car was totalled. My girlfriend gave me a very strange look the next day at school. And I don't wish things like that anymore.

Be careful what you ask for, you may get it. And what you send out comes back to you.

In one more "coincidence" Sunlight describes meeting her ex-lover's twin:

> Judy has an identical twin I'll call Meg, who lived in California. We had never met, but Judy spoke of her often and I was looking forward to meeting her sometime. Judy and I lived in New York, though and our relationship was ending, with a lot of sadness and silence before I had a chance to meet Meg.
>
> I went to California on a trip and had stopped overnight in a Central California town. The next day, I was continuing my trip and had gone to the women's room of the Amtrack station just before the train came. While I was washing my hands, I looked in the mirror and saw Judy coming out of the toilet. It was like seeing a ghost. I knew it was Meg. I knew that their mother lived in that area, but I was completely surprised, shocked . . . It was an uncanny experience, and it was wonderful to meet Meg.

Entering the subject of ghosts and poltergeists as manifestings, here are Sharon's stories. She interprets the shaking bed as a spirit wishing to make communication with her. Sharon also has a sixteen-year-old daughter, who could be the cause of the disturbance, or energy from Sharon herself could do it. Other than to puzzle her and disturb sleep, the shaking has done no harm.

> My bed, for the past three months or so has been shaking at various times throughout the night. Sometimes before I turn off my lamp, I read or write while in bed. The bed will occasionally shake as if someone has bumped into it. Nothing is there—that I can see. I try to sleep and the bed will shake, again, sometimes two or three times during the night. I have been awakened by it and gotten up, looked under and around my bed only to find nothing that could be causing this . . . It disturbs me that if a spirit wishes to make contact or deliver a message, they cannot just state it verbally. A shaking bed tells me NOTHING!

As an adolescent, Sharon had a psychokinetic experience with a moving table. Adolescent energy is often the cause of these events; her family blamed it on her interest in the tarot. The PK happening occurred in a house rented furnished by her aunt:

> I went into the kitchen and began putting ice cubes in glasses and pouring the nonalcoholic drinks. I heard a loud thud to my right and looked in that direction. The heavy table had moved toward me and away from the chairs around it. A planter that sat on the area where the legs crossed was still swaying. I dropped everything and ran into the living room. Everyone could tell something had happened. I was trembling and was told I was very pale. I blurted out, 'The table jumped at me!'
> Of course, everyone had a good laugh. My aunt and a couple others walked into the kitchen. I followed close behind. My aunt stopped abruptly and gasping, she stared at the table. We looked, too. 'Why, it really did move! 'Look at the coasters.' The table legs were a few inches away from the coasters they had been setting in.
> My family decided that there had to be a 'logical' explanation for this, but I was warned, nevertheless, to stay away from the tarot . . .

Manifestings happen for Sharon, including appearances of light-forms and of spirit guides. They have happened for her since childhood.

> I remember those long nights of my childhood when I could not fall asleep. On one particular night when I was between seven and nine years of age, I was in my bed in the darkened bedroom unable to go to sleep. It was late. I turned over and caught a glimpse of a dime-shaped white light glowing in the corner of my room in mid-air. I stared at it noticing that it was growing in size and intensity. I sat up in bed immobilized with fear as my eyes stared at this light. As it grew, I had to turn away because it became so bright that I could not look upon it. My entire room was brightly lit by this light. When it had reached an oval shape of about three feet, I broke free of the paralyzing fear, leaped out of my bed and ran into my parents' room . . . I described the light. My mother walked to my room with me. I fully expected her to see the glowing white light in my room. But, to my dismay, the light was gone. My room was dark.

Chris also saw lights, and she heard music, in a manifesting that was healing:

> It was when I was in Intensive Care with very bad injuries, near death. I was floating in and out of consciousness, in terrible pain, and they couldn't give me painkillers for a couple of days because if I 'went to sleep' I might choke on my own blood. Eventually I did wake up, though and stayed awake (or slept normally, not passed out).
>
> I could hear the nurses' radio playing, the same song every so often (the big hit that week). The other thing that amused me when I was in there was watching the light come in through the little window that was high up on the wall, to my right. As the light came in, it hit the little dust motes in the room and they'd dance, all colors, in the light. It was very pretty and made me feel very good.
>
> Then one of the nurses asked me if I was bored just lying there, and I told her I was listening to their radio and watching the dust motes in the light from the little window. She was surprised and dismayed that I could hear the radio, they weren't supposed to have it on and were playing it softly, she said. And, 'We don't have a window in here—this is the ICU.'
>
> I looked around and saw she was right, it was an inside room and there wasn't a window anywhere. After that I didn't see the lights anymore, but I felt they were a gift from somewhere, to help me heal by keeping me amused. After taking your workshop, I realized that the colors themselves had been healing. Intensive Care Units don't provide patients with colors for healing, so I got them from somewhere else while I was in there.

Chris' lights and music sound like spirit guide gifts. More on spirit guides in Chapter Eleven, and on healing in the next chapter.

Diane describes a similar manifesting, but a human and animal figure appeared. Manifestings and apparitions can be spirit guides or helpers, or the thought-forms at the time of death of a person who is emotionally close. They can also be thought-forms of someone dead who in life lived in the house, animal or human, or telepathic images. This manifesting happened when Diane was thirteen.

> I was asleep and woke up one night to find a pair of eyes staring at me in the window. I rolled over and ignored whoever it was, then realized that I was on the third floor . . . So I rolled over again to determine if the eyes were still there and who they belonged to. The eyes were gone, but in the corner of the room was a human figure in hooded robes of vague brown or perhaps dark grey. I screamed.
>
> Even after my father was in the room and telling me it was only a nightmare, I could still see the figure and was trying to make him see it. After about a half hour to forty-five minutes of this . . . a soft voice came from my pillow and I saw a small animal (later discovered it to be a Fennic Fox) lying there. I think there was a small notch in its ear and it was wearing a collar with a sort of stylized ankh on a pyramid. I don't remember what it SAID, but it informed me that the figure (which was still standing in the corner, waiting) couldn't harm me. So I went back to sleep, determined to find out more about such strange things . . .
>
> Further information picked up somewhere or another—Fennic Foxes are considered good pets and good luck in the Arabic countries . . . and those that have a notch in the ear are considered especially good luck since they are actually djinns and magickal.

I want to save some of these stories for the chapter on spirit guides. In no case, did the "ghost" described to me by any woman offer her any form of harm.

Two women, Irene and Lynn, described seeing their grandmothers' ghosts at the time of her death. Both women were children at the time. Irene and her mother both saw the apparition, and neither knew at the time that the grandmother had died. Lynn has always seen ghosts and thought everyone did. She attributes it to her Celtic Irish/Welsh heritage and the haunted house she grew up in! Her psychic experiences were taken for granted by her family when she had them as a child.

> I saw my grandmother's ghost when I was five years old. She walked up to me while I was on the john; her long hair was flowing loose, and she wore a loose blue gown, and she talked to me about the new puppy I'd received for Christmas. She was in the hospital over the holiday, and she told me how sorry she was that she didn't get to play with my puppy before she died—specifically, she said, 'before I came over here.' And then she left . . .

The appearance of a close relative or mate at time of death could be telepathic or an astral projection, but is at any rate a thought-form.

Apparitions, ghosts or manifestings don't have to be human. Nan describes her ghost cat which I saw for myself on a visit. The cat had lived in the house before its death, and one Hallows, the time for such things, returned there. A good guess is that it will disappear again next Hallows, an astral shell trapped in the wrong reality plane until then.

> We moved into our apartment in July. From practically the minute we stepped in the door, we just had this sense that there was a cat in the house. We didn't say anything to each other, but we were both feeling it just the same. We would find ourselves automatically blocking the way with a leg when we opened an outside door, so that 'the cat wouldn't get out.' We haven't had a cat of our own for over three years. We could see the cat in the doorway to the bedroom or walking around the corner of the refrigerator in the kitchen, sitting in an outside window. As Samhain (Hallows) approached, we both began to see it more clearly. One day, I came in from outside, kneeled by our gerbil cage, and right in clear sight was a cat walking straight up to me. It vanished about a foot away. I told my partner about it: that's when we first compared notes . . . Around Samhain the sightings were much clearer, and we each felt the cat touch us on a few occasions. Nearer Yule we decided to have a ritual and tell the cat it had died and that it had the choice to go on to the other side. We both cried. Since then we've seen it less often and less clearly, but it's not gone altogether. As I was writing this, I must have summoned the cat in my thoughts, because three of the gerbils started doing their 'danger thump' without any noise or sudden movement on my part to instigate it.

The gerbils accept the cat as the real thing. Sleeping in Nan's apartment in March, I felt the cat come to bed with me. It stepped onto the mattress and the bed moved, walked across my leg, stared at me, then curled up against my knees. It definitely was a cat, a large orange one. I had hoped to see it and asked it to come. Tracing its past, Nan found that it had lived in the apartment till its owner moved, and the remaining roommate had it put to sleep. It wasn't ready to leave. Another comment is that Nan is legally blind, and if it were a "real" cat, she probably could not have seen it. Psychic seeing is not physical vision, but the perception of other realities. The appearance of such visions also questions death.

Bonnie had this experience with a manifesting rabbit. Like Nan's cat, it sounds like an animal trapped between worlds or stumbled into the wrong world. Bonnie and the rabbit startled each other thoroughly.

> I was back in college, 1969 or 1970, taking summer classes. It was sunny daylight, and I was studying geography in the afternoon, in my usual study position—lying crossways on the bed, book on the floor. Suddenly this 'rabbit' leaps from nowhere on the right, and lands in a crouch on the other side of my book, no more than two feet away. It was there, but not there, visible exactly like heat waves rising from hot railroad tracks.
>
> It was a piebald, a dark spot around its eye, and a bigger blotch on its back. It *saw* me! The white around its eye showed as it started in fear. Then it leaped toward me (to my left) into the air. It vanished in mid-air, front part first, like it was diving into water.
>
> All this took only seconds. (Leap, plop, see me, eek!, jump for it, vanish). I was so startled, I wasn't afraid until afterward, and then not very much, since it was afraid of *me*. That's what I found so incredibly fascinating about the whole incident—whatever it was not only *saw* me, but reacted the way a real bunny would have done.

Bonnie had seen other manifestings:

> I saw a black curtain before my grandfather died in 1966, and saw a hand signing the bottom of my driver's permit and knew I'd pass my driver's test. That was in 1964.

Mimi tells another story of Lady, the protective German Shepherd ghost:

> I woke this morning to a scratching and weight on my blanket. Looking over the side of the bed I saw Lady. She walked over to the window, whiffed at the air as if the window were open, telling me she wanted to go 'out.' I started to get out of bed and stepped into my slippers when it occurred to me that Lady is not alive. She looked at me as if to say, 'well?' This amused me and I told her, 'Hey Lady, you came in through the wall, now go out the same way.' She looked at the window again and disappeared through the wall. It was four o'clock in the morning, it was dark and cold outside. I went back to sleep.

This latest Lady story happened on October 25, 1986, just before Hallows or Samhain, the time in women's spirituality when the veil between death and living is thinnest. That same year I lost my Siberian

Husky, Tiger a few weeks before Hallows. In my ritual for the Sabbat, I invited her back and she came. I could feel, hear, see and touch her, and was sorry to watch her go when I opened the circle.

Ritual manifestings are the last examples of this chapter. There were many more experiences of all forms of manifesting than are printed here, and I regret the lack of space that excluded them. Cheryl describes this ritual manifesting that happened on a particularly exuberant Full Moon night at the Michigan Women's Music Festival. The Goddess is Diana, a tree image usually located at the Nightstage.

> After the ritual, a bunch of women stayed around the Goddess, unwilling to let go of all that good energy. When we heard other womyn in the distance howling at the full moon, someone said, 'Let's go find them.'
>
> So we took off across the level meadow and over to the tree line, where we found a half dozen women rolling in the tall grass, laughing and howling, and we lay down, too and joined in.
>
> After we had been enjoying ourselves in primal delight for some time, I looked up and saw the mist rolling in like a cloud over the meadow. Then it sort of congealed into a form—a kneeling winged Goddess.
>
> I yelled to the others—'Look over there, it looks like a winged Goddess!' Everybody exclaimed, 'Yeah,' and called out to her things like, 'Thank you for coming,' and 'We called you and you came!'
>
> And when we looked up again, *all* the mist had vanished—no figure, no cloud of mist, nothing—and it was still night.

Several women described appearances of the Goddess, the most powerful thought-form of all. This last experience is Lynn's:

> Once during a Solstice ritual I had a remarkable vision of the Goddess. Although I was in a state of trance, the vision seemed completely physically involving—I could feel cool, damp leaves brushing against my face; leaves and soft dirt gave under my feet. I could hear wind rushing through the trees and over it all an enormous full moon washed the landscape white. The Goddess ran just a few paces ahead of me. Throughout the vision, I was intensely aware of the movement of her hips and the flow of her hair. And the colors! Her hair was palomino red and her skin was a rich, luminous white. Now and again she would glance over her shoulder, look at me lovingly, and beckon for me to hurry. At one point we ran alongside a still black lake, through meadow grasses so lush it felt like I was running on thick, down cushions. I 'woke' from this vision feeling happy, refreshed and charged with energy.

She has appeared to women in every color and culture, and how often on Full Moons!

The skill of manifesting in women's quest for stroking the python begins with the ability to visualize, to create images in the mind that are not words but sensory impressions, dramatizations, pictures. Pictures created in the meditative state are thought-forms powerful enough to manifest, especially if repeated regularly. They change habits and create new realities, bring possibilities onto the linear plane. This is the basis of affirmation or manifesting in women's spirituality.[20]

Achieving the skill requires some solar plexus/rational mind thinking beforehand. The picture needs to be a clear one, stating exactly what you want to happen, in as much detail as possible. Images are totally positive, since that's what you want to manifest, and are never manipulative of someone else, even in well-meaning ways. Images and the verbal statements that go with them are in present tense. If you ask for something in the future—"I will have" instead of "I have"—the goal keeps moving away. "I have" happens in the now. Statements are "I am" instead of "I am not," as in "I am prosperous" instead of "I am not poor." Remember that all time and space are here and now, and "not" is a negative construct.

A woman wants a new job and goes into the meditative state to manifest it. Once she is fully relaxed, she images the job she is looking for. She sees herself going to work, entering the workplace, sitting down at her desk or working in appropriate ways. She pictures what part of the city the job is in, what the work is like, what her surroundings are. Every detail of what she wants in the job, including the pay scale, is included in the image. When asking for a money amount, ask for the wished-for figure *or better*. The woman sees herself after work, having everything she needs, her bills paid, a smile on her face, no worries.

In manifesting, visualizing every detail of the new job, you create it. Make the thought-forms carefully, think about them before entering the meditative state; they shape the reality that manifests and choose which of the limitless possibilities that come real on the linear earth plane. As you do the visualizations, make statements reinforcing the imagery. Say, "I have a job as a _____ . I work downtown at _____ hours and make a salary of $ _____ a year or better. I have what I need and a job that I like. I am part of the abundance of the universe." Visualize yourself at this job, taking home the pay, going to and from work. Make the visualizations in sensory pictures: see the place and yourself working there, hear the sounds that go with the job, experience the touch and scent impressions. If you cannot make pictures, imagine and say the words. Like other psychic tools, the ability to visualize increases and gets easier with practice. Make positive, present tense statements and pictures of what you want to happen, and do it every night in the meditative state until it manifests. Along with the visualizations, do the physical things required—in the example of finding a job, do the job hunting.

Create only images that are positive and perfect, excluding any fears, gripes or negativities from the pictures. Ask for clearly thought-out things, and avoid using "not" in the wording. If unsure of exactly what details to manifest, ask for "the most perfect job for me." Creating the image is vital—it's often not knowing what we want that keeps us from getting it.

Make sure to ask for enough. Women have been trained in patriarchy to roles that are not positive for anyone. In the re-imaging and changing of these roles, women are making things happen that they have always been told they can't have. If you want it, you can have it. Image it and create it, and make sure you get it all. What you believe you deserve is the only limit to what you can manifest. Amy Wallace and Bill Henkin, in *The Psychic Healing Book* describe what they call a "havingness level," a belief beyond which manifesting won't go. If a woman thinks she deserves a salary of $4,000 a year, that's what she'll manifest a job with. If she believes she deserves $40,000, she can manifest that, too.[21] If you need a job that pays the $40,000, changing the belief that says you only deserve $4,000 is necessary. Women create their own realities, and have no limits but themselves. Gloria remained broke and homeless while she felt she had to do that; then she changed it.

Gloria's description of how she manifested her way from poverty to prosperity is a good one to follow. She prepared herself and her green candle carefully beforehand, deciding exactly what she needed and wanted. She wrote the request on the candle and stated it aloud, then lit the candle and in the meditative state on several nights visualized what she wanted to happen. She saw herself counting money, visualized what to spend it on. She visualized using the money for things needed for herself and her daughter, and saw herself sharing it, giving her friend a month's rent. Importantly, she affirmed that the money she received would harm or deprive no one else, and that she would use it in generous ways. She *saw* her daughter's smile, *felt* the warmth of a winter coat, *heard* her friend's thanks for the help. When money manifested for her, she used it as promised and said "thank you." Greed isn't necessary, there is abundance in the Goddess universe for all, enough for everyone without anyone being deprived or hurt. When she asked for money in this way, Gloria got all she asked for.

When she asked for a microwave, she repeated the process of

manifesting, and got what she asked for also. So did Amy, less positively: create only positive thought-forms that harm or manipulate none. In my own affirmation work, I end the meditation with the following, based on the work of Marion Weinstein:

> I ask for these things or their equivalents or better, according to free will and for the good of all, harming or manipulating none.[22]

and this based on the work of Melita Denning:

> Blessed are the laws of the Goddess.
> Blessed is her bounty.
> Blessed is the swiftness with which all is wrought.
> Blessed is the total good with which all is achieved.
> Blessed are my desires, even now fulfilled.[23]

Think through the visualizations and images carefully, make them into positive, present-tense statements and pictures, use them in the meditative state and use them daily, and watch dreams and wishes appear in the concrete world. While the pictures/thought-forms used in this description are visual ones, include all sensory images, and if disabled in one sense, use the others. The skill is not limited to sighted women only, but available to all.

Manifesting is based on the law of attraction, which says that like attracts like, and what you visualize (the thought-forms you create) is what you draw to you. Marion Weinstein, in a mindblowing chapter in her revised *Earth Magic*, takes the law of attraction one step further, into the law of creation. While in the law of attraction, like attracts like, in the law of creation, like *creates* like. What is "out-there," in the asking, becomes here and now in the creating. All possibilities in the Goddess universe already exist, and the woman herself creates the physical reality of what she wants. Visualization/thought-forms are directed perceptions to this end:

> We may now *direct* our perception in three ways: 1. We acknowledge that the process of directed perception is a means to creation; 2. We consciously choose to direct our perception in a certain way; and 3. The way we do this is to identify ourselves as the very goal for which we are working.
> Let's look at step 3 further: What I mean is, we become the thing we are looking for . . . We focus on *being* that goal. We are it. Now, does this mean that we are no longer ourselves, that we have somehow become the goal instead? Not at all. We are ourselves plus the other (the goal).[24]

The way to use this is not to say "I ask for" or even "I have," but "I create myself," or "I manifest myself as the perfect job." By being able to visualize an idea, make the thought-form for it, you have already created it, have actually *become* the job. By using affirmation and Creation Manifestation, women bring what is already there into linear reality. Remember to say "thank you" when it happens.

Wiccans also correlate manifesting with the moon phases. The New Moon is the time of beginnings, when ideas are first born, and what is begun on the New Moon manifests at the Full. Begin affirmations for a particular thing on the New Moon and continue them. The third quarter Moon is called the fulfillment quarter, when ideas born on the New Moon and brought to manifesting on the Full reach fulfillment. The last quarter, Waning Moon, is the time of disintegration and also the time of planning and laying root foundations. Ideas go deeply inward at this time, to be born or reborn at the New Moon phase. Design affirmations, manifesting and Creation Manifestation rituals accordingly.

For additional reading on manifesting, try the following books; the first few are the simplest, and the later ones more involved.

Shakti Gawain, *Creative Visualization*, (New York, Bantam Books, 1978).

Diane Stein, *The Women's Spirituality Book*, (St. Paul, Llewellyn Publications, 1987). Chapters Five and Six.

Diane Stein, *The Women's Book of Healing*, (St. Paul, Llewellyn Publications, 1988). Chapter Three.

Melita Denning and Osborne Phillips, *The Llewellyn Practical Guide to Creative Visualization*, (St. Paul, Llewellyn Publications, 1984).

Marion Weinstein, *Positive Magic*, (Custer, WA, Phoenix Publishing Co., 1978). Chapter Eight.

Marion Weinstein, *Earth Magic*, Revised Edition, (Custer, WA, Phoenix Publishing Co., 1986). Advanced Work.

The skills of psychokinesis, PK or mind over matter are also learning skills, and apparitions are to some extent. They are all thought-forms, and are slightly but not greatly different from affirmation and visualization work. Again the basis is in visualizing (making a thought-form of) what you want to happen and concentrating on it. Knowing that women create their own realities and *can* move dense objects by will is essential.

Try this simple one for starters.[25] Hang a pendulum—a crystal, ring or other small object on a string of at least twelve inches—so that it hangs at eye level and where it can move freely. Sitting or standing in front of it, look at it, knowing it will move when and where you direct it to. Enter the meditative state or at least be grounded and centered, and visualize the pendulum moving as you wish it to. Be very relaxed and totally without anxiety of the outcome: *know* it will happen as you wish it. Give it time to manifest.

When the pendulum begins swinging from side to side, increase its speed, decrease it, then will it to stop. Will it to begin again in the opposite direction. Slow and increase its speed. Feel the pendulum moving, its vibrations in your solar plexus or third eye, rhythmically and evenly. The pendulum moves, just because you wish it to. You've created the thought-form of it moving. The exercise worked for me on the first try, but if it doesn't for you, keep practicing. Keep it fun, and don't get tired. For variations of this, try practicing psychokinesis on a candle flame, on water in a shallow bowl, on a string of bells. Try it alone and in group effort, with one or more other women. Each moves the bells in her own way, so they jangle.[26]

Then try this one, with two versions of it. First, in a lighthearted game type of way, fully relaxed in the alpha state, pick a number and throw a dice several times with the intent of that number coming up. Rather than concentrating on the number, casually remind yourself of it. Chance says your number comes up one time in six, so if it happens more frequently, take note of it. Keep it light, and keep it relaxed and a game.

Second in this, throw the dice again, making a concentrated serious effort of manifesting the chosen number. Put attention and energy into it, visualize and concentrate, will the results to come up. Focus attention not on the game and the throwing, but on the number. After the same amount of throws as before, check the results. How many times did the chosen number come up before, and how many now? The outcome is the same, the numbers picked come up, but the second way is tiring and no fun.[27]

Remember the difference between Nelya Mikhailova and Alla Vinogradova? Mikhailova experiences profound physical distress and exhaustion when doing psychokinesis, Vinogradova finds it natural and does not. The difference is that of the two parts of this exercise. For better and longer sustaining results, and much more fun, keep it light and relaxed. Use the meditative alpha state. Relax into the work, don't force it.

I dis-covered the pattern of this by accident. During a board game of *Rebirth* at a North Versailles, PA, Theosophical Society meeting, I was spending all of my game reincarnations as animals and demons.

Suddenly, I noticed that if I asked for a number on the dice, that number would come up—I wasn't knowing it precognitively, I was creating it. Since it took a one or a two to progress on the board, I started asking for and getting twos. I was fully relaxed, and not being a competitive woman, didn't have much riding on the outcome one way or another. It became a game in itself to see how many twos I could bring up on the dice. I did it five or six times in a row and won the game, coming up fast from far behind. As I threw the dice each time, I said to myself "two" as I threw, not really concentrating on it or forcing it to come up, just letting it happen. Twos came up, and became a pattern that once started was easy to continue.

Something similar is at work in manifesting parking spaces. Riding down the street, nearing the place to stop, say aloud, "I have a parking space near Bloomer's," and the place manifests. Some women invoke a Goddess for this, with several variations.

Okay Mother, I need to park, please.

Shirley Kramer, Goddess of Parking, find me a place.

Hail Mary, full of grace,
Help me find a parking place.

The invocation is another form of visualizing. By making the statement and invoking the particular Goddess, you visualize a place to park and there it is. Remember to say "thank you," and enjoy the convenience and the fun of it. Use manifesting and mind over matter for any number of everyday needs. Invoke Shirley Kramer and watch someone else's car pull out in front of the restaurant. Pull right in.[28] *

In another example of mind over matter, Leonie offers this recipe for levitation. She has done it several times and had it done with her as the subject. It takes five women, and has been a party game at countless teenage slumber parties.

> They do it by placing one person in a chair, increasing the emotional energy of four people standing at all four strategic points around the chair, and then 'lifting' the seated person using one finger under each armpit and one under each knee. I have seen 300-pound people lifted like feathers. There is a great feeling of joy and completeness about the experience, regardless of whether you are lifted or doing the lifting, a feeling of boundary-less-ness. The levitator and levatee become one.
>
> To manifest an apparition, classic psychic development gives directions

---

*Shirley is one of women's many modern "invented" Goddesses. Others are Asphala, Toyota, and the Goddess of Computers-Data. (See footnote 28).

directions that resemble those for astral projecting.[29] Visualize yourself leaving your body, sending consciousness out of the physical body and travelling in the astral. Will it to happen and will the resulting shape to solidify, then to move. To deal with ghosts or apparitions that are not yourself in the astral, that manifest created or not, first remember that these visions are rarely harmful. Protect yourself with light, but if you want one to come, invite it to come. Do this just before sleep in a very relaxed alpha to theta meditation state.

When a manifestation appears, ask it who it is, if you don't already know. Someone you re-cognize and know could be an astral projection or telepathic thought-form of a living woman, or of a person or animal once living that was close to you. Usually you know these Be-ings, living or dead, and have things to talk about with them. If grandmother was benevolent in life, she will be benevolent after it.

Where the apparition is in light-forms or in people or animals unknown to you, ask them what they want, who they are, what messages they bring. Be polite. Women get what they ask for, so in inviting an apparition make sure to specify a positive one. When a Be-ing invited or otherwise is not positive order it to leave, however much it blusters or protests. A thought-form has no more power than you allow it, and remember, you created it. Wait for Chapter Eleven on spirit guides before inviting apparitions, and manifest a Be-ing of positivity, benevolence and real help.

Manifesting and psychokinesis continue in Chapter Seven with healing, where the object "moved" is the state of women's health, and what is manifested is well-being. Visualization, manifestation and psychokinesis are powerful ways for women to stroke the python, to create a matriarchal, limitless reality. They are major tools in women's spirituality, women re-claiming their power and who they are.

## FOOTNOTES

1. Sandra J. Stevens, *Being Alive is Being Psychic*, p. 80.

2. Starhawk, *The Spiral Dance: A Rebirth of the Ancient Religion of the Great Goddess*, (San Francisco, Harper and Row Publishers, 1979), p. 44.

3. Mary Coddington, *In Search of the Healing Energy*, p. 16-17.

4. Annie Besant and C.W. Leadbeater, *Thought-Forms*, p. 6.

5. *Ibid.*, p. 8.

6. *Ibid.*, p. 16. Pronouns are changed to "she."

7. Rodney Marsden, *Psychic Experience For You*, p. 171. His discussion of coincidence is a highlight of the book.

8. Sandra J. Stevens, *Being Alive is Being Psychic*, p. 75.

9. Jane Roberts, *The Seth Material*, p. 123.

10. David Hammond, *The Search for Psychic Power*, (New York, Bantam Books, 1975), p. 43. Hammond discusses a number of women psychics.

11. Sheila Ostrander and Lynn Schroeder, *Psychic Discoveries Behind the Iron Curtain*, p. 68.

12. *Ibid.*, p. 74.

13. *Ibid.*, p. 75.

14. *Ibid.*, p. 71.

15. David Hammond, *The Search for Psychic Power*, p. 161.

16. *Ibid.*, p. 158-159.

17. Rodney Marsden, *Psychic Experience For You*, p. 36.

18. Sandra J. Stevens, *Being Alive is Being Psychic*, p. 107.

19. Sarah Rheam Harris, "Creative Visuals," in *Inner Vision*, (Los Alamos, NM), Vol. I, no. 1, January-February, 1986, p. 3.

20. For more on affirmations, visualization and manifesting, see Diane Stein, *The Women's Spirituality Book*, (St. Paul, Llewellyn Publications, 1987), Chapters Five and Six, and Diane Stein, *The Women's Book of Healing*, Chapter Three.

21. Marion Weinstein, *Positive Magic*, (Custer, WA, Phoenix Publi-

cations, 1978), Chapter Eight.

23. Melita Denning and Osborne Phillips, *The Llewellyn Practical Guide to Creative Visualization*, (St. Paul, Llewellyn Publications, 1984), Chapter Seven.

24. Marion Weinstein, *Earth Magic*, Revised Edition, p. 93.

25. Melita Denning and Osborne Phillips, *The Llewellyn Practical Guide to the Development of Psychic Powers*, (St. Paul, Llewellyn Publications, 1985), p. 45-46.

26. Enid Hoffman, *Develop Your Psychic Skills*, (Gloucester, MA, Para Research, 1981), p. 110-114.

27. Rodney Marsden, *Psychic Experience For You*, p. 40-41.

28. I would like to thank Judi Friedman for introducing me to Shirley Kramer! Shirley of course, is a "Found Goddess"!

29. Hereward Carrington, *Your Psychic Powers and How to Develop Them*, (N. Hollywood, CA, Newcastle Publishing, Inc., 1975), p. 241.

## Chapter Seven

# The Heart Center: Women Healing Giving From the Heart

*At every given moment, our bodies are continually responding to the messages of our minds. So what messages is your mind giving your body? Prevailing wisdom says: You got a problem? Have a drink. Got a stuffy nose? Take Contac. Got indigestion? Take Alka Selzer. Can't sleep? Take Sominex. There is a chemical solution for everything. These messages promote total distrust in the body's own ability to heal itself. We're led to believe that the innate wisdom of the body/mind simply doesn't exist. 'A drug ad denies your ability to cope . . . The result is that you become further separated from yourself . . . Your ability goes for lack of practice and faith in its efficacy.' Instead of believing in your body you probably come close to hating it because it's not the right size or shape . . . What do you imagine your body does in response to your distrust and dissatisfaction?*[1]

I am a healer, and I travel widely teaching other women to be healers, too. We all are healers, of ourselves and others. One night in California, Bobbie called where I was staying and asked me to do a distance healing. Martha had been bitten badly by mosquitoes, bitten all over her head and face. She was allergic to the bites, and miserable with swelling and itching. She was afraid of a toxic reaction. I was extremely exhausted and not sure what I could do, but I promised to try.

Later, near midnight, I went to bed and before sleeping went into a light meditative state. In it I visualized Martha, whom I'd never met, and saw a tall woman with brown curly hair and glasses. I could see the bites and the swelling, red and angry on her face, arms and shoulders, breasts and hands. I surrounded her image with blue light, sending blue light through a crystal to the redness and pain areas. I visualized the red spots shrinking and going away, Martha's skin clear, and a big smile on her face. Too tired to do much more, and there was no more else to do, I withdrew and went to sleep.

The next day I talked to Bobbie and asked her, "How's Martha? What happened with the bites?"

"Oh," Bobbie said, "The itching stopped about midnight and she went to sleep. This morning the swelling and itching are gone. You can hardly see the bites now. She was lucky this time."

I asked her, "What does Martha look like?"

"She's tall and thin and has brown curly hair. She wears glasses."

I asked her, "The bites weren't just on her face, were they?"

Bobbie said, "No, they were all over her, on her breasts and arms and hands, but it was her face I was worried about. Her face was so swollen from them. The last time this happened she went to the hospital."

This time a little blue light, and Martha went to sleep and the swelling disappeared. I hadn't then, and haven't yet met Martha, but could describe her, and could see that the bites were more than Bobbie had explained.

"She knows you did something," Bobbie said, "And she thanks you."

The something I did is something anyone can learn to do. It's called psychic healing. If the power of women's thought-forms can manifest prosperity and parking spaces, call up apparitions and numbers on a dice, they can also affect the state of women's bodies. The energy that creates the unseen bodies and the spaces between atoms in the dense physical also creates good health and well-being when used positively. By the power of prana and women's minds, women create their own health. All women are creators and healers, first of themselves and then helping others if they choose to. Good health is women's birthright and near as a thought, and women use thought-forms and pranic energy to create their own Be-ing.

This whole idea is another great secret kept from women in the patriarchy: the idea that women actively choose and control their states of health. Entering a doctor's office, or turning on the TV, it doesn't seem that way. In patriarchal medicine, women are passive victims. They come to a doctor who tells them what pill to take to mask their symptoms, or tells them what organ (usually a female reproductive organ) he plans to cut out. Women listen and submit, or are judged insane, neurotic or mentally disturbed for refusing. They take the pills and go under the knife, instead of finding healing.

Patriarchal medicine does not heal, it tries to "cure." Cures never ask or care about why something's wrong, they only treat the parts and symptoms.* (See footnote on page 171.) If a woman has chronic headaches, for example, she gets aspirin for pain and nothing more. In psychic healing, if a woman has chronic headaches she herself creates pain relief, or is helped to pain relief that is nonchemical and in her control. In addition, she is asked to look at the stresses in her life that cause her headaches, and given the understanding (and the choice) to remove the cause. Understanding the cause, she has the tools to relieve the stress. Instead of aspirin that masks the symptoms for three hours, her headaches are gone for good. They are not "cured," but healed. The woman participates in the healing work, or does it herself; she makes the changes in her life and health.

A major reason for the difference between medicine and healing is that medicine does not accept women's unseen psychic bodies; it says that women stop at their skins. Medicine treats dense matter, the dense physical body only, ignoring the fact and power of the emotional, mental and spiritual woman. Any changes for dis-ease or health happen in all four bodies, and are visible in the aura before they manifest in the physical. While patriarchal medicine cures the dense physical level, that small fraction of matter separated by vast distances of space and energy, women's psychic healing works in all four bodies, the whole woman. While male medicine dishes out pills, surgeries and tremendous bills to cure, women's healing is nonchemical, noninvasive, nontraumatic, nonharmful, highly effective and transformational, and often free of charge.

Psychic healing and matriarchy base their work on the quality of life and on respect for the beauty, wholeness, worth and autonomy of all that lives. There is wholeness within and a oneness with Goddess and the Earth—all that lives is a part of her. Each woman is the python creation Goddess, with the ability, responsibility and birthright for well-being. She controls her own life and own health, with help when she needs it, but no one else can do it for her. The rights of choice, decision, autonomy, participation and consent are implicit in women's healing. Matriarchy's stance is to live with, help and benefit the Earth (who is Goddess, women, the planet and all that lives), for the good and well-being of all.

Patriarchy's denial of the unseen woman and its manner of treatment are outgrowths of its denial of women themselves. Both patriarchy and medicine take power and control away from women. Women in both are forced to be accepting and passive, not welcome to understand or participate in what's happening to their bodies and lives. Women in patriarchal medicine are given drugs with convoluted names but not the knowledge (or consent) of what the drugs are and do, and what results—particularly negative ones—they may have. Women are offered surgeries as "cures," at great pain and great cost, when often neither surgeries or drugs are needed. Patriarchy's stance is to dominate and conquer disease, conquering women, the Earth, the Goddess and other cultures, too. Autonomy, particularly in women, is not encouraged.

The best things women can do for their health is to stay out of the patriarchal health care system, to see themselves as well and to stay well. More than half the surgeries done are unnecessary, and unnecessary hysterectomies, mastectomies and caesarean section births are a scandal. The poor state of health care, old age neglect and infant mortality in the technological United States are appalling. The West's great epidemic is not AIDS or even drugs, but iatrogenic diseases—illnesses caused by doctors and their "cures." Here are some frightening ideas and statistics from Margo Adair:[2]

> Only modern malnutrition injures more people than iatrogenic disease in its various manifestations. In the most narrow sense, iatrogenic disease includes only illnesses that would not have come about if sound and professionally recommended treatment had *not* been applied.

> One out of every five patients admitted to a typical research hospital acquires an iatrogenic disease, sometimes trivial, usually requiring special treatment, and in one case in thirty leading to death.

> Medications in hospitals alone kill between 60,000 and 140,000 Americans a year and make 3.5 million others more or less seriously ill.

> More than half the surgery performed in this country is unnecessary. This washes an estimated 12,000 lives and $4 billion down the operating room's drain each year.

This patriarchal Rambo style of medicine is obviously not healthy and not working. It separates women from their bodies, the seen from unseen levels, and denies the body's ability to heal itself—which is the same thing. Male "cures" focus on disease (unhyphenated), and like Freud's comparable concept of mental health, sees all health in terms of illness.

> The public image of the human organism . . . is that of a machine which is prone to constant failure unless supervised by doctors and treated with medication. The notion of the organism's inherent healing power and tendency to stay healthy is not communicated and trust in one's own organism is not promoted.[3]

Medicine treats body parts, separating even the dense physical to an eye, a uterus, a broken leg—parts fragmented off from the whole woman. It ignores the crucial effects of mind, emotion and connectedness, ignores Be-ing. Women's healing focuses on wellness, the whole woman with all of her psychic bodies, and on the bodies' natural ability to initiate and maintain good health.

Psychic healing uses women's intuition and stroking the python awareness of energy and the aura bodies to be well. Women's bodies *are* well, and they stay well with women's help. The physical, emotional, mental and spiritual are all intrinsic aspects of women's Be-ing and health, and these bodies work together. Changes happen in the unseen bodies before they manifest in the dense physical, both in the direction of dis-ease and of healing. Where there is a disturbance, block, imbalance or dis-ease (hyphenated, lack of ease), women work carefully to remove the issues and help the bodies' return to natural wellness. Women who see auras and thought-forms see the process at work, and women who don't learn to sense it. They describe the state of woman's health by what they read in her aura, her unseen psychic bodies. Then they use these bodies' natural tendency for well-being to manifest and create good health. Choice, free will and action are involved.

Dora Van Gelder Kunz, noted healer and teacher, describes what she sees:

> I can see the energy fields which flow through your body—there's the physical field, which tells me about your physical condition. Then there's the mental field, which tells me what you're thinking, and the emotional field which shows what you're feeling. The emotional field sticks out about eighteen inches from your body and is more like a kaleidoscope with a changing color pattern. I can focus on someone walking down the street and know in a split second if s/he's disturbed or normal.
>
> The physical field . . . interpenetrates the body like a sparkling web of light beams in constant motion. This energy field flows through the organs of the body in a stream-like motion. When I see blockages, or breaks in the field, I know this indicates a disease process.[4]

Eileen Garrett in Chapter Two described knowing what a woman is like by the appearance of her aura:

> Some people moved in grey shadows and some in glowing lights. For me the important thing about anyone I met was to see and feel the quality of these 'surrounds.' By their colour and their tone, I knew whether people were sick or well.[5]

Annie Besant describes the aura in terms of thought-forms and their effects. Besant and Garrett are not healers, but Dora Kunz and others use this same information for healing. When a block or break in the field exists, it reflects a happening in the dense physical body known as dis-ease. The psychic healer, for herself or with someone else, releases the blocks, repairs the breaks and helps the aura re-turn to normal wellness.

Psychic healing is a heart center ability, a product of the inspirational higher mind. The heart center is the second mental body level, beyond the rational mental of the solar plexus. It's the place of compassion, sympathy, love and universal love, the place of all-important self-love. Its color is green for regeneration and new growth, or rose for openness, love and caring. Women relate to themselves and others from this chakra and aura band, and relate to animals, with a sense of compassion for all life. Imagination and expanded, creative thinking happen here, with openness to more realities and forms than are possible at the concrete solar plexus level.

Women who think with the heart make good healers. They begin with self-love and self awareness and with trust in their bodies,' their Be-ing and in others. They see Goddess in everyone and everything. Heart centered women feel with others, but in a way universal enough to not take on others' pain (it's clairsentience when they do, from the belly center). They can be separate enough, and all-loving enough, to help. Heart centered women use their higher minds, imaginations and intuitions, along with concrete information to heal. They use learned information, information from others, and inner knowing to release aura blocks, mend breaks, offer energy and love. Involving their third eye centers, the place of women's power/knowing/intuition, they access information and use it with compassion. This is psychic healing.

Healing begins with the self and self-love, and most women who do healing work begin it with themselves. Heart center love includes caring and acceptance of the self, and love of women's bodies. Women honor their Be-ing and bodies, inviting health from within and without. Choosing health for herself is the first choice, then comes learning how to do it. Once she manifests her own good health, helping others who have also chosen health is next, and from the many women who are healed and healers comes a healed and healthy planet.

Channeler Jane Roberts says that women choose every facet of their lifetimes, from who their parents are to each illness that manifests in their bodies.

> This applies to every illness, whether it is a broken leg suffered from an accident or an ulcer. This doesn't mean that we *consciously* make a choice in the way

we're used to; we don't sit down and say, 'Well, I think I'll get a broken leg this afternoon at three in front of Rand's drugstore.' Some part of us is upset and chooses an illness or accident as a way of expressing this inner situation.[6]

Says healer Louise Hay, "I believe we create every so called 'illness' in our body."[7] This is not to blame anyone *ever* for her pain or to say that every (or any) illness is consciously created, but to make a statement of women's power: If women create their own illnesses, they also create their own good health, and can choose and create that consciously. Doing it is a form of Marion Weinstein's Creation Manifestation.

Heart center healing is another aspect of thought-forms and psychokinesis. In this case, the object or matter moved is the state of woman's health, her own or someone else's, and either directly or at a distance. As in manifesting, a woman gets what she asks for. Thoughts are things and powerful, as are women's minds. Every negative non-self-loving thought works in the four healthy bodies to create disease; every positive, affirming and self-loving one releases pain and blocks to manifest wellness. Positive thought-forms work miracles, even curing cancer. Women choose what forms to manifest, and they don't take them in a pill but create them in their minds. Once they learn this principle and put it into practice on their own bodies, they become healers that help others and that heal the Earth.

In her healing work, Louise Hay asks clients to look in a mirror, look themselves in the eyes, say their names, and "I love you and accept you exactly as you are."[8] Create that nightly in affirmations and watch a variety of pains, ills and dis-eases disappear. Create nightly in meditation affirmations the visualization of yourself as healthy and happy, and this is what the body manifests. Say "I am well and feel wonderful," rather than "I get rid of my headaches." Accept the size, shape, color and condition of your body as positive and love it as it is. Patriarchy's ad campaigns want women tall, white, thin, young and blonde, an arbitrary sexual designation that is meaningless. All women are beautiful in all our colors, shapes, ages and sizes—love them all and yourself as healthy Be-ings. By Creation Manifestation ("I create myself as a strong and healthy woman"), healing begins.

The image of perfect health, a visualization made in the meditative state, is the essence of psychic healing. This visualization can be done for yourself or someone else, and the someone else can be anywhere on the planet, at any distance, at the time. As in manifesting, the ability to visualize and knowing what you want to create is important. What is created is perfect health, and every healing meditation ends with this image. It begins with visualizing the woman to be healed (self or other), assessing the problem, sending the proper colored light or a visualization of what you want to happen, creating the image of the woman in perfect health, then withdrawing. In the healing with Martha, I visualized her, saw where the bites and swellings were, sent her blue light, visualized the bites receding, then saw her in perfect health. As in every other psychic skill, the work is done in the alpha brainwave state, the meditative state.

This is one form of psychic healing. The other form is direct healing, using prana or aura energy from the healer's hands on or over the area being healed. The woman being healed is present for this, and it can be used on the self for pain areas that you can reach to hold your hands over. This is called laying on of hands, pranic healing or therapeutic touch (among other names) and usually involves two women working together. Full material on how to do both types of healing is covered extensively in my *Women's Book of Healing* (Llewellyn Publications, 1987), and beginning descriptions and directions are given in this chapter. Examples start the teaching and are how-tos.

The first part of treating a disease is to know what it is that's out of balance, in pain, blocked or needing healing. In most cases the logical way of doing this is to feel it, going into the meditative state and asking for more information if needed, or in someone else just asking her what's wrong. Dora Van Gelder Kunz assesses what's wrong by seeing it in auras, even when doctors don't know. She is a psychic diagnostician who works with a receptive medical doctor, Othlia Bengtsson, an ideal combination of medicine with healing.

> Dora examines patients by simply focusing on them and describing what she sees as the physician writes it down. Generally such sessions consume better than an hour because of the detail. Sometimes, however, she is able to do what she calls a 'quickie.'
>
> 'I recall one girl in particular,' she told me. 'I could see almost immediately what the problem was. She'd been to I don't know how many medical centers, but they couldn't find out what was wrong. It turned out to be a very simple, but elusive, allergy. After I identified the problem, the doctor with whom I was working prescribed the appropriate drug, and she was cured.'[9]

To take the healing a step further, before trying drugs, the healer or woman being healed can visualize the problem, the allergy and symptoms, shrinking and disappearing. Margo Adair did this in a similar case, in a self-healing:

> When I was younger, every year I had a runny nose all winter long—that was what winters were for me. During the winter after I learned the techniques of Silva Mind Control, when my sinuses started to act up I meditated, imagining

my mucous membranes drying up—I had a picture that was like cotton evaporating. I did this maybe four or five times. My nose cleared up, and ever since I haven't had a runny nose all winter. Until I learned the power of consciousness it never occurred to me to imagine the problem clearing up. Instead, I continually gave my body the message: 'This runny nose will be here all winter,' for that had been my experience.[10]

As in other manifesting work, make sure to visualize exactly what you want to happen. When she saw herself with a runny nose all winter, Margo had it; when she saw the runny nose cleared up, it cleared up. Don't imagine the negative; imagine wellness.

Another way of doing psychic healing, wonderful for self-healing or distance work, is to ask in the meditative state for a visualization of the chakras. Dora Van Gelder Kunz works with the chakras in this way, as do Amy Wallace and Bill Henkin in *The Psychic Healing Book*. This can also be used for assessing a problem in a healing. The process is meditative, a going into the meditative state and asking for the chakras to appear. When the light/energy centers are visualized, fill each with its color and make sure the colors are bright and clear. If any center isn't clear and polished looking, mentally polish it or send it more light in its chakra color. If anything appears to be tarnishing or blocking the chakra, mentally remove it. Use your fingers. Send light in its color to each chakra center, and when all the centers are clear and bright, end the meditation. Visualize yourself or the women being healed in perfect health.

An example of using this: I worked in a restaurant until last year, and came home every night with a sore throat. Throat chakra blocks are a given in patriarchal society, where women take great risk in saying what they feel. If I said what I wanted to at the restaurant, I'd lose my job, but holding it in was giving me sore throats from what I wasn't saying. I chose to do something about it. Every night before sleep I do meditation work, and every night that I had the sore throat I worked on it in the meditations. After a period of relaxation and affirmations, I asked to see my aura and chakras. When the chakras lit up, I could see the red sticky blotches appearing in my throat center, the sore throat visualized. Using my fingers, I picked out the blotches, pitching them into a visualized purifying fire to dissolve them. I picked them out repeatedly until the chakra was clear, then flooded the area and my entire aura with clear blue light. I visualized myself well, refreshed and in perfect health. By the time I ended the meditation and went to bed, the sore throat was always gone. This can also be used in distance healing, for someone else.

Healer Susan Sheppard and her working partner Judy Burkhammer use light in the chakra and aura band colors to do distance healing. Susan's description of a full psychic healing, a letter also recorded in *The Women's Book of Healing,* is the best how-to on psychic healing I could print.

Judy and I have worked jointly as psychics and healers for about ten years. In our healings, we use colors as cleansing and rejuvenating tools from a distance. In most instances, a healing is requested. We begin our work by putting ourselves into a light trance. After we have 'grounded' ourselves and our subject (who may be in a hospital bed or at home) by imagining our feet being planted in the earth, we then go through the spectrum of colors starting with red at the feet and then spiraling skyward. Red greatly energizes the healing experience. Later, we do the same with orange-yellow-green-blue-indigo and violet. We allow the energies of the colors to surge within and without our bodies. This works to build a cone of power within us. To seal the energies of the colors, we then visualize ourselves in a golden or very white chrysallis of light. This is for protection, as sometimes the illness can be absorbed into our own bodies and will later result as unwanted symptoms.

We then imagine our subject standing before us. Strangely enough, we often see her as if in an x-ray vision. Sometimes we see the eyes or features of our subject. Often, we just see an outline of the patient. That's when we are able to concentrate on damaged organs, swelling, afflicted tissue, strains, broken bones, etc. At this point we rely upon intuition to lead us. In the case of a young man with a bruised and swollen brain, we interjected a cool turquoise to bring down the swelling. After this is done, we may go to a basic green for rejuvenating purposes and then topped off with a brilliant yellow to energize the healing experience and rejuvenate tissue. If in doubt, the entire spectrum of colors is used. In the case of a young woman with leukemia, we were shocked by the amount of red absorbed during the healing: a color badly needed. It is very important not to have preconceived notions as to what color should be used before the healing . . .

Certain colors work best for specific ailments. Grey or silver will quickly mend broken bones. Cool blues and greens will stabilize the body and counteract any swelling. Yellow is a perfect 'all-round' healing color as it has a gentle but energetic feeling. Pink, gold and white will alleviate severe depressions. Pink is used in the case of a person who is recovering over a broken love affair and/or one who feels dejected or deprived of love. Red is not often used, except in cases of a very destructive illness, such as cancer, where the tissues and bloodstream need an aggressive jolt of energy. Orange can be used in the same way, especially with a patient in a weakened state, as it is not so assertive as red. Violet or gold is then used to cleanse the spiritual state of your patient.

After you feel that your healing is near completion, you again interject a pure gold into the afflicted areas. Imagine your subject standing before you completely healed and well. If the illness is serious or life-threatening, imagine your subject standing before you in five years from now, happy and alive. After this time, cover the inner body and outer body with a protective shield of white light. As an extra measure, shield your own body with the chrysallis of white light. Say a small prayer in which you thank the higher power for assisting you. Now you can break your trance. Your healing is complete.

Susan and Judy describe healings that work. They have halted tumors by imagining them shrinking until gone, helped back injuries and sent active leukemia into remission. They describe as easy to work on: "common strains, injuries to a young or healthy body, swelling, infections, aches and pains." Among the hardest are migraines, and of course terminal illnesses.

> In the case of some terminal patients, a complete healing will not be able to take place because of the mass destruction of cells. Since we have the knowledge that we are not just physical beings of this world, it is probably not to the patient's benefit to lengthen her stay in a damaged or defective body. The healing is then used to help your patient feel more vital and comfortable as long as you can: to gently assist her while passing over to the next world.

A few additional comments: my own all-healing colors are blue or green, and these are colors safe to use when not sure what color is appropriate. They are cool and neutral. Be very careful with colors, since what you visualize happens. Red heats, and in the case of someone with a fever, can be harmful. Blue cools, so is not positive for someone suffering over-exposure to cold. Each color has its attributes and you get what you ask for using it. In visualizing a specific thing to happen, as in a tumor shrinking, this is also true. Visualization is a positive tool, but it can harm if used wrongly. Know what you want to happen, and that it's correct, before visualizing it. The safeguard is always to visualize yourself or the woman being healed in perfect, vital health before ending the healing meditation. The whole process of psychic healing is a meditation process, of being able to switch from linear to matriarchal realities. It combines meditation with manifesting, the same manifesting that invokes parking places and "coincidences."

The other primary form of women's healing is pranic healing or laying on of hands. This is direct healing, also involving manifesting and psychokinesis but more in the Nelya Mikhailova style. In this case, the healer "sends" her own radiant aura energy into someone else's aura or pain area, and the woman being healed uses this direct energy to repair her aura bodies. The process is simple, and a primary tool for relieving pain and emotional upset. Used with color and visualization, laying on of hands is powerful, positive, and probably the first form of women's healing.

Laying on of hands, energy transmitted from a woman's hands when held over the aura bodies, is an easy process to learn. In doing it, a woman first grounds herself (with Susan's light aura or a grounding cord), then holds her hands, not touching, side by side and palms down, over a pain area. She does not touch the woman she is healing, and does not touch her hands to each other. Holding hands steady in this position, in a few minutes an energy sensation develops. This can be a variety of feelings, heat or coolness, a wavy or ripply feeling, a sense of magnetism or electricity. Hands placed so that feeling reaches where it hurts, she holds her hands steady until the feeling fades. When it does fade, the healer can withdraw or can physically touch the woman she is healing, lightly placing her open palms on the pain area. The touching is optional; let intuition guide you. In several minutes the energy charge returns, usually as a feeling of heat, and when this fades too, the healing is over. The woman doing the healing places her hands palms to the ground, releasing any excess energy. This grounding at the end is important.

This process, simple as it is, has been claimed by every religion and church in the patriarchy, taken away from women who developed it. Like dreaming, laying on of hands is archetypal, there by virtue of being human, and anyone can do it. Women learn it by doing it, practicing it. As in any skill, it grows with use. The first and primary factor in successful laying on of hands healing is to enter the meditative state, however informally, before beginning. At first this may require the full relaxation routine, but quickly it becomes a simple process of grounding and centering, of shifting into the matriarchal reality.

In pranic healing, the healer is using the small chakras in the palms of her hands, and sometimes the smaller ones at the tips of each finger. W.J. Kilner described women's ability to will aura energy from one place to the other with these chakras. He could see it in his chemical screens, and this is what's happening in laying on of hands. Mary Coddington's list of attributes of prana, energy, or thought transmission are also the attributes for this type of healing. The process calms and relieves pain in the woman being healed, and brings both women, consciously or not, into the alpha brainwave state. It causes an increase in oxygen volume in the blood, and a decrease in pulse rate and respiration—a calming effect that is physically measurable.[11] The process also has the ability to change the loose hydrogen-oxygen bonding of the water molecule, and water comprises 95% of the human body. In the experiments and analysis of Sister Justa Smith, a healer and researcher in New York State, laying on of hands stimulates the trypsin enzyme, the initiator of physical body healing, for the production of new body cells.[12]

Here is a healing force far different from the cutting and poisoning of modern medical science, and a healing force available to any woman who chooses to use it. It is drug free and trauma free, and requires no machinery or technological advances; it is cost free. When combined with visualization it is highly effective for many dis-ease states, and has been known to generate "miracles." Beginning with a mother's touching a child's skinned knee, it is known to women everywhere and used by them, with good success.

Delores Krieger, Ph.D. nurse, has worked with Therapeutic Touch, as she terms it, for many years and teaches it to non-doctors and in nursing schools. Student of Dora Kunz, her goal is to connect psychic healing to medical science, as Dora Kunz and Othlia Bengtsson have done in diagnostics. Such a union would benefit all. Here is Krieger's analysis of what laying on of hands does:

> Therapeutic Touch effects a profound relaxation response; it helps to alleviate and frequently to eradicate pain, and in a large majority of test cases, it does accelerate the healing process. Therapeutic Touch seems to work well with all stress-related illnesses, and in my experience, it appears to have a significant effect on autonomic nervous system symptoms such as nausea, dyspnea, tachycardia, pallor due to peripheral vascular system contraction, and poor blood circulation in the extremities . . . Therapeutic Touch strongly supports the physiological development of premature babies and helps irritable babies to fall asleep—that last, at least, is worth a pat on the back![13]

The process is great for headaches and menstrual cramps, any injuries, and is effective on children, adults and animals.

At times during laying on of hands, pain can increase, but this is momentary. When the healing process is speeded up, the sensations telescope, but when it stops (usually by the time the healing is over), it stops for good. This increase happens only occasionally and to varying degrees, but women should know about it. Be in close touch with what the woman being healed is feeling, and be there to explain, reassure and be supportive of her. Only in burns is this type of healing very painful, and the results are worth bearing with it for the few moments it takes to go away.

Like Delores Krieger and Dora Van Gelder Kunz, Yolanda B. is a healer. She uses psychic healing diagnostic techniques and then laying on of hands to transmit aura energy. She calls this energy or prana by the name the Russians use, "bioplasmic" or "biomagnetic energy." Yolanda B. is a Hungarian immigrant, now living in Florida:

> I know and have demonstrated that I can transmit the biocurrents into the body of any individual in need, at the best frequency which is most effective

and, very importantly, in a manner not the least bit harmful to the living cells.

This causes not only a change in the apparent condition, but literally a change throughout the entire body of the individual, including a change within her emotional field and a change within her mental field. It is apparent then, that healing takes place on many different levels. There are isolated manifestations of human life that sometimes cannot be penetrated by this energy, and those cases are what we call 'karmic.'[14]

The other occasions when laying on of hands or psychic healing fails are times when the healer is unable to reach the centered and grounded meditative state and/or when the woman being healed refuses the energy, consciously or not. Everyone has the right to her own dis-ease if she chooses it, and at times healing is blocked. Sometimes a healing that ends with no immediate change, however, just takes awhile to work. A few minutes or an hour later, or overnight, the changes happen. Sometimes the woman being healed by laying on of hands doesn't realize that her pain is gone until the healer asks her. Often results from a psychic or pranic healing are labeled spontaneous, and as long as healing happens, it doesn't matter. In both types of healing it is ethically necessary for the healer to have permission before she starts. In a distance healing, ask her psychically in the meditative state, and in laying on of hands, a direct healing, simply ask her. If a woman refuses, the healer withdraws.

Most healers perceive this energy, psychic or directly sent, as coming from within themselves, via Goddess. Some see it as coming to them from discarnate entities, spirit helpers or guides that tell them what to do and how to do it. There can be a combination of both. More is discussed on spirit guides in Chapter Eleven; Jane Roberts' Seth and Sheila Reynolds' Gay Bonner are examples of them. Healing results are the same, whether a woman is working through her creation Goddess self or through spiritism, but most healers feel that the closer connection they can make with divinity/Goddess, the more powerful their healings. These are where "miracles" happen. Blanche Meyerson describes her discarnate-guided healing process:

I suppose I'm a spiritual healer, if you need a label for it. The energy is sent through me, from these doctors on the other side. They do the work. I can't control or direct it.[15]

She began the work reluctantly, dis-covering it and being forced to re-cognize its power and her ability. Being "different" in this society is not easy to accept, physically or psychically.

Friends of mine who are psychics kept bringing messages to me from the 'doctors', telling me I should and could treat the sick, that the doctors were ready to work through me. One friend who believed brought her poodle over, asking that I try. That little thing had two broken legs that had never mended. Seeing her drag herself along just tore at me, so I gave her two very weak treatments that day. When my friend came back, the dog ran to the door to greet her.[16]

However it manifests, women's psychic healing is powerful and positive. Accepting the possibility and choosing it is the first step in learning how to heal, and great healers are and always have been women.

Dr. Shafica Karagulla, in her landmark book *Breakthrough to Creativity*, (Marina del Rey, CA, DeVorss and Co., Inc., 1967) dis-covered a large number of medical doctors who diagnose and treat by psychic means, usually by seeing auras. Virtually all of them hide their abilities, backing them up with medical tests and never speaking of them, for fear of censure by their peers. Virtually all of these doctors are known for their superior "medical" know-how and are highly respected in their field. She describes Dr. Gloria, an osteopath in her eighties (in 1967) who uses psychic unseen energy to diagnose:

> Dr. Gloria is able to sense or feel in her hands the flow of energy along the nervous system when she touches the patient. She knows immediately where there is a block or any other kind of difficulty. She senses the circulation of the blood and the condition of the organs and tissues of the body in the same way. When she places her hands on the patient's head she is aware of all the subtle movements of the brain fluids, and much of her awareness of what is wrong with the physical body depends upon what she senses in the brain and the brain fluids. Her diagnoses have been confirmed over and over again by other physicians using the regular diagnostic method. A number of medical doctors send her cases and discuss her findings relative to their own.
>
> Dr. Gloria senses rather than sees an energy field interpenetrating the physical body and surrounding it. She has healing in her hands and she describes this as an energy flowing through her which is turned on and off as she treats patients. She uses the usual osteopathic methods but with a subtle difference.[17]

Karagulla, a neuropsychiatrist, works with women psychics who are healers. She describes a healing precognition made by Diane, who sees auras and chakras but is not an MD:

> A friend of mine and her husband agreed to be guinea pigs in my program for evaluating healthy people. On the first evaluation Diane described them both as being very healthy specimens. A year later the husband stopped by one day, and I suggested that Diane do a second examination . . . Diane was some what hesitant about discussing the total picture while my friend was still present. She made notes and gave me the rest of the evaluation after he had left. She explained to me that there were certain disruptions and disturbances in the energy body which had not been present a year previous. She described this condition and said to her this meant that within a year to eighteen months my friend would have a very serious physical disorder and a serious hip condition.
>
> I had begun to realize that Diane's observations even in predicting the onset

of a disease were pretty accurate. I discussed this with the wife. Since there was nothing we could tell him from a medical point of view, we decided not to discuss it with him. I did make a point of encouraging them to make a trip around the world which they had been planning for many years. Personally, I felt that in case Diane should be right, they should enjoy life while he was in good health. Within eighteen months he had developed Parkinson's Disease which has become progressively worse and he was hospitalized for an operation due to a serious hip condition.

Diane insisted that this was not precognition. The energy web or body showed the condition clearly many months before it became apparent in the physical body.[18]

In the current women's community, many women are healers. Ana, who contributed to this book earlier, is a shamanic healer trained in Native American traditions. She uses auras diagnostically, and can see pregnancy and the sex of the child before the woman even knows she's pregnant. She has a link with her mother, and "told her that she had a cyst in her left breast three months before it was diagnosed as cancer." Like Dora Kunz and Diane, she sees unmanifested dis-ease before it happens and can see in the aura the reasons for the dis-ease. Ana is an herbalist and leads sweat lodges in the Algonquin heritage, ceremonies of strength and women's healing.

In more women's experiences, Chris describes the results of a distance healing, the first distance healing I had ever tried. She asked me in a letter to send energy to her and I did, in the form of golden light. I asked her if she felt anything over more than two hundred miles:

I looked at my calendar and as near as I can figure when you were sending me gold light coincided with a period of a few days when I was feeling uncharacteristically relaxed and energized. I even commented on it to a couple of people at the time. I felt the way I do when I get back from Mallorca, and before the usual tensions set in again—deep down relaxed and *in phase* somehow. In fact it occurred to me to wonder, at the time, whether you were doing a spell for me or something. When I got your letter saying you'd sent me golden light, I wasn't at all surprised!

Judy had this experience with psychic healing—and with clairsentience:

Never having had back problems, I didn't understand the excruciating pain that wracked my back when I tried to get out of bed one morning. I went to a psychic healer that afternoon. He laid his hands on me and did an adjustment. The pain was gone immediately. Later that evening my identical twin sister called. She was overjoyed. She said she had had severe back problems for about a month and they were so bad she couldn't get out of bed that day. I didn't know she was having any back problems. She said all of a sudden that afternoon (at approximately the time of the laying on of hands), the pain was gone and that she was as good as new.

Nancy describes visualization in a self-healing, and first information of spirit guides to use later:

> Around 1980 I had a health problem and was going to need an operation. I had read *Getting Well Again* by Carl Simonton. One of the methods they suggested for visualizing was to ask for a guide, who would talk to you about your problem. Another method was to imagine the disease being eaten up by a bunch of little pac-man kind of beings. I used the latter, and that plus a healing service and laying on of hands, really lessened my problem, which was a benign uterine tumor, to the point where I didn't need the operation.

Nancy describes her spirit guide Elma in Chapter Eleven.

Cindy learned healing in a workshop and put it to use two months later, having never done healing work before the workshop. Her father was scheduled for cardiac catheterization, and Cindy went to work:

> He went into the hospital to find out whether or not he needed to have a balloon angioplasty—a procedure where the lumen of the artery is enlarged by expanding a balloon in it, pushing the plaque deposits against the artery wall. Initially, the cardiologists felt he needed to have it done, but couldn't decide what percentage of arterial blockage had occurred, so decided to run him through some additional tests to find out. The day he was scheduled for his angioplasty, he went for a treadmill to make absolutely sure he needed the procedure. He even took his bag of stones I had given him!
>
> While he was having his tests, I sat in his room and visualized green light bathing his heart, then visualized him on the treadmill having no problems. End result: no angioplasty needed! He was discharged within an hour with new medicine and instructions to resume exercise and drop some weight! What a great success story, huh?!

His doctors will never know what healed him! Cindy also works with gemstones and crystals for healing, and they are important healing tools to use with laying on of hands and distance work. (See *The Women's Book of Healing* for more on them.)

Shekinah Mountainwater did a healing for Cindy using laying on of hands and crystals:

> She had bad menstrual cramps, so I used one hand to soothe and massage her abdominal area and the other to draw out the negative energy with a crystal. I also used the crystal to swirl the energy in a spiral motion to get everything in her womb flowing again. She said it worked and that she felt much better!

Both women had attended the same workshop, one of mine. Many of the responses I got from this chapter came from women who had experienced either my healings or workshops. There is great joy in teaching women to be healers. Lorre experienced both healing work for herself and the workshops. Her pain area for laying on of hands was a stiff hip:

I have been hiking and feeling more confident about my being sure-footed than I have for a long time. I am continuing with the healing using a crystal and carnelian, and also was gifted with a hematite.

I use the (crystal) wand to send healing energy to my family in Minnesota. I envision colors that automatically seem appropriate and am hoping that they are accepting the energy that is offered by the Goddess through me.

Sharon has multiple sclerosis and received indigo light in distance healing, plus gemstones of moonstone, sodalite and amethyst for the MS, and chrysocolla as an all-healer and for writer's block. Here is her response:

After keeping the stones with me at all times, it was the third day, I think, when I awoke early, felt so motivated to work that I dressed and went straight to the typewriter. Except for brief periods to eat and do what I absolutely had to do, I was at the typewriter until eleven PM. This was amazing! Each day was this productive for an entire week. I didn't realize as this week passed that I was working so hard. I enjoyed it, felt unusually motivated to get this work done . . . This book *must* be written and it *will* be written!

Sunlight describes a women's healing ritual in her book *Womonseed*. Maya had been injured in a plant explosion and brought to women's land:

Coyote picked me up like a baby and carried me out of the hut to a clearing where women were sitting in a circle. Like witches. It was strange, like this was a dream, too. She carried me to the center and laid me down on the ground on a bed of moss. Right away I felt strength coming up from the earth straight into my body. I closed my eyes. The women sang:

> *I am the circle*
> *I am healing you*
> *You are the circle*
> *You are healing me*
> *Reunite us, be one*
> *Reunite us, be one.*

They moved in close and touched me very gently all over. Their hands gave off heat and warmed me too, like the ground I was laying on did. The heat soaked into me and made me stronger. It filled me until I couldn't lay there any more. I wanted to get up. I opened my eyes and saw the circle around me, shining like a light. I sat up and breathed deep and it didn't hurt. I moved my arm and shoulder and they felt like part of my body again. I stood up and that felt good. Betsy hugged me. Kahuna did, too. Then the circle closed in and we were all hugging. They enveloped me, all those warm women bodies and spirits. It was like heaven . . . I'd been to hell and now I was in heaven. Sure. I heard the angels singing.

> *We are the circle*
> *We are healing us . . .*
> *Reunited, we are one*
> *Reunited, we are one.*

The light from that circle was bright like the one I saw in my dream, and I

knew that healing magic was made out of love.
The next day I walked out of the healing hut and it was like being born.[18]

## Selena Fox describes the New Moon healing rituals at Circle Sanctuary:

We begin a Healing Circle with a short, silent meditation to prepare us for the healing work. It is important to purify, ground, and center before working with magickal energy, and we use this meditation time to do this. We breathe deeply, each of us at our own pace. With our breath, we relax our bodies and cleanse our minds and hearts. We focus on the Planet Earth beneath us and the Sky above us, and on being clear channels of the healing force in nature.

During the meditation, we also pass incense around the circle as part of our purifying work—usually it is sandalwood or frankincense, both of which are excellent for cleansing the energy fields of people and places, as well as aiding in healing energy channeling. As the incense comes to each of us in turn, we breathe it in and move it around our auras and the spot where we are standing.

When all of us have finished our meditation and are ready, we join hands briefly for a few moments to center and connect ourselves as a group. Then we create sacred space for healing by turning to the four directions and calling forth the forces we associate with each direction into ourselves, into our circle, and into our healing work.

We begin by facing North and calling the Spirits of the Element Earth to bring forth strength and prosperity and to aid the physical healing work we will do. Then we turn to the East and call the Spirits of Air to bring forth mental clarity and intelligence and to aid mental healing work. Next we call the Spirits of Fire from the South to bring forth energy and the will to be well and to heal. Then we face West and call the Spirits of Water to bring forth understanding and intuition, and to aid emotional healing work . . .

Now we call on Goddesses, Gods and Spirit Helpers to aid in the healing work. Each of us has an opportunity to call forth in this Circle those Divine Forces we work with in our own personal rituals. Some invocations are spoken, some are sung, some are silent. This approach not only brings more power to the ceremony, but it aids in group attunement.

After the invocations, we begin doing healing work itself, by focusing on any special healing needs of those present at the circle. We usually do this by working on those needing healing one at a time. A person comes forth and stands in the center of the circle and describes her or his healing need and any preferences about how we should work to channel energy for the condition to correct not only the symptoms, but also the cause.

One method we often use for direct healing is this. The person relaxes and stands or sits in the center of the circle where the rest of us are standing. We start combing the aura of the person, beginning at the top of her head and working down to her feet. We imagine our fingers as combs. When we sense clogged energy, we pull it out and dissolve it.

When we are done with the auric cleansing, we pause a few moments and center ourselves, then direct healing light into the person's aura through our fingertips. Sometimes, some or all of us also do laying on of hands, touching the physical body as well. Sometimes we chant as we are doing a direct healing. We keep channeling healing force to the person until group energy for this working peaks and is fully released into the person's aura or until the person signals us she has received enough by closing her arms over her chest, in which case any extra energy built up is sent into the earth. We ground and center after each direct healing we do.

... When there are many people to be healed, especially in circles where a large number of people are present to do the healing work, we form a circle of those needing healing in the center and have healers in the outer ring direct energy one-on-one, going clockwise around the circle. We have found this method works well for groups of twenty to three hundred, although with several hundred people in a circle, it also is necessary to adapt the whole circle format to facilitate group attunement and focus.

After completing the direct healings, we move on to absent healing work—sending energy to people who are not physically present. Each month people in need of healing from around the USA and other parts of the world send us written healing requests. We place these in our healing chalice as they arrive, and at the New Moon circle, the chalice and the written requests are brought into the center of our circle... After a short meditation, each of us selects a request, senses it, reads it, and channels energy to the person. When a healer finishes with a request, she then places it in a larger ring around the chalice, and takes another request ... Each request gets the personal attention of two healers present, as well as the group as a whole ...

We then move on to the third and final aspect of our healing work—Planetary Healing. The work we do here varies from circle to circle. Sometimes we send energy for a particular need, such as protection of an endangered species of animal or plant life. Sometimes we just focus on the larger picture—the planet as a whole. Most of the time we do a combination of these approaches—beginning with specifics and ending with the general.

One visualization we have used frequently is that of the Earth as seen from outer space surrounded by light instead of physical and spiritual smog—this is sending healing to the aura of the planet. We usually do chanting during the Earth Healing part of our ritual. When we finish raising energy, we touch the ground and direct our cone of power there.

After doing Planetary Healing, we come together as a group in silent meditation and group embrace, for a moment. Then we give thanks to the Goddesses, Gods, and Spirit Helpers we have called upon during the circle, we then turn and face the four quarters and give thanks to the guardians of the four directions and to our own group spirit. As we face the four quarters again, we send the columns of light we have visualized there back into the Earth and we dissolve the circle that we have set up as a force field to bless and protect our work.

Following the Healing Circle, our custom is to share food and socialize. This is an important part of the Healing work, for sharing food helps center and ground us, and socializing shifts our attention from the intense healing we have been doing into a lighter space.[19]

Group healing work can be intensely beautiful and intensely powerful. The New Moon healings at Circle Sanctuary are perfect examples of wiccan ritual, and of what wicca or witchcraft really is. Sandra Pastorius writes about another healing ritual, led by Laeh Maggie Garfield for Sandra's daughter, Cindia. The ritual was part of a workshop weekend:

When I began working to produce Laeh's workshop, I felt strongly that Cindia should be there. I knew it could be a healing for her to experience and learn about women's Native American spirituality. I had recently learned of the extent to which my daughter had used cocaine. She had been addicted for about five years. Leah suggested that Cindia be the 'healee' for the Moonlight Healing Ceremony that would be a part of the weekend Intensive. I invited her to come for the weekend and to have the healing, and she opened up to the idea.

I gave Cindia a small beaded medicine bag to wear. She really liked it and wore it constantly for many weeks after the healing. I was anxious about the possibility of her withdrawing herself from the healing, but she was steady and seemed to grow stronger in her desire to grow into this experience. I felt proud of her openness to listen and share. Laeh drew her in with stories and humor, and made her feel accepted and cared for.

On the next evening ten of us gathered, hidden in the folds of sand dunes, exposed to the Full Virgo Moon during Pisces. A large fire was started by Bonnie, our fire-tender for the ritual. As we watched, Patti and I sang together, 'Sweetly, Deeply,' a song about coming back home. Then Laeh told Cindia it was time to take off her clothes, and we gave her several blankets to wrap up in. I put my bulky white sweater down on the cold sand for her to stand on while we prepared for the ceremony. The waves were white-capped and crashing with full moon intensity. As I watched the surf I remembered Cindia romping here in the polka dotted bathing suit she used to wear when she was eight years old. Still lingering was her enthusiasm, health and freedom. I wanted to will that image back into her body and spirit.

Laeh began the drumming and we all danced around the fire. Most of the other women were mothers, with one eight month old wrapped snuggly against her mother's bosom. Laeh burned sage and other herbs in a shell, and had Cindia stand next to her, with me standing just behind my daughter. Laeh began singing her Healing Song as she spread the smoke all around Cindia's body and head. She stood shivering and watching the fire while Laeh's singing became louder. Then she brought out her eagle's feather, and swept Cindia's aura all around while singing soft and loud, preening her with sound and feather. I felt so many feelings surge up as I watched my firstborn in a healing rite. I did my part by watching the surf and seeing how innocently she used to hop around at the edge of the water. I saw the life force strong and full. The drugs had sucked enough of her; now she would be free to be her best self.

Laeh walked forward with her arm around Cindia, and we all turned towards the white presence in the night sky. Laeh told Cindia to open up her blankets and bathe her body in moonlight three times, and to yell out her pain to the moon. Later Cindia told me that on the third scream Laeh told her to throw all the drugs out of her mouth and send them up to the moon. She said she could feel the moon reaching her and her throat empty. Her screams pierced my heart. I saw all the pain I never wanted her to have cast out into the still dark night and get absorbed by the moon. There was a rush of guilt for not being there for her enough, mixed with pride for how she showed her own mothers' and grandmothers' strength of spirit. I felt angry about the landmines of modern life that get set for our kids as they begin adult life. It felt like the eye of the earth was here watching this passage of girlhood giggles and romping joy in the surf, to a woman's crying out in the pain of recognition for her temptations at death's door. As Laeh held and comforted my daughter, tears fell into the sand for the love of them both, and for the support and caring of my sisters surrounding the fire. I was in awe of our woman presence.

Then four women danced with shawls around the fire, spreading their arms together like great wings. They seemed to seal in the healing with their movements, invoking the purifying fire. I had already prepared for doing a 'giveaway' to Cindia. I soaked the amethyst ring that I had worn for the last ten years in salt water. I had gotten this ring just after she had moved in with her father after our divorce, and I was healing and discovering new parts of myself. I wanted this symbol of my freedom to pass on to her as she took back her own power, and set herself free from addiction. It was my gift of love for myself to her. I'll always remember the look in her eyes when I slipped it onto her finger.

When the giveaway was completed we sang, and settled. Laeh brought out her fur pipe pouch, and shared the lore of the medicine pipe. She filled the antler bowl with the rare species of angelica root cut fine earlier in the day, and told how this root was used for visions and knowledge. She lit, smoked and sent the pipe around the circle, from woman to woman. The menstruating women passed their turn, being full of their power already. We all watched the fire quietly, then shared our insights, and gave them to the fire. I tasted the fullness of motherhood, and felt grateful for this coming together, the deep sharing between us all. It was a bond that honored the power of the Earth Mother to heal her children. I experienced the most significant merging of my own spiritual path with my role as mother in my life. I felt the power of the moon as witness and healer. I am grateful to Laeh for facilitating this crossing point in our lives.

Before I was able to recount this experience I found that I needed to wash Cindia's medicine pouch, which she had stopped wearing. I put some renewal energy in it, so Cindia can affirm again her best self. She feels healed, but yet not finished with the healing process.

I send the pipe to you and bless you in your book. Thank you for your patience and encouragement. This writing has been and will be a seal of spirit over the experience. I hope it will inspire other mothers and daughters to create healing ceremonies between them.

So may this blessing be ... Laeh Maggie Garfield's work, from her book *Companions in Spirit*, continues in later chapters. Her newest book is called *Sound Medicine*.

In doing individual healings, I use a combination of laying on of hands, visualization, trancework, psychic healing, gemstones and laying on of stones. (More on all of these in *The Women's Book of Healing*). Some of the work is for others, but much is self-healing. On one occasion I worked with burns, which are painful. I had spilled boiling tea, splashed it so drops fell on the backs of both hands, one more painful and extensive than the other. This was at my restaurant job, and there was no privacy and little time for healing work. I worked on the more severe burn, on the right, but hadn't time for both hands. I rested a crystal and a peridot (a green stone, all I had with me) on the burn and used my left hand only over it. I visualized green light, but the intensity of the energy was extremely painful. In no other case than burns does laying on of hands cause significant pain, but this was bad. The energy was too strong and tears ran down my face. I kept going. There wasn't time to do the left hand, but I knew I'd go home in three hours to my altar where I could use the meditative state and psychic healing. At the end of the laying on of hands, the pain was still strong, worse in the hand I'd treated.

When I got home and went to my altar, I dis-covered that the pain in my right hand had completely gone, and the only pain remaining was in my left, which I hadn't treated. Both burns were red, but the untreated one was redder, though a smaller burn. Just to see what would happen, I didn't do laying on of hands work with my left hand or much psychic healing. I went into meditation and filled my aura with blue light, nothing else.

The next day, the hand I had treated was nearly healed. There was a red spot there but no more, and no pain. The left hand that was untreated was quite painful and very red, though a much smaller burn. It blistered that day. In thirty-six hours, the hand I had treated was completely healed, even the red spot gone. The untreated hand remained painful for another week, blistered and the blister slowly healed. The red spot and mark of where the burn had been remained for several weeks. However painful the healing had been, it had pre-vented the burn from blistering and healed it in a fraction of the time of the untreated hand. Despite the pain it was worth doing. I men-tioned the incident to Susan Sheppard in a letter and here were her suggestions. Burns are common injuries for healing:

> Try an icy-pale blue on burns. It's possible that green is 'too hot' of a color for a burn because of the warm, yellow element. Also, I imagine your energy is very intense. Imagine something soothing the next time—like the image of icy mountain water rushing over rocks, (hot ones).

Another suggestion is to use hands-only on burns, not touching, and not with a crystal. If available, try using a cool blue gemstone—blue topaz, chrysocolla, lapis lazuli—instead. When healing with others and pain occurs in the healing, ask her to breathe into the pain, and explain to her what's happening, that the pain will stop. If she chooses to end the healing, end it.

Susan describes the tingling sensation that happens doing healings. She feels it in her hands during psychic healing as well and more recently all the time:

> During the healing, you will often feel the palms of your hands begin to tingle or itch. This is your healing energies building. You may even feel as if you are floating outside of your body. At this point you must trust it and go with it. You are probably linking up with a higher, more direct force.
>
> My hands are constantly tingling, especially the palms. I can feel the nerves leaping and shimmering at all times. I think I am gaining some type of a greater power—This is psychic and not physical in nature. It feels especially strong

> whenever I submerge my hands in water. I feel there is so much energy in my hands!

As the chakras open and develop, sensitivity increases. There have even been women able to determine colors and read by using these chakras, rather than visually, in a skill called "eyeless sight."[20] More on eyeless sight in Chapter Ten.

The how-to for this chapter has been intrinsic in it throughout. For an exercise in beginning psychic healing, go into the meditative state and ask to see your chakras. Watch them light up in their colors, and brighten each color. Clear them by removing with your fingers or with colored light anything that appears to cloud or obstruct their brightness. Women who do not see the aura or chakras visually learn to do this easily. If you think you can't see this, imagine it, and with practice it happens. Psychic healing at first feels contrived, but the results are real. Cast colors of light around your aura, experiencing what each feels like and what it invokes. Try each color of the chakra rainbow, then pick a color that you need and fill your aura with it for as long as you need it. When you have enough, change the color to clear and come out of the meditation.

When doing a psychic healing meditation, begin with relaxation and relax fully before doing healing. Use an aura of light, clear or blue around you and a grounding cord before starting. Make a visualization for yourself of something to heal. If there's a wart to remove, for example, visualize it shrinking and disappearing. If there's a cut to heal, see it zippered shut and gone. Then cast light around yourself, green or blue this time, and withdraw. When finished, place palms down to the Earth to release excess energy, and surround yourself with clear light at the end again. The groundings are important safeguards, preventing you from absorbing other's symptoms or re-turning your own. The best way to learn psychic healing is to practice it on yourself.

To begin laying on of hands, rub your hands together briskly until friction builds, then hold your palms facing each other but not touching. Feel the energy, bouncing it between your hands like a spongy ball. When the energy fades, place palms to the Earth to ground, then start again. Practice on houseplants and pets. At the end of a laying on of hands, run your hands in cool water to clear the energies. When using crystals for this work, hold the crystal in the right hand, sending hand for most women, over the palm chakra. Be sure to clear the crystal in cool water at the end of each healing, too.

Practice starting and grounding until the energy comes at will, then try a healing by placing your palms on opposite sides of a pain area on yourself or someone else. Hold them over the pain area, both palms, until the energy fades. When it does, place your palms directly on the pain area, touching, and hold them there gently until another surge of energy builds and fades. Be sure to ground. This is the process of laying on of hands; it grows stronger, longer and more focused with use.

There are several important books on healing. I've mentioned my *Women's Book of Healing*, (St. Paul, Llewellyn Publications, 1987), for laying on of hands, psychic healing, color work, the chakras, gemstones and crystals. For doing psychic healing, also try:

Margo Adair, *Working Inside Out*, (Berkeley, CA, Wingbow Press, 1986).

Benjamin O. Bibb and Joseph J. Weed, *Amazing Secrets of Psychic Healing*, (W. Nyack, NY, Parker Publishing, 1976).

Amy Wallace and Bill Henkin, *The Psychic Healing Book*, (Berkeley, CA, Wingbow Press, 1978).

For laying on of hands, read *The Therapeutic Touch* by Delores Krieger, RN, Ph.D., (Englewood Cliffs, NJ, Prentice-Hall, Inc., 1979). Books are a good beginning for women who want to be healers, but the important thing is to do the work, to practice it and make it happen.

Women's healing is as old in herstory as women are, and uses the energy force of life itself. Women who are healers stroke the python in the ways of our matriarchal foremothers, using this form of Creation Manifestation for the good of all.

---

*Patriarchal law requires a medical disclaimer for this chapter. Healing and medicine are two different things, complementary at best in present times. In medical difficulty seek medical attention; this information is not medicine, but healing.

©Francene Hart

# FOOTNOTES

1. Margot Adair, *Working Inside Out*, p. 165.

2. *Ibid.*, p. 158. These are quotes from various sources.

3. *Ibid.*, p. 160. Quote is from Fritjof Capra.

4. Dora Van Gelder (Kunz), in David Hammond, *The Search For Psychic Power*, p. 49 and 51.

5. Eileen Garrett, in David C. Knight, *The ESP Reader*, p. 198.

6. Jane Roberts, *The Seth Material*, p. 134.

7. Louise Hay, *You Can Heal Your Life*, (Santa Monica, CA, Hay House, 1984), p. 127.

8. *Ibid.*, p. 25.

9. Dora Van Gelder (Kunz), in David Hammond, *The Search for Psychic Power*, p. 52.

10. Margo Adair, *Working Inside Out*, p. 162.

11. Delores Krieger, RN, Ph.D., *The Therapeutic Touch: How to Use Your Hands to Help or to Heal*, (Englewood Cliffs, NJ, Prentice-Hall, Inc., 1979), p. 153-156.

12. George Meek, *Healers and the Healing Process*, p. 196.

13. Delores Krieger, *The Therapeutic Touch*, p. 89-90.

14. Mary Coddington, *In Search of the Healing Energy*, p. 120 and 121. Pronouns are changed to "she."

15. Marcia Gillespie, "Healer Meyerson," in *Ms. Magazine*, Vol. XIV, no. 6, December, 1985, p. 58.

16. *Ibid.*, p. 60.

17. Shafica Karagulla, MD, *Breakthrough to Creativity: Your Higher Sense Perception*, (Marina del Rey, CA, DeVorss and Co., Inc., 1967), p. 76-77. This is an amazing book.

18. Sunlight, *Womonseed*, p. 169-170.

19. Selena Fox, "New Moon Healing Circle," in *Circle Network News*, (Mt. Horeb, WI), Fall, 1984, p. 11.

20. See Sheila Ostrander and Lynn Schroeder, *Psychic Discoveries Behind the Iron Curtain*, Chapter Fourteen.

## Chapter Eight

# The Throat Chakra: Telepathy
# Sending and Receiving

*Words have not the value to me that others place on them. I can, in a flash, by sensing, communicate to another all my thoughts and wishes, as well as perceive those of others, without uttering a single word. The inadequacy of words, to express emotions, thoughts, and feelings has, from time to time, created a barrier between me and others . . .*

*From my earliest memory, I have been able, by lying quite still with my head in the crook of my arm, to reach out and touch the flowers and the sky. I have also, in this way, sensed the breath of a distant bush, the flesh of a far-off flower, or the sap of some remote tree . . . I can to this day, by lying thus within myself, know 'oneness' with all Light and Life . . .*

*While the girls at school were not aware of such matters, I was sure that the animals understood them . . . As a mouse reacts to the presence of a hawk before it sees its form, so did I know that all animals reacted to their enemies and friends . . . [1]*

Women send and receive, telepath with other humans and with animals. Telepathy for me is animals, is Tiger. Tiger was a Siberian Husky dog, black with white legs and belly, striped chest and masked face. She was small for her breed, as small as a large Cocker Spaniel, and had bright aqua eyes. From the time of her birth, Tiger appointed herself as my mother and teacher, and since her death, reappears as a spirit guide. During her life, we talked to each other constantly. Talking to that dog, with her wisdom and smart-assed comments, was a way of life for me for eleven years. Her ascerbic wit and different perspective are sorely missed since her death.

Tiger saw as her job my training and upbringing, though I was an adult and she a fuzzy puppy when we met. She was often very funny, and got away with most of the things she wanted from me, but only rarely did she get me to change clothes for her. Dressing to go out one night and being silly, I asked her, "Well, what do you think of this?"

Tiger's reply was a sour, "Yuck."

"But Dog," I said, "it's my new dress, and I like it."

Tiger, staring at me from my bed where she could see everything commented, "You're human, you would."

I asked her, "Well, what's wrong with it?"

And she said, "Why don't you wear your fur?"

Often at night she would cuddle against my legs to sleep, grumbling if I moved around too much. She woke me by washing my face every morning, and humming. I had a lover she was jealous of once, and being a smart adolescent, Tiger committed the one sin that would always get my notice—she peed on her. Tiger did that to discipline me. When I'd been away on a trip and left her at the vet's, her first act getting home was to pee on the rug. Greeting her after being gone, she'd turn her face away and tell me, "I'm not talking."

Tiger saw me as a healer, and in the early days of learning to channel energy, she'd use herself as a receiver. One afternoon in the park, I sat in a swarm of yellow jackets, and woke up in the night with an allergic reaction, similar to what Martha was afraid of. I had chills, muscle and stomach cramps, and was very dizzy. There were no antihistimines in the house, so I drank some cranberry juice and came back to bed; Tiger curled against me as always. I began to visualize the reaction as red thorns and circle them through my body, drawing in blue light from my left hand and releasing the thorns through my right. As soon as I began to do this, Tiger moved and placed her body against my right hand. Fearing to hurt her, I moved it, and she turned to place herself there again. I sent the thorns out. In a few moments, the dog got up and went into a convulsion, and I became terribly frightened. It was over as fast as it started. She shook off, curled back beside me and went to sleep, and I realized I felt fine, the reaction was over. Tiger had done a healing.

When Tiger died, at eleven years old, she simply withdrew. She stopped eating and I tempted her, cajoled her, raged at her for three months as she got weaker and weaker. For the first time in eleven years, Tiger broke the communication between us. When I tried to use crystals and laying on of hands with her, she pushed them away, and when I pleaded with her, she shut me out. One day, frantic, I asked her, "Tiger, why are you doing this?"

And she said, "I'm an old dog, and I want to die. Let me go." When I wouldn't accept that and kept trying, her words to me were, "Go away, I'm not here now. Leave me alone." That was the only message for almost three months. I began to realize what she had given me all her life.

The dog became so weak that I carried her in my arms to take her outside and to bring her into bed with me. She didn't make one puddle in the house, however weak she was—she wasn't mad at me. One night doing meditation work, something Tiger approved of and always joined, she lifted her head and put it into my lap. I stroked her as I'd done so often and told her I loved her, what a good dog she was. Tiger talked to me then, said, "I love you, too. You keep me here, but I have to go now. You don't need me anymore." The next day she was unconscious, truly "not here anymore," and it was time to put her down. I had done all my crying for the last three months, now all that was left was to miss her terribly.

Tiger appears from time to time. She turns up in Hallows rituals, when in scrying I invite a friend to come from this plane or the next. When I picture one of my spirit guides, Tiger is always with her, sitting beside her grinning and wagging her tail. A week after she died, she went to a friend of mine in her dreams and asked Kathy to take care of me. The day will come when in another fuzzy puppy I find her again.

Women have a knowledge of the oneness of life, and they use that oneness to merge or link with other Be-ings, to share living with them. These are human or animal, and usually others that share closeness, love and emotion together, openness and trust. They can be lifetime links as with Tiger, momentary knowings that happen once, or anything in between. Thoughts sent out by one are received and understood by the other, and words are not needed between them. One is sometimes stronger at sending or receiving than communicating the other way. Thoughts cross all boundaries in their communication—time, space, distance and even death. The ability to send and receive is called telepathy. In its parts, sending is to telepath; receiving is to empath.

Telepathy is a throat chakra, lower spiritual body psychic skill, along with clairaudience (clear hearing). Where the heart center (healing) is the place of feeling oneness, the throat chakra receives others into the self and expresses the self (oneness) to others. The brow chakra, the next level, is knowing what has been received, and is also the place for sending. Therefore, three chakras and aura layers figure in telepathy, the heart, throat and third eye, though the skill is listed at the throat. Beginning even closer to the physical body, the thought-forms sent in telepathy are made at the solar plexus and third eye level. Transmitted outward they travel through the mental to the spiritual body; transmitted inward, they travel through the mental and emotional bodies to the etheric double and dense physical levels.

The throat center is the place of physical and psychic hearing, the clear hearing of clairaudience. In this receiving skill, a "voice" known or unknown transmits information and messages the woman could not otherwise have heard. The information can be a warning, a piece of knowing about the self or someone else, a direction, inspiration or reassurance. At the throat center, women receive and "hear" others, in physical and nonphysical ways; they open to others with trust. Once the throat center is active, and emotions held in the self are opened, expression happens and creativity takes place. A reaching out to share the self with others, every form of creativity from speech, music and acting to writing and dance occur. The throat chakra and lower spiritual aura level are the connecting point between heart center feeling and third eye knowing. Telepathy, clairaudience and creative expression are located at this level, where oneness with the self and others meets.

Along with receiving others and sending from the self, the throat chakra and lower spiritual aura level are the place of listening to yourself. Being in tune with the self and accepting what your inner self tells you is a major part of throat center psychic ability. For telepathy to happen, not only must the messages from others be received, but they have to be re-cognized and accepted, given validation, listened to. In sending, not only is a message formulated, but there has to be acceptance in the self of the process. Listening to the self also includes accepting intuition, following hunches, validating what you know. Knowing is a third eye skill, and skills are transmitted from their specializing chakra through each layer in turn to the physical body. In the throat chakra, knowing is validated and transmitted to the heart. In the heart chakra, feeling is transmitted upward to the throat and given acceptance and expression. The self-love of the heart is accepted and validated at the throat, as is oneness with others and all life.

Emotions, the belly chakra and astral body level, are also involved in telepathy. Messages that matter, that come from someone loved, are the most likely to be received telepathically or sent. Most telepathy occurs between women who care about each other, have deep emotional ties, and know each other well. The link between mothers and children is a classic one, and between lovers. People with karmic connections, soul mates or otherwise, often share a telepathic link, and women often share links with animals. In any psychic skill, this emotional connection operates. When something matters, is emotionally powerful and important, the information is most effectively transmitted.

Sending your thoughts outward to another is telepathy, and the receiving portion, hearing thoughts and messages from others, is called empathy. Many healers are empaths, receiving others and understanding, knowing how and what they feel. Some women absorb the feelings and thoughts from others around them, bringing themselves unease and disturbance until they understand what's going on. Some of this is clairsentience, the absorption of others' emotions, while some is empathy, the absorption of feelings and thoughts. Much telepathic reception involves the receiving of feelings and emotions as well as thoughts, and the two skills are difficult to separate.

Some women who are empathic, including myself, have difficulty being in crowds—the confusion of receiving so many impressions of others' thoughts, emotions, feelings and physical states is overwhelming. Surrounding yourself with an aura of blue or gold light helps to screen the impressions, as does wearing a fluorite gemstone. When re-turning from a crowd situation where the impressions received are an upset, go into the meditative state and clear the throat chakra. In some kinds of crowds or groups, as in groups of friends, the influence of being empathic is positive and a mood-raiser. A woman who enters such a situation feeling down or indifferent absorbs the thought-forms and impressions around her and leaves feeling good.

Telepathy/empathy begins with thought-forms, that energy from the lower mental body that radiates outward from it, to have effect on the auras of the self and others. Thoughts travel as vibration and if they are thoughts of someone, the vibrations reach her emotional and mental bodies and affect her.[2] Thoughts with enough emotional strength reach her, transmitting to her etheric double and physical brain. Thought-forms of less emotion or not of someone else gradually fade, their energy exhausted with nowhere to go. Thoughts of the self remain close to the self, affecting things like health and emotional state. If a woman is receptive to someone, she is likelier to receive her thought-forms than those of someone she does not like or isn't open to. Like also seeks like in thought-forms, and similar ideas attract together. A woman in a relaxed, meditative state is likelier to receive thought-forms and to send them effectively; thought-forms can be consciously directed.

In describing what happens in the aura bodies, there are three kinds of thought-form transference. Thoughts transmit between two women's etheric bodies, two women's emotional bodies, or between two women's mental bodies.[3] In the first type, mental body thought passes from the mental to the emotional body, then to the etheric double and finally to the physical brain. Physical brain electrical thought vibrations then pass to reach another's brain. The woman receiving accepts these thoughts in her physical brain, transmits them into her etheric double, emotional body, then mental body aura. The lower mental body is the conscious mind, and the thought is understood and received. This is the least-evolved method of telepathy, not involving the spiritual body.

The second form of transference involves thought-forms passing from emotional body to emotional body, and this is the place of clairsentience, clear feeling. The woman transmitting sends emotions, and the woman receiving feels them, rather than hearing words or ideas. A woman entering a room where someone is depressed suddenly becomes depressed. She may not know why it's happened or where it's coming from, or even think to analyze it. She suddenly is depressed, having accepted another's feelings as her own. Healers who absorb others' symptoms experience this, and it can hurt them. Protect from it by the grounding cord and casting an aura of clear, gold or blue light around you, or using such gemstones as amber, tiger's eye or fluorite.

Occasionally in this form of telepathy/empathy link, someone can sap the energy of another. This virtually always happens unconsciously and unintentionally. Shafica Karagulla describes it:

> I made the discovery accidentally when a sensitive described an incident to me during a social gathering. One of the people there, for no apparent reason, got up and left abruptly. I commented on it to the sensitive, who said to me, 'Couldn't you see what was happening?' Since I couldn't she told me that one of the guests had been sapping the energy of the person. She saw it and stopped it by trying to help the person block the sapping. It took me two years to verify that what the sensitive said was correct.
>
> Since then I have discovered that energy can be pulled through the solar plexus, the eyes, and the voice. Distance doesn't matter. Many people have written to me saying that this was valuable information in helping them to understand themselves and their problems with other people.
>
> What kind of people are energy sappers? Self-centered people. Their flow of energy is always inward, not outward. They're takers, not givers . . . Instead of taking from nature and giving to life, which will replenish them automatically,

they want to take predigested energy from someone else for their own use.[4]

This is a negative form of emotion to emotion telepathy, but there are positive forms, as well. What happens between a fine actress or singer and her audience is also emotional telepathy:

> When an . . . actress is performing before an audience, the emotional field of the actor seems to glow and expand and extend outward until it includes the whole audience. The emotional fields of the audience blend with the vastly extended field of the performer, and what might be called a unified emotional field results for the duration of the performance.
>
> When the performance is over, the clapping of the audience breaks the unified field, and each person is seen by the psychic as again functioning within her own separated emotional field. If the performer is not able to achieve this unified field, she does not reach her audience, and they will say the performance was mediocre or poor. All good performers are able to do this.[5]

In any form of telepathy, the transmission of thoughts is stronger, and is made possible, by the emotional content. If there is no emotion, there is likely no telepathy or empathy.

In the third type of telepathy, the thought transference is from mental body to mental body, with reception sent from the mental body to the spiritual levels. This is the place of instantaneous thought-form transmission and reception at any distance, and where telepathy/empathy links can be consciously created. In transmission through the etheric, thoughts are received at random and usually from nearby people; the transmission and reception are uncontrolled. In mental body telepathy, with reception through the throat chakra (lower spiritual body), and transmission through the third eye (middle spiritual), transmission comes from any distance and is received. It can be asked for in the alpha meditative state successfully, and two women can plan its happening.

These three types or stages of thought transmission are an evolutionary process in women's psychic development and awareness. Etheric body transmission happens first, and the woman first realizing that telepathy is happening—that she is "hearing others' thoughts" may scare her. If two women with affinity for each other are in proximity to each other, this type of telepathy occurs. Intensive emotion is not needed, or intensive emotional links to each other. The telepathy seems to happen only when the two are in the same building or room, and stops when one or the other is not present. Neither woman is asking for the event, but both are aware of it.

When I worked in the restaurant with Dee, this happened frequently. I enjoyed it but it frightened her at first, became more comfortable to her as time passed and we continued to work together. She came to accept it and use it, as I did. The examples were routine ones. I would hear her telling me to come to the kitchen, and when I did she would be standing there with something for me to do, a meal ready or a message. She didn't have to call me in words, I knew she wanted me. In one case, it was a warning to watch a slippery place on the floor; I had gone to the basement and she was upstairs. She would remind me of things forgotten and offer all sorts of friendly advice. She seemed to be a stronger telepath, and I a stronger receiver/empath in these events. The roles occasionally reversed, with my calling her mentally from the other end of the building—once she had called a cab and it was there. In every case I was aware of who was calling me, why, and what she was saying. When it happened that she was receiving me, she was aware that it was me and heard me in words. Once either of us left the restaurant, the link was ended. It always surprised her that when she thought about me, I would come. We are very different women, different ages, backgrounds and lives, but the affection, respect and telepathy between us was strong.

Telepathy from emotional body to emotional body has been explained in Shafica Karagulla's paragraphs. Everyone has experienced a creative performance and become fully involved in it, enthralled with it or with the woman performing. The magick of a play or musical performance, any sort of performance, is one of the joys of Be-ing. Some performers are aware of the aura explanation for what happens, but most work toward it on other levels. The stage charisma of Odetta or Judy Garland, Rhiannon or Lucy Blue Tremblay are examples. Both performer and woman in the audience open to telepath and receive the energy and thought-forms, and the magick happens. They are one aura, one Be-ing for the moment of the performance, and the memory of that oneness retains the glow after. The thought-form created is retained.

Oneness with animals is usually on this emotional body level of thought-transference. In receiving from a dog or other animal, the woman picks up impressions, feelings, emotions more often than clear words. With Tiger there was much more, and this can happen, but most empathy with animals is a linking into feelings. Tiger has a daughter, Dusty. Dusty has a rose colored aura and is made of pure love and joy, but when I try to link with her I rarely pick up words. She is a total air-head, but all love. This type of telepathy with animals is emotional-body based, and is frequent. Leonie's ability to draw wild animals to her as a child is an example of this. The link is emotional rather than intellectual, and the transmission is in feelings.

Mental body to mental body telepathy is the place where women hear each other at any distance, and in clear words and feelings received through the throat chakra. When two women are psychically linked, something both have to be open to, they have a mental and emotional bond that tells each at all times what's happening to the other. If one is in danger or emotionally upset, the other knows it. Sometimes this is a one-way transmission, one woman being able to send and the other to receive, but not working the other way. Such bonds are by choice; if one woman refuses it, the transmission is not received or is not sent. Clear messages come through, and the telepathy can be consciously or unconsciously created.

In an unconscious telepathic transmission, I have a friend who is a performer, and on the day of her performances I can become highly aware of her emotional state and stagefright. She is telepathing, not consciously and probably not directly to me, but I receive her. In the example of a conscious telepathic transmission, a woman asks her roommate to bring home a quart of milk, and comes home to find she has done it. Or a woman asks her friend to call, telepathically, and the friend phones her that day. Many "coincidences," apparitions and clairvoyant events are telepathic, consciously sent or not. Psychic healing is an example of consciously created and sent thought-forms and telepathy.

The woman who sends a thought-form/telepathic message does so by visualization and creating a thought-form, an image of emotional power. When she does this consciously, she uses the same forms of awareness as in manifesting or healing, creating carefully what she wants to happen. If that thought-form is to be directed at a particular woman, she visualizes that woman and sees or hears her thought-form message reaching her. The woman who receives is open to impressions and open to the woman sending. If she is not, she does not hear her message, whether it is aimed at her or not. She is able to sort out the message of her friend from other impressions, from her own inner voice and stream of consciousness, and from the general din of impressions that surrounds her continually in everyday life. The receiver/empath knows who is sending the message, hears it, and accepts it into her self.

While sending is from the mental body in this form of telepathy, receiving telepathic transmissions happens in the throat chakra, the lower spiritual body. This aura level is the Crone level of women's psychic knowing. The three spiritual body levels are the Maiden, Mother and Crone, and the Crone at the throat center is the place of experience and ancient wisdom. Telepathy is an ancient tool, and as the Age of Aquarius opens, this form of communication begins to take on greater emphasis again. It's a goal to work for, and a skill that women in women's spirituality are dis-covering and using. As development increases, a woman moves from etheric to emotional to mental forms of telepathy, until in the third type she learns conscious control of her thought-forms as a means of communication. In this type of telepathy, sender and receiver become psychically advanced.

Russian scientists experimenting with telepathy/empathy have sent messages thousands of miles to have them correctly received. They have sent the information in words, numbers, visual pictures and in feeling sensations (a glass of warm tea held in the hand). They have put subjects into hypnotic trance from a distance, sometimes again and again, and often without warning her it would happen. In one experiment, a woman named Olya was hypnotized into sleep, and awakened by telepathy in six of eleven attempts.[6] Work on telepathic communication has been done with both Russian and American astronauts. The Russians claim success, but the Americans refuse to comment.

Research in Russia finds that people who are deaf make the best telepathic senders—they have learned precisely and thoroughly how to visualize, have trained that skill to perfection.[7] In working with telepathy, the Russians gain the best results by asking the sender to visualize what she is sending, and then to visualize the woman receiving it. The receiver is less emphasized in these experiments—the sender is considered to be the psychic—but without the empath's receptivity and psychic hearing (not physical hearing, she can be physically deaf), no telepathy takes place. As in psychic healing, which uses telepathy as its medium, both women are necessary to complete the circle and both are psychics. It's interesting to note that in the Russian experiments, men are always the senders and women the receivers. Are women more receptive/empathic than men? More than likely. But women are also good visualizers and senders, and are telepaths.

Telepathy/empathy links with animals are frequent. Part of it is the issue of oneness with all life, the woman's acceptance of what the animal wants to say. Eileen Garrett opening this chapter writes of this oneness extending to plants as well. Leonie in Chapter One wrote about the deer who came to nuzzle her as a child, and a moth that was there for several nights. I have always been able to converse with animals, and thought everyone could, but Tiger is my fondest example. Women who can open to, accept and be empathic with animals find that animals come to them, trust them and give them much in return.

Animals have the ability to know who is beneficial to them and who is not. Dogs know to hide when the dog catcher's truck is in the neighborhood, especially if they've ever been caught. As Eileen Garrett commented, the mouse knows when the hawk is near. Animals also know when someone is there who accepts and loves them, and who accepts her oneness with them. In women's spirituality, all that lives is seen as a part of Goddess, from a blade of grass to a woman, and women in this thinking often have animal stories to tell.

J. Allen Boone writes of this, dis-covering it through the teaching of Strongheart, a celebrity German Shepherd. Once the principles were understood, the simple idea that animals, birds, reptiles and even insects respond to love, it opened whole worlds. Boone is a man for whom such ideas were a revelation; women already know that all life is one. In the wiccan rede that "what you send out comes back to you," send out thoughts of love to another living Be-ing and watch that Be-ing respond. In his book, *Kinship With All Life*, Boone put it to practice with snakes, horses, skunks, worms, and even a housefly. Strongheart taught him well:

> When I was willing and ready to be taught by a dog, Strongheart shared precious wisdom with me, wonderful secrets having to do with the great dog art of living abundantly and happily in the present tense regardless of circumstances.
>
> Strongheart broke me of the bad habit of mentally looking down my nose at other living entities and other forms of life as inferior, limited or unrelated to me.
>
> Out of this teaching there developed a mental bridge, so to speak, between us. It was a bridge for two-way, not one-directional, thought traffic. A bridge extending from where I appeared to be operating as 'a human' to where Strongheart seemed to be functioning as 'a dog.' With this invisible bridge connecting us, it was possible for my thoughts freely to cross over into his thinking areas and for his thoughts freely to cross over into mine. But there was a strict obligation in this; I had to learn never to permit anything but my best thoughts to cross our bridge in his direction; and he, I know, never allowed anything but his best thoughts to come across to mine.[8]

The rest of patriarchy should hear about this!

Boone describes Grace Wiley, a herpetologist (snake specialist) and her ability to tame wild poisonous snakes into pets. She telepaths to these dangerous creatures her love, respect, caring and admiration and the snakes respond. Here is a session of this:

> After a while you would notice a marked change in the snake's attitude. The fast rattling of its tail was slowing down. Its head, which had been glaring in all directions at a fast, nervous tempo, was steadying itself in the direction of Miss Wiley, even though it could not clearly distinguish the motionless woman from the motionless wall behind her...
>
> As Miss Wiley continued her reassuring talk, but now in low, soft vocal tones... You would see the big snake slowly uncoil and cautiously stretch itself the full length of the table, finally resting its head within inches of where Miss Wiley was standing. Then the first physical movement by Miss Wiley as she reached across and began gently stroking the snake's back...
>
> At this precise moment in the gentling process, another 'deadly poisonous snake' had become a member in good standing of the Zoo for Happiness.[9]

Most women have more access to cats, dogs and the occasional forest creature than to poisonous snakes, but the process is the same.

One example of this is the cat, Fagin. He paid little attention to most people, but wanted to be held by me anytime I was with him. When I held him and reached in, he presented me with a touch as soft as moth wings in his mind, and paws that reached up to hug around my neck. His owners, not particularly liking me, decided that he must be getting senile to act like that. Fagin himself said no, he was lonely.

On another occasion, traveling in a national park, I was with a friend who wanted to stop and take pictures. Getting out of the car and wandering, I came upon a small mule deer, a young two point buck, and walked right up to him feeding oak leaves. The deer and I stared at each other, and gingerly I reached out to touch him, put my arm around his neck. He held still. I stroked him, then feeling my friend come back, returned to the car. There I was given a lecture about approaching wild animals—"Didn't you see the doe and fawn there? He could've turned and pounded you to death with his hoofs." I had thought these were "tourist deer," but was told otherwise. Concentrating telepathically on sending love to the buck, I never noticed the rest of the family behind him.

A home I visited in Indianapolis had cockatiels, tropical birds free to fly, a mating pair and a nest of four fledglings. The adults and young came and settled on my hand and shoulder, with no hesitation in the least. Said Ida who raised them, "They know they have nothing to fear here. This is a house of love."

In a channeling session, Gail Fairfield asked Nadal about animals:

> Well, it is a very interesting question—who is the teacher in those situations? Who is the wise one? ... Spirits sometimes choose to have experiences as human beings and sometimes as animals and sometimes even as trees or

flowers. And so even you can do an experiment if you allow your consciousness sometime to feel part of a tree or a flower or a cat—then you know what the experience is like of letting your spirit, or having your spirit inhabit a different form of being than human. It is not that the lower spirits do come as animals or trees and the higher spirits as human beings. There is no such thing as lower and higher spirits—they just are. It's about the choice of what kind of experience you want to have. And so, usually the spirit that is part of the cat, or the dog, or the bird, or whatever, or the squirrel outside, usually that spirit is here to have some kinds of experiences and to learn some things just as you are and if your paths cross each other and you interact with each other, then you are teaching each other just as surely as when you interact with another human being, and so these relationships are to be treasured as well, and acknowledged.[10]

Women write about their experiences with telepathy, oneness and communication with other lives. There were lots of animal stories, along with the human ones, and some of these start the telling. Mimi writes about Lady, before the big German Shepherd became the "ghost" of Chapters Four and Six:

She would amaze me when she scolded me if she thought I was doing something dangerous. She would bark when I went up on the ladder to repair something. She barked noisily when I used the lawnmower telling me it was dangerous. She would really scold me when I used the electric saw to cut a few pieces of wood, or cut unwanted branches off a tree. I would talk to her like a friend and we understood each other. Sometimes it was my turn to scold her when she made deep holes in the lawn or my garden. A big dog has big feet so the holes were unsightly. She would look at me and let me know that she too had some rights, she liked the cool soil under the grass and under the bushes, and I had better put up with it. Well, no way was I going to argue with her. I knew that and so did she, and I respected a force greater than mine.

Matriarch of the neighborhood, Lady remained there after she died, just to keep her people in line and safe. Mimi says, "Not all animals are telepathic. They vary as do human beings."

Lynn has rapport with wild things:

You asked about 'rapport with animals,' which is something I've always taken for granted. For example, I find it simple to win the affection of a supposedly vicious dog. Injured animals quietly trust me . . . Among these were several wild animals and birds. Once I found a hawk with a badly injured wing from a gunshot wound. I talked to it and stroked it, and the bird allowed me to handle it. It perched quietly on my fist and allowed me to restrain its damaged wing, 'hood' it with a towel, and drive it to the university veterinary school. It turned out to be a rare species, so I was doubly happy to know it had trusted me to help it.

Rebecca Crystal tried conscious telepathy with a nest of bees, and it worked:

My grandmother was living with my family and she was senile. She loved to go outside but there was a bee's nest right by the door. It was decided that was too dangerous and a date was set to kill the bees. I went to the backyard and explained what was going to occur if they didn't leave. I sent a picture of flames and destruction. I told them when it would happen. To my surprise, they left! Since then I have been able to talk to bees, but not to flies.

There were several dog stories, and this is Ana's:

When I was a child I had a deep rapport with one particular dog. She would come when I called mentally and do things that I wanted her to do as I thought them. She was a Redbone Hound. I took her with me everywhere. I lived in Maine at the time.

I remember that when I begged my father to camp out and 'live off the land' he reluctantly agreed to let me stay, provided the dog was with me, (which she always was). She and I were left (years later I learned that my uncle and father were shouting distance away) to go through my fast for vision, my first vision quest. I was to stay out for three days with my water and berries if I really needed them. One day was all I could stand and I went to nearby raspberry bushes for a feast. I suddenly could 'see' a bear but could not really see one— and I climbed a tree. The dog, Freckles, started barking like crazy. There was a female bear and cub about twenty yards away. The dog made the bear chase her; she doubled back after leading the bear away. My conclusion is that the dog telepathed to me 'danger, a bear.' My father believes that happened, that the dog sent a message to me, since I could not explain why I would spend an entire day in the tree waiting for the dog's return.

Chris writes about Buffy, her familiar and teacher, and their trips to the woods on Full Moons:

Oh, she loved those excursions. So did I. We were like Diana and her hound. Buffy would lead me around through those thick woods. She'd flush out rabbits and run them right in front of me and I learned from her to run both with the hare and the hounds. I also learned a lot just from observing her natural doggy behavior. She was a very successful dog, unusually intelligent and so forth, the sort of dog that other dogs always defer to. As a dog, she was far in advance of me, as a human being. Anyway, she taught me a lot.

Maggie is not an "animal person" but has a rapport with animals nonetheless, and has since childhood. Like Leonie, wild animals approach her:

As to animals, I seem to be completely unafraid of them, even in situations where common sense tells me (or might tell me) I should be. When I was a child I played with snakes, would walk up to a snarling dog. I certainly don't 'love animals' in any general (or sentimental) sense, but I feel connected to them. I also find I am approached by wild animals on my walks in the woods—deer, rabbit, squirrel, etc., and birds. I feel plants and trees as individuals and talk to them. I also listen to what they are saying and feeling.

I find as I write about plants and animals that this is a very private thing I am sharing here, and that I don't want to talk about it at length. I guess I have to protect that.

All of these animal stories are not to forget telepathy with humans. Women are highly telepathic and highly empathic. Where the emotional link is strong, women's telepathic links follow, and women have the gift of re-cognizing and using their emotions. Ana and the women of her family have carried a psychic link over several generations, from her grandmother through to her granddaughter.

> In my family it is accepted that we 'link' together. As a child, my mother and grandmother (we all lived in the same household) could tell whenever I was hurt long before I got home with my injury(s). I was knocked out around four years of age by a fall—my grandmother found me within minutes with no real search. She knew where to look.

She could communicate with her mother or grandmother without speech, and also her dog. She continues the link with her mother today, whom she diagnosed psychically for breast cancer.

> I also communicate with my daughter and granddaughter—they have no phone but will call me whenever I think about them doing so.
> I can send as well as receive messages. They are strongest between those I have a close bond to. My family members, although some can receive, they do not send. My abilities are in proportion to my efforts to fine-tune and use them. I meditate and use altered states to retain my own harmony and grounding essential so as not to be bombarded with too much data. I use some protection in isolation now.

Ana's small granddaughter is psychic, and Ana is training her. Ana's grandmother taught Ana,

> Because you always train those who have natural ability and aptitude. I plan on training my granddaughter who is now three years old as she grows, just as I was trained, provided she wants to learn . . . I practice her telepathic abilities with 'games.' I visualize an object and she guesses what it is, or a color or a word. Then we reverse roles and she is quite good at this, with very high scores for 'hits.'

How many of us wished for a grandmother like this, a healer and medicine woman of wisdom and beauty.

Leonie writes about telepathy experiences as a child. She is an empath, a receiver:

> I remember once, when I was about ten, walking with my father down a street in town. We ran into an acquaintance of his and they had a conversation about a new business the man had just opened. When he left, I turned to my father and said, 'Well, Dad, are you going to do it?' 'Do what?' he asked. 'Why, invest, the way he wants you to,' I said. He thought it was clever of me to figure it out. But I didn't; I had actually heard the man thinking it while he and my father were talking. I even knew how much he wanted to talk my dad into investing.
> I . . . was a 'wise guy' kid, or so my teachers thought. Some seemed to think I had stolen their notes or books, or that I was cheating on tests . . . I couldn't spell, but I could paraphrase what I had heard them thinking, or 'know' the answer to a math problem without doing the work. Sometimes I really didn't know where the answer came from—it was just there.
> One day, when I was about twelve, I woke up one morning, seeing things

through the eyes of someone else—a boy I knew from school. He was feeling very ill—in fact he had the flu and wouldn't be back at school for three days. I had seen him a day or so earlier (he wasn't in my class, so I didn't necessarily see him every day). I could see his room, the furniture, and I could also feel his nausea. When I got to school that day, he wasn't there. He was back on the fourth day, saying he'd had the flu.

Leonie and her mother also have a link, her mother knowing when Leonie is in trouble, regardless of distances. Many women who are psychics come from psychic families; the ability seems handed down from mother to daughter. The link also works from her mother to Leonie, now that Leonie is an adult.

I have also had empathic/telepathic experiences with my mother. Some months ago, I woke up knowing she was ill because I could actually 'feel' a phantom pain in my intestines that I knew was not mine. I 'knew' it was my mother's pain, and called her to find that she had had an attack of diverticulitis during the night.

She had this link also with her lover. Feeling others' pain as one's own is clairsentience.

In another mother and child link, Judy describes this experience:

When my son was eighteen months old, he was hospitalized. The hospital pediatric unit was across the street from my office in the hospital's accounting department. He was being fed intravenously with a tube in his head. His hands and feet were held still by elastic bandage restraints so he could not remove the tube.

While working, I was overcome by a sense of urgency and danger to the boy. I left my desk and ran across the street to his room. When I got to the bed, I found him strangling and already turning blue. He had managed to pull one restraint loose (on his arm) and had wrapped it around his neck. As he struggled, the restraint tightened around his neck, choking him. I called a nurse after unwrapping his neck and she re-secured the restraint.

My psychic experiences are part of my daily life and I think a part of many lives.

Carol has a link with her mother, and directly or indirectly with her father, as well.

My mom and dad moved to Florida. I wrote to them two to three times a week for almost twenty years. I would answer one of my mom's letters and be asking her questions and our letters would be crossing in the mail. She would be answering my questions to my letter and vice versa.

My father and I were also close enough for me to pick up the phone—call down there and ask my mom when did he go in the hospital or when did he get sick? She would never let me know in her letters if they weren't well, because she didn't want me to worry. I just knew.

Pat grew up in a psychic family, and shares these stories:

I grew up Catholic, in a strongly traditional Irish family with a mother who we now realize is highly psychic. My sisters and I—one is so psychic that friends in California call on her to exorcise ghosts and suchlike—used to have a game with Mom. We'd come home and all think about something for dinner, chicken, say. Mom would be busy making, oh, say hamburger. (This game is easy if you're poor and have few choices). Sometime before dinner she'd sigh, look distressed and say, "Gee, I wish I was making you chicken."

Mom has such incredible tracking ability with her kids—I don't know how far beyond them this extends—that we refuse to play Trivial Pursuit with her. If we are on the other team and we steal a peek at the answer, it will suddenly flood into Mom's mind. It's damn frustrating. I remember one time, end of the game, the question was 'how many yards are there in a Canadian football field?' We were sure to win—Mom knows nothing about sports—and somebody looked. Mom gets this glassy look and says, '110? Not 110? A statement of fact.

I was with my sister in California once and we were in a fairly serious car accident. When we got home from the hospital, the phone was ringing. Of course, Mom. We lied, said everything was alright. 'Well, why did I feel I should call you?' As if there had to be a reason.

Consider that this woman has worked for more than a decade as the parish secretary and is a devout Catholic. If you told her she was psychic she'd get very embarrassed. Yet she is—at least as far as her kids go. She thinks this is just normal motherly behavior—tracking your kids' actions 3000 miles away. She sees nothing unusual about it at all.

I think that's a very common phenomenon: a woman who is deeply psychic but doesn't experience it with Twilight Zone music playing in the background. It's just a fact of life. Isn't every woman connected to her kids? Isn't it just natural? Nothing spooky or strange about it at all.

I also think this is very healthy and has allowed women's psychic skills to continue through generations of the Enlightenment's divorce between mind and body. It has helped me greatly to know that my mother, although she would wince at my writing these words, is a psychic as I am—and that I am as psychic as my mother. It is a bond and a source of strength.

As we were growing up, we sisters didn't ever think of ourselves as unusual or different from others in this way. We just knew there were differences. It was only after I became an adult that I realized what a pool of psychic talent our family represented. We make jokes when we make long distance phone calls, 'I knew you were going to call tonight, mom, but I thought I'd save you some money,' or more usually, 'Hi Mom, I was waiting for you to call. I figured I'd hold out and make you pay.' It's a standing family jest, this kind of phone trickery, trying to get someone else to eat the phone bill. These comments also show you just how casually psychic talent is taken by women of the family.

When you write about women having their psychism beaten out of them, I thank the Goddess for my mother and her strong matriarchal hand in this area. We were never discouraged in any way I can remember—how else would the five of us have come out as we did?—though we were never particularly encouraged, either. Simply, nothing much was made of it. It was like telling stories or telling jokes—something we all do with aplomb. It was a fact of family life.

Had I been discouraged from using this talent, I think life would have been harder than it has been. When I was a young woman I had intense psychic experiences, so intense I would frequently not leave my room for days, just lie there in a sort of trance and watch the spheres break open. I didn't try to tell anyone about these experiences. I would tell Mom I 'didn't feel well,' and she'd leave me alone. There was no particular pressure to say what was going on—although Mom, psychic as she is, surely knew—but no punishment either.

Instead, I could stay in my room and occasionally be brought toast and tea, and lie there and watch things happen.

Pat's last story in her letter is clairvoyance, "watching the spheres break open." More on clairvoyance in the next two chapters.

While Pat and the women of her family both send and receive, some women are stronger at one or the other, or send and receive alternately at different times. Diane describes telepathy, sending, which is a third eye skill, and receiving, which comes from the throat chakra:

Occasionally people know when I'm on the phone or they'll be looking for me and find me. When asked how they knew it was me, they just shrug and say, 'I dunno.' Or as two friends have put it, 'You let me know.' They say they can't do this with everyone, just with me. Often they will say they 'know exactly what I am thinking.' This is sometimes aggravating, since I can't tell what they are thinking, except generally by body signals and facial expressions. I've asked, and generally they don't read my body signals.

On Full Moons, instead of sending, Diane receives:

Around this time I know who's on the phone, if anyone is in any kind of trouble—emotional, physical or monetary—and needs a listening ear. I pick up upon people who are interested in magic, strangers out of the blue. I seem to be at the right place at the right time.

Karen and her circle concentrated on receiving chocolate chip cookies—and got them:

I don't recall why, but we started concentrating on getting one member's roommate to bring us some cookies (chocolate chip, I believe) and milk. Well, her roommate had the cookies all right, but we didn't find out about that until the meeting had ended and we were getting ready to leave. She hadn't wanted to disturb us. Of course, we did get to share in what was left of the cookies!

Karen has a link with her lover, and this was one of their experiences:

A few years ago, I had to attend a family wedding. Since I wasn't out to my father's side of the family, I drove to my hometown for the wedding, while my lover stayed at our apartment. I spent most of my time during the ceremony being pissed off that my stepsister and her partner could have such a public and legal ceremony, while my lover and I couldn't. This was on Friday afternoon. When I got home on Sunday, my lover asked me if there had been anything wrong on Friday, about 5 PM. Apparently the anger I felt at the wedding had gotten channeled into our link and woke her up from the nap she had been taking then.

Some things are important to note here: Karen's strong emotion and her lover's relaxed state of mind, in or near sleep. These and their closeness, their openness to each other, made Karen's telepathy powerful and her lover able to receive it.

A few of the women writing to me described clairsentient (clear feeling) reactions, and others' clairaudience (clear hearing). The first is feeling others as oneself, and the second is hearing others' messages in words. The first is emotional body telepathy, and the second is mental body transmission. Examples of each are given here, and Leonie's feeling her mother's pain is also an example. Irene describes clairsentience, and her ability to receive from others:

> I don't see things about the person, I don't even think about them in the sense of mentally forming a thought—it just happens. I get a strong feeling about the person—if they are troubled, I feel troubled. If they are sad, happy, hurt or whatever, I 'feel' it. If they are insincere or selfish, I 'feel' it, too and automatically stay away from that person. I've never gotten a ticket because I've always felt there was a police car and slowed down. Again, it's not something I decide I'm going to do—it just happens. My fourth grade teacher, a woman (I do feel their thoughts easier), told me I was very empathetic. At the time I really didn't understand what this meant. Since then I've learned. If a woman confides in me, I feel with her. It's just the same as if it happened to me.

Maggie, looking at her childhood, sees her ability to sense negative vibrations as her only psychic ability then:

> I could tell when something very painful or destructive had happened in a house or in a location by the horror and grief that would rise in me. This I always feel and have felt all through my life.

Louise had this clairaudient experience, probably prompted by her uncle's ability to telepath, and hers to receive. Again, they are two people who are emotionally close.

> One day—I don't recall if it was day time or night—my friend and I had been talking together. We were standing in the bedroom, hugging each other . . . All of a sudden I heard something coming from inside of me. Not a voice, per se, of someone talking to me, but rather just something inside me that kept saying: 'I'm dying . . . don't you know I'm dying?' The voice/feeling kept saying that phrase over and over, and it was so strong and distressing I finally moved my head from where it was resting on my companion's breast. She asked me what was wrong, and all I could tell her was that I kept hearing this voice or something saying, 'I'm dying . . . don't you know I'm dying?' I told her I knew *I* wasn't sick, or heavens, dying so I didn't know why I kept hearing or feeling these words. Was *she* sick, and hadn't told me about it? She assured me she wasn't.

Almost three years later, Louise was visiting her grandmother and

> One of my uncles, a Franciscan priest came to visit a day or two after I arrived, and his first words to me were: 'I was dying . . . didn't you know I was dying? I kept trying to tell you. Didn't you hear me?' His words just kept coming as he told me how he had almost died, had had a triple by-pass surgery . . . He was operated on in New York, and yes it all happened at the time I was in that small town outside of Syracuse. We hadn't kept in touch with each other, and I had no idea he was in New York. When he was getting ready to go into surgery, he told me he kept saying to himself: 'I'm dying . . . don't you know I'm dying,' trying to send a message to me. We always felt close—he being a Franciscan friar, and me

having been in the cloister for seven years as a Franciscan Poor Clare contemplative nun. He had helped me get through some difficult adolescent years, and he was with me and my family when I entered the cloister . . .

Louise's mother also received a clairaudient experience with her uncle, but knew where it was coming from.

> My mother and I were doing something in the kitchen, when she suddenly said, very quietly, 'Louise, go and open the door. Your uncle, Father Benedict, is here.' I stopped what I was doing, and told her I didn't hear anyone at the door. 'Did he write and say he was coming?' I asked her. 'I didn't know he was coming to visit?' . . . She told me he hadn't written, but that he was coming, and to open the door. Sure enough . . . I heard the downstairs door open, and a familiar voice was asking if anyone was home. I opened the upstairs door and there he was.

Louise traces her psychic ability through her mother and her grandmother.

Bonnie had this clairaudient incident, a warning of danger:

> I worked in the summer of 1985 at the Mount Hope Winery, doing art for their Renaissance Fair. My 'studio' was the second floor of a huge old barn. This is a Pennsylvania Dutch type barn, so one side has dirt up to the second story for loading vehicles to go up there. It has bay doors at the top, but it was raining, so I only had the regular door open.
>
> Abruptly, it started to thunderstorm and rain. I have *never*, even in a hurricane, seen rain that hard and that heavy. It was awesome, and so was the thunderstorm. Usually they don't last long, but this one went on for two hours without slacking.
>
> I was happily painting signs in the waterfall roar of the rain on the barn's metal roof, when suddenly I heard a far away voice yell, 'Bonnie, get out of the barn.' I blinked and it 'shouted' the same thing. It was directional, I only heard it in my right ear. It sounded far away and slightly behind me, and it sounded like *me*.
>
> I thought lightning was going to strike the barn, but that unbelievable *rain* was outside (words just don't conjure up the *force* of it). No umbrella could have stood it. There was no *way* I was going out of that barn. So I did what I could and put my chair right next to the door, ready to jump out.
>
> Then my chair actually vibrated on the floor. The whole barn shook. Had I been standing, I'd have been knocked over. I thought 'Wow! We had an earthquake!' Driving home after work, I passed through a town three or four miles away. Houses and trees were knocked down. A *tornado* had gone through. It must have just been coming down when it hit my barn.

Bonnie luckily wasn't hurt—but she was warned.

In one last experience, Sharon, with her ability to perceive discarnate entities, had this clairaudient incident of someone calling her name:

> At age eighteen, while sleeping overnight in another aunt's home, a male voice whispered directly into my ear, 'Sharon?' I leaped off the bed and turned on a lamp. I had my aunt up half the night searching for the entity who called my name.

This happened again when I was twenty-one years old. My infant daughter slept while I folded clothing in the bedroom. It was early afternoon. A male voice called, 'Sharon?' . . . No one was there.

When our name is called like this by an invisible entity, should we answer? Should we run?

The experience is clairaudience without a manifesting, and possibly a spirit guide. No experience related to me by women has ever brought harm to them, no "ghost" or discarnate entity.

From the number of letters I received on telepathic or clairaudient experiences, they are common ones for women to have. The power of thought is immense, creating "coincidences," manifesting objects and visions, directing healing and good health, and connecting women to each other and to other living Be-ings. Telepathic/empathic ability runs in generations of women, linking women together with lines of communication and of love. The ability to communicate with animals is also frequent, and something many women know from earliest childhood. The oneness of all life, re-cognition of Goddess within, connects women with animals and plants, and with other women.

Telepathy and empathy, sending and receiving, can be learned. For most women the skill is there, waiting to be opened and used. The first skill in learning it is the meditative state, and the second is the ability to visualize what you want to happen. If this sounds like psychic healing, it is. Try it first on a Full Moon for added psychic power, and try it first by linking with women everywhere who are also celebrating the Esbat. The power of many minds together at once is very strong.

Enter the meditative state, casting a circle of protection and drawing down the Full Moon into yourself.[11] Do your usual Full Moon ritual, then telepath and receive others:

The woman looks up to the moon, or visualizes her again in her candle. She thinks of how the moon shines on women everywhere, how the Goddess is everywhere, and how women planetwide are invoking and wishing on her tonight. The priestess asks that her heart be open to other women in their full moon rituals, that she feels their presence and knows she is not alone. She visualizes the women she knows personally who have drawn down the moon at this time, sees their faces in her mind, feels them invoking the Goddess as she did, and feels her own pull of love toward women everywhere. Her heart and throat chakras opened by the ritual, she channels the moon-lit energy of her love toward greeting her friends and feels their greetings in return. Quietly and surely, she knows they are there. Then visualizing women everywhere, known and unknown, she sees the thousands of women of the earth who alone and in circles and covens, from Africa to Chicago to Belgium to South America to China, are drawing down the full moon. Radiating love from her heart, she touches them in greeting and feels their love and greetings in return.[12]

This is a powerful exercise in group telepathy, a beginning in sending and receiving. The results will delight and astound you.

In an example of emotional body telepathy, transmit a feeling, rather than an idea. Sit facing another woman, and as both enter the meditative state, become as relaxed and open as possible. Clear your minds of any outside thoughts. Visualize your separate auras, "surrounds" of light that envelop you, and making those auras orange reach out and merge them. Feel each other's Be-ing, then one woman sends a feeling to the other—of joy, love, well-being (nothing negative). Send the feeling for at least a full minute, then separate your auras and withdraw. Notice how the other woman feels, and how it feels to send to her. Ask your partner what she felt. Repeat the exercise, this time reversing roles. The woman who sent the last time receives. Notice how it feels to receive and what you felt. Take turns sending and receiving a few more times, but stop before getting tired.

To re-turn from the exercise, separate your auras completely from each other, then turn the color from orange to clear. Allow the light to fade completely, and come back to the present. Place both palms to the floor, releasing excess energy and any emotion and feeling not your own. This grounding at the end is important. Emotions and the emotional body are located at the belly chakra, and feelings are sent from there. They are received at the throat center, the lower spiritual body. The ability to send and receive emotions grows with practice, but if a woman feels she receives others' emotions too much, she can protect herself with an aura of blue light, or with visualizing her belly chakra partially (never fully) closed.

For mental body telepathy, try this one.[13] Enter the alpha meditative state, becoming fully relaxed and clearing your mind of as many thoughts as possible. Think of someone you would like to call you, someone who calls at least occasionally. Visualize her in her home, see her walk to the telephone and dial your number, imagine the sound of your phone ringing and see yourself picking it up, imagine the two of you talking together. Concentrate on this image, but for no longer than five minutes. Withdraw from the meditative state, and ground as before. Let go of the thought.

If the woman you visualized doesn't call you by the next day (and she probably will), call her. If she doesn't say she was thinking of you and planning to call, I'd be much surprised. If the exercise doesn't work at all, try again, perhaps with someone else. Remember that women have free will and no one has the right to violate that. The woman you first tried may not be open to you, or may not be someone who notices her feelings and thoughts. Always be careful not to violate anyone's free will in these experiments.

In a similar one, seated in a restaurant become as grounded and centered as possible. Take a few deep breaths and close your eyes for a moment to do this. Concentrate on the waitress, asking her to turn around and look at you, and come to your table. This may not happen at the first try, but keep trying and it will. Do it only legitimately, when you need her to come. With practice, this ability to use telepathy to attract someone's attention grows.[14]

For another mental telepathy exercise, arrange with a friend a time and date to contact each other telepathically. At that time, each of you in your homes enter the meditative state. Once there, visualize the other doing the same thing, and open to each other, first sending a message, then listening for one. Concentrate alternately on sending and receiving, allowing at least a couple of minutes for each. When you feel you have both sent and received, leave the meditative state and ground. Be sure to leave enough time to listen and receive. Later check with your partner and compare results and messages. Send emotions, words, a visual picture, or a feeling. You will know when you've received the message.

Enid Hoffman has an exercise for using telepathy/empathy with children. Studies show that children absorb their parents' emotions and feelings, often their fears, and these fears affect their actions and lives. A child's aura does not fully separate from her mother's until nearly adulthood, when she is independent and autonomous on more than the concrete level. Children need reassurance until they are able to understand the adult world.

> Sometimes at the end of the day, we regret some of the transactions between us and our children, and wish we could remedy the negative results from them. Sit quietly, by yourself, at a time when the child is asleep, and beam toward her mind what you feel. You can ask for forgiveness, or just send reassuring thoughts concerning your love. Or you might want to go into the bedroom and look at your child's sleeping face as you transmit your messages of love and reassurance.[15]

Use telepathy to call a child home if you don't know where she is or to tell her at a quiet time what you need her to understand and know. Do this relaxed or asleep, directing your thoughts and words to her and repeating this for several nights, as above. There is influence in these messages for behavior changes. Since the ability to telepath and receive seems hereditary from mother to daughter, chances are good that your child is listening, and hearing every word you say.

In working with animals, even wild ones that don't know you, the process is similar to working with children. Holding physically still and speaking with your mind, tell the animal that you love it, respect it, have caring for it, appreciate it. Send this in images and feelings, as well as in words. If you know the animal's name, use it in directing your thoughts. For a wild animal, emotions and images are more effective; for a domestic one, add words that she knows. Send your love in any way you know how to express love, and mean it. Tell the animal how beautiful she is.

Watch body language to see what effect your messages are having. Grace Wiley and the snake is a good example of this. An animal that lives with you will come from another room at hearing your telepathy, glad you've finally decided to talk with her. I could call Tiger that way, never commanding, but using her name and inviting her to come. An animal is Goddess and your equal—don't order her, ask her. A bit of teasing in the message works for Dusty, who takes much longer and much more concentration to "hear." Telepathy works wherever your pet is, including outdoors. In a crisis however, as on the rare occasions my dogs have gotten loose in the city (Siberians are not reliable for voice commands), my own fear for them blocks their willingness to respond. If your emotions scare them, they will run, and this is doubly true for wild creatures or for domestic animals that don't know you.

Sit very still during the process of sending, and use your physical voice only after your telepathic one has been received and accepted. Make no moves with a wild animal for some time, and if using voice, keep it very low. When you move, move slowly, showing the animal in your mind first, in a visualization, what you intend to do. Keep your thoughts positive and loving, voice gentle and movements minimal and slow. Hold hands out, rather than up.

Sit quietly in a park, under a tree, telepathing "squirrels" and an image of peanuts. Image the squirrels coming, climbing onto your lap, taking the nuts from your hand. Image dozens of happy squirrels, playing with you and being fed. Watch the squirrels answer your broadcast. Sit quietly again, and image the birds coming to you, feeding from your hand. Transmit the image of love for birds, and their perfect safety with you. Show them the goodies you have. Remain physically still. Birds are wary, far more so than the squirrels, but will come. As long as you continue sending love and remain still, they approach, feeding on seeds put in front of you. Make no attempt to reach for them or touch them; they will fly at any movement. Done repeatedly over days and weeks, they gradually approach, learn to know you, and feed from your hand. Experiencing this is worth the work and patience.

With a litter of puppies or kittens, sit on the floor, mentally calling, "babies, babies" and sending love. The whole litter will use you for a jungle gym, and you might find your own Tiger in the bunch. If there is one infant more receptive, more drawn to your thoughts, or one who answers in re-turn, welcome it and love it. Anne McCaffrey, an Irish science fiction writer, has based her *Dragonriders of Pern* series on such a relationship. Her puppies and kittens are "dragons," with Queen Dragons only accepting strong and independent women for their partners.[16] Women who know and honor rapport with animals enjoy these books, and find rapport with animals right here in the linear world.

Telepathy/empathy skills are there for women who stroke the python and are basic skills. Every woman has in her thoughts and thought-forms the ability to communicate with others. Where her love is strong and her thoughts are positive, making the link is easier than most women realize. Using the power of thought-forms and the meditative state, distance and space are no barrier between women's minds. A woman sends her message or emotion to another, and the other understands, hears her and receives it. Where the attitude is for the oneness of all life, the understanding of Goddess within all, women using telepathy make contact with and learn from animals, as well. Where there is love and the power of women, everything is possible.

# FOOTNOTES

1. Eileen Garrett, in David C. Knight, *The ESP Reader*, p. 192. (three separate paragraphs).

2. Annie Besant and C.W. Leadbeater, *Thought-Forms*, p. 16-17.

3. A.E. Powell, *The Mental Body*, p. 65-67.

4. Shafica Karagulla, in David Hammond, *The Search for Psychic Power*, p. 57-58. (See Shafica Karagulla, *Breakthrough to Creativity*, p. 162-169.)

5. *Ibid.*, p. 59-60. Quotes are from Karagulla's Book, *Breakthrough to Creativity*, (Santa Monica, CA, DeVorss Publishing, 1967), p. 161-2. Pronouns are changed to 'she'.

6. Sheila Ostrander and Lynn Schroeder, *Psychic Discoveries Behind the Iron Curtain*, p. 104-107. See Chapters Nine and Ten.

7. *Ibid.*, p. 120.

8. J. Allen Boone, *Kinship With All Life*, (San Francisco, Harper and Row Publishers, 1976, original, 1954), p. 74-75.

9. *Ibid.*, p. 97-98.

10. Cobra, "Channeling Interview with Gail Fairfield," in *Goddess Rising*, Winter Solstice, 1986, p. 7.

11. See the Full Moon ritual in Diane Stein, *The Women's Spirituality Book*, p. 113-118. The telepathing is adapted from a meditation by Light-Works, Tel-Empathy Network, Fairfax, CA.

12. *Ibid.*, p. 117.

13. This exercise has several sources, primarily Enid Hoffman, *Develop Your Psychic Skills*, p. 97. Also Rodney Marsden, *Psychic Experience For You*, p. 69-70.

14. Rodney Marsden, *Psychic Experience For You*, p. 68-69.

15. Enid Hoffman, *Develop Your Psychic Skills*, p. 101.

16. Anne McCaffrey, *Dragonflight, Dragonquest, The White Dragon*, (New York, Del Ray/Ballantine Books, 1968, 1971, 1978). Also, *Dragondrums, Dragonsinger*, and *Moreta*, same publisher. Dragons and strong women in these books are a delight, and McCaffrey also writes psychic short stories.

Francene Hart

## Chapter Nine
# The Third Eye: Clairvoyance
# Women Knowing

*A ten year old girl was walking in a country lane near her home but out of sight of it. She was studying geometry. 'In a moment, I saw a bedroom known as the White Room in my house, and upon the floor lay my mother, to all appearances dead. The vision must have remained some minutes, during which time my real surroundings appeared to pale and die out; but as the vision faded, actual surroundings came back, at first dimly and then clearly.'*

*Unable to doubt that what she had seen was real, the child did not go home, but went immediately to the home of the family physician. When he came back with her to the home, the vision was found to be true 'even to intimate details.' The mother had had a heart attack and would have died without quick medical intervention.* [1]

May, 1967, I was nineteen years old, ending my freshman year in college, and my best friend Laurel was in Israel. Tensions were building in the Middle East, and Americans had been asked to leave. I assumed that Laurel, with her group of students, were on their way home and I expected, hoped, to see her at any time. Her mother was notified that the group had left the country. Despite common sense and reassurances, I was terrified. I lay on the rug in the living room, my stomach tied in knots and a pounding headache. When anyone spoke to me, I broke into tears, and when they asked I said, "It's Laurel, she's being shot at." Whatever anyone said, of comfort or otherwise, I couldn't let go of the feeling that Laurel was in danger.

That night I went to bed early, but slept little. I'd tried to talk about what I was feeling with others, with my mother, with women where I worked for the summer, with other friends, but no one took it seriously. They said I had an overactive imagination, that there was nothing wrong, and they asked me why I worried about it anyway. I woke about four A.M., frozen with fear and crying. This time I could "see" wide awake what was happening.

I saw Laurel and her group in a cellar, underground, hiding and frightened with other people. I saw rockets, or I thought they were rockets, streaks of red light through the air that landed in a burst of flames. I could hear them, whistling and then dropping with a loud thud and explosion. I knew that Laurel was in danger, was watching bombs fall, and was afraid. I turned on the radio at about six o'clock, to hear that the Six Days War had started and that bombs were falling in the Gaza Strip. My feelings of terror and extreme danger continued all day. I called Laurel's mother to ask if she'd heard from her, but she hadn't. She only knew that the group was on its way home, and thought that Laurel would call her from New York. She said she wasn't anywhere near the Gaza Strip, anyhow, but in Tel Aviv where there was no fighting. Her mother thought I shouldn't worry, but I worried.

My panic continued through that day and into the next, when about four o'clock that afternoon, I suddenly relaxed. I fell asleep in the first sleep I'd had in days, knowing everything was fine. There was something about school buses, yellow buses, driving along an otherwise empty two-lane road. I knew it was okay, that I could sleep now, stop watching. I woke feeling good, more refreshed than seemed possible in a short sleep, ate a good meal that was also my first in days, and went back to my life.

Laurel had not left Israel, but the war was over quickly; she came home in the late summer. Her group had in fact been in the Gaza Strip visiting a kibbutz (or was it a moshav?) when the war broke out. The residents and college group went to the land's bomb shelter, an underground cellar, and heard the war's first bombs fall entirely too near them. They were still there the next day, when the bombing stopped and school buses took the students out of the war area, on the road to Tel Aviv. Comparing times and places with Laurel later, the events matched her fear and what was happening to her. We had to figure out the time difference between Pittsburgh and Tel Aviv. Everything I'd seen had happened when and as I saw it, and when I knew it was over was when the group was on the two-lane road to Tel Aviv in yellow buses.

During the period when all of this was happening, I was seriously in pain and Laurel was in real danger. Other clairvoyant visions have happened to me, but this was the most intense and the most frightening, and probably the first. I had no name for what was happening, no knowledge of what was going on. I only knew at the end that I had seen something real, and it was verified, and that I would never forget it. I didn't know what being psychic was, or have that term for it then, but I knew that I was "different." I wasn't sure I wanted to be different, to see things no one else could see.

Clairvoyance is the ability to see events that are not in reach of the physical senses, simultaneous to when the event is happening. The definition of the skill also includes precognition, which is seeing and foreseeing an event that has not yet happened, and retrocognition, the seeing of an event past. In each case, the woman experiencing this has no rational way of knowing the event, yet sees it in details usually possible only to someone who is there.[2] The term means "clear seeing" and is most often experienced in visual terms, but also can come as a feeling of *knowing*, a certainty beyond doubt that something has occurred. Occasionally the knowledge comes in the form of an apparition or spirit guide bringing information, and manifesting or spiritism is then involved. Much clairvoyance is also related to telepathy, information coming through "seeing" another's situation, being linked with her. The scene can be viewed through her eyes or your own. It is often difficult to separate the means and see how clairvoyant information has come.

There are people who experience clairvoyance as a way of life, and most of them are women. Jeane Dixon is a familiar example in this country, and in Bulgaria people stand in line for readings by Vanga Dimitrova. Susan Sheppard, a contributor to this book, is clairvoyant, and so are many of the other women in this book. In classical Greece, the best known clairvoyant was Cassandra, daughter of fallen Troy, who was blessed with the gift of prophecy, and cursed in that none would listen to her. Women experiencing prophecy or clairvoyance often feel the same rejection, and think of Cassandra as almost a patron Goddess. The great women mediums of the last hundred years were also clairvoyants, and found much of their information through spiritism. They included Eileen Garrett, Eusapia Palladino, the probably lesbian Eva C., Gladys Osborne Leonard, and Leonora Piper. More on these women in Chapter Twelve.

Clairvoyance is the psychic skill most tested by scientists in laboratories and the most elusive to test successfully. Numerous runs of Zener guessing cards (described later) measure a woman's ability at precognition, but women lose interest in the boring tests and as psychic skills depend greatly on emotional involvement, the testing is unreliable. It is a very different thing to predict what pattern or number will come up next on the turn of a card than to have the foreknowledge that someone will die or see a distant event as it occurs. Nevertheless, some psychics' hope for acceptance by science hangs on this kind of testing. This book de-emphasizes testing for the greater reality and significance of real experiences. Women have no need to prove to the patriarchy that they are psychic, they only need to know it themselves.

Clairvoyance is a third eye/brow chakra skill, coordinate with the middle spiritual aura band, the indigo dark blue color. This is the place of sight beyond physical sight, and all of the psychic unseen senses, the senses beyond the concrete physical information level. The center is the Mother, the mature woman who has wisdom and capability, knowledge and the skill to use it. This is the place of women's intuition, women's power and women's spiritual will.

The third eye is reality, how women perceive reality and shift between reality levels. Visualization occurs here and in the solar plexus, and both chakras are connected with the will. Images are made in the lower mental body, but *visions* in the third eye/middle spiritual. Higher knowing and higher will come at this level, beyond the consciousness of linear reality to the reality of knowing what is possible. Vicki Noble defines this center as "the window of your soul," and says it can be active or receptive. When receptive, visions enter and are received; when active, visions are transmitted and willed outward to others and the world.[3] This third eye center alone is cold and analytical in its power, all intellect, but when combined with the heart it's in balance. The power to see and create realities comes with the caring, compassion, love and feeling of the heart center to form women's intuition and clairvoyance. These are the most re-cognized of stroking the python skills; they are "being psychic," or ESP. The third eye or brow center is women's psychic knowing.

Among third eye skills is the ability to telepath, the sending portion of the telepathy/empathy link, and Vicki Noble's active "window." Seeing auras and chakras comes from third eye knowing, as does seeing pictures in your mind.[4] Healing is a combination of third eye knowing with heart center compassion, and opening the third eye is a goal of several mystical traditions. Amy Wallace and Bill Henkin comment that a blocked third eye causes headaches, and this is a frequent dis-ease in women. Perhaps if women accepted their clairvoyance, precognition, retrocognition, their ability to telepath, to see pictures and auras, and their ability to know intuitively, the aspirin companies would go out of business. Patriarchy is afraid of women's third eye knowing, repressing it brutally, repressing women, and headaches are only one result.

Theosophists define three types of clairvoyance: simple clairvoyance, clairvoyance in space, and clairvoyance in time.[5] Simple clairvoyance is the opening of psychic sight, the ability to see apparitions and entities, to see auras and energy flows, and view the chakras (self or others) in healing work. In full use of simple clairvoyance, solid objects are no longer a barrier to perception: women know what's inside a box or behind a wall; they know what's in a letter before opening the envelope. Helen Blavatsky called this the "fourth dimension," the permeability of matter or of concrete realities. In it, the woman:

> Sees not only the inside as well as the outside of every object, but also its astral counterpart. Every atom and molecule of physical matter has its corresponding astral atoms and molecules, and the mass which is built up out of these is clearly visible to our clairvoyant. Usually the astral part of any object projects somewhat beyond the physical part of it, and thus metals, stones and other things are seen surrounded by an astral aura.[6]

Women see auras, thought-forms, and other realities, shifts of plane from the concrete to the matriarchal/multi-possible. The psychic unseen portions of matter, the energy spaces between atoms, are perceived not with the physical senses, but with the psychic (extended, unseen, nonphysical) ones. Meditation and the alpha state cause this shift to the fourth dimension, and the skill increases by practice.

Divination, the ability to gain knowledge by scrying, dowsing, psychometry, casting stones, shells, I Ching coins or dealing tarot layouts, is a simple clairvoyance skill. So is the ability to see those who are dead, apparitions, "ghosts" or spirit guides. Children who see "faeries," "brownies" or "angels" are using simple clairvoyance, and are usually seeing nature elementals or devas. In the case of divination and of manifesting spirits, the solar plexus is also involved.

Simple clairvoyance happens in the here and now, and directly for the woman experiencing it. The skill can be partial or full, involving some or all of the items listed, and in varying degrees and uses of perception. Leonie sees auras, but Ana uses them diagnostically. Sharon does not see auras, but sees apparitions and manifestings. Susan knows what's inside a letter before opening it, and I invoke views of the chakras to open energy blocks. In simple clairvoyance, no space or time boundaries are crossed, the work is present and here.

Divination and clairvoyant divination are discussed in the next chapter.

The second category of clairvoyance is clairvoyance in space. This is the ability to see events far away, far beyond the physical senses' ability to perceive them. The woman sees these events, usually in visual images and as they happen. My experience with Laurel in Israel was such an event. Telepathy may be involved in these experiences, but not astral projection—the woman perceiving the event is not there, either in her physical or astral body. These experiences can be intentional or spontaneous, and most women are more familiar with the intensity of spontaneous experiences. The visions come unasked for and unexpected, are physically and emotionally overwhelming, and prove on checking out to have been true in every detail.

These experiences can happen in waking or sleeping, but always are accompanied by a definite shift in realities. The ten year old girl whose experience opened this chapter describes this shift as the real world paling out for the length of the vision, and the vision appearing vivid and more real than "real." The experience is too intense to ignore it as a daydream or dream, and is remembered years after. Telepathy can be involved and clairaudience, the receiving of another's thoughts or voice. Astral projection is not clairvoyance, but can happen. Some women experience these events regularly, others at long intervals, some once in their lifetimes, and others not at all.

Three years ago, I shared a weekend with friends who left the city that day by van. I was driving elsewhere, and in an opposite direction, when suddenly I "saw" their van in trouble by the side of the road. The impression was so strong that I nearly stopped my car, then realized nothing was there. In the flash I saw their van facing downhill and stopped at the side of a highway, on a grassy berm. I saw the women get out of the van, knew who was driving and what each was wearing. My vision was focused on one of the women, the one I felt closest to. I seemed to be watching her, and heard her say as she walked to the hood of the vehicle, "What are we going to do now?" I felt her fear and worry, her sense of responsibility for the group, and their need to be in another city in a set amount of time. I saw all of the women of the group except one, and realized later that it was through her eyes I was viewing the scene.

From here my sense of fantasy took over, and I saw myself being there to help them, though I had no idea where they were. I saw myself helping them, sending them protection and energy. I continued my drive, very shaken, and the scene would not leave my awareness for all of the next week. At that time, I talked with someone who had further contact with the group, and found that the breakdown had happened. Others rescued them, housed them overnight until their van could be repaired. Later talking with the women I felt close to, the one whose panic I'd heard and the one I had linked with, both confirmed the events and one said she felt my presence there.

This type of clairvoyance can happen in dreams, where it's said that everyone travels astrally in sleep. Some happen wide awake as mine did. In both cases for me, the rational mind was disengaged at the time of their happening, by driving in one case and by relaxing near sleep/daydreaming in the Israeli incident. Emotional connection with much loved friends opens the way for linking with them, as in telepathy/empathy links. Says Leadbeater:

> A commoner instance is that in which strong affection sets up the necessary current; probably a fairly steady stream of mutual thought is constantly flowing between the two parties in the case, and some hidden need or dire extremity on the part of one of them endues this stream temporarily with the polarizing power which is needful to create the astral telescope.[7]

Links between mothers and children and between lovers are common, but some cases of clairvoyance in space that are spontaneous seem to have no good explanation.

Great medium Gladys Osborne Leonard describes her clairvoyant vision of "The Happy Valley" as an unhappy child:[8]

> Every morning soon after waking, . . . I saw visions of most beautiful places. In whatever direction I happened to be looking, the physical view of wall, door, ceiling, or whatever it was, would disappear, and in its place would gradually come valleys, gentle slopes, lovely trees and banks covered with flowers of every shape and hue. The scene seemed to extend for many miles, and I was conscious that I could see much farther than was possible with the ordinary physical scenery around me. The most entrancing part to me was the restful, velvety green of the grass that covered the ground of the valley and the hills. Walking about, in couples usually and sometimes in groups, were people who looked radiantly happy . . . I remember thinking to myself, 'How different they are, how different from the 'Down Here' people, how full of love and light and peace they are. No fear, or doubt, or dreadful mystery is there.'

She tried to convey these impressions to others, and at first disbelieving her, her persistence with her parents won out:

> At first they thought I was making it up, but as I was so persistent, and described many of the visions so minutely, they were forced to the conclusion that there was something in it—something which was not in line with their conventional way of looking at things. I was sternly forbidden to see or look at the Happy Valley again!

Gradually her visions disappeared, and she was aware of the loss, but reclaimed her psychic abilities later. She never knew where the "Happy Valley" actually was, never found it in real life or the earth plane, but it was there for her through childhood, clairvoyantly.

Clairvoyance in space can be semi-intentional or fully so as well as spontaneous and unasked for. Crystal ball gazing (scrying) is discussed in the next chapter, and is an example of this. Women also enter the trance/meditation state asking for visions and information and describe what they find. In spiritism, women are shown these visions by a guide or helper, taken to places that they need to see. In a simple clairvoyance example of this, with the visions brought to the woman, Gay Bonner manifested the "angel and colored lights" incident for Sandra Stevens (Chapter Six). Had Sandra gone to the "angel," it would have been clairvoyance in space.

Intentional Clairvoyance in space is using meditation, thought-forms, telepathy/empathy links or divination/crystal gazing as an "astral telescope"[9] for seeing a specifically asked-for woman or distant scene. As in other terms of stroking the python psychic skills, intentional clairvoyance is a function of the alpha brainwave state and the ability to visualize.

Clairvoyance in time is the third category of clear seeing, where a woman sees an event that has not yet happened, or an event of the past she wasn't present at. Different women have different degrees of this ability, and clairvoyance across time often comes in isolated pictures difficult to place or trace. When the event happens later, or when a description of the past event is met with, the woman re-cognizes what she saw. In women trained to accept, understand and use their psychic abilities, the ability to understand these pictures grows.

Some women become highly accurate at prophecy or foretelling, predicting future events, yet the future is not static and a vision of something that's coming is reversible. Disasters can be averted, the doomed plane not boarded, etc. Women create their lives by free will, not by predestination, and there is an element of choice in every event. A vision of the future is a warning, a picture of one of the many possibilities. Nett in her dream of her friend's child was accurate about the illness, but the child in real life did not die. Frequent stories are told about precognitions of plane or auto disasters; the woman with the "feeling" does not board the plane or drive that day, or is extra cautious, and the disaster doesn't happen.

Some disasters that could be averted, though, aren't. Several psychics, including clairvoyant Jeane Dixon, attempted to warn President John Kennedy about the trip on which he was assassinated. No one who could reach the President was willing to carry the warning. In another assassination example, Abraham Lincoln, working with medium Nettie Colburn, knew beforehand of his coming death, but chose not to take precautions.[10] A woman seeing an event she does not wish to happen, can in some but not all cases avert it. Maggie tells about one of these incidents later. When precognition averts it, a woman is often accused of fraudulent predictions; when it cannot, there is often a feeling of unnecessary guilt, and always someone who accuses the seer of causing it. Clairvoyants do not create the future, only foresee it. Their knowledge averts some disasters, but not others.

In the days preceding the explosion of the Space Shuttle Challenger, a number of people talking about the coming launch made the statement, "Oh, it's going to blow up." This idea was in my own mind as well, and in so many others' minds, that the thought-form of it alone must have had influence. Some tried to warn NASA, but were ignored, repairs were not made, and the Shuttle exploded, killing seven astronauts, two of them women. Certainly none of the people that *knew* of a coming explosion actually caused it, but the thought-form of the disaster was available to anyone sensitive enough to read it. If in a patriarchal society, women's intuition and precognition were re-cognized and valued, the Shuttle disaster and probably the deaths of two Presidents need not have happened.

Clairvoyance of the future is called precognition, and clairvoyance of the past, retrocognition. Both are a function of simultaneous time, the idea that all time is now. Says spirit guide Gay Bonner, speaking through Sheila Reynolds:

> You can predict future events by staying totally in the present and realizing there is no future, and there are many probabilities to explore in your so-called future. If you can begin to focus on the present only, you will have a good sense of the strongest probability now, and there is no future to concern yourself with. This is one thing that does strongly motivate you—a need to control what will happen to you, and to know what is to be. What is to be is now, and this is all there is—only now. You are too concerned with the future and its implications for you.[11]

According to Gay, and to Jane Roberts, and other mystics and psychics as well, there is only one time, which is now. The future or past are here in the present, and neither is frozen. Future and past events are subject to change by free will and action. When a woman sees a precognitive or even retrocognitive event, she is seeing only one possibility of its manifesting. With her free will and visualization/manifesting ability, she can change the outcome (even of the past). In Nett's precognitive dream of the house fire, her dream showed her what was to come, and how to escape with her life. Yet, when a precognition comes to be, the woman did not cause the event or disaster, only witnessed it.

Here is another example of choosing which possibility manifests:

> Mrs. Hannah Green, the housekeeper of a country family house in Oxfordshire, dreamt one night that she had been left alone in the house upon a Sunday evening, and that hearing a knock on the door of the chief entrance she went to it and there found an ill-looking tramp armed with a bludgeon, who insisted on forcing himself into the house. She thought that she struggled for some time to prevent him from doing so, but quite ineffectually, and that, being struck down by him and rendered insensible, he thereupon gained ingress to the mansion. On this she awoke.

Nothing happened until a full seven years later, when one night Hannah Green, home alone, heard a knock at the door.

> All of a sudden the remembrance of her former dream returned to her with singular vividness and remarkable force, and she felt her lonely isolation greatly. Accordingly, having at once lighted a lamp on the hall table—during which act the loud knock was repeated with vigour—she took the precaution to go up to a landing on the stair and throw up the window; and there to her intense terror she saw in the flesh the very man whom years previously she had seen in her dream, armed with the bludgeon and demanding an entrance.
>
> With great presence of mind she went down to the chief entrance, made that and other doors and windows more secure, and then rang the various bells of the house violently, and placed lights in the upper rooms. It was concluded that by these acts the intruder was scared away.[12]

No one was hurt, and no violence done to validate the dream. Instead, Hannah Green used the dream for warning to avert a disaster, as Nett did in knowing from her dream how to escape the possibly fatal fire.

Clairvoyance of the future, or any clairvoyance, contains numbers of stories of disasters, the reason being that strong emotion is more likely to be transmitted to consciousness than no emotion or desire. This effect has given precognition a bad name, of knowing disasters women can do nothing about. The vision of a loved one's pending death or of a national disaster is difficult to witness, and many precognitions come true. However, the reason for the information being given is often to make it easier, to soften the shock or the blow, to show the woman how to deal with something. A clairvoyant precognition can save lives, as it did for Nett and for Hannah Green. Some negative precognitions come true, no one can prevent them, yet few of them are not in some way preventable. On the other hand, some precognitions are highly positive and not of disasters. In my dream opening Chapter Five, my efforts to be at Bloomer's that night, spurred by the dream of being with my friend, helped to make a positive event manifest. In free will, I could have decided not to go.

There's an adage that says "Hindsight is better than foresight," and that's what clairvoyance of the past, retrocognition, is. The woman sees a clairvoyant vision, but the event has long since occurred. The mechanism for this is an astral imprint that every event leaves behind, thought-forms that a sensitive can perceive to re-create the scene. The Akashic Records are the "record book" of these imprints, both in lives and in happenings. The example of an event happening on the Sun, with its perception on Earth occurring only after several minutes, is one way of looking at retrocognition. Every perceived beam of light from the Sun is a retrocognitive experience—the beam was generated eight minutes ago, to be perceived "now." Some stars are so far away in space that it takes years for their light to reach Earth. They could be out of existence for centuries before this is seen, and their end a retrocognitive experience centuries old.[13]

This astral imprint is most readily perceived by psychometry or crystal gazing (see next chapter), but also can happen in spontaneous visionary experiences. Ginny's dream of her grandmother and the Mothersingers was a dream of the past, triggered by her mother's receiving her grandmother's box of memorabilia. Spontaneous past life experiences, as mine with the pottery shard in Chapter Three, are also retrocognitions, that one probably triggered by psychometry with the piece of pottery. "Ghosts" are retrocognitive thought-forms; Nan's "ghost cat" had once lived in the house. Generally, something triggers such experiences, and as in other clairvoyance, the information often, but not always, comes in dreams.

Two classic examples of retrocognition, both of them waking examples and probably the result of thought-forms on a place, were the Moberly-Jourdain Versailles case, and the Dieppe Raid case. Both were women's experiences, recorded in David C. Knight's, *The ESP Reader*. In the Moberly-Jourdain Versailles case, Charlotte Moberly and Eleanor Jourdain together visited the Gardens of Versailles in 1901, as sightseers:

> As they walked along the twisting paths, the scenery became unreal, stagelike. They felt as if they had entered a strange 'circle of influence,' an eerie world of shadows and fears.
>
> The garden around them was not the showplace of 1901, it was the garden of

Marie Antoinette. This was the garden in which one of the great dramas of all time was building towards its last scene, when a piece of falling steel would meet a queen's white neck.

For some time the two women wandered through this scene which was correctly placed in space *but misplaced in time*. Figures moved in the garden, figures out of the past. They saw before them buildings as they existed in those last days when the tolerance of the French masses was fast running out. They observed people who belonged to that long dead time.

Then they walked on, and suddenly entered the normal world, whose time agreed with the calendar. Both women had observed the same scene . . . For ten years the women searched through documents, trying to identify each detail of the vision . . . Everything was checked, location of trees and shrubbery, dress of the court, hundreds of minute details. After a decade they believed they had succeeded in completely verifying the vision.[14]

The Dieppe Raid case is auditory only, where the experience of Charlotte Moberly and Eleanor Jourdain was a visual one. It occurred in 1951, this retrocognition of a 1942 battle from World War II. The unidentified women, called simply "Sally and Jane" were sisters-in-law, sleeping at a small French hotel a mile from where the battle took place. The women were English.

At 4 A.M., Sally awoke, having heard an uncanny sound. At first she thought it was far-off thunder heralding a storm. Then it grew louder and more insistent, seeming to come from the beach.

There was shouting and distant rumbling. Then Jane woke, too. 'What is that noise?' she asked. For a while they lay in the dark listening, as the noise grew louder still . . . 'It sounded like a roar which ebbed and flowed. We could distinctly hear the sounds of cries, shouts and gunfire.' Jane had served in the WRNS. There was no doubt in her mind what the noise was: it was the sound of battle.

They got out of bed and went cautiously out onto the balcony outside their window. Nothing moved; there was not even a car on the road leading to the beach. There were no troups; they could hear the crackle of exploding starshells but could not see their dazzling light.

At 4:50 A.M. the noise stopped abruptly and started again 15 minutes later. This time it reached a new pitch of violence . . Until 7 A.M., the noise of battle continued in varying degrees of intensity. Then the last shot was fired, the noise of tanks and aircraft receded into the distance. And birds began to sing.[15]

The women reported their experiences, separately and in writing to the Society for Psychical Research in London. The events of the night, including the times of action, corresponded precisely to the actual Dieppe Raid of Allied troups against German occupiers of France. The Society, with great care in its investigations, felt that the psychic event had been verified. The women's experience was both clairaudient and retrocognitive. The two cases, both by women, are considered to be the classic examples of retrocognition in psychic literature. Retrocognition is far less frequent an occurrence, unless past life experiences are included, than precognition or simple clairvoyance.

According to Jane Roberts and her channeled entity Seth, both the past and future can be changed. Visualization and physical action can avert some disasters seen precognitively, as will be seen in Maggie's experience, but the idea of changing the past is a new one. In linear thinking, the past has already happened and is irrevocable, but not according to the "all time is now" theory. Says Jane Roberts and Seth:

> The past exists as a series of electromagnetic connections held in the physical brain and in the nonphysical mind. These electromagnetic connections can be changed . . .
> The future consists of a series of electromagnetic connections in the mind and brain also, and this is the only reality that you are justified in giving the present.
> In other words, the past and present are real to the same extent. On occasion the past can become more 'real' than the present, and in such cases past actions are reacted to in what you call the present. You take it for granted that present action can change the future, but present actions can also change the past.
> The past is no more objective or independent from the perceiver than is the present. These electromagnetic connections that compose the past were largely made by the individual perceiver, and the perceiver is always a participant.
> The connections, therefore, can be changed, and such changes are far from uncommon . . . They happen spontaneously on a subconscious basis. The past is seldom what you remember it to be, for you have already rearranged it . . . [16]

I have not seen conscious psychic work done on this, but it's an intriguing thought. According to Jane Roberts:

> A change in attitude, a new association, or any of innumerable other actions will automatically set up new electromagnetic connections and break others. [17]

To summarize the chapter so far, clairvoyance is a third eye/ middle spiritual body skill that occurs in three forms. There is simple clairvoyance, in which women see psychically: see auras, thought-forms and chakras; the insides of envelopes and boxes; apparitions, ghosts, spirit guides and faeries; and achieve information by divination. There is clairvoyance in space, where the woman sees a present event happening from a distant location, and clairvoyance in time, where the woman sees past or future, retrocognitive or precognitive events. The forms of seeing can mix, with distance clairvoyance perceiving a future or past event, or auras seen on someone far away, as in psychic healing. These happenings are the skills of ESP or extrasensory perception, and are what comes to mind for most women in the word "psychic." Clairvoyance is only one form of stroking the python psychic ability, but many women experience it. Like other psychic skills, it happens spontaneously and in partly or fully controlled ways, and past and future are subject to willed changes.

Vanga Dimitrova, a Bulgarian woman who is blind, is an example of a psychic clairvoyant. Seldom leaving her home and yard, she locates the missing, solves crimes, is a psychic diagnostician, and reads the past and future.[18] She is described as a peasant woman, age near fifty (in 1977), who wears black and a shawl. She gives dozens of readings a day for people from all walks of life who wait in her courtyard. She was sought heavily after World War II to locate missing soldiers. Vanga Dimitrova has the ability to foresee the future twenty years ahead, and to predict with inexorable accuracy the dates of people's deaths. Her predictions are accurate 80% of the time, a phenomenal record. She sees pictures; images and hears voices.

> Vanga says she has no control over the mental images that form in her mind's eye. They have to come naturally. 'I can't force them. They may be about the past, the present, or the future.' She has no way of knowing which triad of time will suddenly light up for her.[19]

She makes her predictions, often not knowing of their outcome.

A woman describes prophecies made to her father when she was twelve years old:

> Vanga told him all sorts of things about his past. My father was married three times. She described the marriages correctly, told him details, private, small things that only he, not even his later wives, knew.
> Then Vanga started speaking about the future. My father, she predicted, would die in fourteen years, in 1958, of cancer. She also spoke about my younger brother and me. Of all his children, we were his favorites. Vanga said I would make a happy marriage, but that my husband would die shortly after. I would be left with a baby to raise. She said I'd marry again and this would be a mistake. It would turn out badly for me. My brother's fate would be even worse, according to Vanga. He would be killed in a freak accident when he was in his twenties.[20]

Every item in the reading came true, including her marriages and the date and manner of her father's and brother's deaths. Vanga Dimitrova had predicted details of the woman's adult life when she was a child, and the woman had never met her.

While few women devote their lives to clairvoyance, most have some spontaneous clairvoyant or precognitive episodes to relate. Nan says she dreams of having an argument the night before she runs into someone she doesn't like. Loren, a midwife, dreams beforehand what will happen at a birth, and uses the information in her healing. Says Elizabeth Lynn Cox on tape:

> I seem to always know certain events will happen, nationally or on a state level or personal level, with friends or with people I don't know at all.

Amy and I wrote letters that crossed in the mail, and there was one woman with whom this "coincidence" happened regularly. She wrote to me, knowing that my letter was coming. Susan Sheppard, a veteran psychic, comments that

> The only difficult task in being psychic (and also being an artist/imaginative person) is being able to tell the difference between real psychic influences and kicks of the imagination. Usually, the psychic thing will be more unexpected, with details not typical in your imagination. In a psychic vision, you will 'see' or 'feel' things that go beyond usual imagining and fantasizing.

Women who experience a clairvoyant event have little difficulty in paying attention to it. The dream, vision or feeling is too emotionally intense to ignore.

Maggie, in her past life regression work, saw the recurrent image of "a dusty country road with trees on one side and a ditch and beer cans in the ditch: Schlitz and Coors and something else I can't read." The regressions connected her with Cheryl, a past life connection with a woman living at the farm she was visiting. She knew that the image and Cheryl were connected.

> I heard myself saying to (my sister) out of some desperation, 'I feel as if I've lived my whole life to be here, now, as if I've come here to do something. It's terribly important that I do this thing—and I don't know what it is!' It made no sense to her but she heard the urgency in my voice and said that although she couldn't help me she could take me to someone who would, a kind of medium, she said. A medium? Me? Now I was really going crazy, I thought. But I followed her and she took me to meet a weekend guest who had just arrived at the Farm. I knew when I saw her that she *wouldn't* think I was crazy, that I could trust this craziness of mine *to* her. So I did.
>
> I told her everything that had happened since I had come, and said, 'I think I need to do something. I think something is going to happen to Cheryl, and I will not let it happen. I think she might have an accident and I think I am here to prevent it—because we need to live this time, we need to finish.' I couldn't believe what I was saying, but Susan believed me. She seemed totally unsurprised and suggested to me that together we create a protective shield around Cheryl—and asked me how long I thought she would need it. I thought it would be soon, in the next few days, but asked for a week. We knelt facing one another, held hands, repeated her mantra, envisioning the clear bubble around Cheryl. When it was done I sank back, exhausted. And relieved. It was going to be all right. There was nothing more I could do. Or was there?
>
> I debated with myself about how much of this, if anything, I should tell Cheryl. I was afraid of self-fulfilling prophecy and also didn't want her to be feeling some obligation to me or gratitude. It was a risk. She could so easily see me as deluded or manipulating, or both. However, I felt that she had to know, at least enough so that she would, if she chose to, be aware of danger, be careful. To my relief—shouldn't I have known?—she was interested and receptive, a little

puzzled, but certainly not judging.

This was on Friday. On Thursday morning I woke up thinking to myself that this was the day. But for what? Cheryl, I knew, had left early to go to a part-time job helping a mother look after her children. As I got up I realized that it was essential for me to see no one, to speak to no one. I knew, too that I couldn't eat. Instead I took myself to a small rock-garden in a little clearing under some trees. To my right, as I sat on the ground, was a stone Buddha, about eighteen inches high. I didn't look at the Buddha but was aware of it. Instead I focused on a smooth, grey, granitic rock, not thinking, just waiting, empty-minded. In the waiting something happened that had never happened to me before. When I read now descriptions of what people call a religious experience, I know that's what it was. I felt lifted out of myself and yet was totally *in* myself. I knew that everything in the universe was one, that everything had life, was animate, and that I was one with it. There was no time, no past or present or future, but only now. That 'now' was eternal. In a sense, 'I' didn't exist at all, and that made 'me' inexplicably and entirely happy and at peace. When I did become aware of time I looked at my watch to discover that it was shortly after four in the afternoon. I remember 'coming back' to ordinary life, knowing that whatever was to happen had happened, and that life could now go on. I was suddenly hungry and feeling the need of a shower.

While I was standing in the shower in the barn, my sister came to tell me that Cheryl had been in an accident and that the entire community was going to the hospital. Did I want to come? I wasn't at all upset because I *knew* she was unharmed. When we got to the hospital it turned out to be true. What had happened was that another car had crossed the center of the road, had come straight at her. It had been a head-on collision. Her car was, essentially, totalled. Her head had broken the windshield, but she had not even a bump. Nothing. Miraculously, the other people involved had only minor (relatively) injuries. She told me she had been watching, had been driving more slowly, more cautiously, than she would have been ordinarily. With more speed on her part, less ability to control her car, it could have been much worse.

The next day she asked me to drive her to the scene of the accident. A girl in a nearby farmhouse had been kind to her, and helpful, and so Cheryl wanted to thank her. The country road—I'd never seen it before—became more and more familiar. We parked where the accident had happened. There was glass on the road, pieces of metal. I got out, stood in the sandy road, in the dust, trees to one side, and looked at the ditch. There were the beer cans just as I had seen them: Schlitz, Coors, and one so rusted I couldn't read its name.

The initial image, of the beer cans in the ditch, had come to Maggie during the past life regression meditation tape. The full experience was a waking precognition, a disaster averted by using the information and "knowing" to take action.

Amy, a Wisconsin midwife, also totalled her car without being hurt. She had warning in advance of the accident, had dreamed it:

Actually the whole accident was a very psychic experience for me. I'd had dreams of it for weeks before and knew it was going to happen before it did. Would you believe I was on my way to a ritual in full costume as The Fool? Talk about dangling on the precipice, as Vicki Noble calls it! I adore spiritual irony!

Other women wrote to me of precognitive dreams, some of which are printed in Chapter Five. Here is one of Lori's:

> A very disturbing dream began to haunt me during the summer of 1971. In it, I saw my then-fiance clearly. Then he fell backward, violently. In my dream, it appeared that he was pushed, although I couldn't see by whom, striking the back of his head. I would wake up crying, knowing that he was dead. I tried to warn him that he was in danger, but he didn't believe in such things and wouldn't listen. In January, 1972, he died in precisely this way, although no foul play was ever proved.

Had he taken notice of Lori's precognition, he would likely be alive now, as Cheryl is and Amy.

Ginny "linked into" a national disaster, the worst bridge accident in United States history. It was the ramming and collapse of the Sunshine Skyway Bridge in Florida, at 7:30 A.M. Friday, May 9, 1980. A cargo ship hit the bridge at midspan, ripping part of it away, and causing several vehicles to fall through the gap, 140 feet into Tampa Bay. There were thirty-two deaths, with no survivors from the vehicles. Ginny had "seen" the disaster in a dream about half an hour before it happened, and her experience was written up by psychologists as a verified precognition. Ginny sent me the transcript of the report:

> At approximately 7:00 A.M. on Friday, 9, May 1980, a 23 year old woman in Cincinnati, Ohio dreamt that an 'expansive' bridge 'somewhere in Florida—perhaps in a city,' suddenly cracked in the middle, creating a gap through which 'about ten' automobiles plunged. The bridge was quite long and extended as a gradual, gently arching span 'high above' a body of 'blue water.' It was supported from below by an indeterminate number of 'pillars' anchored in the water. Except for the hole in its middle through which the vehicles fell, the bridge remained intact. Weather conditions, so far as the percipient remembers them, were 'normal' and 'sunny.' She recalls feeling that the bridge cracked 'sometime in the morning,' probably at rush hour; at any rate, she remembers that traffic was rather heavy. She recalls no auditory phenomena and the dream was not lucid (i.e., she was not aware that she was dreaming during the actual dream). Finally, she has a vague recollection that 'Cubans' were somehow associated with the dream.
>
> The percipient awoke after the dream, but just as quickly went back to sleep until approximately 8:00 A.M. She does not recall being particularly upset over the dream, either immediately upon experiencing it or afterwards. She reported the dream later in the morning, at approximately 9:00 or 9:30 A.M. to two colleagues who were leaving Cincinnati that day to attend a medical convention in Florida. She recalls telling them about the dream not so much to 'warn' them as to report what at the time she took to be merely an interesting coincidence to their pending trip. It was not until later in the afternoon, after her friends had left for Florida, that she first heard news reports about the Sunshine Skyway Bridge disaster in St. Petersburg, Florida. Even then she was not particularly upset over what she at that point accepted as a precognitive dream. Her Florida-bound friends, however, who first heard of the disaster themselves on their trip south, told her upon their return to Cincinnati that they had

been quite unnerved at receiving media confirmation of the dream she had earlier reported to them.

Every detail of the experience/dream was verified. Ginny says that while she has had a few waking precognitions, most of her experiences come in dreams. This experience was her first, and there have been others since. Most of her dreams have been more "mundane."

Dee described an event in the restaurant where she works. Two waitresses had spent much of their evening shift packing a huge takeout order for a party on a boat. While packing takeouts, the waitresses lose time from serving tables, and it's tables that give the tips waitresses live on. The women hoped the boat owner would tip them, so they could earn something that night. When he didn't, Dee said, "He'll get his. His boat's going to burn down tonight after the party." She said she could see it happening, a waking precognition, and that night it did. The party was over, and everyone gone; no one was hurt. Dee had seen it happen several hours before, and wondered if she had caused it. The experience frightened her. She says she's never wished ill on anyone again, and the experience could have been a manifesting. In clairvoyant experiences, the seer is a witness, rather than the cause of the event—but "be careful what you ask for, you may get it!"

Some women are able to predict deaths before they happen, as Vanga Dimitrova does. Eileen Garrett had such an experience as a child. The manifesting of her aunt's "ghost" may have been telepathic or a thought-form:

> I was sitting lazily on the porch at home, turning over the leaves of my school book when, looking up suddenly, I saw my favourite Aunt Leon approach me. I had only seen her a few times in my life . . . I knew that the aunt I lived with cared for her sister, Leon, very much and had been worried of late about her health. Often I had heard mentioned in the household that Aunt Leon had not been as well as usual. I had not been to visit her for several months, so I was naturally pleased when I saw that she had come to see us like this. I noticed, as I got up to greet her how very tired she looked and fearing that she was really ill, I reached out to take her hand and help her to walk indoors. I shall always be sure that she said to me, 'I must go away now and take baby with me.' I waited to hear no more and fled within the house to fetch my other aunt to help Leon . . . She hurried outside with me. When we reached the door I saw that my Aunt Leon was gone. I went into the garden and down the lane in search of her but she was nowhere to be found . . .
>
> My story told, I was full of questions as to what could have been happening to Aunt Leon. My aunt did not seem to believe anything that I described and told me that I was cruel to play such a practical joke on her. In vain I assured her that I had really told her exactly what I had seen . . . [21]

The next night, her aunt woke her with the news of Aunt Leon's death, in childbirth and along with her baby. "Before I could say anything, my aunt said to me, 'Don't ever speak again of the things that you *see*, for they might come true.' "[22] Eileen, given no comfort, was fully frightened.

Other women have experienced foreknowledge of deaths. Meg wrote of dreaming of her father's death four days before it happened. Diane knew of the pending death of a child, not as a dream but a "knowing." In 1972, I dreamed of my grandfather's death, and it happened suddenly that morning—and I was terrified. Lola had this precognition of her grandmother's death:

> My first real experience was when I was twenty. My maternal grandmother lived with us and was seventy years old at the time. She had no medical problems whatsoever. She was in perfect health and quite lucid. We shared a bedroom, she and I. I recall vividly lying in bed one night, she was asleep, and I looked over at her. A feeling very strong told me she was dying. I cried to myself. I tried to dismiss it but couldn't. Needless to say, within a very short time she became ill and was diagnosed as having a large incurable brain tumor, and died within six months.

Joanne foresaw the death of her dog, a child's precognitive experience. A great many of the psychic experiences of this book happened when the women were children. The knowings were so intense that even as adults these women remember them in detail.

> I guess the first thing that happened to me did concern an animal that I had been sort of raised with. He was a beautiful black and white border collie . . . I remember suddenly seeing what looked like a movie in my mind, and on this movie screen, I saw how my pet was to be killed. I was scared and hurt and it seemed that my dog knew also and was trying to comfort me by licking my hand and whining. The next day my dog was killed by a car, just as I had seen the day before in my vision.

Most "knowings" don't involve death, and more everyday things abound. These are less easily remembered than traumatic events, the emotion connected with deaths and traumatic events makes them unforgettable. Llynn talks about some of the less dramatic ones.

> Minor events strike me as being remarkable and curious experiences—*knowing* who is on the phone, for example, or thinking suddenly of someone I haven't thought of in years, and then moments later, physically bumping into them. I also have this funny relationship with the mail—I know, before I go home and look in the box, exactly what has arrived in the day's mail. This happens quite often. I'll be driving along and suddenly I'll think, 'A letter from Ellen arrived today!' The letter will be there when I get home.

Carol had this knowing about her children:

> We had a little ritual after supper that both children could go out and play for an hour or so before preparing for the next day. Besides cleaning up the dishes, I

could sit and watch the news without anyone disturbing me from 6:00-6:30 P.M. I had a flash of injury to one of the children at 6:10 P.M. I ran out and down the street and saw a neighborhood child riding my daughter on a two wheeler. I stopped them and reprimanded both of them and thought I had stopped the injury. At the same time, my son and friends were coming along with baseball bats, gloves, etc. to play baseball. As my son was saying 'Hi mom,' one of the boys was taking a real good swing with the bat without looking and connected with my son's head. I couldn't stop it. That was the injury I had the flash about.

In a similar situation, Judy's precognitive dream about her sister's children prevented a disaster:

While living in Colorado several years ago, I dreamed of my sister's two sons and another boy, named Damon, playing in a tin shed. The boy Damon I'd never met or heard of, but he was very vivid in the dream. The boys were in the shed and upset some paint and chemicals which exploded. The shed was consumed by flames. The boys perished. I awoke crying and screaming.

I called my sister in Dallas and told her of the dream. Knowing our psychic link, she did not laugh at me. Her boys had gone that day to spend the summer with their father, some five hundred miles away. When I told her of the boy Damon, she said they had a best friend named Damon who fit the description of the boy in my dream. He lived near their father.

She called her sons and told them of the dream and told them to stay away from the shed, in which they were accustomed to playing. That night she called me back. Her sons had called her that evening. The shed at their father's house had burned to the ground that afternoon after her warning call in the morning.

Precognitive dreams are discussed in this chapter and in Chapter Five. Dreams are a vehicle for clairvoyant information.

Lola had this precognition about her mother's new apartment, another "hunch" that proved out. Foreknowing can prevent or prepare for trouble. Unfortunately, Lola's mother refused to listen:

My mother asked me to go and see an apartment she was interested in renting. As I walked up to the building, in my head I saw 'fire' all around this building. I felt afraid to tell her this. I don't know where it came from, this vision I had. I told her what I saw and felt, and she indeed told me I was crazy. She went ahead and rented the apartment.

After she moved in, sure enough the fire . . . The fire was in the incinerator on her floor about two doors down and was under control. For the two years she lived there the incinerator caught fire three-four times. This had to have been what I saw and felt, but had no way to pinpoint where it came from.

Her mother and her belongings were unhurt.

Another Amy, not the midwife, had this experience as a child. It was a warning that she also didn't heed.

I was eight or nine years old. My family and I had returned from a city baseball game and I was going to go down to a friend's house with my younger brother and sister. The friend's house was two blocks away. Something told me that if I went I would have to walk my bike home because I would be hurt. Being eight or nine, I didn't listen to it and went anyway.

> While at this friend's I was in a fight with a boy my age; my brother had arranged the competition because I always would beat him up at home. During the fight I kicked at the boy and he grabbed my foot. I went down landing on both palms of my hands behind me. This cracked my wristbone, and I had to go home walking my bike because of the pain. The next day I had a cast on my left wrist and hand.

Women remember their tomboy childhoods! Adult now, Amy says she's learned to listen to her feelings. In a happier incident, Pam was introduced to a friend's father, and had an immediate vision of him standing beside her mother. They hadn't met yet, but four months later they were married.

Cheryl had this clairvoyant experience:

> When a young womyn disappeared jogging in Schenley Park in Pittsburgh, the news announced every night for a week or so that she had not been found.
>
> As I was driving by another park, Frick Park, some miles away, a vision kind of *hit* me in the head as if a TV screen had been turned on suddenly in my head—and I saw a picture of her body lying somewhere in the bushes of Frick Park.
>
> When I arrived home, I told my lover about what had happened. The TV was on, and just then, they announced that the womyn's body had been found—in Frick Park!
>
> I'd never experienced this feeling before, and in fact am quite a sceptic when it comes to psychic phenomena.

Gloria describes her visions as "pieces of film being run across my mind's eye," and several women have used this image. For her, it takes about three months before the visions come to manifest in the real world, while others see them happen in varying lengths of time, years to immediately. Gloria's stories are keynotes of Chapters One and Six, and she is a psychic reader. Here is the result of one of her readings, and a reminder again that clairvoyance and disasters don't always come together.

> This past winter an old friend wrote to ask if I'd give her a reading. We had been college buddies, but had drifted apart through the years. She went on in her letter reminding me of a special incident that had taken place while we were in school. Jean and I were close and she had been very upset over a broken romance.
>
> While comforting her, I saw a piece of time and space. Since she was so broken-hearted, I decided to tell her. I saw her clearly. I described how she looked, how the room looked, what she was wearing. It was an unusually designed shirt, customized obviously. The place was in a log cabin somewhere. But the important thing was her happiness. The warm contented feeling of that time, was as real as the pain she felt that day. I relayed to her all that I saw. It didn't give her much comfort at the time, but she wrote that she had never forgotten.
>
> The first paragraph read, 'I didn't rent the cabin, but I was there. I didn't buy

the shirt, but I was wearing it. Everything you described came to pass. I'm impressed.'

That was about ten years after I saw it.

Virtually all of these experiences have been of distance and time clairvoyance, precognitions. There were no retrocognitions in this group of letters, but many past life experiences (Chapter Three) are retrocognitions. Some of the manifestings of Chapter Six could have been simple clairvoyance experiences, as are the stories of seeing auras. Healer Susan Sheppard sent me this experience of simple clairvoyance, as she describes her on-going psychic development:

> I am able to 'see' through everything—I can see through peoples' writings, even religions like Zen. (I think, yes, that's nice—BUT). I can see people just the way they are and how they feel about me. It's something akin to being cynical, yet it's not. It's like a wide panorama view of everything—very little is hidden—I can see waves of things about to happen . . .
>
> It seems as if in my solitude I have become part of a greater mind, a greater knowing, . . . as if I am part of the fabric of all life. I guess this must be a period of enlightenment. It must be.

Being psychic, being clairvoyant, being female, is definitely part of the fabric of all life, and women's experiences with clairvoyance begin with this feeling of transcendence.

While most clairvoyant experiences are spontaneous and are emotionally connected, the ability can be stimulated and trained. As in other psychic skills, meditation and visualization are the basis for clairvoyance, and this is the place to begin it. Enter the meditative state, becoming as relaxed as possible, counting down into the relaxation state. When you feel fully relaxed, do one more countdown. Then, visualize an astral telescope, a telescope at least a hundred yards long, that extends your vision to wherever you wish it to go.[23] Direct the telescope to a place or person you wish to see, in the present, past or future. Watch the scene, noticing as many details and surroundings as possible, and understanding the "when" and "where" of it. When you have seen what you want to, return to now, and come out of the meditative state. Write down what you saw, for later verification.

Another version of this, by Enid Hoffman, enters past and future in the same exercise:

> Begin counting yourself down into a more relaxed state of awareness. Count from ten down to one. Pretend you are on an escalator, riding easily into the depths of your own consciousness. After the first countdown, ask your inner self to present to you a past event of an impersonal nature, something on a newsworthy scale that you have experienced in the past. Wait until something appears. Note and observe carefully when it is, when it was, and your own reac-

tions to the memory.

Now do another countdown. This time tell yourself you are moving ahead instead of back, and while counting, imagine you are poised on a leaf that is floating into the future. If you prefer, imagine yourself on a magic carpet, but it is important that you clearly state you want to move into a future time, into a time when events have not yet become objective. At the count of one, silently state that you are in the future now, and ask your self to present to you an image or idea of some event. Wait patiently, without trying, for something to arise in your mind.[24]

Again, experience the event fully, then come out of the meditative state and re-enter now. Remember to record what you saw. This meditation is similar to a past life regression technique, with a similar goal, to transcend linear time.

On a more mundane basis, try this one. Taking a few moments for this at the same time every day and using a notebook for the purpose, become grounded and centered and make a list of predictions, whatever comes to mind. Don't try too hard on this, just do it, and write down impressions that come when you state the intent, "I write a list of things to come." Most of these will be very mundane: who will call on the phone, whose letter will come in the mail that day, what will happen at work, etc. Even if an item seems ridiculous, don't scratch it out. Put the date and time beside each day's list, and leave space to verify later. As in the dream journal, go over the lists frequently, first at the end of the day and then every few days, to see which items have come true and how long they take. Make a note of every item that verifies and when it happened, and compare the predictions to the time of the moon and to your dream journal, if you keep one. Some predictions will be closer to "hits" than others.[25]

In another way to do this, every time the phone rings, make a prediction of who is calling before you lift the receiver.[26] Write down the prediction before answering the phone, then verify a hit or a miss. Do this when the phone rings, or make the prediction before of who will call next. Be sure to write it down and verify it when it happens. Do these predictions for other things: when you meet a friend, guess beforehand what color clothes she will be wearing. When you leave her and unless it's pre-arranged, guess when you'll next see each other. Guess who will win a sports event or a race, or what performers will appear at the next music festival, before the flyers come. Write down all guesses and verify them as they happen. Don't be afraid to miss. Getting it wrong harms no one, and is part of your training process.

Impressions of an object or event are influenced by memory, women's past experiences of similar things. Third eye knowing is perceiving reality, and individual versions of reality are based on experience and therefore on memory. Clairvoyance is an extension of memory and an extension of the physical senses to psychic levels. Psychic impressions are filtered through each woman's own memory processes and are subjective. What I visualize as an apple is different from your visualization of an apple. Some psychics experience clairvoyance as memory, seeing the future as if it has already happened and they are remembering what they already witnessed. When seeking a clairvoyant impression, look within,[27] the information is already there. Follow first impressions and hunches, and write them down.

While psychic testing is de-emphasized in this book, using Zener Cards or even playing cards to test precognitive ability is an interesting exercise and experiment. Zener cards are a pack of twenty-five cards, in five designs. There are five each of cards showing a circle, waves, square, cross and star. These cards can be homemade, and showing any simple designs you choose, including five animal shapes. When there are five each of five designs, the probability of guessing each card correctly is one in five, or random guesses would hit 20% of the time. When precognitive ability, or retrocognitive, manifests in using these cards, the accuracy rises beyond the guesswork at a one in five level. Tests with these cards were used heavily in the 1930's to bring psychic development into scientific notice. The testing gave more than ample proof of psychic ability, but science continues to discredit and ignore other consciousness than patriarchal reality. Women's reality, intuition, clairvoyance and stroking the python psychic sensibility are too threatening to re-cognize. Zener cards are otherwise known as ESP cards.

It takes two people to work with Zener cards, one to make the predictions and the other to handle the cards. The woman guessing becomes as relaxed as possible, and enters the meditative state or a state of being centered and grounded. The other woman shuffles the cards, turns them over one at a time, keeping them from the vison of the woman who is predicting. The woman predicting writes down each time what card she feels has been turned up; the woman directing the experiment writes down what card *did* come up. After at least two hundred cards, they end the exercise and compare lists. Shuffle the cards after each run of twenty-five, and stop before getting tired. Effectiveness increases with interest, decreases with boredom.[28]

Hits of more than 20% show clairvoyant ability. If the number of hits is high with the dealer looking at the cards, try doing it when the woman turning the cards does not look at them. Telepathy can be at work, and if this is the case, enjoy it. Sometimes the woman guessing consistently makes hits that are one card back or one card ahead of what the woman turning them produces. These are evidence of retrocognitive or precognitive abilities. When a woman's scores are lower than the 20%, one in five random probability average, check to see why. Is she feeling self-conscious about the exercise? Is she afraid to know or show others she is psychic? Is she afraid of failing? Is she consciously or subconsciously blocking herself? Talk about it, then try again.

Try a run designed specifically for precognition. Instead of guessing which card *has* come up, guess instead which card will come up *next*. Do it by stating this intention at the beginning of the run. Scores probably increase.[29] When using standard playing cards, guess whether a black or red card will come up, or guess which suit, but keep it simple. Don't try to guess numbers, colors, suits at once. Try this with the tarot major arcana, if you are familiar enough with tarot cards, but use red or black on a standard deck for first tries.

Card tests become boring rapidly, so don't overdo them. Effectiveness drops greatly when the woman guessing loses interest, and the tests themselves are not exciting. Make one series of two hundred cards, the twenty-five of the Zener pack shuffled and gone through eight times or a regular playing deck, four, and then stop. Do the card exercises relatively quickly, in a comfortable and unpressured rhythm. Examine results at the end.

I tried this one evening in an unplanned-for way. I was babysitting for a nine year old girl who liked card games. She said I should guess red or black as she turned the cards, and I agreed to go along. I had no expectations or caring in the outcome, but the game after a few minutes caught my attention. At first, I made no hits at all, I wasn't trying for any, only doing it to pacify Kim. When the idea caught my interest, something felt like it clicked into place. Suddenly I got every card right, more than twenty in a row. Kim told me right or wrong after each card. Then the phone rang and my link was broken for the rest of the deck. When we started it again, I found the link once more, and after a few cards got all of them right. Kim thought I was cheating.

The girl looked at each card as she turned it. When she decided that she wasn't going to look and turned the cards over face down without seeing them, looking only after I had guessed, my ability to guess accurately stopped. Apparently my clairvoyance in this game was telepathic; I was receiving the images empathically, hearing "red" or "black" in my mind. It was in interesting thing to note. We were using ordinary playing cards, just guessing for color. I have no idea who taught Kim the game.

Lola also tried this with her sister, and came up with forty right of the fifty-two cards. With random probability being five out of twenty-five or ten out of fifty, forty "hits" is high. Ways to increase the hits are as follows: 1) avoid conscious thinking; don't let your rational linear mind interfere. 2) Try lifting the card to your third eye, without seeing it visually (hold it so the image side faces away from you). And 3) say the first thing that comes to your mind, follow impressions.[30] Try using short runs of cards with a few seconds break in between, it lessens the boredom. Make it a game, and do it without embarrassment. After being told so often in childhood that being psychic is wrong, many women have conditioning to overcome in this direction.

Psychometry and crystal gazing, divination skills, are tools used to focus clairvoyance, and these are discussed in the next chapter. They help to bring what is often a random experience into women's control by providing the vision when she asks for it. Women are naturally clairvoyant, and precognition, retrocognition, and psychic vision are a part of women's stroking the python realities.

# FOOTNOTES

1. Anonymous child, in Lawrence LeShan, *The Medium, the Mystic and the Physicist*, p. 9.

2. David Hammond, *The Search for Psychic Power*, p. 9-10.

3. Vicki Noble and Jonathan Tenny, *The Motherpeace Tarot Playbook*, (Berkeley, CA, Wingbow Press, 1986), p. 72.

4. Amy Wallace and Bill Henkin, *The Psychic Healing Book*, p. 29.

5. C.W. Leadbeater, *Clairvoyance*, (Madras, India, The Theosophical Publishing House, 1983, original 1899), p. 29.

6. *Ibid.*, p. 45. Helen Blavatsky was the founder of Theosophy, a psychic, scholar, writer and mystic. Material on the types of clairvoyance comes from Leadbeater, much of it derived from Helen Blavatsky and Annie Besant.

7. *Ibid.*, p. 110.

8. Gladys Osborne Leonard, "My Life in Two Worlds," in David C. Knight, *The ESP Reader*, p. 156-157.

9. C.W. Leadbeater, *Clairvoyance*, p. 72-79.

10. Nettie Colburn Maynard, "Seances with Abraham Lincoln," in David C. Knight, *The ESP Reader*, p. 46.

11. Sandra J. Stevens, *Being Alive is Being Psychic*, p. 87-88.

12. C.W. Leadbeater, *Clairvoyance*, p. 182-184.

13. Swami Panchadasi, *Clairvoyance and Occult Powers*, (Chicago, Yogi Publishing Co., 1916), p. 169. The information here mirrors that of Leadbeater's *Clairvoyance*.

14. David C. Knight, *The ESP Reader*, p. 149-150.

15. *Ibid.*, p. 151-152.

16. Jane Roberts, *The Seth Material*, p. 218.

17. *Ibid.*, p. 219.

18. Sheila Ostrander and Lynn Schroeder, *Psychic Discoveries Behind the Iron Curtain*, p. 259.

19. *Ibid.*, p. 267.

20. *Ibid.*, p. 261-262.

21. Eileen Garrett, "My Life As A Search for the Meaning of Medium-

ship," excerpted in David C. Knight, *The ESP Reader*, p. 200-201.

22. *Ibid.*, p. 203-204.

23. Hereward Carrington, *Your Psychic Powers and How to Develop Them*, p. 125.

24. Enid Hoffman, *Develop Your Psychic Skills, p. 89.*

25. *Jane Roberts, The Coming of Seth*, p. 136-137.

26. Zak Martin, *How to Develop Your ESP*, p. 48-49.

27. *Ibid.*, p. 52-53.

28. Rodney Marsden, *Psychic Experience For You*, p. 85.

29. Melita Denning and Osborne Phillips, *The Llewellyn Practical Guide to the Development of Psychic Powers*, p. 194.

30. Rodney Marsden, *Psychic Experience For You*, p. 86.

# Chapter Ten
# The Third Eye: Divination
# Crystal Gazing and Psychometry,
# Tarot and I Ching

All time is now. *It is our perception of time which defines an event as 'future'—to be experienced later. But we can choose to experience the event 'ahead of its time'—by seeing it now. Then we are free to choose again—to re-experience the event later in its original form, bypass that form entirely, or experience it in changed form. Divination is one way of transcending our linear perception of time; and perceiving time from the occult frame of reference, the overview, in which linear time does not exist. (This is what psychics mean when they say, 'The future has already happened.')*[1]

Hallows, 1985. I priestessed a ritual with three women and a four year old girl. The room was decorated for the occasion, dried corn, pumpkins and gourds, chrysanthemums, apples, nuts and a pomegranate. There was a glass bowl in the center, for a cauldron, green translucent sides and three crystals at the bottom, filled with spring water. Black and white candles lit the ritual. In a meditation, I asked the women to go to a time in their pasts and experience the joy of a past time. Then I asked them to go to the future, experiencing a joy to come. There were pauses in between. Then, "Come into the center and look into the scrying bowl, the cauldron for this ritual. Invite the presence of someone to be here, someone loved, living or not. Invite but don't command. Give them welcome."[2]

I looked into the bowl after two powerful past and future meditation visions. For the past I saw last year's Michigan Womyn's Music Festival, a place I love. For the future, a love affair, yet to happen. Who would come next? Usually in leading rituals, I remain outside of them, a watcher and a monitor, but not in this one. I looked into the bowl, took deep breaths and waited. Suddenly Tiger ran in through a closed door. She had only passed over two weeks ago. She entered the room, a grin on her doggy face, her tail waving high in a plume, running widdershins once around the circle. Then she plopped down beside me, her head in my lap, the way she did in life in countless rituals and meditations. I could feel her weight and warm fur, hear her snuffing and breathing. I rested my hand on her head, as I always did, welcoming her. She was there for the rest of the ritual.

When I opened the circle, the dog was gone, seeming to just disappear. I'm sure there were dog hairs on my long skirt. The child in the ritual said she saw her, asked me who she was. The women said they felt her, knew something was there and that I was happy about it. They'd had visions of their own from the scrying. It was a memorable Hallows.

Scrying or crystal gazing—in water, fire, a crystal ball, pool of ink, mirror, or in any number of other ways—is a form of divination for seeing the past, present or future. It's a tool for stimulating clairvoyance, creating an astral telescope into the fourth dimension of other time frames. Psychometry, the art of reading astral imprints by holding an object in the hand, is a way to stimulate retrocognition, past clairvoyance. Other forms of divination abound, as well. Divination includes a variety of tools and methods for far-seeing, including tarot, I Ching, lithomancy (stone casting), the African Table of Ifé (shell casting), the Nordic runes, dowsing and drawing dominoes. I'm probably missing a few methods.

In women's spirituality, tarot and I Ching are the best known of divination methods, and are covered in detail in many books. For tarot work, see any one of several decks and books by women, particularly Vicki Noble and Karen Vogel's *Motherpeace Tarot* book and deck, Gail Fairfield's book *Choice Centered Tarot*, and Mary Greer's book, *Tarot For Yourself.*[3] See also *The Women's Spirituality Book* for a chapter on beginning tarot and I Ching. In the I Ching, see Marion Weinstein's work in *Positive Magic*, and my own *Kwan Yin Book of Changes* (Llewellyn, 1985). In these systems, the layouts of pictures in tarot or casting of coins to locate a written passage in I Ching, answer a question clairvoyantly. Instead of receiving an image in the mind, a pictorial or written standard message is offered, the prepared message to fit the issue. Runes, lithomancy, Table of Ifé, and dominoes operate on a similar basis.

While these methods provide tools for indirect clairvoyance— messages written by someone else, applied to your situation or question—crystal gazing and psychometry are direct clairvoyant tools. By using these objects, clairvoyance within is unlocked, and the woman connects with her own visions. She uses these methods to receive images, pictures and impressions that "run like a movie" and offer her the information she is seeking. It is up to the woman scrying or reading the psychometrized object to interpret, understand, apply and verify what she perceives.

Crystal gazing and psychometry are aspects of clairvoyance, ways of tapping into every woman's ability to be psychic. The whole herstory of an object or its owner or past owner unfolds in psychometry. In crystal gazing or scrying, information of the self or others, precognitive, retrocognitive, distant or present are seen. Crystal gazing is the astral telescope of the last chapter, a tool of women's knowing. Both skills are basically simple to do, simple to learn and develop, and are highly exciting and rewarding. Neither requires complicated preparations, beyond the familiar meditative state and ability to visualize, operative in every psychic stroking the python skill.

Clairvoyance by psychometry or scrying is a third eye skill, while divination by tarot or I Ching combines third eye knowing with solar plexus psychokinesis or manifesting. The ability to visualize, used in psychometry and scrying is also solar plexus involved, with interpretation and understanding of pictures and transcending time located in the third eye/middle spiritual level. I define *clairvoyant divination* (scrying and psychometry) as third eye skills that offer direct pictures and information of the scene requested. I define *divination* as the cards, coins, runes or shells that come with predetermined meanings assigned to each item, and that offer information symbolically, rather than literally.

Divination tools (tarot cards, I Ching, runes, Table of Ifé, lithomancy) have a predetermined range of meanings that individual knowing uses and extends. The Tower card in the tarot always means traumatic change, the Star card a new beginning. In the I Ching, *Interesting Times* is traumatic change, and the *Peace* hexagram is harmony and rebirth. In clairvoyant divination, psychometry and scrying, the images are wide open, with few symbols predetermined in scrying, and none in psychometry. The scene itself is shown, and the range of possibilities and visions from them is endless and limitless. The images received are seldom static or the same twice, unless the question or object is the same. While tarot and I Ching give symbolic information that is applied to a literal situation, psychic clairvoyance tools offer literal pictures of what is, was or will be. Both divination and clairvoyant divination are stroking the python skills, but are different from each other.

Crystal gazing and psychometry are the active and receptive third eye skills of Vicki Noble's quote in Chapter Nine. In psychometry, the woman holding an object receives impressions from it, impressions put there astrally, by the owner or a former owner's past condition, emotions, thoughts, knowings and spiritual development, all her unseen psychic senses beyond the physical ones. The woman holding the object uses her own psychic sense to "read" what she discovers. In crystal gazing, the woman invokes what she specifically wishes to see, or simply asks for a far-seeing. She may get what she asks for, or other images, but has gone actively to seek the visions she gets. In both skills, understanding, interpreting and communicating her impressions is the other half of the process. The information reaches her visually, in images or pictures.

In divination, the process is slightly different. In casting coins for an I Ching reading, for example, the woman uses visualization to link her question to an I Ching hexagram, a pattern of six lines that are part of a written passage. As she does this, she also uses psychokinesis, mind over matter, to make the coins come up in ways to give her the passage and information her question seeks. In reading the passage, she applies its symbolism intellectually to her situation. The process is indirect; she does not see the information happening before her, but interprets it from symbols and written material, through her rational mind. The solar plexus is involved more primarily than the third eye, and synchronicity/manifesting is involved.[4]

A woman in an I Ching reading asks "What is happening to Betty?" She throws her three coins six times to derive a pattern of six lines that match a written passage/hexagram. That passage, in symbolic terms, tells her what is happening to Betty, but it doesn't tell her specifically. If there is a crisis pending, a period of withdrawal, the I Ching tells her. It doesn't tell her that Betty has lost her job or broken up with her lover. The information in I Ching is present-tense always, but can change. It is not future or past oriented. When the same woman in a crystal gazing/scrying exercise asks, "What is happening to Betty?", she is shown in pictures what is happening to Betty. She is shown Betty's breakup with her lover and her unemployment, or shown how Betty feels about them, a picture of Betty. These pictures can be present, past or future, and with experience, the scryer learns to distinguish between them. The pictures are sometimes in symbols more often in visual images, film clips out of time. They are waking clairvoyance. When the woman holds a ring to psychometrize that Betty wears, or a gemstone she carries in her pocket, and asks, "What is happening to Betty?", she gets a mix of feelings, images, symbols and visual impressions that may or may not be clear and coherent. By interpreting the images of the psychometry, the woman knows how Betty is, what she is feeling, and may see images of present or past. She may also see images of who wore the ring before Betty did, and what that woman saw and felt.

Psychometry gave me the spontaneous past life regression of Chapter Three, the piece of pottery shard I held at Mesa Verde a connecting link with the woman who made the water jar. The image was intensely visual and totally coherent. The same information and vision could come in a scrying or crystal gazing, and in crystal gazing I used the technique to invoke the astral imprint of my recently deceased dog. This was a spontaneous manifestation, semi-intentional in that I asked for a manifesting but not a specific one. This type of event is most frequent at Hallows, but can be sought in the crystal ball or scrying bowl at other times. Scrying usually provides visions rather than manifestings, visions as in watching a film or fleeting impressions.

I Ching, in contrast, does something different. It would not give me a picture of Tiger or invoke her, but offers instead directions and possibilities, gives advice in specific situations. Psychometry or scrying/crystal gazing, clairvoyant divination, shows outcomes, rather than trends, but both are based on what the situation is now. The information in I Ching is symbolic and intellectual, requiring intuition to apply it; it is printed on a page. In scrying or psychometry the image is visual, presented in living scenes. Tarot is a pictoral I Ching; the pictures have set meanings as do I Ching hexagram passages, and tarot also invites/asks for intuitional interpretations. In clairvoyant divination, the intuitional material is given first, the process (unlike divination) is not apparent. I Ching and tarot have been the entrance to psychic development and women's spirituality for a great many women, including myself. They bridge the intellect with the intuition and are valid for both, and clairvoyant divination (psychometry or scrying) take the skills of divination further, for use in similar but more direct ways.

Divination and clairvoyant divination make the past and future, karma, available to the present. Marion Weinstein calls karma the law of cause and effect, and this law is also the natural law of women's spirituality. Seeing it in advance does not mean that fate is arbitrary or unchangeable. In an I Ching or tarot reading the trends are developed and made clear, but what a woman does in reaction to these trends is her free choice. If she does not like the direction the future is taking her in, she changes it. The same is true in clairvoyant divination. Nett saw the basement fire in her dream, and in the dream saw how to escape it. When the fire happened, she used the information to save her life; if she hadn't made that choice, she and her infant brother would have probably died. When Maggie knew that there was danger coming for Cheryl, she and Cheryl took measures to prevent it— Cheryl to drive more carefully, Maggie to send her protection—and Cheryl came through it unharmed. The same is true when the future is seen in crystal gazing; what is seen is only one possibility, and choice, free will and action definitely affect what manifests. In the case of psychometry, where the impressions are often retrocognitive, see the discussion in Chapter Nine about the past. It too is changeable by free will.

Says Marion Weinstein on karmic law, the law of cause and effect:

> The idea may seem inexorable—a law of nature which cannot be changed! And perhaps the workings of this Law are difficult for us to avoid. But *the Law is neutral*. We are not in bondage to its whims, the law does not set things up for us— *we* do. The Law has no whims, or ideas, or directions, or will—or qualities of its own. We ourselves supply each Cause for our own futures and the Law merely carries it out to the next step: Effect. We can just as easily work consciously, with a full understanding of this process as live in ignorance of it, or in fear of it. In fact, the Law of Cause and Effect is so predictable and trustworthy in its function that it makes the process of divination possible.[5]

Divination or clairvoyant divination show women the trends, what will happen if trends continue in their current direction without change. In seeing the trends, women take actions and at least some of the events that are not to be wished for are averted. Remember the psychics who predicted the deaths of Kennedy and Lincoln; a refusal to take action allowed the visions to manifest. When Maggie took action to protect Cheryl, a possible (probable) tragedy was averted. Divination shows women the trends, and clairvoyant divination the outcomes of cause and effect/karma, but neither are predestined and both are subject to women's action, choice and free will.

Scrying or crystal gazing is a fascinating clairvoyant skill and one of the oldest in recorded herstory. Its first use was probably in gazing into a pool of water for impressions and visions. Traditional wicca uses the scrying mirror, an ordinary makeup mirror, round and concave, painted black. Scrying is also done in a bowl of water, the sides of the bowl should be dark, and a quartz crystal or cluster placed in the bottom enhances its effectiveness. Gazing into a fire, into a pool of dark ink or into an actual crystal ball are other ways of scrying, and it's the crystal ball that is discussed further in this chapter. The descriptions of scrying with a crystal ball also apply to other ways of scrying.

A crystal ball is almost the key symbol of being psychic, though only a few psychics actually use them. For women working with crystals and gemstones, the idea of scrying with a crystal ball is logical and possibly the next step in working with the stones. In the European Dark and Middle Ages, crystal balls were made of quartz crystal or the beryls (aquamarine, emerald, golden beryl),[6] and were obviously very expensive, out of reach for most of the witches and Goddess women of the times. Today, the balls are of natural materials, quartz crystal and sometimes obsidian, but also of synthetics—glass, lead crystal, even plexiglass. Some women use balls that are not round but are "eggs," and some use tumbled crystals or even natural quartz points.[7] The argument of whether or not a ball has to be of real quartz crystal—which is not cheap but probably cheaper than women imagine—is a personal one. Women who use synthetics say they work. Natural crystal is not totally clear or totally without lines or flaws; glass or lead crystal is completely clear but seams or flow lines are visible. Natural quartz crystal is far heavier than any synthetic material, but lead crystal is also heavy. A quartz crystal ball may put scrying out of reach for some women because of its expense and less availability, but synthetics and other methods than balls are cheaper and easier to find. I tell women to use what works and what they choose to, having had success with the scrying bowl, quartz crystal points, and a mirror backing a large raw crystal. I'm hoping for a quartz crystal ball in my future.

William Fernie, expert on gemstone healing in early times, comments that, "Persons of the male sex are not so readily developed into Seer-ship as the female." He says that women are better crystal ball clairvoyants, and especially women not tied to men, "virgins see best; and next to them in order, widows."[8] He says that children before puberty, especially girls, see crystal visions the most easily. Women who are:

> of a magnetic temperment, being of the brunette type, dark eyes, brown skinned, and having dark hair, will charge the crystal more quickly, (but not more effectively), than those of the electric temperment, such as the blonde.[9]

The Waxing Moon phase is the best time to work at crystal ball gazing or scrying, and Full Moon rituals offer great possibilities. In women's spirituality, Hallows, the October 31 ending of the old year and beginning of the new in the wiccan calendar, is the time when "the veil between the worlds is thinnest," the traditional time for scrying. At this Sabbat, life and death are barely separated from each other, and visions of the past, present and future, nearness to other realms of time and space, are easiest to reach. Says Fernie, personal purity is an issue, and "therefore, food, digestion, sleep and what drinks are taken, all must receive a proper degree of attention."[10] The scryer should be in good health.

In crystal gazing, the scryer goes into a rapport with her tool, the crystal ball. She focuses her concentration on the ball, in the mirror or bowl of water, clears her mind and enters the alpha state. By her shift from linear reality to the clairvoyant reality, she allows information to come through to her conscious mind, from her subconscious mind and from her unseen psychic bodies. The chakras of the eyes are in operation here, and the third eye is opened, the place for clairvoyant and psychic sight, psychic knowing. As in the ability to see auras, lighting conditions are controlled, and the ball is arranged on black velvet to remove any reflections. The surface of it is fully dark. All of the conditions for doing other meditation work apply: a comfortable sitting position, comfortable clothes and room temperature, dim natural or candle lighting. (Gazing into a candle flame is another way to scry). A two-to four-inch ball is the easiest size to work with.

Says crystal gazer Korra Deaver,

> Crystal gazing can be defined as the science of inhibiting normal outward consciousness by intense concentration on a polished sphere. When the five senses are thus drastically subdued, the psychic receptors can function without interference. Exactly why this alteration of consciousness works so well with crystal is not precisely understood, but many researchers believe there is an energy interchange between certain portions of the brain and the stone. Thought waves are energy very similar to radio waves. These waves of brain energy trigger the crystal into activity which in turn stimulates the dormant psychic centers to awaken and function. In a sense the crystal acts as a filtering antenna and amplifying reflector to the psychic centers.[11]

The idea of thought waves and energy are Mary Coddington's list of attributes all over again, and what turns on these waves is once again the meditative state's opening of matriarchal, psychic or clairvoyant reality. Crystal gazing or scrying with other reflecting objects is the astral telescope of clairvoyance or clear seeing, and the space-unlimited timelessness of "all time is now." Active visualization is also involved.

The woman beginning crystal gazing develops a rapport with her crystal, keeping it covered when not in use and not allowing others to touch it until her rapport with it is complete. This is the same process as in bonding a new pocket crystal (see *The Women's Book of Healing*). The stone when first purchased should be cleansed of others' vibrations with salt or salt water, and should only be purchased if it feels good to the woman who will use it. The stone should be kept clean, washed in soap and water if necessary. The seer adds her own vibrations to the ball, using her hands as in laying on of hands: her right hand passes over the surface of the ball, not touching it, to transmit strength, and her left hand to increase sensitivity.[12] This is done several times a day for five minutes in the beginning. When not in use, keep the ball on its stand and covered, preferably in black silk. The entrance of others' vibrations confuses the images of the ball, and the entrance of the seer's vibrations enhances her rapport with it.

To use the ball, the woman places it about ten to twelve inches from her eyes, on a stand and surrounded by a black cloth placed to remove reflections. There is a dark patch within the crystal when gazing into it. Zak Martin calls it the "blob," and it appears near the base of the ball, an optical effect. The woman finds that "blob" or dark spot, using it as the movie screen for her visions to appear on. Enter the meditative state, and look into this "blob," keeping the eyes steady and attention on the ball—and wait.[13] For the first several sessions, nothing may happen. When clairvoyance occurs, the ball seems to fog and then clear, with sometimes points of light inside it, colors, ripples or rings. Then the visions appear.[14]

Do scrying sessions daily at the same time, and for forty-five minutes to an hour at a time. Several sessions pass before an image appears in the ball. Control over the images grows slowly and over time and practice. After an amount of experience, the scryer can choose the visions she receives, but not initially. Scrying is a learning process, sometimes a long one; though some women receive visions immediately, others take several weeks of patience through daily sittings. Two to three weeks is average. When the images come, they come suddenly and sharply. A woman describes the process:

> For perhaps forty-five minutes nothing at all happened, and I was becoming quite bored and restless with the exercise. On several occasions I became aware

that my thoughts had wandered and I had to consciously drag my mind back to what I was doing. This was my fifteenth attempt at scrying . . . I was ready to give up when, quite suddenly, the 'fog' cleared and I found myself gazing in fascination at a tiny 'TV screen' on which a series of images—people, buildings, outdoor scenes—came to life. Each scene lasted only a few seconds, faded, and was replaced with a new image. The detail and clarity astounded me, as did the contrast between each scene and the next. There didn't seem to be any connection between them, which made it all seem the more eerie. There must have been a hundred scenes in all . . . the procession lasted five or six minutes, then finally the images just faded away completely, and that was that. I tried for a further half hour to bring them back, but with no success.[15]

No images that were clairvoyant information came through on this woman's first success. These take time to develop.

Korra Deaver offers thirteen suggestions, thirteen steps in the process of crystal gazing. They are summarized here:[16]

1. Practice in a plain room, comfortable for meditation, and without distracting mirrors. Use daylight, moonlight or candlelight, soft natural lighting or drawn curtains. Light should not reflect into the crystal.

2. The crystal can be on a stand or held in the hands, but should have a black or deep blue velvet or silk cloth under it. Drape the cloth so there are no reflections in the ball.

3. Wait at least an hour after eating to scry, several hours if possible. Avoid alcohol or drugs, and times of illness or anxiety.

4. Begin in a centered and grounded state of mind, at least, preferably a deep meditation state. The alpha state is essential to scrying.

5. Use aids to distract the physical senses: crystal gazing itself does this for the sight; use incense to distract the sense of smell; quiet places to mute sounds; hold the crystal for touch.

6. Use active visualization to begin. Visualize a simple object, holding it first then closing eyes and visualizing it fully. Use all the senses in the visualization, then transfer the visualization and image into the crystal ball.

   In scrying work, nothing is actually seen inside the crystal, but in your own third eye and mind. The vision from within is projected outward and seems to appear in the crystal ball.

7. Look into the depths of the crystal, without staring. Blink as

little as possible.

8. Concentrate on what you're looking for and expect to see it. Keep your eyes from wandering from the ball; keep attention on the subject you wish to see. It's fine for your eyes to unfocus, as in seeing auras.

Spend only five to ten minutes concentrating on the ball at first, (this differs from Zak Martin's directions, use what works), lengthen the time later, with practice. Don't be discouraged if nothing happens for several sittings. Continue to practice and visualize; be patient. Scrying is a skill that takes time to begin and develop. You may also see things clearly one day and nothing the next, especially at first. Complete control comes with time and practice.

9. Use deep, rhythmic breathing while crystal gazing. After finishing, rest for five minutes with the eyes closed to prevent fatigue. Also do this before starting. Use protection and a grounding cord, and ground with palms to the Earth at the end. Be receptive and alert, at first not asking to see something specific; later write your question or what you wish to see down before starting, but remain receptive during the work itself.

10. Do not force yourself to see things. Relax fully and be receptive, allow the visions to come and go. There is a sense of limitless space, and time, of looking into the depths of the universe. Sometimes answers come without pictures, they just are there inside. There are no set rules for interpreting symbols when symbols appear.

11. Try to visualize your dreams in the crystal ball. Make telepathic contacts using the crystal ball. Invoke the presence of spirit guides in it. Ask for past life information.

12. In seeing the future, don't expect or ask for traumatic events or dangers. You get what you ask for. Be open and receptive to what comes, but don't let your imagination create it or give trouble a place to manifest. Don't project outcomes, and only scry in a calm, rested mood.

13. Be responsible in giving information to others. Don't say, "I see an accident," say, "Take special care." Don't make self-fulfilling prophecies unless they are positive ones. If you see something to avert, work with the woman on averting it, if

she is someone receptive. See Maggie's discussion on this subject in her precognition experience with Cheryl, in the last chapter.

Bevy Jaegers, in *The Art of Crystal Gazing*, (Sappington, MO, Aries Productions, 1983), presents these six categories of the material seen in scrying:

1. Daydreams or imaginative visions. Crystal enhances and amplifies, so use positive thought-forms only.
2. Memory recall of forgotten events, linking the conscious and subconscious mind. Use this to find things and improve memory.
3. Past occurrences, retrocognitions, past life regressions.
4. Present clairvoyance of which the gazer has knowledge, telepathy/empathy links.
5. Present clairvoyance of which the gazer has no knowledge: clairvoyance, spirit messages, empathic reception, either near or distant. These can be preplanned and set up between two women.
6. Future scenes, precognitions, predictions. These are often blurred or symbolic, recalled later when the event happens. This skill takes time to develop but clear images happen and can be learned.[17]

Most or all crystal gazing images come under one or another of these headings and using them helps to clarify what you see.

In advanced work, crystal gazing can be used to channel information, contact spirit guides, perceive a living person in spirit form, even invoke a manifestation as in the one that opens this chapter.[18] In doing this, make sure you are protected by clear or blue light, and arrange to have someone with you as a monitor. Use only positive images, in any use of the crystal ball or scrying. Hold your focus, allow the images to flow, prevent the rational mind from interfering. If a session is interrupted, wait a few days before trying again. Be sure to ground at the end. In using crystal gazing, keep a notebook and write down the session's impressions each time. Verify them later, whatever can be verified. The impressions are so many and so fleeting that writing them down helps to retain them.

Crystal gazing is a natural for women, and it surprises me that more women haven't dis-covered it. So many women use divination, tarot and I Ching in particular, and crystal gazing/clairvoyant divination is a natural next step. With the popularity of crystal work, scrying too seems a natural outgrowth. Antiga is a crystal gazer from Minneapolis who also works with other forms of divination and clairvoyant divination. She does readings for herself and others:

> For me, crystal ball gazing is a way of looking at the world and my life in that world from a different perspective. This perspective is round and whole—no part of it is split off from the rest. As with the actual physical act of gazing into the crystal ball, the question, action or problem that one chooses to deal with is first magnified, then blurs and fills the whole ball, then goes to the edge. This is the turning point after which the image becomes smaller and is seen upside down. If one is open to it, seeing a problem or question in these different ways can give her new insight. It can reveal new ways in which she can act in her life.
>
> I do not use crystal ball gazing to foretell the future. I use it to allow the gazer to get in touch with her own internal knowledge that may be hidden from her. This requires the active participation of the gazer. The reader is simply a guide, one who does not tell but rather points the way. It is always up to the gazer herself to take the actions that can change her life.
>
> I do not attempt to give anyone answers from the outside. I use crystal ball reading to empower the gazer to find her own answers. I use the images that I see in the ball or show the gazer how to see images to help explore any question that is puzzling the querent.
>
> I find crystal ball gazing a lot of fun, a way of approaching serious issues with a lightness that opens up creativity. I invite anyone who is interested to play with the crystal ball, to let out the child inside, to recapture the joy of seeing the world for the very first time.

Who says that learning and being psychic aren't fun? They are fun if we let them be, and they should be fun. Opening up women's natural, psychic stroking the python abilities is opening new worlds.

In the *Mists of Avalon*, Marion Zimmer Bradley's book on Arthurian England told from the point of view of women and the Goddess Craft, Viviane seeks a vision from the mirror pool. Scrying by looking into a pool of water was probably the first form of crystal gazing:

> She set the lamp on a flat rock near the lip of the mirror pool, so that its light would reflect, as would the crescent moon, into the water. Now there were present the four elements: fire, in her lamp; water, from which she had drunk; the earth where she stood; and as she invoked the powers of air, she saw, as always during this invocation, a vagrant breeze ripple across the surface.
>
> She sat for a moment in meditation. Then at last she formulated to herself the question for which she would consult the magical mirror.
>
> How is it with Britain? How is it with my sister, and her daughter who is priestess-born, and with the son who is the hope of Britain?
>
> For a moment, as the wind stirred the surface of the mirror pool, she saw only confused images, flowing—were they within her mind, or on the restless surface of the pool? She caught glimpses of battles, blurred by the restless water; she saw Uther's dragon banner and saw her Tribesmen fighting at his side. She

saw Igraine robed and crowned, as she had seen her in the flesh. And then, in a flash that made her heart pound faster, she saw Morgaine weeping; and in a second and terrifying flash of Sight, she saw a fair-haired child lying senseless, motionless—dead or alive?

Then the moon sank out of sight beyond the mist, and the vision was gone, and try as she might, Viviane could summon nothing back except mocking glimpses: Morgause holding her second son, Lot and Uther pacing in a great hall and hurling angry words, and the confused memory of the bruised and dying child. But had these things been, or were they only a warning of things yet to come?[19]

Many women have learned psychic work from the "novels" of Marion Zimmer Bradley, psychic work of all sorts. Try her Darkover series.

Psychometry, reading astral imprints from an inanimate object, is another form of clairvoyant divination. This is another process of sensing directly, rather than through the medium of written passages, pictures or symbols, and in formal ways or not, it's a familiar skill in women's spirituality. As women become more psychically sensitive, their ability to use psychometry grows, consciously or unconsciously. How many times on shaking someone new's hand do you get a feeling of like or dislike that's inexplicable from someone you've had no dealings with? How many times on taking a letter from the mailbox do you have an impression of good or bad news in the letter, usually felt as an emotion? If you use gemstones for healing, receiving their energies is a form of psychometry, and so is the touch sensitivity of a massage therapist. How many times have you picked up a crystal and known it's right for you, or not right, or picked up a piece of jewelry and were attracted strongly to it or totally repelled by it? How many times have you tried to guess what's inside a wrapped package? All of these are psychometry.

Unlike crystal gazing, which is totally visual, psychometry does not require physical sight, though the impressions from it come most often as images and pictures. These sense impressions are psychic sight, rather than physical sight, and go beyond the visual. Says Shafica Karagulla,

> I believe psychometry is a most important aspect because four components can manifest through it: seeing, feeling, hearing, and sensing. Some clairvoyants who see energy fields may not hear sounds or feel emotions or sense attitudes. Maybe, through the people who have a higher level of perception, women can reach out and become aware of higher dimensions of the stars and galaxies. I'm sure there are intelligent beings who have these capacities . . . [20]

Women are dis-covering these capacities, partly through psychometry. Emotions, fragrances, sounds, visuals and sensory feelings come through psychometry, where most other clairvoyance is visual.

In crystal gazing, the chakras in the eyes are activated, and the third eye psychic center. In psychometry, women use the palms and fingertips chakras, the same chakras opened in laying on of hands, with information interpreted through third eye knowing. The third eye center is all of the psychic senses, beyond the physical and concrete sensory. When a woman holds an inanimate object that has absorbed impressions from a living Be-ing, she uses psychometry to read the astral imprints left in the object. If solid matter is not so solid, and is composed more of energy spaces between atoms than of dense matter itself, and if that energy between atoms is transmissible as described by Mary Coddington's list, then it is logical to assume that women can become sensitive to the information left in these energy spaces. Women who use crystals know that crystals absorb energy and have to be cleared of impressions periodically. It's this build-up of information, energy, emotions and impressions that women feel in an object when they hold it to psychometrize.

It's not surprising that jewelry, particularly necklaces that are worn at the sending/receiving center of the throat chakra, are highly powerful for use in psychometry. Gemstones of all sorts are highly readable, as are precious metals, particularly silver and gold. Diamonds are highly absorbent of astral energy from the woman wearing them, and the impressions of everyone who wears a diamond remain within it. Cloth that has been worn as clothing holds psychic vibrations, a personal lucky piece kept close to the wearer of any material, and even furniture. Objects held or used by one owner are easier to psychometrize than objects used by several; when there are several women handling something the impressions can be highly confusing to read.

What a woman reads when she psychometrizes an object is its astral imprint. This is basically the aura imprint or astral energy of the owner. Objects that have been held in the owner's aura, as in a necklace she wears all the time, absorb and hold a record of the woman's aura. If the woman removes the necklace and someone else wears it, the first woman's aura energy held in it becomes confused with the energy of the second woman's.[21] If several women have worn the necklace, the psychometrist can be totally confused with contradictory impressions. Energy from all the aura bodies is held in the object, the woman's full four-bodied Be-ing. When a woman psychometrizes an object used by only one other woman, she receives impressions that are physical, emotional, mental and spiritual in nature. All the senses and all the bodies are involved.

Impressions from psychometry are usually present or past, since they are received from energy already held in the object. Precognitions are not unkown, but the information is usually retrocognitive—where the woman has been, more than where she is going. Information from psychometry can be literal or symbolic. It pictures the woman herself or even the making of the object, the mining of the stones. It can carry an emotion or feeling, rather than a direct visual scene, or can simply feel good or bad. Emotional states from an object can manifest in the woman reading it: if someone wearing a bracelet is depressed, the woman psychometrizing the bracelet can feel depressed, and she should be aware that this is possible and protect herself with light and grounding. Allow such emotions to flow through, not to stay or remain. Acknowledge their presence, then release them.

In some brief examples of psychometry, I received past life information from holding a piece of pottery made at Mesa Verde before 1298 AD, saw it in intense visual ways, my psychic orientation is usually visual. Every time I hold the shard, I see the information again. My friend Goldie held an amethyst from my pocket and picked up from it not visual images, but a feeling of dizziness that almost overwhelmed her. Being disabled by dyslexia, that dizziness is my natural state, almost unnoticed by me but new to her. Susan found a beautiful silver bracelet at a flea market and brought it home, but had intense headaches and depressions every time she wore it. Once she connected the emotions and headache to the bracelet and took it off, the feelings went away. The bracelet could probably have been cleared in salt water. In contrast, Janet found a ring in an antique shop, not of great value, but feels so good wearing it that she never has it away from her. I have the same feelings for a turquoise nugget necklace.

Susan Sheppard does past life readings and psychic readings by asking her client to send her a scrap of cloth she has worn on her body for a week. Her readings with this method are highly accurate, usually involving past lives and present circumstances, often with future predictions. I received a letter from Susan once that felt so angry I was afraid to open it—but when I finally did, I found she was angry with someone else. Impressions from using psychometry are emotional, visual, auditory or sensory, and they access moods, feelings, events in all time frames, most often the past, and sometimes reach past lives.

In May, 1964 Lawrence LeShan tested Eileen Garrett in psychometry. He brought her three objects placed in transparent plastic boxes: a lock of his daughter's hair, a rosebud, and a tuft of doghair from a neighbor's dog. Eileen Garrett knew what the objects would be, but not in what order they would be given to her in the boxes, where she could not see them or directly touch them. LeShan's daughter's name is Wendy, and the dog, a Welsh Terrier, is Charlie. She identified the objects with these comments. Her comments are first, and LeShan's discussion follows:[22]

*Item #1: Eileen Garrett's Comments:*
Oh, that's your daughter. I think I'll call her 'Hilary.' She'd like that.

*Discussion:*
When my daughter was four years old (eight years previous to this date), she had a 'crush' on a girl named Hilary. For a year she begged us to change her name to Hilary . . . It had certainly *not* been mentioned in at least four years by any of us.

*Eileen Garrett:*
She should ride horses. There is something between her and horses. They understand each other.

*Discussion:*
This is true. My daughter rides like a cavalry officer and can gentle the most upset horse. However, many girls of her age enjoy horseback riding and are very interested in it . . .

*Eileen Garrett:*
She has a special relationship with her father. She loves her mother but is particularly close to her father at this time.

*Discussion:*
True, but this is valid for a very large number of girls of her approximate age.

*Eileen Garrett:*
She is nice. She's better and more interested in art and literature than the sciences.

*Discussion:*
This is true. (I certainly believe she is a 'nice person'). The 'interest' statement is true, but rather general . . .

*Eileen Garrett:*
She has been very interested in American History these past few weeks, hasn't she?

*Discussion:*
Three weeks before my daughter had been given an English assignment in school to do a book review of Howard Fast's book on the American Revolution, *April Morning*. For the first time in her life she became interested enough in a subject to go to the school library and ask for more books about it. During these last three weeks she had read several other books on the American Revolution and the period . . .

*Eileen Garrett:*
The Peace Corps? She wants to join the Peace Corps this summer. That doesn't seem right.

*Discussion:*
We had recently decided to send Wendy to a work camp the following summer. She had heartily disliked the idea. The night before, my wife and I were discussing the matter. My wife said, 'it's a sort of junior Peace Corps.' Wendy immediately grasped this concept, became quite excited at the idea and began to look forward to going to the work camp. The discussion had not been mentioned to anyone else by my wife, my daughter, or myself.

## The second object was a tuft of hair from Charlie's tail:

*Item #2: Eileen Garrett's Comments:*
Oh, he's a nice dog. I'd like to take him hunting. He gets a lot of burrs in his coat.

*Discussion:*
He does often get burrs in his coat, but so do most dogs in the suburbs and country, I imagine.

*Eileen Garrett:*
I think he once had a very bad pain in his paw. It really hurt him badly, didn't it?

*Discussion:*
That evening I asked the neighbors if the dog had any trouble with a paw. They answered that the previous year he had cut a forepaw on a piece of glass in the garden of their home. It had become infected and they had expected it to be fatal. He spent six weeks at the veterinary hospital.

*Eileen Garrett:*
Tell me, didn't he once have a Sealyham companion?

*Discussion:*
That evening when I asked our neighbor about this he replied, . . . 'He's a purebred Welsh Terrier with Kennel Club papers to prove it, but there is something in his bone structure so that every time we show him to a real dog fancier, he says, Oh, come now, there's a little Sealyham in him somewhere.'

## The third item was a rosebud from LeShan's garden. Eileen Garrett did not touch the objects, only their boxes, or know which item was being given to her behind a screen.

*Item #3: Eileen Garrett's Comments:*
It's the rosebud. It comes from a very small garden. The garden needs a lot of work before it's ready for summer.

*Discussion:*
These statements are true but could have been intuitively guessed by anyone who has formed a fairly accurate picture of my personality.

*Eileen Garrett:*
The soil is too acid for it to grow well.

*Discussion:*
I had been told this several times by people who knew something about gar-

dening. However, it is entirely possible that someone raised in the country—as Mrs. Garrett was—could have known this from looking at the rosebud. Further, this soil condition is very common . . .

Despite Lawrence LeShan's quibbles, Eileen Garrett's psychometric impressions were entirely accurate.

Psychometry is operative in reading Braille, and can even be developed into what Sheila Ostrander and Lynn Schroeder call "eyeless sight."[23] This is a technique developed by Rosa Kuleshova, a sighted Russian woman who worked with the blind in the 1960's. Kuleshova dis-covered that different colors feel differently, and that the blind can be taught to perceive colors and even letters and numbers by touch.

> Colors divide into smooth, sticky and rough sensations. Light blue is smoothest. You feel yellow as very slippery, but quite as smooth. Red, green, and dark blue are sticky. You feel green as stickier than red, but not as coarse. Navy blue comes over as the stickiest, but yet harder than red and green. Orange is hard, very rough, and causes a braking feeling. Violet gives a greater braking effect that seems to slow the hand and feels even rougher. (Experiments noted that the fingers of trained students actually did move with greater difficulty over the braking violet and 'sticky' red than over the 'slippery' yellow) . . .
> If you start on each side of the middle color, green, the sticky, rough feeling increases as you finger your way toward either end of the band.
> Black, according to the Soviets, feels the most sticky, viscid and braking of all. White is smooth, though with a coarser feeling than yellow. Rosa, in her self-taught way, developed a different description of what her seeing fingers felt. She sensed various colors as crosses, straight lines, wavy lines, dots.[24]

Blind children taught this system learned it easily, some faster than others, and children learned it where adults had difficulties: they already *knew* it was impossible. Colors once learned are felt at a distance, as the human aura is felt at a distance. To teach it, the children start with sensing two different colors, rather than the whole spectrum. It takes time and practice. Once the sense is awakened in the fingertips chakras, try sorting black from red playing cards or checkers into black and white piles.[25] Then expand into other colors, learning one color at a time. Letters and numbers come later, with practice. Scientists believe that aura fields are involved here, along with psychometry that reads the aura imprints.

Shafica Karagulla, a woman neuropsychiatric doctor, found examples of eyeless sight in her studies of psychic ability. Joan and Mary (pseudonyms) were her subjects:

> I had taken pictures from magazines at random. Some were photographs and some were advertisements with lettering or whole sentences over the pictures or under them. I blindfolded Joan and placed one picture at a time in front

of her. She would place her fingertips on the picture and move around over it, describing a tree here, water there, a boat, a child on the bank, flowers, and in most cases she read the letters and words very clearly. Some of the things that she described in the pictures were so minute that I had to look closely at the picture to see them. She did this with picture after picture.

The second subject, Mary, was not as sensitive and her perception was somewhat different. She sensed 'wetness' over water, 'stickiness' when she touched a picture of chocolate frosting, 'bubbles' when her fingers moved over a glass of foamy beer. Mary seemed to sense the texture and quality of things rather than seeing a visual picture as it would appear to the eye.

It occurred to me to find out whether this sensitivity which Joan and Mary exhibited was limited to the finger tips. I had each one of them use her elbow over the pictures. Joan could still read the pictures with the tip of her elbow, but not quite as well as she did with her fingertips. Mary sensed the quality and texture of things in the pictures with her elbow but again not as clearly . . .

Shortly after my experiments with Joan and Mary, someone gave me a clipping which had been taken from the *Miami Herald* in September of 1957. The article was about a teenage girl who could read blindfolded by passing her fingers along a line of print. In spite of the clear evidence that the girl could read blindfolded, the whole thing was dismissed. The psychiatrist said it was impossible.[26]

Dr. Karagulla investigated psychic phenomena in her book, *Breakthrough to Creativity*, (Marina del Rey, CA, DeVorss and Co., Inc., 1967).

Standard psychometry, slightly different from eyeless sight, simply holds objects, and uses the familiar stroking the python skills of meditation and visualization. To do it, take an object used by only one woman, a ring, pocket crystal, piece of jewelry, and hold it in the left hand. For most women, energy is received from their left side, transmitted from the right. Take some deep breaths and enter the alpha brainwave state, the meditative state, clearing your mind of any outside noises or distractions and relaxing as completely as possible.[27] Focus on the object, visualize it in your hand without looking at it, then go deeper into it. Ask yourself questions about it: who wore it last? What did she look like? What was she feeling? Did anyone wear it before her?

Start talking about the object saying the first impressions that come to mind, immediately and as they come. Don't stop to think rationally about what you are saying, don't analyze the statements, and talk without stopping for a few minutes. Use a tape recorder to record the impressions or have someone else take notes. The other woman remains quiet, not interrupting or speaking until the woman who is giving impressions stops.

When the talking stops and all the impressions are stated, the woman who owns the object or someone else acting as guide can discuss or verify. The other woman asks questions, taking the psychometrist further, as in past life regressions. To prevent absorbing traumas or negative feelings from the object, protect yourself with a grounding cord and an aura of light, and be sure to ground at the end. Running your hands under cool water after ending the session is another safeguard. Traumatic events appear first and strongest in psychometry, often negative events—so don't judge the woman by her object, as these are emphasized disproportionately. As in telepathy and clairvoyance, events with the most emotion make the greatest impressions. To clear these emotions from an object, or from your hands, rinse in clear water or salt water, the same principle as in clearing gemstones and crystals. This clears negativity (or impressions) from an object permanently, except for diamonds, so use with awareness on objects.

Lola describes her experience with psychometry and suggests an exercise for others to try:

> One time my sister and I were fooling around testing our ESP. While I would wait outside the room, she would pick up an object and hold it. I would come back in and go directly to the spot of the room where the object was. After handling and holding a few objects, when I came upon the 'right one' it would tingle and be very warm to my touch so I knew it was the one.

Hereward Carrington suggests other ways of developing your fingertip chakras for sensitivity in psychometry. Hold your hands over a bowl of body temperature water. With eyes closed, lower your hand and try to distinguish when your fingertips have actually touched the water. It's not so easy as it sounds. Or using an almost-closed drafting compass, touch the two points to your fingertip, trying to guess how far apart the points are without looking at them. Like the first exercise, this develops sensitivity.[28] Working with crystals enhances sensitivity in the palms and fingertip chakras, also. Develop your ability to act on first impressions when doing psychometry, and only after these are given analyze the impressions and feelings from an object held. Practice and use increase this skill, as all others.

Clairvoyant divination offers direct, internal impressions and sensations, information that could not be known simply by looking at an object. Psychometry is mainly for past or present material involving all the senses, and crystal gazing/scrying is visual, for past, present or future information. Both are astral telescopes on clairvoyant knowledge.

Divination as opposed to clairvoyant divination, provides information in less direct ways, bringing internalized information outward by external means, and giving advice and analysis. The issues are usually present or future, but can involve the past. For more on this type of divination, see *The Kwan Yin Book of Changes* for a women's I Ching, and for tarot, Vicki Noble's *Motherpeace: A Way to the Goddess Through Myth, Art and Tarot*. Women interested in African heritage may wish to study the Table of Ife or Marie de la Gou, systems of casting cowrie shells similar to the I Ching. Shekinah Mountainwater has a beautiful women's rune set and rune interpretation system.[29]

Since women are more familiar with divination than with clairvoyant divination at present, a few of their tarot experiences are included here. The how-to for crystal gazing and psychometry are given with their sections, so this chapter ends with some of women's other divination experiences.

Susan is a psychic and healer who works in several media. For her, the cards (she uses standard playing cards, rather than tarot) are a linking key to clairvoyant information. They open awareness, but are not really needed for clairvoyance.

> I use various methods of divination: card reading, aura reading, psychometry and some intuitive mediumship.
>
> I guess my most exciting divination story has to do with the time I made a literary friend a millionaire—by sheer accident actually! Cathy and I had been 'poetry buddies' for several years when she asked me to look at her cards for a 'light' reading. She was doing 'okay' financially as she was the partner in a popular grocery store in a small West Virginia town—but wished to know more about her financial future . . .
>
> I'd never visited Cathy's farmhouse. However, I could 'see' the farm with my inner eye as I was doing the reading. The funny thing was, I also envisioned a working oil well on her property. I asked her, 'Have you ever thought that there might be a large amount of oil on your property, Cathy?' She looked puzzled and said no, that she hadn't really thought about it . . . I was given the 'message' that the oil was upon the hill several yards from her kitchen. I could also see in the cards that Cathy was going to be an unusually wealthy young woman and told her this.
>
> A few weeks later, an oil company came to Cathy's farm asking for permission to drill. She was shocked, but not surprised. Cathy looked into her land deed and saw that she had also bought the mineral rights to the property so immediately said yes. A few days later they had an enormous gusher on their hands. It turned out to be one of the largest oil wells in the entire state of West Virginia . . . Needless to say, she soon retired at age thirty as a millionaire . . . As usual, I never asked a nickel for the card reading as I believe the best of the physical and the spiritual can never truly mix.

Pam had an interesting precognitive/clairvoyant experience as she opened to reading tarot. Pam is from New York State.

Last fall, I bought a tarot deck and book—they were traditional, male oriented, but I found that I have a real gift for reading and interpreting the cards. During the fall and winter cycles, I also have a strong urge to create my own needlepoint designs. I bought a blank canvas and started a very interesting abstract picture. Upon completion, it looked very Native American.

She ordered a Motherpeace Tarot deck by mail, and when the cards came, she took them to her writing/workroom.

I lit one of my candles and a stick of incense, and proceeded to spread the beautiful cards out on my table. I was enchanted by them! Loved them! You can imagine my surprise when I looked at the Nine of Discs—it was my needlepoint! Or, my needlepoint minus the medicine woman on the Nine of Discs was so much like the card, it was uncanny! Colors, symbols, and I knew *I* was the woman. I bought the Motherpeace book at a local New Age bookstore, and there it was, the healer/shaman working and studying as a solitary figure. And that's what I'd been doing. Needless to say, I've been working with the Motherpeace deck ever since, and studying with the Greer tarot workbook. I've done some great work in the last few months.

The Greer workbook is Mary Greer's *Tarot For Yourself*, (N. Hollywood, CA, Newcastle Publishing Co., 1984), and along with the Motherpeace books and deck is highly recommended.

Corinne had this experience with tarot while she was pregnant:

Before my daughter was born I kept getting the Death card. I assumed it meant she was going to be born under the sign of Scorpio, which she was. But I also almost bled to death. I received fourteen pints of blood, then I contracted childbed fever. Because of the Death card, I am the only woman I know that had her Last Will and Testament written before the birth of a child. The pregnancy had been normal.

Corinne also works with a crystal ball, dreams and past life regression.

Terry told me this story, and I asked her to write it for inclusion here:

First let me explain that I only use the major arcana and I never ask the person what their question is. I have found that many times people want to ask a question but are embarrassed to say it aloud. They ask a 'safe' question instead. This is fine but the tarot cards answer the question they really wanted to ask and not the 'safe' question. So I just hand them the deck and say, 'Think of the question you want to ask. Don't tell me the question. All I will ask at the end of the reading is, Did the reading help?' I usually hear a yes.

Rose asked for a reading. We selected her representative card and she shuffled and concentrated on the deck. I spread the cards and told her that around the time of the next full moon there would be a 'change'; something that was worrying her would alter and not be so worrisome. It would involve advice and help from another woman. It would also have something to do with travel. There were a few other minor things but these were the most obvious in her reading.

The month passed and I saw her a few days after the full moon. I hadn't thought of the reading until the day before I was to see her. I wondered what, if anything, had happened. As soon as I walked in and said hello to everyone, I asked Rose if anything had occurred. She said, 'You'll never guess!'

The weekend before she had heard bad news about her car. It was in very bad shape and she just couldn't see throwing more money into it. At the same time, she couldn't see her way clear to getting another car, the payments were so high. A car was not a luxury, it was a necessity. She went to work as usual, feeling pretty low. One of her clients that day noticed her glum mood and asked why. Rose explained about the car. Her client turned out to be a loan officer at a bank. Rose was told to go down to the car lot and find what she needed. Rose could *not* believe it! They found her a car. Her client helped arrange the loan. There were a few problems, but the client continued to tell Rose not to worry.

That evening Rose drove home in her 'new' secondhand car. It was the night of the full moon, and Rose's client was a woman. When Rose told me, I was *so* happy for her.

Like Terry, Leslie has worked with tarot for many years; she is designing her own deck. Leslie describes reading cards for others:

When I read someone's cards, I get very warm and kind of 'out of it,' not really a trance though pretty close to it. I become tuned in to the imagery, and also try to remember the academic explanations of each card. I use my intuition mostly. I don't adhere strictly to the book definitions of the cards. I find it difficult to tell someone a negative reading. I'd rather have them re-draw the spread. I use the Celtic Cross but am working on a Kabbalistic spread.

In my readings I have seen a lot of truths come to pass. The querents pick their own cards and lay them where I direct them to in the spread. Their energies 'make' them pick the 'right' cards . . . I am only the translator. I can't explain how this all works, all I know is that for me the Tarot is a connecting thread to what was, is and will be and tells us *how to control* things, too. The symbolic Tarot is a key to mastery of our realities through our own powers. The hard part is that in its simplicity Tarot is as complex as a foreign language. Learn the vocabulary and you'll get by, but fluency requires practice and grammar and nuances. Years of study, the more you learn the less you know!

Maggie helped to interpret a tarot reading done for me the day I started this book, on the book, its focus and successful completion. I'll list a few of the cards, but not the whole reading, with Maggie's interpretations. The first card, the focus of the reading, was the Sun card:

I find myself wondering if you chose or drew the focus card . . . I'll assume you drew it. The Sun, focus, I read symbolically as birth, the rising of a wholly new daughter, the Sun. The garden on the card is the womb of the mother/virgin, the children signifying the fruit of creation. So this is a time when the new is brought to birth, and you are justified in confident hope and expectation. The Sun is the creative (feminine) energy and the children are the book. The enclosed garden is the necessary, private, restricted, safe place in which the birth can happen. You may also be choosing to make creative changes in the way you normally do things, altering your approach. This may have to do with the way you are composing the book or the way in which you are dealing with other people who are in some fashion connected with or involved in the making of the book. This new approach should be trusted altogether.

Though reading began for this book almost two years ago, its writing has happened incredibly quickly. Maggie's comments on a new approach and dealing with new people are also correct, as many many women have had input in this book. I did not choose the Sun card, it manifested itself first in the reading, was drawn for me by the original reader.

In one more card, on the question of how to best nurture the writing of this book, the card that came up was the Queen of Cups. Maggie gave this interpretation:

> The Queen of Cups (how to nurture) has to do with self-defense and with defense of one's offspring, the book-child. It means not allowing the masculine world and its demands to intrude in any way until the child, the book, is weaned. It may be necessary, important, for you to be protective, stubborn, obstinate. The Queen also signifies emotional and intuitive maturity, skill in processing what is happening in relationships, empathy towards others tempered by self-protection, (as a compassionate but experienced mother guards herself during pregnancy). It is the ability to cleave to one's self and to repel invaders. This might mean any number of things including care of your own energy in giving out, refusal to accept inappropriate responsibilities, refusal to listen to 'masculine' precepts, doubts, worries. You have the maturity to do this.

All of this applies, has applied and will apply to this book, to seeing it through the writing, submitting and publishing process. That you are reading it tells you I've succeeded.

Divination is powerful for women and well-known in women's spirituality. Clairvoyant divination, the skills of crystal gazing/scrying and psychometry are new and gaining. Both are important ways for women to stroke the python, open the psychic creation Mother Goddess in themselves. Clairvoyant divination tools continue into mediumship, with automatic writing and ouija boards. Where the astral telescopes of divination connect women to past, present and future, the astral telescopes of mediumship connect women to other planes of existence, Be-ings beyond the linear plane and earth bound lives. Mediumship and spirit guides, automatic writing and ouija boards are the subjects of Chapters Eleven and Twelve.

## FOOTNOTES

1. Marion Weinstein, *Positive Magic*, p. 151.

2. This ritual is in *The Women's Spirituality Book*, p. 96-97.

3. Vicki Noble, *Motherpeace: A Way to the Goddess Through Myth, Art and Tarot*, (San Francisco, Harper and Row, 1983), book and deck; Gail Fairfield, *Choice Centered Tarot*, (Seattle, Choice Centered Astrology and Tarot, 1982), book; and Mary Greer, *Tarot For Yourself*, (N. Hollywood CA, Newcastle Publishing Co., 1984), book.

4. Rodney Marsden, *Psychic Experience For You*, p. 127.

5. Marion Weinstein, *Positive Magic*, p. 151.

6. William T. Fernie, MD, *The Occult and Curative Powers of Precious Stones*, (San Francisco, Harper and Row Publishers, 1973, original 1907), p. 204.

7. Korra Deaver, Ph.D., *Rock Crystal, The Magic Stone*, (York Beach, ME, Samuel Weiser, Inc., 1985), p. 15-16.

8. William T. Fernie, *The Occult and Curative Powers of Precious Stones*, p. 208.

9. *Ibid.*

10. *Ibid.*, p. 205-206.

11. Korra Deaver, *Rock Crystal, The Magic Stone*, p. 16-17.

12. Sibyl Ferguson, *The Crystal Ball*, (York Beach, ME, Samuel Weiser, Inc., 1979), p. 7.

13. Zak Martin, *How to Develop Your ESP*, p. 89-91.

14. Korra Deaver, *Rock Crystal, The Magic Stone*, p. 21-22.

15. Zak Martin, *How To Develop Your ESP*, p. 91.

16. Korra Deaver, *Rock Crystal, The Magic Stone*, p. 18-24. Material is condensed.

17. *Ibid.*, p. 24-25, material here is paraphrased from Deaver.

18. Barbara Powell, "Ghost Chasing With a Crystal Ball," in *Psychic Press*, (Franklin, NC), March, 1987, p. 4.

19. Marion Zimmer Bradley, *The Mists of Avalon*, p. 115.

20. In David Hammond, *The Search for Psychic Power*, p. 87. Feminized.

21. Hereward Carrington, *Your Psychic Powers and How to Develop*

*Them*, p. 84-86.

22. Lawrence LeShan, *The Medium, the Mystic, and the Physicist*, p. 17-25.

23. Sheila Ostrander and Lynn Schroeder, *Psychic Discoveries Behind the Iron Curtain*, Chapter Fourteen.

24. *Ibid.*, p. 170-171.

25. *Ibid.*, p. 171.

26. Shafica Karagulla, MD, *Breakthrough to Creativity*, p. 101-103.

27. Zak Martin, *How to Develop Your ESP*, p. 62-63.

28. Hereward Carrington, *Your Psychic Powers and How to Develop Them*, p. 87-88.

29. Shekinah Mountainwater, POB 2991, Santa Cruz, CA 95063. Send SASE for inquiries, or $1 for catalog.

# Chapter Eleven

# The Crown Chakra: Mediumship
# Spirit Guides and Channeling

*Spirit beings are as interested in us as we are in them, if not more so. They're interested in our physical world and in us as individuals. They hold us in the light and love of the cosmos, and they have just the right vantage on our position to be excellent teachers and helpers. They can assist us to center our creativity, or attract abundance, to find what we desire nonmaterially, and to cultivate liberating qualities such as tolerance and forgiveness. In return we can do a great deal for them, not by giving up our integrity, but by treating them as they treat us: with consideration and respect.*[1]

Helen has curly, flaming red hair and brown eyes with an auburn tint. She comes to me dressed in fringed black dresses, fringes flowing and waving, a young flapper from the twenties when my grandmother was a teenager. Helen moves brusquely, talks seductively and always has a big smile. She was a prostitute in the life she appears to me from, an elite call girl, she informs me, and tells me that love and erotic love are her reasons for being my spirit guide. On nights when I ask for her comfort, or when she comes of her own accord, I feel her beside me holding me. In matters of love and affection, she has ready advice, and in loneliness she comes the most often, to console. Helen is always laughing, and a tease. I tease her, laugh with her, hold her and have fun with her. She's a playmate and a friend. There is no formality with Helen.

Hutseba is my wisdom and writing channel, healer and serious problem solver. She appears middle aged, in a grey homespun dress with white apron and a veil that semi-covers her shoulder length black hair. Hutseba has grey eyes and work-worn hands, and wears sturdy black shoes. She is a healer connected with Elizabeth Seton in ways that I'm not sure about. I also haven't understood whether she is a nun, a Quaker, or simply an olden-times nurse. She usually brings a basket of herbs with her, appears in a garden, and often Tiger sits by her side, watching both of us but not interfering.

In physical or emotional pain, Hutseba comes, is a solver of hard problems, a soother, a creative source. When I do healing work for others or myself, I feel her there, guiding and teaching me. She is quieter and graver than Helen. In times of emotional stress, the women appear together, Helen to be there and rub my back, to make me laugh, Hutseba to offer good advice. When I write, I feel Hutseba with me; her voice is these words on the page. She comments and advises in a myriad of situations, and is my second guide. Hutseba tells me that Helen is there because Helen can be more accessible to me, has experiences to teach me that she doesn't. Touch and the erotic are commonplace to Helen, foreign to shyer Hutseba. For many years, knowing I was being guided but not yet able to contact them directly, I thought Helen and Hutseba were one.

There is a third entity among my spirit guides, one just coming into Be-ing and contact for me. He is male, and tells me he remained unseen until he thought I could accept his maleness. I am still ambivalent about it. For about a year now, I have known him in the background as indefinite light, something or someone there, but was not sure who or what. He has made contact now, but little more, as a Native American shaman, well past middle·age. I know little else about him yet.

Spirit entities have always been with me, back to the days of childhood. Helen has been there since adolescence, appearing by the name and face of every woman I've ever been in love with, for the duration of the love affair. When information came to me as a voice in my mind, I early called it my conscience, later my inner self, and still later yet, the Goddess. Through learning, reading and meditation work, I know them now as spirit guides, who are all three. They protect me, heal me, provide me with ongoing advice, company, encouragement, moral support and comfort.

Spirit guides are there for everyone, though women have more openness to receiving them, as they have for all other stroking the python and spirituality skills. Says Laeh Maggie Garfield, "None of us comes here alone; it is not permitted,"[2] and everyone has spirit guides to help her all the way. Women call them a variety of names, from conscience to guardian angel, and I called them Goddess. They are not

Goddess, but come from women's oneness with her. Spirit guides also manifest as totem animals or animal helpers, and as ancestors. They appear as presences or manifestings, ongoing companions seen or unseen, and in dreams, meditations or quiet times. Children's invisible playmates are their spirit guides.

There are several types of spirit guides, some that come and go, but women's lifetime guides are permanent.[3] All children enter the world with a lifetime guide, a "guardian angel" that takes care of them. The relationship fades as they grow up, but lifetime guides return in adulthood. Most children's lifetime guides, their invisible playmates, are banished by school age. Some children hide them from their parents—and are happier for it. Many children are taught to internalize the helping voices, as I was, into what my mother called "your guilty conscience." Advice, directions, warnings, play and encouragement come from spirit guides, but never negativities. In matriarchal cultures, Native American and others, children are sent on vision quests to make contact with and know their guides. These are animal or human, and are the children's helpers throughout their lifetimes. In patriarchal cultures, children are told their playmates don't exist, and they are silenced, to the children's greatest loss. In women's spirituality and matriarchy, guides are re-claimed, re-gained, re-cognized and welcomed, given deepest respect.

Guides come for a purpose, and come lifelong or until that purpose is fulfilled, but no one is ever alone. Women have a variety of guides. Some can appear just once, if once is sufficient, to bring information, comfort, healing. Occasionally a guide can appear as an archetype, a Goddess or mythological figure, or as a fairie or pixie; they can appear as a Christian Saint, if that is what the perceiver needs to see. There are women who know Mary or Isis as their spirit guides. Ancestors appear frequently as guides, whether it's a grandmother who returns to comfort a child, a deceased spouse to her mate, a distant mother or even an unborn infant. In Africa and China, ancestors are worshipped and honored for their ability to help their children, and they are their children's and grandchildren's spirit guides. Children especially have visions or dreams of helping animals, the totem animals and animal helpers honored in Native America. There are family guides who watch over family karma. Everyone has a lifetime guide, who appears to her in any way she can accept and relate to, and often several more. Mine are ordinary people, as most are, appearing as they did in one of their reincarnations. Until now mine have been female, since that is how I can relate to them the most comfortably. Occasionally, and usually only for a limited encounter, a spirit guide can manifest as a famous person of the past.

Along with lifetime guides and guides that appear temporarily for short or long duration, there are also Matron Guides (what Laeh Maggie Garfield calls Master Guides).[4] These are not contacted as early as regular spirit guides, and are not individual. Matron Guides watch over higher development, great advances in thinking and spirituality, and oversee numbers of individuals and regular spirit guides. When a woman channels information from discarnate entities, the information is often coming through a Matron Guide. When someone experiences a situation or crisis that threatens her life or ability to survive and succeed her life's plan, and is "rescued" or saved from that suddenly, a Matron Guide is often behind it. These are the aides and supporters of women doing Goddess work on more than an individual level. Perceived in meditation, Matron Guides appear more often as Be-ings of light than in human or animal form, sometimes as archetypes, and women advanced in working with spirit guides can be aware of and make contact with them elusively.

Spirit guides appear in male, female or androgynous form, often first as a voice received empathically from the throat chakra. The ability to hear spirit guides is located at the throat, the ability to perceive them is from the third eye, and the ability to work with them, know and accept them is from the crown chakra. All of the spiritual body and spiritual body chakras and aura levels are involved. Once a woman becomes aware of the presence of her guides, accepting them and wishing to make contact, she learns more about them and may see them visually through meditation.

The crown chakra is the center of communication with Goddess and communication between the linear and nonlinear world. This is women's spirituality center, the center through which all energies and light are channeled into women's Be-ing. While oneness is felt in the heart center, received and expressed in the throat and seen/perceived in the third eye, oneness is intrinsic and becomes manifest in the crown chakra. How women perceive Goddess/divinity and themselves as part of her, how they perceive their own Goddess within, is through the crown chakra. The color of this higher spiritual body, and of advanced spiritual development, is violet, and the Native American Hopi call this center the *kopavi*, the door to the universe. In women's spirituality, this aura band is the Maiden, the prime creator of the Earth and women, the Creation Goddess within and without.

Women become a clear channel for oneness, knowledge, creativity, healing, energy, sexuality, and incarnation (all of the chakras), by opening from the crown. Light travels from the crown center through each of the other chakras in turn, from the spiritual body through the mental, emotional and etheric double, to the dense physical level. Information opened to and received at the crown affects all Be-ing. This information is spirituality, divinity, oneness, Goddess and Goddess within. Spirit guides are links between the individual woman and creation/Goddess. Through this center comes women's connection with the guides that comfort, help, advise and protect her all of her life, and that help her both enter into and to leave this life. From birth and through the process of death, spirit guides teach and protect, and they help women through the between-life choices and learning each soul makes. They guide her experience on Earth and her learning and choices beyond. More on these choices in Chapter Thirteen.

For many women, becoming this channel for Goddess also means becoming an actual mediumistic channel for nonphysical entities—spirit guides or Matron Guides—carrying their teaching, information and messages from the nonlinear world into the earth plane. This is a further development of the crown center, the higher spiritual body, and of connecting with spirit guides. These women, through voice, seance work, automatic writing, creativity or healing skill, bring information from other planes to share. Sheila Reynolds channels entity/guide Gay Bonner in this way, Jane Roberts channeled Seth, Eileen Garrett channeled Uvani, and Gail Fairfield channels Nadal and Siran, Erika and Bella. Healer Blanche Meyerson calls her channeled entities simply "The Doctors," and hears them not singly but as a group. These entities' information is brought from what Annie Besant terms the "fourth dimension," through the chosen ability to receive them and speak for them by various women. The psychic skill of channeling, becoming more frequent in women's spirituality, is a crown chakra opening and skill. Another name for it is mediumship.

Eileen Garret, medium, psychic and author of several now out of print books on the stroking the python world, worked with spirit guides and discarnate entities all her life. She was a channeler and seance medium. In her autobiography, *My Life as a Search for the Meaning of Mediumship*, she talks about her childhood and her spirit guides, "invisible playmates" as a child. She called them "The Children," two girls and a boy:[5]

I believe that I first met 'The Children,' some time before I went to school, at about four years old. Out-of-doors the next day, I saw them again. They stood, as children will, intent on looking; I joined them and after that they came to see me daily. Sometimes they stayed all day, sometimes but a little while, but no day passed of which they were not a part. When I looked for 'The Children,' I had to see them out-of-doors; sometimes they would come within, but I grew to know that they were unhappy inside the house. Until I was thirteen, they remained in touch with me, coming and going. I regarded them as 'My Children.' . . . Like the growing things around me, which I loved, I loved 'The Children.'

'The Children' never changed. I dreaded, lest I should lose them, when school began, but they assured me that school had no terrors for them, and they promised to remain with me. So the days went on, 'The Children' and I talked and laughed and played together and were very happy.

Like most adults, Eileen's guardian aunt told her there was no such thing and accused her of lying about them. She said they were imagined, just made up.

'The Children' laughed when I told them how my aunt doubted their existence. 'We are wiser than she,' they seemed to say. I never doubted the reality of 'My Children,' or the fact that we spoke in ways that no grown-up understood. I touched them and found that they were soft and warm, even as I. There was one way in which they differed from other people. I saw the form of ordinary humans surrounded by a numbus of light, but the form of 'The Children' consisted entirely of this light.

"The Children" taught her to validate and value what she saw, though others could not see it and ridiculed her. A very unhappy child, Eileen Garrett protected her "Children" at all costs. They in turn kept her from being lonely and were her playmates and teachers.

I have also been asked to tell how 'The Children' communicated with me when we met. 'Did they use words?' is often asked. I can only answer by saying that I conversed with the children as I did with everything that was alive; for it seemed that I knew what the flowers and the trees were saying without the use of words.[6]

No adult believed her, and she learned gradually not to talk of "The Children" with others.

Noted seance medium, (more on seances and woman mediums in Chapter Twelve), Eileen Garrett channeled an entity called Uvani, her major spirit guide as an adult woman. Lawrence LeShan attempted to analyze, in his gentile but linear way, who or what Uvani was, labeling the androgynous Be-ing "he," just to be polite. LeShan talked of two types of entities, structural and functional.[7] He named structural entities those on the linear plane, subject to time and space, and having linear (height, length, depth) dimensions. Functional entities are outside of the linear realm and entering into the matriarchal/

clairvoyant reality. They are not measurable in ways that structural entities are, in sensory perceptions and measurements, and are not bound by time and space. Spirit guides and medium "controls"—a control is an entity that speaks through a woman when she channels—are functional entities. In LeShan's theory, these Be-ings do not have continuous existence, but only exist when the medium shifts to the altered consciousness of the matriarchal reality, through the meditative state. When Eileen Garrett enters the meditative state and shifts to the matriarchal/clairvoyant reality is when Uvani exists.

> Of this class of entities we cannot ask the question 'What is it?' and expect a reasonable answer. We can, however, ask other questions such as "When is it?' and hope to obtain a satisfactory reply . . .
> The question 'where' a functional entity is 'when' it exists cannot always be answered . . .
> In essence we might say: A functional entity *is* what it does and when it does it. Further, it only *is* (does anything) when it is being conceptualized by a perceiving and conscious entity.[8]

The analogy given is of an emotion: an emotion is definitely real, through something unseen and unmeasurable in linear ways, but where or when does it have existence on the earth plane?

This is a provocative concept, but I feel an incomplete one. When questioned about it, my own spirit guides tell me they could appear in any form but come to me as they appeared in their own past lives and in forms acceptable to my reality. Spirit guides appearing in manifestations as something inhuman (not human or not animal), as two glowing eyes or as Be-ings that could frighten, are not behaving according to the spiritual laws they all universally obey.[9] Guides have existence and past existence, they tell me, and are always there. Their "there," however, is a different world, and their reality is different. It is not our viewpoint of a space-time linear reality that they appear from.

Guides have existence of their own, in their own worlds. They come as we need them to, and when we need them to, and come in ways we can accept. Their reality is androgynous and in the form of light. Seth tells Jane Roberts that he is extremely busy, has other things to do when not making contact with her, and he is perhaps a Matron/Master Guide. Gay Bonner, Sheila Reynolds' guide and "control" speaks similarly. Yet, when a psychologist interviewing Eileen Garrett asked Uvani how "he" had been since their last meeting, Uvani was obviously confused.[10]

LeShan says that spirit guides and medium "controls" are functional entities, which partly makes sense—they are beyond the linear and part of the nonlinear, not physically measurable world. But do they only exist when summoned, as LeShan believes? My own guides and *The Seth Material* tell me no. They seem to be Be-ings who have once had life on the earth plane, though not all of them have had that experience. They are Be-ings that have incarnated or have the capability of incarnating, are what religions call souls. By experiencing the oneness of all life, women make contact with entities that are beyond linear reality. These are spirit guides or controls. They have existence in their own plane of reality in the same sense that living women do in theirs, but it's a different form of reality than is known on the earth plane.

Jane Roberts' channeled entity is male and calls himself Seth. He is probably the best known channeled entity, and Jane Roberts the best known medium, of modern times. Late in 1963, through automatic writing and the ouija board, (both discussed in the next chapter), Roberts made contact with an entity, who when pressed to pick a name, chose Seth. He described several past lives with both Jane Roberts and her husband.[11] Roberts found her consciousness and psychic abilities expanding at an amazing rate at this time, and the outline for a book on psychic development, *The Coming of Seth*, (New York, Pocket Books, 1966). With the ouija board slow to spell out messages, she dis-covered that the full messages were appearing as voices in her mind, and began to speak them before the spelling caught up with her. Later, she started speaking without the board, channeling Seth by shifting to the altered state and allowing him to come through her consciousness. In a year's time, there were over 2,000 pages of session transcripts, 5,000 by 1969.

Jane Roberts made contact with Seth through the ouija board on December 8, 1963, and by December 15 she was channeling. From this point, a distinct personality manifested through Jane Roberts as Seth, looking, acting and speaking differently from her self in linear reality. Seth had a very different physical expression, body language and method of speech from Jane's. He asserted his independent Be-ing, and in cooperation with him, volumes of information on the psychic world were channeled by Jane Roberts. The material ranged from psychic development of all sorts, to the nature of life after death, reincarnation and karma, alternate realities and simultaneous lives, the dream world, healing information, and the nature of time and space.

The material came through Roberts without hesitation or pause despite the involvement of some of the ideas, in a deep voice and mannerisms not her own. While speaking these lectures of philosophy and metaphysics, she could hear herself only, "Dimly, as if a radio program were going on in my head from another station."[12] Her own Being removed from what she channeled as Seth, the material coming through her rather than from her, she was not aware until returning to linear reality what was said. Seth described his role initially as that of teacher, and the teaching continued. In Jane Roberts' several books before her 1984 death, her channeled material changed the nature of the Western psychic and metaphysical seeking world.

Seth and Jane Roberts describe the reality of spirit guides and "what" Seth is:

> To say I am energy is no lie. It is actually truer than many designations that would sound more authentic and complicated. I am a personality in essence-energy form. This in no way implies that I am a 'spirit,' some sort of a granddaddy longlegs of science fiction. What I am is difficult to explain because of the limits set not only by your own knowledge but by the present method of our communication . . .
>
> I do have a structure nevertheless, and I can change or interchange the components of that structure so as to appear or operate under vastly different conditions. During these sessions I use my basic energy components in a manner other than I would under other circumstances. In other words, I can change the alignment of my components, focusing my powers into one particular direction . . .
>
> Your idea of a spirit, I believe, is something without a form, and I can have form. I certainly have structure. It is true at this point that under ordinary circumstances you cannot see my structure. This does not mean that I have none . . . You see, the inner senses provide direct experience. The outer senses provide camouflaged distortions of translated, second-hand experience.
>
> You or your scientists are simply not aware yet of many basic laws that govern such things as my structure, though already some of these are glimpsed by the more original thinkers.[13]

Seth states that he has had other lives, and so had his channeler Jane Roberts. Their coming together as a control (Seth) and a medium (Jane) was a working partnership, occurring by the free will of both of them.

Like Seth, Gay Bonner is a channeled entity, a control working through Sheila Reynolds and Sandra Stevens. In *Being Alive Is Being Psychic* (Barrytown, NY, Cordella Books, 1983), Sandra describes her and Sheila's relationship with Gay as their spirit guide and teacher, and their meeting of each other and of her. Both Sheila and Sandra were developing psychically and working to know more when they first contacted Gay through the ouija board. As did Seth, Gay described her past lives and where she had known the women before. She chose the name and persona of her past life as an eighteenth century Welsh-woman. The sessions began in Spring, 1977 and became channeled sessions that summer. Sheila is the medium, with Sandra guiding and recording the material.

In August, 1977 Sandra asked Gay about Gay's relationship with Sheila:

> Gay: I am the you who refuses to face all the power, and I am the know-ing part of you.
> Sandra: Are you also Gay Bonner who lived in 18th Century Wales?
> Gay: I am also Gay Bonner, and those were to be my next words. Do you see? We are one, yet two or sometimes three or four. In life we were meeting as one—then we split.
> Sandra: You were coming from the same source?
> Gay: As we all. We came so close as to be one person.
> Sandra: You and Sheila?
> Gay: Yes.
> Sandra: In the life in the 1700's you were two?
> Gay: Now we are two.[14]

In the same session, Gay spoke of her first appearance to Sheila, as an "invisible playmate" or spirit guide when Sheila was a child:

> Gay: I have been around, and she (Sheila) didn't choose to have a relationship with me . . .
> Sandra: Earlier than this?
> Gay: Only when she was six years old. I was there, and we spoke.
> Sandra: In physical life?
> Gay: No, spirit form, and we spoke. She has no memory of spirit friends. She was laughed at for talking to herself.
> Sandra: You left her until now?
> Gay: I had no choice. I did stand by in dreams and fantasies.[15]

Many women have invisible playmates, lifetime spirit guides, who were refused because of peer or parental pressure in childhood. Some of these are lost fully, some regained in adulthood by the woman's growing awareness and receptivity, and a few become con-trols for channeling mediums. A spirit guide remains internal, within the woman she guides and counsels, while a control speaks through her medium student, coming outward to the linear world and teach-ing more than her single charge. In her past life as Gay Bonner, this control entity was sister to Sheila and cousin to Sandra. Reincarnation information says that entities reincarnate in groups to teach, love and help each other, and for the working out of karma. And everyone has guides.

Sheila and Sandra's growing psychic development is Gay's pur-pose in contacting them, and her own curiosity about them and their physical world. As to who or what she is, Gay calls herself a thought-form, created by Sheila's channeling and Sandra's questions, but also an independent Be-ing with her own herstory:

| | |
|---|---|
| Gay: | You both (Sandy and Sheila) gave me my name and lives. |
| Sandra: | Explain that please. |
| Gay: | You create me and made my history also. |
| Sandra: | Are you independent from us all? |
| Gay: | That is a question of considerable thought and requires an answer that may seem difficult to understand. It is not possible for me to be independent of you. |
| Sandra: | But I (Sandy) am independent of Bob sitting here next to me? |
| Gay: | You may very well feel that way if you choose, but you are not independent. |
| Sandra: | You mean that when he leaves I will be different? |
| Gay: | Yes. |
| Sandra: | Are each of us thought-forms as you? |
| Gay: | Yes, and you are people too, which means that you are also responsible for a physical existence.[16] |

Asked if there are laws governing her existence, or any limitations placed on what she could tell them, Gay replied:

First, there are no rules for my existence, just as there are none for yours. Any limitations are self-imposed. You contribute even to my limitations as I contribute to yours. This is because we are one. What I say is what you can hear at any given moment. That is the way it operates always. That is, not that there are things I can't tell you, only things you do not hear. You know everything anyway. I can say nothing new. All laws can be transcended. Even natural laws can be transcended in other 'realities' that you are free to enter at any given time. You have chosen to operate within a given framework of existence. So do I . . . Any forces that appear outside of you have been placed there in order that you may feel more comfortable than you would if you realized they are you . . . [17]

Is this another version of Lawrence LeShan's functional entities? And do medium controls or spirit guides exist by his definition or definitions of their own as individual Be-ings? No one can say. On the subject of spirit guides, Gay says this:

You all have a greater soul and power. Your guides are connected psychically and, as such, represent the wise parts of yourself. They are not magic or mysterious.[18]

Seth said something similar. In readings, Gay connects people with their spirit guides and says that everyone has them. She emphasizes that incarnate or discarnate, we are all one, and that none of us are alone on the planet. Guides are separate entities, but also a part of each of us:

You have created us just as you can create your physical friends; and we, in a

> sense, have created you and wish to help and send love. This is a feeling of love, and it means much to have it accepted. When you offer friendship and love to a physical person, it feels bad to have it not accepted; and this is the same, but your guides are also you, and you hurt yourself by refusing love . . .
>
> Your guides are close to you all, as close as a change in frequencies or consciousness, and all send you love . . .
>
> Understand that your guides are a part of you. Many of the everyday thoughts you have are now coming from this higher self. You often live in this consciousness and you are not aware that you are already there. You are in constant communication, but unaware. Look around you and know that your life is the answer, as it unfolds.[19]

A "change in frequencies or consciousness" is the meditative alpha state.

Sandra Stevens and Sheila Reynolds operate Mind Matters, a psychic development and reading/channeling organization they developed together with the help of Gay. It's located at Washington Crossing, Pennsylvania, near Philadelphia. Gay has helped and promoted the business from its start, and through it Sandra and Sheila teach what they have learned from her.

Another contemporary channeler, and a member of the women's movement, is Gail Fairfield. Known for her work with astrology, neurolinguistic programming, and her book *Choice Centered Tarot*, she is also a channeler whose work is reaching public notice. She lives and practices in Seattle, has been working as a trance medium for ten or twelve years, and is writing books on astrology and mediumship with a choice and how-to slant.

Like Jane Roberts and Sheila Reynolds, Gail dis-covered her ability to channel through the ouija board. As with Jane Roberts, she began to anticipate the slowly spelled out ouija board messages and to speak them. In one session, the board spelled out, "Gail in trance, Gail in trance," and

> I didn't know what to do, so I lay down and I relaxed, and I thought, 'Oh, I should compose myself. The messages came very slowly, one word at a time. Gradually, though, we would get sentences out of them. I was very conscious that if it came to my mind before it came out of my mouth, I might be making it up. Was I forcing it to happen? Is it real? I was very cautious.[20]

She would sometimes get images, sometimes words,

> And there were times when I had different experiences—there was a level of information that seemed fairly accessible; then, there was another level that felt like it was coming from far away and it seemed like five minutes between words . . . I felt as though there were different entities, but I didn't have a conscious sense that these were entities, or beings, who had personalities.[21]

Two years ago, her main channeled entity, Nadal, came through:

And she had a name, and personality, and an accent, and a whole way of being . . . All of a sudden there was this new energy that started to happen. For about the next year or so I practiced, working more with people I did not know, instead of friends.[22]

Four major entities channel through Gail Fairfield, Nadal first, who was a mute teacher/healer in Nepal in the early 1800's. She had learned English from a British doctor. Her son Siran, his mother's translator, appears after Nadal speaks, answering questions and discussing his mother's channeled lecture. Siran sometimes invites other entities to speak and offer specialized information. Among them is Erika, a Swedish, lesbian doctor from the 1800's, and Bella, an Italian child who died at eight years and who appears when someone is upset. The personalities are very different from each other, with Nadal severe and not accepting interruptions, Siran humorous and talky, Erika speaking primarily on health issues, and Bella, a sweet and very tender child.

Gail believes in taking control, even in a channeling situation, and is not open to energies from negative entities. This is a choice; the trance medium can refuse and ask an entity to leave. Entities have their own natures and own personalities; their information is not infallible, and the woman channeling them chooses what entities come through her and how much of their advice to accept. Entities have the biases of their own lives, along with a broader than linear perspective often beyond what women on the earth plane can perceive. Working with a discarnate entity, however, is a mutual cooperation and mutual choice; if you don't want one to be there, or don't like that Be-ing's energy, the medium can and should refuse it. Gail Fairfield also chooses to avoid entities that claim to be masters or to have absolute truths, and to avoid "celebrity" entities:

I have enough of the rebel in me that a big name has less validity, that's how I operate. If some entity came through and said they were Buddha or Kwan Yin, or whatever, I'd say, 'Yeah, you've got to be kidding.' My own belief structure doesn't operate that way, so it'd be less possible that I'd channel one of those types.[23]

She is present and aware of what's being channeled through her, and questions seriously and constantly "what is real?" There is a physical sensation in the process, and the choice to be a channel and to receive the entities. Over time, Nadal has taught her to trust herself and her intuition, and the question seldom comes up for people she channels for. The need to trust is a real one. In the process of choosing to channel:

> My consciousness moves over a little to the left, and Nadal or Siran or whoever it is comes in more to the center of my body and uses my vocal cords. I feel that they also use my mind; they use my vocabulary, they use a lot of my phraseology. I find words for them if they don't know how to describe something. It's a dialogue, an interactive process. A lot of the time I'm just observing. I feel that I'm watching and listening, as I think, 'Oh, that's interesting . . . well, I wouldn't have thought to say it that way' . . .
>
> I don't feel taken over. I don't feel out of control. I do feel I'm sharing with somebody, I'm communicating with somebody. I have a definite sense of when they're there, and when they're not there.[24]

The only limits to the information received are the limits of women's questions and understanding:

> I have the feeling if we were to stretch the scope of our questions we would get more. In terms of response from other different levels, I feel that anything is possible. I have no idea where it's going to go, but I sense this is really just the bare beginning of it.[25]

With her emphasis on women's creating their own realities and making free choices, Gail Fairfield works with entities that won't tell others what to do, that give advice in terms of philosophies and possibilities rather than commands and directions. With my own spirit guides, I also find this happening—frustrating though it sometimes is. Discarnate entities are not sent to women to make their decisions, but to help them reach their fullest potentials. Only by taking responsibility and exercising free will is real learning gained. Whatever a control or spirit guide tells her, women make their own choices and take their own actions. Gail Fairfield fosters this perspective, refusing to use channeling to make herself or her controls into gurus.

Nadal's comments on the relationship between humans and animals was given in Chapter Eight. Here is her comment in June, 1986 on the importance of completing tasks. Her ideas are another way to look at time and timelessness, the difference between linear and matriarchal realities:

> When you are not in this reality there is not time, and therefore tasks do not exist outside of this reality. But when you are here, within time and within space, then it becomes important to have tasks, otherwise how would you know that time had gone by? It is one of your ways of measuring the progression of time. When you come to a time when it seems that the tasks are larger than the amount of time that you have, it simply means that you are wanting to be in an experience of another kind of time than earth. Think of the possibility of being in a reality in which the amount of a day would be what you consider 28 hours, or 30 hours, or 50 hours and if you, in fact, had existed in one of those realities in another time, your conception of how long, or how much you could accomplish in one day would be quite different. So sometimes it is disorienting

to be here, and all of a sudden it is night and there are still things to do. This is true for some of you. For many of you, the dilemma also has to do with the amount of future that you are trying to cram into the present. If you allow the future to remain in the future and simply deal with the present now—it will be simpler. What is here now. Even five minutes from now is the future, it is not the present.[26]

Nadal, Seth and Gay Bonner are all in accord on this issue. All time is now in the clairvoyant or matriarchal reality.

When channeling for an individual, Gail talks with the person for ten to fifteen minutes about her issue, channels for half an hour to forty-five minutes, then does some debriefing at the end. In her work and writing, Gail Fairfield also teaches people who wish to be channels themselves:

It's the big thing right now and, relatively speaking, is an easy tool to learn. Astrology takes three or four years to understand the whole system and how it works, it's really complex. Tarot doesn't take quite as long, but channeling is something that if you really decide you want to do it, and have somebody teach you, you can decide today and start channeling tomorrow. The quality of information, or the types of issues you can deal with may not be sophisticated yet, but if you want to do it, all you need is your body. All you need is yourself and the desire. I think people have the mythology that it is more real, that information gotten from a nonphysical entity is more real, or of higher quality than a tarot reading or astrology reading. I have doubts about that ... because I know that Nadal and Siran have their own prejudices and their own points of view, and certainly also do Jesus Christ and Buddha—they have their own perspectives, and who's to say ... [27]

Gail Fairfield is working to take the mystique out of channeling, to make it accessible for any woman who chooses to do it. This is what women's psychic ability, and psychic development, is all about.

Women write about their experiences with discarnate entities, usually the spirit guides that help and protect women in lifelong ways. While the terms vary, the experience is one known to all. Irene writes about her guardian angel:

My mom was really responsible for my belief in spirit guides—although I knew them as angels. We prayed every night asking for their guidance and protection, and my mom laughed because I always added one line, 'and don't go away.' I could hardly speak, yet I remember feeling there was an angel there with me, and I loved that thought. We lived in a three room flat, because we were newcomers to the country and my father couldn't afford more then. The area was run down with rats in the neighborhood. I must've been about three or four years old and I remember playing and feeding the 'kitties' in the backyard. Whenever I came back in and told my mom how the 'kitties' came out and how happy I was to see them, she would get angry and scared and not let me out again. How I never got a rat bite, I don't know—it must've been my angel. There were no cats, only rats.

When an aura reading was done for her, the woman described
Irene's guides:

> She said I had four of them: a small druid-like dwarf behind me trying to push
> me forward; a shorter Indian guide in front of me; a vague figure on my right,
> and a large, energy filled grandfather type on my left.

Flyin thunda cloud writes about her spirit guide, Isis. She is a
Black lesbian who experiences Isis as her Goddess or orisha:

> During the year 1983, I underwent surgery, very dangerous surgery on my
> heart, and I was so frightened that I wouldn't come out of the surgery. But one
> night this female form appeared to me and this very female voice spoke to me
> about not being afraid. At that time I think that my experience of the Goddess
> Isis was a very third-world experience (since that's the way I've always been
> able to experience Goddesses). Anyway, she took hold of my hand, helped me
> to lower my blood pressure, and talked me ever so gently through the surgery.
> To this day we remain very close and she's not only my orisha but my pal. She is
> the Goddess that justifies my madness and surrounds me in her loving warmth.
> She gets me through the hard spots and helps me to get over the intense hatred
> and anger that I feel both as a Black lesbian and Indian (Native Amerikan
> mixed) lesbian. I rarely feel good about expressing my closeness to her, because
> most people think that I am crazy, but I know that I'm not. Without Isis in my life
> I would never be calm or centered. Without her in my life, I don't think I'd be
> writing you now . . . She's got her hand of love upon you and she's helping you
> to share her love with all womyn.

Nancy is an artist who works deeply with visualization techniques,
and increasingly with her spirit guide:

> I'm an artist, and I studied at the Pennsylvania Academy of Fine Arts—1967-71.
> I've used visualization in a number of ways in my work. At first I would get
> spontaneous flashes and attempt to paint what I'd seen. Then I let the vision
> come through the painting, applying washes of this color and turpentine, find-
> ing images in the shapes that resulted.

As she learned more about psychic development, Nancy dis-covered
her spirit guide:

> I decided to call on a personal guide, in meditation, to help me through life
> challenges. I started my journal of guided visualizations. I've now gone through
> two volumes with this guide. My guide is a small, androgynous being, with
> scraggly hair, smushed up top hat, striped sox and Mary Ann Shoes. Some-
> where down the line my guide let me know that she was a *she*, and her
> name is Elma.
> Elma takes me through landscapes and stories, meeting a variety of charac-
> ters, and after the visualization I write it down and maybe try to figure out what
> it means, although I don't always. I just figure that keeping that channel open is
> an end in itself sometimes.
> In May I started drawing a story that is one of these visualization segments. In
> it Elma, who had not yet revealed her name, takes me through scenes that show
> me how I can 'Make Ready the Harbor'—because my ship is coming in. (That
> was good news to me after so many years of struggle). In the story I meet

characters who are parts of myself—I rescue them and my guide shows me what they're each about. This book is drawn in frames, showing the scenes and characters, somewhat like a comic book. I have over forty pages now, and it will probably go to around sixty pages.

I can't wait to see Nancy's book! Many artists describe their work as guided, but few so directly.

Catherine writes about her spirit guide, Doug, who taught her to take risks. When a discarnate entity tells you to do something that feels wrong, don't do it. In this case, whatever she did, Catherine was protected and survived.

When I was a child I had a voice in my head which used to communicate with me. I called this voice 'Doug' and considered *her* a friend. We usually talked in the privacy of the bathroom (who knows why, but that's what I remember). Anyhow, when I was a child there were times that my life required me to do something daring or dangerous or in other words, something that I consciously thought might require hurting myself, if circumstances went wrong . . . Whenever I got myself into a situation where my conscious mind said danger and my peers said 'do it,' Doug would pop in my head and her message was basically, 'Oh, what the hell, the worst that can happen is I can die'—no big deal, right? So 'Doug' prompted me to defy the death potential.

Diane's guide appeared to her in a dream, helping her to find her "power tools." She bought a clear crystal from me at a craft fair, and later at another one a piece of gem rose quartz.

First, I bought my large clear crystal from you. Then, at a craft fair in Minnesota, I found a rattle with Kali's image on it and was drawn to it with the same force as the clear crystal.

Later that night I had a dream where my spiritual guide gave me two crystals and the rattle. I played first with my clear crystal, and then the clay rattle, feeling them in my hand.

Then I picked up the triangular pink quartz crystal. It shimmered and had prisms in it like my clear crystal. I was amazed and calmed by its beauty.

My guide said, 'Now you have your three power tools.' I thanked her for them. Then I suddenly realized that I didn't own the pink crystal in my waking life. 'I don't have this one,' I told her.

She gave me one of those 'Oh ye of little faith' looks and said, 'Then you'll find it.'

And at the last vendors' night I found it on your table and knew that it belonged to me.

Sharon, who perceives manifestations, had this spirit guide experience crossing space and time, and also involving dreams:

I turned over in my bed and gasped as I saw a transparent woman who looked to be around 25-28 years old. She had long, dark hair and wore a flowing white gown. Her smile radiated much love and was so extremely pleasant and comforting that I fell asleep as she looked down at me.

What intrigues me about the above sight is a dream I had when I was 28 years old. In the dream, I had gone to a child's aid who was struggling constantly in the darkness. I handed her a flashlight to help her find her way. I knew that she was the child I used to be and wanted to assist her. The next morning as I dressed for work, I was caught up in surprise at my reflection in the mirror. It was the same face I had seen all those years ago as a child. Did I, as a child, receive help from my future self? Did I, as the adult, go back in time; I wish I knew. I have never understood the theory of the ever-present NOW. I do not understand how everything past, present and future can exist simultaneously. How could the child I was receive help from the person of today? Yet, this experience seems to relate, somehow, to that theory.

If spirit helpers can be ancestors, why not also living women taking jumps in time? Channeled entities again and again say this is possible, and Jane Roberts discusses the idea extensively. There are simultaneous reality and time frames, and simultaneous lives.

Pam's spirit guide Anthony became St. Anthony. He is there to help her find things, to comfort, calm, protect and be company. Assimilating into her beliefs, spirit guide Anthony became a saint.

I've always been psychic, but as I've heard *many* others say, it was discouraged and laughed off by the adults around me, so I squelched it early on. However, since I was *very* small, I've always had a good relationship with St. Anthony. Anthony and I 'believe in' one another—so I've had extremely good luck in finding lost objects . . .

It seems he's always been with me, although as a child, I remember calling him 'Anthony' (instead of St. Anthony). Perhaps he's a guardian angel? I'm not sure of when I *first* contacted the one I call 'Saint.' I guess I'll have to leave it, as I can't remember a time when Anthony/St. Anthony wasn't around. I get in touch with him by closing my eyes, calling him, and asking for help. It has to be a conscious, actual, request: i.e., 'St. Anthony, I need your help. My ring is lost and you know how much it means to me. Please help me find it. Thanks.' Sometimes I'm led to where it/the object is, other times, I 'see' it and go to the place and find it. I always say 'Thank you!' I truly believe that 'an attitude of gratitude' (although sounding trite) is a real plus . . . and I work at being grateful for everything I'm given or accomplish.

She describes two other spirit guides that have come to her in meditation work:

One is a high guide called D'ar, and the other is a Native American woman. I've received some interesting information from both.

Pam also connects with her guides through automatic writing, particularly with D'ar, who may be a Matron Guide.

Nan connected with her totem animal/guide in a shamanic journeying meditation, an experience with her circle:

I went into the cavern expressly to meet my totem animal. I ran into a few others first, but there's a way to know which one is it. I even saw a tarantula, an animal I have great terror of, but was relieved to find it wasn't it. I finally got to this trio of big cats, a jaguar, a puma and a panther. They directed me further, and there was a lion! I had to laugh because I'm into lionESSES, but my circle told me afterward that totem animals represent all the animals in a species, so it could just have easily been one. Well, to make a long story short, I asked the lion what to do about writing again. It said, 'Just DO it!'

Then later I asked about my eyes, why I have so much trouble accepting my poor vision and all. I explained none of my other sources could/would help me. The lion said my problem is that I'm afraid, paralyzingly afraid of death! It said that I have to come to grips with that, to accept and trust that Pine and I and my other loved ones will die and that it's okay and not the END. I actually cried right there in trance.

More on death, its process and what comes after it from the terms of matriarchal/clairvoyant reality, is discussed in Chapter Thirteen. Totem animals are another form of spirit guide.

Susan Sheppard is part Native American and becoming a Lakota shaman. She had this experience:

Oh, what happened last night! My car broke down at the post office at nine o'clock in the evening—three miles from home. I had to walk through the worst part of town, a very dangerous section to even drive through. I started walking and before I knew it, I was singing in Lakota! I can do this now and I don't know how I do it. I felt my two spirit guides on both sides of me. No one bothered me at all and even the most dangerous looking hoodlums smiled and spoke to me. They probably thought I was a crazy woman because I was singing as loud as I could. I sang parts of the Sun Dance song. I could feel the cone of power within me and walked with great confidence. No one can hurt me or break this power. I thought that over and over, and it worked.

In a healing experience, Susan saw the spirit guide of a woman she and Judy were doing healing with, Judy's daughter Margo:

In my mind's eye, I saw a woman always standing at Margo's bed. She looked English and wore a crown. When Margo was able to talk, she told Judy the exact same thing. Of course, none of this was surprising at all. She is Margo's guide.

Oak Sky tells how she found her name, in a shamanic vision experience that she felt was guided. A feeling of at-one-ness happened to her, the oneness Gay Bonner talks about:

I was feeling a little bit detached from the group, the circle of women—my mind was wandering from the critiquing process, when all of a sudden I lost all awareness of the group and everything else except the following. Without consciously willing any of this, my head turned slowly (felt like it was being turned by an outside force), until my eyes reached the trunk of a large beautiful Live Oak tree we were sitting by. My eyes moved up the trunk and I experienced the sensation of the tree as being vibrantly alive—it was like I could see its molecules vibrating and I felt them, as though the tree and I were not separate. After a moment of joyous wonder (but no hysteria or analytical thought), a voice—not seemingly my own said, 'Oak.' Then my eyes moved up along a branch into the leaves, and I was drawn to a beautiful segment of blue sky between leaves and branches. I experienced the sky as alive and with it At-One-Ness, and the voice said, 'Sky.' Immediately after I heard the words 'Oak' and 'Sky,' and was utterly filled with the sensation of both; my own mind said, (I said to myself in my head)—'Oak Sky'—and knew immediately beyond the shadow of a doubt, that this was my name. After a moment, I began to return to ordinary awareness and the poetry group.

This story could also have been included in Chapter Eight, on telepathy and the oneness of life. Oak Sky considered the experience a vision quest, with guided information showing her the name she had been looking for.

JoKasha had this channeling or mediumship experience spontaneously:

On July 4, 1985, I decided to have a day in solitude since both of my sons would be with their father for the day. In the afternoon, I took a nap. After waking, as I lay in bed, I became aware of an entity in me. I began to speak in a thick Italian accent and did not have access to the vocabulary that I normally have. I was able to switch between this entity and myself and carry on a conversation. (I am accustomed to doing gestalt work, so this style is comfortable and familiar to me).

This woman told me that she died when I was born. She told me that she lived outside of Catania, which I later learned was in Sicily, and that she had been a prostitute. She told me that she wanted me to take care of her daughter who was now in a nursing home. I asked her how I would find her daughter. She said, 'That will be easy.' I have not yet come across a woman in a nursing home who needs my care.

JoKasha sees past life overtones in the entity's manifesting through her. In this life, she is a psychologist and teacher, director of a halfway house for women on probation.

As I thought about my current life, it made sense. My work at the halfway house had been with prostitutes. My pain with my husband was that he had a sexual addiction and frequented prostitutes. Somehow once I had this experience, the 'why me?' questions decreased and I felt more peaceful about my current lot in life.

Such experiences can be of past lives, ancestors or other discarnate entities, with information important for this life, and for the woman experiencing it.

Ancestors are also spirit guides, a theme strong in African and Asian religions. Luisa Teish writes about this in Dahomey, from the view of the Fon people:

The Fon people believe that the *se*, the soul, has many layers. The core of *se* flows into the *Da* at death and rejoins the *Voduns* (the Goddess, nature). The *joto* is a layer of spirit/intelligence handed down from the ancestors of the person. Under the right circumstances, it is *joto* who has been the guardian spirit of the person in life. In rebirth the *joto* blends with the *selido*, the peculiar personality traits inherent in the person to be born. Thus the new person is both *joto* (ancestor) and *selido* (a new being). The *ye* (physical characteristic), the shadow that leaves the body at death, also reblends itself with *joto* and *selido*. Together, these three form a new person who has physical characteristics of the ancestors (*ye*), an individual identity (*selido*) and a source of inspiration and protection (*joto*). *Se* who has been revitalized by her stay with the Mother Creator blends with *kpoli* (destiny) and becomes *sekpoli*, the destiny of the newly formed soul in body.[28]

In theosophical terms, the *se*, the soul, is woman's spiritual aura body that flows into oneness and rejoins the Goddess at death. *Joto* is part of that oneness, woman's spirit guides that travel with her on her journey into life, and women are part *joto* and part their own personalities, the *selido*. The shadow that leaves the body at death is the etheric double, the *ye*, and *kpoli* in other terms is karma. *Sekpoli* is Be-ing. Women's spirit guides are therefore the passed over spirit/intelligence of ancestors who have gone before them.

In these terms, Luisa Teish describes her own spirit guide, She Who Whispers from her book *Jambalaya*:

> Her voice is gentle, rich, but different from my own. We have similar personalities, but She is wiser and offers me information, advice, and instructions on charms and rituals. Periodically, through disbelief, I have lost contact with Her, but She has been my steady companion since 1974.
> I don't know when She first showed up really. She might have been the Wind that blew gently past my ears, as I opened the bathroom window of my mother's house. This simple act made me feel, unreasonably, that I should have been born in the remote past or the distant future. She could have been that girl in my mother's bedroom mirror. She could have been that *feeling* I got from stalking the Lady, the one of Perpetual Help. Maybe I heard Her scream in the library, 'He's lying. Don't believe it' . . . She could be Moma Ruthie. Maybe She's Big Moma Jones. Perhaps shes my 'little soul'—my *anima*. For sure She's the one the priest mentioned when he said, 'Listen to your head, *mi'hijada*, my daughter.'
> But trust in her is not a matter of blind faith. I don't believe in the stuff, myself. Like everybody around me, She has been tested.[29]

Stories of She Who Whispers weave in and out of this beautiful book.

Other women have had ancestors for their guides. Jokasha describes an out of body experience where her deceased brother took her to a special room and gave her a message for her mother, and Carol describes her father's appearance as her guide:

> My father died a few years ago and he has helped my daughter and I all the time. One day we had to be somewhere and the car wouldn't start. Fifteen times, we would get it going, once we took our foot off the brake—it died. My daughter asked him for help, and the next time it started.
> I had to take my mom to the doctor's, but my dog got loose. I drove for two hours looking for her. It was getting too close to my picking my mom up. I explained to my dad how I felt and asked for help. My car wheels started taking

streets I hadn't planned on going—he led me to the dog in less than two minutes.

My father was a carpenter. I take after him as far as fixing things. I was driving a huge nail in a wall. I had spent half an hour driving it and still had an inch and a half to go. My arm was dead—I didn't have the strength. I asked his help— within two minutes the nail was in.

My daughter was visiting a family for the day. She gave a young boy ten dollars to go to the store a couple blocks away. He came back crying because he lost the ten dollars. His family was angry with him and about fourteen people went to look for it. When they came back without it—the boy was still crying— she told him not to worry about it, her grandfather would find it. She proceeded to ask for help and went outside and was led directly to the ten dollars.

Many of the death manifestations women see are ancestors acting as spirit guides for them. More on the connectedness of life and death in Chapter Thirteen.

Guides can come singly or in groups. Blanche Meyerson channels a group of guides, who she calls "The Doctors," and they direct her healing work:

Blanche explains her 'doctors' as six spirits who work through her. She knows their names and can describe each of them, even has her favorites. At one time, they communicated directly with her but now send messages only through psychic intermediaries. One reason for that: Blanche has not heeded their admonitions to stop smoking—something they stay on her case about.[30]

Sharon has also been visited by a board of guides, telling her to quit smoking:

In 1972 . . . I was sleeping in the bedroom I shared with my daughter. I was awakened by someone whispering my name. I quickly sat up in bed. In the darkened room, I saw five beings standing at the foot of my bed. They appeared to each look the same, with heads larger than ours, their bodies shorter than ours. I couldn't see what they wore or their features well, but I did see that they were without hair on their heads. Telepathically, they gave me a message in unison. I can't remember the exact words, but they said something to the effect. 'You must quit smoking, now. You quit smoking and when you do, the world is yours. You must quit smoking before it's too late.'

In utter terror, I eased my way over my daughter's sleeping body and ran to the living room. Realizing I had left my daughter in the room with these beings, I tip-toed back to the door of the bedroom. My daughter was sleeping soundly and undisturbed. The beings were gone. There was no one in the room. Unnerved by the incident, I lit a cigarette. I had been offered the 'world' if I quit smoking and I cannot believe that I am still smoking in 1986. But, I am trying like hell to cut down and to quit.

Blanche Meyerson has not quit, either.

In one more group guide experience, Rebecca describes being in contact with the "entities I always knew were there":

I was in a circle of coveners and we were doing the OM chant when I heard other noncorporeal entities singing. I asked who they were and with a laugh they directed my attention to my womb. That's how I first knew I was pregnant.

I remember that little girl I once was who yearned to be able to talk to animals, entities and other people in ways that, at that time, I had only read about. Now I act as teacher and proof to others that they too can be psychic.

The last spirit guide to meet in this chapter is Gunther, friend and companion to Lynn. Though she speaks with him primarily by ouija board and automatic writing, there is also the direct, intuitive, voice-in-the-mind type contact.

I depend on Gunther, my guide, for a lot of insight, the way one might depend on a good friend for an objective opinion of a life situation. I don't find Gunther to be any more omniscient than an ordinary human with regard to day-to-day matters, and he stubbornly refuses even to hint at upcoming events—something I'm usually grateful for in retrospect. He has a remarkable talent for finding objects that I lose and for drawing my attention to important things in my physical environment. He often alerts me to traffic dangers, for example, causing me to brake when I have a green light at a blind corner, a second before someone runs the red light. He likes to 'manipulate' small physical objects—for example, if a mosquito is annoying me, he will distract it away from me if I ask. With regard to spiritual matters, he is an excellent guide, always direct, clear and to the point. He has a marvelous sense of humor, and he loves to coin 'quotable quotes,' if you will.

Two of my favorites are:

'Some people go to great pains to achieve truth. Most go to greater pains to avoid it.'

'Being dead, as you put it, is a lot like the LSD experience: the senses are all enhanced incredibly, one's sense of time is unreliable, and mundane things seem profound. The only difference is that there are no narcs on the astral plane.'

Gunther is fairly typical of spirit guides and a good place to end women's stories of them. These psychic companions and discarnate helpers figure prominently in the remainder of this book.

Every woman enters this existence with a lifetime guide and probably several other spirit helpers. To come alone is not permitted. Possibly, if you were not aware before of your guides' existence, reading about spirit guides has put you in contact with them, helped you to know them through others' experiences. Many women are aware of their guides, knowing them as their "inner voice" or "inner bell" or "conscience." Whether guides are a new idea or an old one, it is amazingly simple to contact them through meditation. Meeting your guides in this way brings women to know them for the first time or increases women's knowing of them if they've already met. The process is familiar and simple for women who have read this far.

Find a quiet, protected spot to do the meditation, indoors or outdoors, but following intuition and being especially choosey.[31] Either sit tailor fashion or lie down flat with your knees bent and feet on the floor. Close your eyes and become very relaxed. Some women experience a feeling of spinning or of their legs shaking, and this is nothing to worry about. Ground fully, using roots or rods from the soles of your feet, or the umbilical grounding cord. When fully relaxed and grounded, invite your guides to come forward, or use this affirmation, "I am ready, able and open to receive my life guide on the conscious plane."[32] Telepath feelings of compassion and love, open your heart, and open your crown, third eye and throat chakras. Wait and receive. It's that simple.

Impressions and responses come in a number of ways, mostly sensory. You may see your guide visually in the meditation, hear her words telepathically, experience a fragrance, a touch sensation, a feeling of stationary presence. It can feel as simple as an intuition of someone being there, someone known and loved. Guides appear as light, or more usually as male or female; your own psychic receptivity gives them their appearance and gender, as light is their actual form. When you feel someone there, ask her name.

For many years, perhaps always, I have been in contact with Helen, but knew her only as a voice and presence. I knew my writing was guided, and assumed it was all one guide. I had no visual images or names, not realizing these were available to me. The first time I did this meditation, I saw Helen, in full twenties regalia and laughing, and welcomed her like an old friend. "So that's what you look like!" I said. I asked her name and she told me. Until now, she had taken on the name of any woman I was in love with at the time. When I asked her why she had done that all these years, instead of telling me who she is, she replied, "You never asked my real name."

Later that night, in bed before sleep when I feel most in contact with my guides, I asked Helen to appear again, and she did. I was not in the meditative state, just grounded and centered. This time I was aware of a second presence, a Be-ing separate from Helen who became more separate and distinct over the next few nights. This was Hutseba, who came forward visually when I asked who she was. Both women appear together now most of the time, Helen there first, more boisterous and physically closer, and Hutseba waiting quietly behind us.

After a few nights using this meditation, then continuing it in the quiet time before sleep, I only need to feel grounded and centered to contact these Be-ings or ask them for advice. I daily feel the presence of one or the other, speaking telepathically at most quiet times, but visually they appear only at night before sleep or in meditation when I ask for them. Over a period of about a month, I asked each woman to tell me who she is and what she does, and there were ready answers.

Several months after her death, Tiger started appearing with Hutseba. When I talk to her, she grins at me and wags her plumey tail, but so far she hasn't talked with me. I know she's listening and watching, and maybe it's time to ask her. The new guide, the Native American man, has appeared in the background for about a year now, as a form of blue light. He has only now come forward, still surrounded by light, in the time I talk with Helen and Hutseba before sleep. I have talked with him once, and in his presence the women moved to the background for the time he was there. I don't yet know his name, and have only made verbal contact with him once. My friend Ida Shaw, who sees auras visually, saw him there a year ago, predicting we'd make contact this year. She says he is a Matron/Master Guide.

Sometimes in the meeting meditation, more than one guide appears, and this can be confusing. Ask your life guide to appear first, and the others to wait. Meet her first and ask her name, then ask the others to come one by one. It may take more than one meditation session:

> Should you be blessed with more than one guide, they'll all want to be known by you while you're in a receptive state. Later in the day you might do a second session and call in someone else. But it's less confusing and less threatening to get to know your guides one at a time. Usually they're sensitive to this, and the others will wait patiently in the background until you have met and made acquaintance with your life guide (an encounter which poses minimal difficulty, inasmuch as you're already accustomed to your life guide's energy, having felt it around you since infancy).[33]

Hutseba held back until I'd met and begun to know Helen. When you've met and named each guide, go first to your life guide, asking her why she's there, what her purpose is in being with you. Ask each of the guides in turn. Concentrating on your life guide first, ask her any questions about your relationship that you have. Ask her about the life she appears to you from, and/or in what other lives you have known each other.

Most women contact guides readily, but for some there is a block or resistance. If this happens, go deeper into the meditative state, and try running energy or clearing your chakras before asking your guide to appear. It may take a few nights of doing the meditation before something happens. Are you fully relaxed? Fully grounded? Do you have the will and intent to meet your life guide? Is there resistance? Why? Examine what worries or prevents you: is it your upbringing in traditional religious values? Your fear of the unknown? Your worry of losing autonomy in your life? Your teenage fears that no one could ever want you? The repression of your invisible playmate or your psychic abilities/realities as a child? Being aware of the resistance and re-evaluating it can open the blocks.

Accepting a spirit guide, or even the ability to channel, does not mean you give up your Be-ing or autonomy.[34] Guides only advise, they cannot and do not make your choices or force you to accept theirs. Guides interact with you in a friendly relationship, and with the same type of interaction as friends who are incarnate. A guide you don't like can be asked to leave; a guide that appears at a time you don't want to talk with her can be asked to return later. Sometimes guides are sent to help you realize things you don't want to see or make changes you need but resist. Be aware of what's really good for you before refusing the presence of a guide showing unwanted truths.

Guides are not permitted to appear in a form that frightens, but from the number of apparition stories in this book, it seems that they sometimes do. In no woman's story has any harm come. Laeh Maggie Garfield shares this one:

> One night I woke out of a blissful sleep. Something had roused me and I glanced around the room. Suddenly, just above my face, two green eyes blinked down at me. At first I was scared; then I got angry. I said, "You know the rules. How dare you appear in that form?" The green eyes, attached to nothing else that I could see, blinked all the way across the room and out into the hall, diminishing as they went. The next night I was awakened by a beam of golden light so beautiful and peaceful that for a while I just basked in it. This time the entity had found the right way to approach me.[35]

As with any friend or Be-ing sent by the Goddess, treat it with love and respect. But remember that you are in charge of the situation and you make the choices.

Working with spirit guides has been for me one of the most rewarding aspects of developing psychically, of connecting with Goddess, Goddess within and the matriarchal reality. The feeling of being wanted, protected, cared about and supported in all I do is a coming home. In doing healings or in writing I know what to do, how to do it and when, with spirit guide help. Women who perceive their guides as the Goddess are not so far off the mark; they are part of Goddess and part of Goddess within, and a link between them. There is everything here of comfort, friendship, love and help in the woman/spirit guide/spirit control relationship. As Gay Bonner teaches, incarnate or discarnate, we are all one. And women are all part of Goddess, as their guides are.

The next chapter continues work with discarnate entities, and discusses channeling through the ouija board and automatic writing. Women begin voice channeling with these methods. Also included is work with seances and an introduction to the great women mediums of the last century. Now that you have dis-covered and met your guides, and know they are always with you, they will continue to be prominent in the rest of this book—for the peace, beauty and good of all.

Francene Hart

# FOOTNOTES

1. Laeh Maggie Garfield and Jack Grant, *Companions in Spirit*, (Berkeley, CA, Celestial Arts, 1984), p. 1. This is a beautiful book.

2. *Ibid.*, p. 44.

3. *Ibid.*, p. 44 ff.

4. *Ibid.*, p. 118 ff. I have feminized Master Guides to Matron Guides, as the term implies ownership and hierarchy.

5. In David C. Knight, *The ESP Reader*, p. 192-193.

6. *Ibid.*, p. 195.

7. Lawrence LaShan, *The Medium, the Mystic, and the Physicist*, Appendix B, "When is Uvani: An Approach to a Concept of Spirit Controls," p. 211-215.

8. *Ibid.*, p. 213.

9. Laeh Maggie Garfield, *Companions in Spirit*, p. 42-43.

10. Lawrence LeShan, *The Medium, the Mystic, and the Physicist*, p. 216.

11. Jane Roberts, *The Seth Material*, p. 15-16. Also, in *The Coming of Seth*, Chapter One.

12. *Ibid.*, p. 20. Also, P. 25.

13. Jane Roberts, *The Coming of Seth*, p. 209-211.

14. Sandra J. Stevens, *Being Alive is Being Psychic*, p. 19.

15. *Ibid.*, p. 20.

16. *Ibid.*, p. 26.

17. *Ibid.*, p. 27.

18. *Ibid.*, p. 26.

19. *Ibid.*, p. 53.

20. Jennifer York, Ph.D., "Gail Fairfield: Astrologer, Channeler, Tarotist," in *Spiritual Women's Times*, (Seattle, WA), Vol. I, no. 1, Spring, 1987, p. 3.

21. Cobra, "Channeling Interview with Gail Fairfield," in *Goddess Rising*, Issue 15, Winter Solstice, 1986, p. 6. Gail Fairfield has revised her words for this book.

22. *Ibid.* Much of this section is from Cobra's article, and from personal communication with Gail Fairfield.

23. *Ibid.*

24. *Ibid.,* p. 3.

25. *Ibid.,* p. 6.

26. *Ibid.,* p. 7.

27. *Ibid.*

28. Luisa Teish, *Jambalaya, The Natural Woman's Book,* (San Francisco, Harper and Row Publishers, 1985), p. 68-69.

29. *Ibid.,* p. 43.

30. Marcia Gillespie, "Healer Meyerson," in *Ms. Magazine,* December, 1985, p. 58.

31. Laeh Maggie Garfield and Jack Grant, *Companions in Spirit,* Chapter Four. The exercise is from their book.

32. *Ibid.,* p. 39.

33. *Ibid.,* p. 40.

34. *Ibid.,* p. 42.

35. *Ibid.,* p. 43.

## Chapter Twelve
# The Crown Chakra: Mediumship
# Ouija Boards, Automatic Writing
# and Seances

*Pretend that you hold a flashlight, and the flashlight is consciousness. You can turn this light in many directions, but instead you are in the habit of directing it along one certain path, and you have forgotten that there are other paths.*

*All you have to do is swing the flashlight in other directions. When you shift it, the path upon which you have been focusing will momentarily appear dark, but other realities and images will become available to you, and there is nothing to prevent you from swinging the flashlight back to the earlier position.*[1]

This book, and all my books, are channeled writing. When I begin one, given I've done the reading and the research first and thoroughly, I sit at the typewriter and calm myself into a meditative state. I begin consciously thinking each word to go on the page, but that gradually stops. After awhile, I just type, and can go for as long as several hours, several pages at a time. I may start with an outline of what I want to write, but often there is just the subject. Beyond chapter headings, I understand the book's structure only by looking back at it. I "hear" each word as I type it, or slightly before, forgetting it on conscious levels as soon as it's written. I do some revising, but very little, as I go. Every morning I sit at the typewriter and for several hours I write, my first and primary activity of every day. I write five to twelve pages in a four to ten hour day, and do that seven days a week until the book is done. Each book has her own rhythm, her own pace and joys.

When I come back to "now" each day, there's a pile of variously neat pages, turned face down on my desk. There are typos and misspellings to correct, and sometimes grammar to fix up, but the basic material or chapter is in the pile. When I stop, I have little memory of what it is I've written until I read it later outside the alpha state. While writing I leave the space-time continuum, and feel safe and monitored in doing that. I have no concept of how much time has passed and little awareness of events around me.

When I begin writing each morning, I start by revising what I've done the day before. For the first time, I see fully what I've written and work consciously to revise it. I retype, make corrections, complete quote references, polish it up. I'm usually surprised at how little of this there is to do. The revising takes half an hour to two hours, depending on how many pages, and by the end of it, I've entered the meditative alpha state again, ready to receive information by going deeper, ready to continue the writing for several hours and pages more.

I feel spirit guide presence when I write, of course. The words are coming from a spirit source (is it Hutseba or Helen?), and I feel Hutseba, the healer, at my left shoulder, supervising and protecting. Hutseba eases me into the alpha state and decides when it's time to come out of it. She's the one who sends me for a glass of water or a bathroom trip, still in trance. Some days she frustrates me with interruptions and distractions, until my will to write calls a halt to it. She applauds me when I refuse the telephone and the letters to answer, and go back to receiving at the typewriter. The words flow again, and peacefully.

Writing is the deepest trance state I go into, the most pleasant, and my greatest awareness of outside help and channeling. When I finish a day's work and come back to now I'm exhausted, but the draw to keep going and to start again is the most intense need in my life. When I finish a chapter, I revise it completely, and then the whole manuscript at the end, with a less intense discarnate presence and less deep the daily channeled writing state. Being a channel for the automatic writing of Goddess books and skills is my calmest, most centered, most satisfied time.

Spirit guides and discarnate entities speak to women from within, and come forward to the linear plane through channeling. While voice channeling was discussed in the last chapter, there are other ways to channel, and the other ways often lead to voice channeling. Automatic writing, the ouija board and doing formal seances that invoke discarnate spirits are other ways of channeling and mediumship, bringing discarnate information to linear reality. Voice channeling is the form most women know now, and many women today are tapping into it. In our grandmothers' times—and remember that many women inherit their psychic abilities in motherlines leading back to their grandmothers, skipping a generation or not—the skills of the ouija board and automatic writing were more known and used. At the turn of the century, mediumship by seances was being worked at extensively, and the great mediums of the time were mostly women. For about seventy-five years, from the pre-Civil War until after World War I, mediumship was an honored skill, bringing several great women psychics into prominence in the United States and Europe. Spiritism or spiritualism, as it was called, then declined.

The ouija board has degenerated into a parlor game, yet through it Jane Roberts, Sheila Reynolds and Gail Fairfield all made contact with their spirit controls and began voice channeling. Automatic writing is a skill from which many women begin to voice channel, also. Women at or after menopause often tap into automatic writing for the first time; several women have related that experience, though many younger women do it. For the women who commented on finding this form of channeling only as they reached their crone years, it's a new wisdom, a new linking into stroking the python. Remember that the priestesses of Gaea at the Delphic Oracle could not become the Pythia until after age fifty.

Seances are something from women's past, but in psychic reality there is no past. Opening up the skill, and meeting the women of other times who were great mediums, is an entry into herstory. If the skill was important to our foremothers, should it not be something to understand? If contact with spirit guides means so much of comfort, companionship and information to women on the linear plane, wouldn't contact with specifically invited spirits—a deceased mother or grandmother, or a spirit guide—not also be significant? The connection of time and space into matriarchal wholeness where all time is now, is also a connection between the worlds and between the living and the dead, life and death as separate but existing realities. Spiritism and seances, as beginning understandings of what death is (for greater understanding of what life is) are things women need to know about, choosing to practice them or not.

In automatic writing, ouija boards, channeling or spiritism/seances, women connect their own Be-ings on the earth plane to women who are "dead," who have their existence on other planes. Spirit guides describe their past lives, virtually all of them do if asked, as do channeled entities such as Seth, Nadal and Siran, Gay Bonner. Entities connected to by automatic writing or the ouija board are also channeled entities or spirit guides, discarnate spirits, Be-ings that have existence outside of the linear reality/earth plane. In spiritism and by way of seances, women invoke a particular spirit, rather than whoever comes. In any of these cases, lives and past lives are dis-covered, and the knowledge of movement among planes of existence. The living are "here" (wherever that is), and the not-living, the "dead" have carried their awareness to somewhere else.

Seth explains these changes of dimensions, or levels of realities:

> Consider a network of wires, a maze of interlocking wires endlessly constructed so that looking through them there would seem to be no beginning or end. Your plane could be likened to a small position between four very spindly wires, and my plane could be likened to the small position in the neighboring wires on the other side. Not only are we on different sides of the same wires, but we are at the same time above or below, according to your viewpoint. And if you consider the wires as forming cubes . . . then the cubes would also fit one within the other, without disturbing the inhabitants of either cube or iota. And these cubes are themselves within cubes, and I am speaking now only of the small particle of space taken up by your plane and mine.
>
> Again, think in terms of your plane, bounded by its small spindly set of wires, and my plane on the other side. These, as I have said, have boundless solidarity and depth, yet to one side, the other is transparent. You cannot see through, but the two planes move through each other constantly. I hope you see what I have done here. I have initiated the idea of motion, for true transparency is not the ability to see through, but to move through.[2]

The lines and cubes are imaginary, but "things behave as if the wires and cubes existed."[3] Jane Roberts and Seth call the other, unseen side of the model the fifth dimension, Annie Besant calls it the fourth dimension, and Lawrence LeShan calls it the clairvoyant reality, what I have called the "stroking the python matriarchal consciousness" throughout this book.

With this structure, unseen though it is and a functional rather than structural reality (though Seth and Gay Bonner both assure us there is structure, too), planes of consciousness exist simultaneously. All time is now, and all space is here in this structure or reality, and carnate and discarnate Be-ings are all, as Gay Bonner stresses, one. There are hints of Goddess and Goddess within in this model, as well, and the idea of the oneness of all life stretches to include Be-ings who have passed beyond life, to other planes of existence, through the wires and the cubes.

The force that connects the planes, connects Be-ings on the linear plane to each other, and Be-ings from one plane to another (living and discarnate) is emotion. Remember that in all psychic reality, the *desire* to connect is necessary for connection to happen. In telepathic links, for example, the link occurs most often between mother and daughter, lovers, or other two women who have strong emotional attachment. Without the desire to make an object or affirmation happen, manifesting doesn't occur. In conscious astral projection, separating rather than connecting, the woman must will to leave her body. In meeting spirit guides, or other discarnate entities, the desire to do so is necessary for the contact to occur. In the case of connecting the living and the discarnate, Seth and Jane Roberts say:

> What you call emotion or feeling is the connective between us, and it is the connective that most clearly represents the life force on any plane, under any circumstances. From it is woven all material of your world and mine.[4]

It is this desire to find oneness that makes connection possible, that makes automatic writing, the ouija board, channeling, connecting with spirit guides, and seances happen.

Mediumship of all sorts is a crown center skill, involving just this connecting of planes of reality, this awareness of oneness. It includes connecting the linear to the matriarchal, woman with Goddess and Goddess within, life with death, and incarnate with discarnate Be-ings. Where all of the chakras from the heart center deal with the concept of oneness, the crown reaches beyond the barrier of the planes, the separation between life and death. In the crown chakra, the learning is to bridge the separateness between life and death, and in the transpersonal point, Chapter Thirteen, women discuss Goddess and death itself. Death is part of the continuum that leads to rebirth, and to full circle awareness of the root chakra and past lives. The spiritual connects to the physical. Women who have crown chakra awareness of discarnate entities, and the ability to contact and gain information from them, have awareness that there is no death as we know it, no separation but only connectedness.

Connecting with spirit guides in the last chapter is a beginning of spiritism, and channeling is a beginning and form of mediumship. The way channelers make connection between the planes, open themselves to receive information from discarnate Be-ings, is often through automatic writing or the ouija board. The process of opening the mediumistic channel, the connectedness between a living woman and a discarnate spirit, goes by the quaint term of "sitting for development" or simply "development." This is a term from the era of the great women mediums.

Ouija boards can be bought at game stores or homemade. In a bought one, the board is about twenty-two by fifteen inches,[5] and printed with the alphabet in two rows of large letters. In the upper left-hand corner is printed "yes," and in the upper right-hand corner is printed "no." Numbers from 0 to 9 are printed in a row beneath the alphabet, and at the bottom of the board is printed "goodbye." In making one at home, the board can be printed on oilcloth or heavy paper, paste-on letters used if wished. Make the letters fairly large, in simple printing.

A pointer comes with the board, looking like a flat triangle on legs, or a three-legged miniature table. In France, this is called a planchette. When it comes with a commercial board, the planchette or pointer is made of plastic, with a window. Women making a ouija board at home can use an inverted whiskey glass or a small wine glass. The board and planchette need to be smooth, as the planchette glides over the board pausing at letters and numbers, pointing them out one by one. The planchette should be lightweight to make this movement easier, and the letters need space between them.

Two women operate the ouija board, and a third woman with pencil and paper records the letter-by-letter message. The first two women place their hands on the planchette or wine glass, and all three attune to each other and enter the meditative state. They become grounded and centered at least. The women make an affirmation of what they want to happen: "We receive messages from a positive spirit," and they surround themselves with protective light. The pointer, seeming to move by itself, draws the wine glass or planchette with the women's hands to touch one letter or number after another. The letters spell out the message, and the woman recording writes each letter down. Messages can come quite rapidly, challenging the women to keep up with the letters, requiring deciphering when the pointer stops. If one woman moves her hands from the planchette, the spelling ends.

Contact can happen on the first try or require several tries. The first messages may be garbled, and a series of o's or 8's can be the first contact. An attitude of open receptivity helps; if you don't believe it can happen, it won't.[6] Place the board between the two women touching the planchette, on a table or held across their knees, touching both of them. Keep your eyes open, and both rest two hands on the pointer, the pointer resting on the board. Use the alpha state, and work in sessions of about twenty minutes at first.

Begin the session with the affirmation, specifically stating the invitation of only positive/serious spirits. As on this plane, there are discarnate spirits of all sorts, and a few bad eggs. If a prankster or negative entity comes through, simply refuse it, breaking contact or asking it to leave. Spirits claiming to be Joan of Arc or Eleanora Duse are usually pranksters. In starting a session, either remain quiet and open after the affirmation, or start with a question: "Is anybody there?" When contact is made, the two women's hands follow the pointer while the third writes the letters down, and the women decipher the answer. Once understanding the first message, continue asking questions, gearing the questions to the messages as in any conversation. Use respect; serious questions get serious answers.

When contact is made, ask the entity for her name, who she is, when she was born and died, where she lived, etc. Ask her for relatives' names, and ask her if she knew any of the women at the board in this life or other lives. One woman at a time should ask the questions, speaking aloud in a normal voice or asking mentally. Keep the questions simple and one question at a time, giving enough time for the answer to be spelled out. If nothing happens after asking a question, repeat it. The women holding the planchette do so lightly; too hard and the pointer cannot move.

Keep a notebook of the messages, recording even garbled ones, and date each session, listing who was there. Write down the women's questions and the entities' answers. Messages are not punctuated and often words are not separated, so some decoding may be needed. Things like "4" instead of "for" and "u" for "you" occur, and sentences run together. Some messages are indecipherable, and there can be distortions and contradictions. A number of entities, one after the other, can make their presence known, and the operators can choose who is to speak. According to Jane Roberts, women may or may not make contact in the first session but many do, and most are getting complete sentence messages by the third or fourth time after making contact. After a month's work, she and her partner got as much as ten typewritten pages from a session on the ouija board.[7]

Jane Roberts explains the information as coming through her subconscious mind. She sees the subconscious as more than what is stored underneath the conscious rational, and the subconscious is also the emotional body, a storage place for women's intuition. The subconscious or inner self is the place where the *se* and the *joto*, the self and the inner self or spirit guide merge. Other researchers have called the ouija board, use of a mechanical device to link the planes of existence, a motor automatism.[8]

In this theory, an inner impulse below the rational/conscious level directs the women's hands to move the planchette. In using the ouija board or automatic writing, another motor automatism, the operators receive information from discarnate entities, through the barrier between the planes, and by way of their subconscious minds. As to who's moving the pointer in this explanation:

> Watch any two people operating it for the first time. First one, then the other, will accuse (her) partner of being the culprit who moved the tripod. But this 'You're doing it; no *you* are' syndrome does not last for long, especially if the two continue to practice with the ouija and are in the habit of trusting each other. Both operators soon come to realize that neither one of them is 'doing it'—at least consciously.[9]

As in channeling, women learn that discarnate spirits from the ouija board are not infallible information sources, and also that they have little knowledge of the material world. Asking them about money or the stock market gains little. Asking them about the spirit world, their own world, gains much. Though active in the time of spiritualism's popularity and height, the ouija board was known to ancient Greece. How far back to matriarchal knowledge that it goes, to Goddess stroking the python knowledge, no one knows. Most women have used the ouija board at some time or another as a parlor game, not taking it very seriously, fallible or not. Yet, Jane Roberts connected first with Seth through it, Sheila Reynolds and Sandra Stevens with Gay Bonner through it, and Gail Fairfield also began channeling by voice starting with the ouija board.

For Sheila Reynolds, the first contact with Gay on the ouija board went like this:[10]

| Q: | Is anyone there? | | |
|---|---|---|---|
| A: | GAY BONNER | DEEFJC | WAS GAY |
| | BONNER | | |
| | GOT EFHAURTHAWAY | | QGAT |
| | SHEILA | RUN | F  WO  YES |

and soon

LISTEN TO GAY, LONG TIME TO LISTEN. PATIENCE. JUST REACH OUT AND U WILL NOT BE HURT. THINK FOR URSELF. CRY HATE RAGE FEARS MOLD. UR MUCH HEALTHIER THAN YOU BELIEVE. IT IS WITHIN U. SAY WHAT YOU THINK. CAN HELP MANY PEOPLE RAISE THEIR BELIEFS. U HAVE TIME BEFORE US.[11]

At this time, Sheila worked on the ouija board with other women.

Then Sandra entered:[12]

Q: How did you die?
A: HEART STOPPED
Q: Heart attack?
A: YES
Q: When?
A: 1838
Q: Is there a connection with anyone else in the room?
A: SANDY
Q: Relationship to Sandy?
A: COUSIN
Q: Sandy's name at the time?
A: FRANCES
Q: Last name?
A: BONNER TOO
Q: What year was Sheila born?
A: 1750
Q: Year Sandy born?
A: 1751
Q: Were they close?
A: VERY

After time on the ouija board, Sheila switched to voice channeling of Gay Bonner, with Sandra guiding the questions and recording the sessions. Their original contact with Gay had been on the board.

Jane Roberts met Seth by ouija board, too.[13] For their first several sessions, a variety of deceased relatives and other entities came through, along with a session of nonsense, a few coherent words among it. Then a person called Frank Withers (Jane gave him that name, not the name he gave himself), someone who had lived in their town, came through. She verified Frank Withers' history, including the death date he had given on the ouija board, as a real person, dead in 1942. In the next session, Frank Withers became Seth, choosing that name and persona, and recounting his past lives. Frank Withers arrived on the board on December 2, 1963, became Seth on December 8, and Jane Roberts first channeled Seth by voice on December 15. For a time, she opened Seth sessions on the ouija board, then eventually switched totally to channeling.

The story is similar for Gail Fairfield:

How many years ago—ten or twelve, I really can't pinpoint the exact time. I was reading a lot of Jane Roberts' Seth books and started experimenting with the ouija board with some friends. I decided that's what Jane Roberts started with, so that's what I would start with and see what happened . . . Very early on with the ouija board I started to know what it was going to say before it said it. At first I thought, 'oh, am I making it say that?'—then I realized, 'no, I was just getting the information.' Because it was still weird information, or it was still 'why would I know that . . . I don't know that in my consciousness.'[14]

One day the ouija board spelled out, "Gail in trance, Gail in trance," and Gail began voice channeling.

These women went from the ouija board to channeling, but others go from ouija board to automatic writing. The most classic case of this was two women's, Emily Hutchings' and Pearl Curran's connection with the discarnate entity Patience Worth.[15] The women made their first ouija board contact with Patience in 1912, a seventeenth century Englishwoman who emigrated to America and was killed by Indians. She dictated educated literary English from which Pearl Curran wrote six highly successful novels. The contact switched from ouija board to automatic writing for the channeling of these novels that described a life Pearl Curran could not have known about.

In the early sessions, Emily Hutchings and Pearl Curran operated the board and Mary Pollard recorded the messages for typing later on by Emily. The following early contact was recorded on July 18, 1913:

> Many moons ago I lived. Again I come—Patience Worth my name.
> Wait, I would speak with thee. If thou shalt live, then so shall I. I make my bread at thy hearth. Good friends, let us be merrie. The time for work is past. Let the tabby drowse and blink her wisdom to the firelog . . .
>
> Q: Patience, where was your home?
> A: Across the sea.
> Q: In what city or country?
> A: About me you would know much. Yesterday is dead. Let thy mind rest as to the past.[16]

Patience was consistently difficult to pin down about her past. She gave her dates of incarnation as 1649-1694. She also channeled poetry through the board. After Pearl Curran, a St. Louis woman with an eighth grade education began channeling Patience Worth through automatic writing, she published channeled novels and poetry that were critically reviewed and well received. Her personality, language and style far different from Pearl Curran's, Patience came alive in the writing.

Automatic writing is considered the most common form of mediumship.[17] To do it, women need only a free-flowing pen or pencil and large sheets of paper, or they can do it at the typewriter or computer if they are good typists. Women who use paper and pen/cil like lots of paper, and in our grandmothers' days, the unprinted backs of wallpaper rolls were used. No one is needed to take notes since the writing itself is the notes, so this is a skill that women can perform alone.

As with the ouija board or channeling by voice, the meditative state is required for automatic writing, some women needing to go deeper than others. When working at a conscious, or near-to conscious level, the conscious mind has to be distracted away from what's being written. The woman writes while talking with someone, or even while watching television, disengaging her rational mind. To do automatic writing in the meditative state (and the "conscious" form is still a meditative alpha state), become as grounded and centered as possible, as quiet inside as possible, making the affirmation, "I receive writing from _____ , or about _____ ."[18] Then sit quietly and write down what comes, when it comes. You may hear the words in your mind first, or only at first, but let them come through you, rather than from you. Wait until the writing stops before you read it back.

If you are handwriting, rather than using the typewriter or computer, you may be surprised to see a handwriting different from your own, or even writing that is upside down or backwards (mirror writing). Occasionally words in a different language show up. The question of "who's doing it" is the same as for the ouija board, but you will realize soon that it isn't you, or at least isn't your conscious mind. Contact entities in automatic writing by asking for them as with the ouija board, using the question "Is anyone there?" A question and answer dialogue occurs.

Being in the meditative state or trance state has never precluded free will in any other psychic skill, and it doesn't in spiritism, either. Remember that you are in control and you remain so. If an entity you don't like comes through, ask it to leave, or break contact with it. If it returns, be stern about it. Take your power and take your control of the situation. If an entity insists that she's someone unlikely and famous, assume it's a joke. Joan of Arc or Sappho are not usual controls. Don't believe everything, or everyone, you read in automatic writing anymore than you would in the newspaper.[19]

Enid Hoffman, usually quite open psychically, insists that mediumship is unhealthy, that "You are here to live your own life,"[20] and not to let other entities control you. Where the medium and control relationship is a healthy and positive one, and where the medium has a good perspective and uses free will, there can be no harm. According to Hoffman, automatic writing and ouija board work are for contacting the subconscious inner self only. Yet, if Jane Roberts and other channelers are correct, and if Luisa Teish is correct (and I see no reason to doubt four women of good repute whose work does not contradict each other), the subconscious mind is the link between this plane and the rest of the universe. It's a vast universe indeed, and women who have access to it grow by exploring it. Enid Hoffman presents two rules for safe use of mediumship: work at the same time every day, and work for only reasonable periods of time. I add a third: accept channeling only from positive entities and take charge of who comes. Use common sense and free will as to what you believe. Avoid channeling if you are emotionally upset or not feeling well.

Jane Roberts suggests going to automatic writing from the ouija board.[21] When you begin to anticipate what the board is spelling out, take a pen and paper and write it down. This was the point where Roberts, Sheila Reynolds and Gail Fairfield went to voice channeling, so do whichever feels right. To try it by automatic writing, have a pen/cil and paper handy, placing the paper on or next to the ouija board or in your lap. Hold the pen or pencil over the paper, put your name and date at the top of the page, then wait. The pen moves, seemingly of itself. Avoid watching the paper or yourself writing, but distract your conscious mind in some other way. Read the material only after the writing is finished.

On the subject of Joan of Arc, Eleanora Duse or Sappho appearing in automatic writing, Jane Roberts attributes them to the subconscious mind not reaching through the planes, but indulging in sheer wish fulfillment. The subconscious is women's child-within. No one's going to believe it if you tell them you've been channeling Sappho, and usually neither should you. Reaching the inner self, subconscious mind, is a step in connecting to matriarchal consciousness, but it's only part of the journey. In stroking the python, women reach past this level, going deeper and further in channeling. Having a sense of humor also helps; channeling is serious, but also fun.

When is the material received by channeling invalid? When it vents personal prejudices, satisfies repressed needs, comes with a sense of superiority over others or power over; when it's excessively emotional, sexual or religious, or when it expresses negativity or hate.[22] Outside of patriarchy and the linear plane there is no racism, sexism, ablism or hierarchy; there is matriarchal power within and Goddess within, and love for the oneness of all. When these things come through, trust them for real. Also trust new ways of looking at things, and superior insights on a creative, psychological or intellectual level, information and Be-ings that you know at an intuitional level to be real. Over time the validity of the material grows, rather than diminishing. This is true for all forms of channeling, psychic automatism, and mediumship.

Keep automatic writing or ouija board sessions to about half an hour, especially at first. In ending a session, make the affirmative, aloud statement, "I will resume this tomorrow at the same time." Returning to now, ground yourself, as after any meditation or psychic exercise, surrounding yourself with light and placing palms to the Earth to return to now. If you feel shaky coming back, eat something, but not white sugar. Never go so long as to become tired, or to make it hard to come back. When back in the present, read over the results of the session keeping them in a running notebook, entries dated.

In the 1920's, "Betty"—Elizabeth Grant White—began to develop as a medium. Her husband's books, *The Betty Books*, three volumes first published in 1937, describe the process. Betty went from the ouija board to automatic writing to trance mediumship as a channeler. In the beginning she had no knowledge of her psychic abilities, and was reluctant to dis-cover them, but curiosity and growing awareness won out. Early in the process the ouija board repeatedly spelled the name Betty:

> Immediately her fingers touched the glass it began to move in circles. Around and around it went, faster and faster until she and her partner could hardly keep their fingers on it. So comically like a dog frisking in delight was it that we all burst into laughter.
> It's glad to get Betty,' said we.[23]

Then the board spelled, repeating intermittently, "Get a pencil," and Betty, several days later and privately, tried automatic writing. The pencil moved as the whiskey glass on the ouija board had:

> The pencil moved very slowly and it wrote curiously formed script, without capitals or punctuation, or even spacings, like one long, continuous word. It was necessary to go over it painstakingly, dividing the words by vertical marks—when we had determined them. Sometimes we interlined more plainly, in our own hand, what we made them out to be. The result made sense.
> Betty assured me that she had, consciously, nothing to do with moving the pencil. Furthermore, she said that she did not know the sense of what had been written until we had puzzled it out. As I knew Betty's complete honesty, I believed her . . .
> The seizing and using was by a force outside her own consciousness . . . [24]

A number of women have mentioned that they began automatic writing, almost spontaneously, after menopause. They have not used a ouija board or done other psychic work to start it, or been otherwise aware of their psychic abilities before it. Some women, like myself, have done automatic writing for years, probably since adolescence, without having a name for the process or paying much attention to it. Many women who are performers or artists are also channelers, aware of it or not. They feel their performance coming through them, and often at the end have only a vague idea of what it is they've done. The feeling of being this type of channel is entirely positive, rewarding, and something to be sought.

Other women have experienced mediumship and channeling through seances, the spiritualism that brought so many women to notice in the past century. In this process, a circle sits for development, combining their energies.[25] Two key members of the evening are the facilitator, a woman who remains outside the meditative state to act as a monitor for the group, and the medium, the woman the discarnate entities or spirit guides choose to speak through. When a group first begins, it is often unknown who the medium/s will be. More than one woman can develop as a sensitive, medium or channel. The monitor of the group can be a rotating position. She never enters trance, but is a safeguard for the well-being of the others, sensitive to women's needs.

Mediums can be of two types in the seance setting, mental mediums who are basically voice channelers or automatic writers, or physical mediums whose psychokinetic focus is used in producing actual apparitions, sounds or moving objects. Rappings and table tiltings are the most frequent manifestations of this type in a seance setting. Each woman who experiences seance mediumship experiences it in her own way. While the medium is the central focus of a seance circle, the need for an attuned group of women whose energy supports her work is fully necessary. The medium is a channel, but only a channel, and any woman can develop as a medium.

Spirit guides are also present at seances, and their protective presence is asked for by each member of the circle. They are only one means of protection. Women beginning a seance cast a wiccan circle of protection, asking the guardians of the four directions to protect and help them. The directions and spirit guides screen out negative controls from entering the circle or the seance. Handled as a women's spirituality ritual, taking care to purify, cast the circle and invoke protection, seance work is highly safe. These beginnings and precautions taken, the facilitator invokes discarnate entities to speak through the medium or manifest rappings or psychokinetic effects. When the spirit messages have been received, the spirits are thanked and released, the directions thanked and released, the circle opened, and the women ground and come back to now.

Here is the process in more detail.[26] The women sit in a circle on the floor or on chairs at a table—comfortably, for a seance takes time, and they hold hands. The circle is not broken or hands dropped during the entire seance, and women sit with legs uncrossed. Do ritual purification with incense, but do not use salt or salt water, as these repel discarnate spirits. Cast the circle and invoke the four directions, asking for protection and positive contact from the spirit world. When the circle is declared cast, make the affirmation/invocation, "We connect tonight with positive discarnate spirits, and gain learning from them." Do guided meditation to bring the women deeper into trance, and invoke the presence of their spirit guides. Different women in the group can do different parts of this structure, or one woman act as priestess. The controls manifest through someone they choose, rather than who the women choose or who chooses herself, especially at first. A woman can dis-cover through seances that she is a medium, if she doesn't already know, and act as a channel in other circles after.

In the seances of the last century, incense was used as a sensory signal for the ritual, a way of disengaging the rational mind. Song was also used at the opening, in those days prayers and hymns, but any type of song that is positive is possible. Try some of the Goddess songs familiar in women's spirituality. These are not recordings but are sung by the group—don't worry about your singing voice. Sometimes a spirit guide will choose the song, or try this one:

> She is the Spirit,
> She is like a mountain.
> Tall and strong,
> She goes on and on and on.

A red or blue light is also traditional, particularly red, and can be helpful to the group.

The appearance of a spirit or control in the circle is similar to the voudoun concept of possession. The spirit takes control of the physical body of the medium, speaking through her. The medium invites this and does it by her own choice and free will, in partnership with the spirit. A form of this in women's spirituality is called Aspecting, where a woman, rather than invoking Hera or Isis or Oshun, becomes her for awhile.[27] Her own mannerisms and speech give way to the control entity's, and the spirit, orisha, ancestor or Goddess speaks through her, using her body and vocal cords to do so. This possession or mediumship is temporary, of course. The control finishes what she wants to say and leaves. If she doesn't, she is asked to leave, and spirit guides help with this. She only acts as control of the medium while the medium consents.

Women in the circle can invoke a particular entity or ancestor, deceased friend, mother, etc. They can also be open to who comes by asking, "Is anybody there?" as in the ouija board, automatic writing, or other voice channeling. A spirit guide can be the channeled control. A woman who finds herself being the medium of a seance may find that she can channel a control in every seance. Other women who wish to be mediums can develop through the ouija board or automatic writing, and may do so.

When a control manifests through a medium, the group one at a time asks her questions, who she is and what she wants to say, what her message is. Sometimes the manifesting is physical rather than mental, as when a visual apparition appears, or when there are raps, knocks or table tiltings. Knocks or raps can have a code, or the women in the circle can establish a code. One rap for "yes" and two raps for "no" are standard, or a rap for each letter of the alphabet; one rap is "a," two raps are "b," and so on This brings messages similar to those of the ouija board. The raps can come from the table women are sitting at tilting and thumping, and they sit at a table for this. It is generally believed that apparitions at a seance come from the extruded astral material of the sitters or the medium, and they are a less frequent happening.

When ending a seance, the women open their circle. They stand, thank the directions, their spirit guides, and the manifested entities, bidding them a farewell and a blessing. Then the circle is declared open:

> This circle is open but not broken,
> May the peace of the Goddess go with you.
>
> Merry meet and merry part,
> And merry meet again.

The women rise from the table or seated position, drop hands, and ground themselves by placing their palms to the Earth and reconnecting with the physical plane. The monitor, who has not gone into trance, claps her hands loudly several times, in the traditional seance way of bringing the circle back to linear consciousness. Food is a good way to end; it's a grounder, and women discuss the evening before leaving.

Some women find themselves a channel at every seance, the controls or their spirit guides picking them each time as receptive Be-ings. This is not to start a star system, but to utilize available skills. Every woman of the circle who chooses to can sit for development with a ouija board and automatic writing, as well as other psychic develop-ment, but some women seem chosen for it. Remember that the seance medium does not act alone and needs the rest of the circle working with her, a careful monitor, and her own spirit guides for protection. Mediums are channels for connection with other realms and God-dess; they are not the Goddess themselves any more than any other woman, or any less.

There have been some great names in mediumship in the last hundred and fifty years, some interesting women mediums. Eileen Garrett, whose work appears throughout this book, was one of them and a later one. The women given credit for starting the spiritualist movement in 1848 were children, Kate and Margaret Fox,[28] who heard rappings in their home and interpreted them as spirit com-munications. They developed a code and alphabet for the rappings, and received control messages in this way. At the beginning, Kate was twelve and Margaret fourteen years old. They were Americans living in New York State, who carried their work into adulthood and for most of their lives, giving public seances. They were physical mediums, rather than mental voice channelers.

Nettie Colburn worked as a trance medium, a voice channeler, for Abraham Lincoln, channeling material in seances that affected the course of the Civil War and Lincoln's decision to repeal slavery and give the Gettysburg Address (1863). Nettie Colburn channeled entities known as Pinkie and Old Dr. Bamford, as well as a female control who was a Native American woman. In the waking state, Colburn had no knowledge of what had happened in trance, what had come through her or who. She warned Lincoln of approaching death, and he chose to take no precautions.

Eusapia Palladino, a physical medium from Italy, uneducated and of peasant stock, worked with scientists from 1888 to 1908 to prove or disprove the authenticity of her mediumship. No con-clusions were ever reached. There were times when this controversial and interesting woman was declared a fraud, and other times when she was given the patriarchal seal of approval. The verdict changed from week to week. She began mediumship and seances at age four-teen, and was known widely throughout Europe and the United States. Her major control entity was called John King.

Leonore Evelina Simonds Piper went by the name of Mrs. Piper in her work as a medium, and no one called her anything else, including her close relatives. Her daughter Alta Piper was her biographer. She was born in New Hampshire in 1859 and lived to be ninety-one years of age. Most of her work was in New York City seances in the thirty years preceding World War I. Also working with researchers and scientists trying to prove or disprove her mediumship, none ever found reason to doubt or disprove her channelings. She worked by voice mediumship and automatic writing in seances; in conscious life she was known as a powerful psychic and clairvoyant. Her earliest control was a Native American woman named Chlorine, and later controls were male, Phinuit, G.P., and lastly the Imperator Group. Biographical material by her daughter, and accounts of some of her mediumship and clairvoyance are in the David C. Knight anthology, *The ESP Reader* (New York, Grosset and Dunlap, 1969). They are worth looking up.

Marthe Beraud, a Frenchwoman who went by the name of Eva C., was a physical medium who produced apparitions of ectoplasm (astral matter from her own aura). These began in 1906, in the form of full entities. There was a Hindu, helmeted warrior from the seventeenth century named Bien Boa and an Egyptian woman. Eva C. was investigated thoroughly by researchers, convincing even the most skeptical. She is said to have had a Black woman as companion, Aischa (no last name given), who may have acted as monitor for her seances and who participated in and enhanced her apparitions and effects by her presence. Eva C. is described as living with a woman, a Mme. Bisson (was this Aischa?) who "rarely leaves her; the two ladies take their meals together and sleep in the same room."[29] It is possible that Marthe Beraud (Eva C.) was a lesbian.

Eva C., like Eusapia Palladino, Leonore Piper and Eileen Garrett, went to great lengths to prove her mediumship authentic to authorities and researchers eager to find fraud. The investigations were extensive:

In these experiments, which lasted over four years and were conducted with admirable care and patience, minute precautions were taken against fraud. At each seance the cabinet was closely searched, Eva was completely undressed and in presence of the experimenters clothed in a close-fitting garment covering her from head to foot. Her head was covered by a veil of tulle sewn to the other garment. Her hair, armpits, nose, mouth, and knees were examined; in some cases even examination *per rectum et vaginam* was resorted to. As the materialized substance frequently comes from her mouth, syrup of bilberries was administered, whose deep colouring powers are well known, but notwithstanding this the extruded forms were absolutely white. Experimental rigour was even pushed to the point of giving her an emetic before a seance.[30]

Despite all this, and with wonder as to why she allowed it, Eva C.'s manifestings and apparitions in seances were never proved fraudulent. Her work ended around 1920, when her mediumship, inexplainably, diminished.

Gladys Osborne Leonard was a more recent medium, living until 1967 and the age of eighty-five. Her account of the Happy Valley, taken from her autobiography, *My Life in Two Worlds*, is given in the chapter on clairvoyance. Gladys Leonard's major control was female, a woman named Feda, and it was Feda who convinced Gladys to become a professional seance medium, saying, "Something big and terrible is going to happen to the world and Feda must help many people through you."[31] The time was 1916, and the happening World War I. She connected with Feda through the mediumistic circle and table tilting, using the alphabet, then developed into a voice channel in the structure of the seance. Gladys Leonard describes her first voice channeling attempt:

> Suddenly I felt a tingling in my hands, which were resting lightly upon the table. The tingling spread through my wrists, up my arms, then began in my feet and legs, till my whole being felt as if filled by a gentle electric current. Then came a strange feeling in my head—a pressure on my temples as of a band tied round them, and also on top of the head.
>
> The pressure ceased, and I felt a curious force pulling me up from my chair impelling me to stand. What I was to do in the event of my standing up I seemed incapable of imagining. It was like a dream in which I was neither conscious nor unconscious, but yet aware that somebody outside myself urged me to do one thing at a time, telling me not to try to think what the sequence of events might be.
>
> I was drawn up on to my feet by a strange magnetic power which seemed to operate from just above my head. My mouth opened; a sound issued from my lips. What it was I do not know, for at that moment the president touched me on the hand, saying, 'All right, friend, don't worry, you'll be able to speak in a moment or two.' He was addressing the spirit who he knew was trying to control me, but I . . . thought he was speaking to me. That and the touch on my hand broke the spell.[32]

A friend suggested she try again, and in this next try Gladys became a medium for Feda. During the seance,

> I lapsed into an unusually sleepy state. I felt more pessimistic than ever about my psychic possibilities. The drowsy, tired feeling increased. I lazily thought, "It's darker than usual tonight. I'm sleepy. They won't notice if I sleep for a little while.'
>
> I slept. I awoke . . .
>
> Agnes and Nellie were leaning across the table holding my hands. I noticed they were agitated. Nellie turned the light on and I saw that tears were glistening on their cheeks.
>
> 'What on earth's the matter?' I asked.

> 'Matter!' said Agnes. 'Feda has been controlling you and giving us messages from our relatives. Nellie's mother has sent her some messages, too. We have had a wonderful time.'[33]

Gladys Leonard had become a medium.

Whole books have been written about these fascinating women, virtually all of them now out of print. More could be written, much more, and their books would be well received by women today. Women mediums of the spiritualist era are a special interest personally. With space short, however, and the how-to's given in the chapter, modern women's experiences with automatic writing, the ouija board and seances come next and close this section.

Mimi writes about using a ouija board:

> When a friend and I started with a ouija board many years ago, we got more fun and more trouble than we anticipated. But we also have just thousands of pages of nonsense and practical information. I enjoy reviewing these 'telepathic messages' occasionally.

Here is material from a ouija board telepathic message of August, 1971, coming from a place quoted as Ramar:

> Our main purpose is to advance in the realm of adversities. We practice problems as you might experience them, then make improvements on the outcome. When these souls are again born they will remember this knowledge and unconsciously apply it to problems. In this way they have taught a new solution to earth people who profit and advance through this knowledge. The earth people have a very limited knowledge and conception of their former existence in the spirit form. Remembrance would only hinder their progress. The advancement they make must be of their own volition and desires as humans. How they apply the instructions and knowledge gained here is up to them. Should they not advance in earth life they must again relive spirit life on the same level or plane. Earth life is a continuing phase of existence. After each term of learning in spirit life it is necessary to put this practical information to use. When the lesson has been well learned the outcome is very satisfactory, if not, the lesson must be learned again in spirit life.
>
> Spirit life is one level of learning after another. Concentrate on these levels of learning in your experiences in life and apply each phase with concentrated effort, and you will begin to feel and to know that this information comes from within, a knowledge that can be called forth to benefit you. In many areas of life you find answers and are surprised how they came about. You were born with them but it takes deep concentration and effort to bring this memory to use . . .
>
> One day in the far future, earth will experience a life very advanced and beautiful, with peace, no suffering and no hardships, which are all necessary for advancement but not for an enjoyable and beautiful life. Hardships are for learning, not for living.

Mimi sent dozens of pages of ouija board transcripts, all extremely interesting. Her control gave no name or identity. This material on the spirit world works closely with the subject of the next chapter, death and beyond.

Irene also tried the ouija board, looking for answers:

> I read anything I could get my hands on. I went through Buddhism, Existentialism, Satanism. I got wrapped up in mind over matter and meditation. Then I bought a ouija board, reasoning what answers I couldn't get out of books, I'd get from my board. I had decided I was a witch, because too many unusual things always happened to me. I knew things I shouldn't have known . . . In the meantime my ouija board progressed from strange named spirits to Satan or Beelzebub. Whenever I asked it who it was, those were the answers I got. I knew there was more to living on earth, and going to either heaven or hell. I wanted to know what it was.
>
> Then Mary came into my life—first through the board—giving me some answers but never enough. By this time I was in my first year of college and had to do an English paper. I chose Nathaniel Hawthorne. When I went to the library to research it, I felt almost like I was led to the section with his life story. Then I found it—Nathaniel Hawthorne became involved with the occult and visited a medium. He had communicated with my Mary.
>
> I knew she died a violent death, but through Hawthorne I found out she was burned in Salem for being a witch. Then Mary came out of the woodwork, so to speak, she told me she wanted to live again and could do it through me. I was eighteen and terrified. I thought this was the price of what I had received. I felt that to get the ultimate knowledge I wanted I had to give up my soul to Mary and Satan. I didn't want this. It was my soul and my life and I wanted to live it! . . .
>
> Mary was becoming an obsession and I was terrified. I went to a philosophy professor and told him my whole story. He told me I hadn't lost it and wasn't schizo, that somehow I had bridged a gap in existence and may very well have attracted another soul. He told me not to deny or fear what was going on, but to accept it and use all my inner strength and fight it—tell it NO—no matter what.

In the ouija board, mediumship, the craft, or in any aspect of stroking the python, women take charge of their lives. When using the ouija board, use protection, and refuse any entity not positive. Limit sessions to under half an hour.

The board predicted accurately that Trudy would marry Bill, and Sheila, Paul. Here is Sheila's story. When the girls used the board as a parlor game, not taking it seriously, it replied with gibberish:

> My mother bought me a ouija board. At the cabin, we girls took turns asking the obvious questions: Who will Trudy marry? Where does he live? Will I ever get married? . . .
>
> Usually it answered. Sometimes we couldn't understand or it stopped midway. We did establish that Trudy would marry a Bill from Boston. I would marry someone named Paul.
>
> When the board wanted to send us a letter somewhere and we laughed, we got some obscenities, some gibberish, and we didn't have much luck after that.

Sheila did marry Paul, meeting her soul mate through the ouija board.

In one more of these, Rebecca from Texas' mother had a ouija board, and broke it in embarrassment!

> I've tried the ouija board, but . . . it doesn't tell me anything. The board mumbles gibberish and an occasional naughty word! My mother broke her beautiful antique board into four pieces and buried them because it kept telling her, 'Fuck you, fuck you, ha ha, fuck you!' My mother is a rabid Baptist. I thought it was hysterically funny. Mom was not amused. *If* it's true that the ouija board only reflects one's own subconscious, then it's even funnier!

Again, there is need for invoked protection when contacting other planes, and the willingness to take control, refuse and banish, order gone, any negative or prankish spirits. Says Susan Sheppard,

> Ouija boards aren't for just anyone. They have a bad reputation—which in some instances is well deserved, since the ouija board lets down the floodgates for many destructive 'thought-forms' and negative entities to enter in consciousness. A disturbed person should stay miles away from a ouija board . . .

She herself occasionally uses them, "as a way to reach a deeper and higher level." Remember that Sheila Reynolds, Jane Roberts, Gail Fairfield, Betty White, and Pearl Curran all contacted their controls by the ouija board initially, all positive entities.

Sunlight uses automatic writing as a way of problem solving. Here is how she began:

> Long ago, I'd learned of and had been using a way of contacting my inner guidance for solving problems, to have the question ready in my mind . . . meditate, then after meditating to focus on the problem and listen for an answer. I think I wrote down the question and maybe then began to write the answer, the guidance as it came.
>
> I used this before the channeling workshop and automatic writing workshop I'd taken that spring and summer of 1984, but didn't have a name for it. After the workshops, I saw it as channeling/automatic writing and began to use it more often and more extensively. It was easier and broader than the yes/no of a pendulum which I had used before . . . This inner voice has given me wisdom that I am not aware of in my conscious mind and answered questions I hadn't given shape to.
>
> Always, I think, I've seen it as an inner voice, Goddess within, my higher power coming from a place of knowledge in me, rather than an 'external' guide. It is that part of me that is one with everyone, with the universe, my connection with the Whole, the All. So this voice understands how I fit into the Whole and guides me accordingly, in ways that are mutually beneficial for all concerned. It is always a gentle, loving voice and very sensible—as opposed to the chorus of demeaning and conflicting views that come from some of the beliefs imprinted on my childhood. I find a lot of peace in the guidance from this Source, and when I have followed, it has led me to a good place. I trust it now and find it comforting.

Here is part of an automatic writing transcript, where Sunlight first used her word processor:

I am a part of you, the central, eternal part of you, what is there, always there when you let your ego fall away . . . my voice is and has always been there for you. Long ago, you used to listen to it because that is what you came with, only as the layers of conditioning built up, each with its own voice to add to the insistent chorus, my voice disappeared in the static . . . that is what growing is, getting through the chorus of imposed voices back to the one that is You, that is a part of the Whole, the part you have been seeking for so long . . . inner voice, higher power, god, goddess, holy spirit, call me what you want—love, yes, call me love, for that is what I am, the voice of love in you, because love is the energy of the Whole and the Whole is energy . . .

Marion Former contacted her spirit guide Moon by automatic writing in July, 1984:

His name is Moon and I think of him as being male, although he has told me that when a soul is not in physical form, it is androgynous. I have compiled a tremendous amount of written information on many varied subjects, and in 1985 I wrote a book, telling of this psychic experience, and included much of Moon's writings up to that time. I have never really done anything with the manuscript, but perhaps one day I will. Moon has made predictions at times which have come true. One very sad one was the Space Shuttle disaster. He has also given past-life readings for several people, most of whom were strangers to me.

Marion began doing automatic writing after reading about Ruth Montgomery's experiences in contacting her spirit guides with it (in *A Search For Truth*). She made a conscious attempt, with successful results on the first try:

I sat and meditated for about fifteen minutes, as Ruth Montgomery suggested in her book, and then I lightly held a pencil to a sheet of blank paper, closed my eyes, and waited for something to happen. After about five minutes, I could feel my hand begin to move across the paper. At first, the movement was slow, but then it became quite rapid and I felt as though I were writing words. Each time I reached the edge of the paper, I would consciously bring my hand back to the other side, but as my hand scribbled across the page, it seemed an involuntary action and I had no idea what, if anything, I was writing. When I had repeated this action a number of times, I opened my eyes, put down the pencil, and looked at what I had written. The page contained several lines of very small writing, which was joined together, and because my eyes were closed, some of the lines had run into one another. On closer inspection I could see that I had written some words, but it was difficult to distinguish many of them because the letters were so small and there were no spaces between the words. Some of the writing appeared to be in another language, but one of the English words was quite legible and it was repeated on several of the lines. The word was 'moon' and I remember thinking that it was an odd word to find there. Although I didn't realize it then, that was my first written contact with the being whom I have come to know as Moon.

Calling Moon "he" was a personal choice, as the entity is androgynous. Moon writes about mediumship and channeling, in an automatic writing transcript dated February 21, 1986:

There are many groups of melded facets within the inner levels of my domains and these are the levels over which I truly have power. These groups may consist of two or more facets and they meld themselves for the purpose of instructing those in the physical plane. A single facet may also pursue this work, as I sometimes do with you, but only a few have the power to manifest this contact in some physical form, such as automatic writing or speaking through ouija boards or mediums. The larger the group, the stronger the power, particularly if all the facets are of the same supersoul. There is always at least one watcher within the group . . . Please understand there are imperfections in my domains as there are in all of the levels of the spiral, duality is the nature of all that is . . .

The channels for each of these groups also completely believe the experience of which they are a part and their belief strengthens the bond. Again, I tell you that a soul's belief system creates its own realities, all is possible, all can be actualized! When the channels of these groups are no longer in the physical plane, then the facets of these groups may well unmeld and re-group with other facets. If, however, they determine that there is another within the physical, with whom they can communicate, then the initial contact will be made through the watcher or watchers of the group, during the dream state. Even when this form of contact has been executed, this will not guarantee a continuance of the communication. The physically-oriented facet must desire this contact or nothing comprehensible will be accomplished when the trance state, the automatic writing, the ouija board, or whatever form of divination is being utilized. This rule is verifiable in cases of contact with that which your world would call both good and evil. There is always free will!

Moon here answers the dilemma of unwanted entities making contact through the ouija board . . . S/he also warns of the risk of obsession for deep trance mediums, something to guard against, and says that "mediums who channel through light trance or self-hypnosis are melded with their guides. Those who are only able to utilize the alpha state are still melding, but here there is a distinct difference":

Now to those who channel through the alpha state. These teachings are usually given through the ouija board, automatic writing, or some other form of physical divination (Note: motor automatism). Here only a small part of the 'me consciousness' is being laid aside, therefore, there is the strong possibility of the mediums flavouring, as it were, the teachings with their own consciousness. They will block what is unacceptable in their present incarnation and present questionable information in a manner which is acceptable to them. Please understand that I do not wish to imply that what is given by these channels is false, rather it is brought into the validity of their present belief system. This is more prevalent with some mediums than with others . . . The process of censoring the teachings, as they are being given, is indiscernible to the medium, but it transpires during each session of channeling. It is a definite strain upon the medium's physical brain and this is why sessions should not continue too long without some form of break, and also why the teachings must be given slowly and over a long period of time, in terms of the physical.

Since Marion has been channeling by automatic writing, there have been other entities:

In the early days there was also a female entity, named Yolande, who was sending messages. These stopped after a couple of months, but about a year later, Moon said that Yolande was merely a facet soul of his supersoul. For almost a week (I used to write more frequently in the beginning because I had more time then) Moon didn't write and instead it was two entities, named Niger and Naomi, who were writing. Moon wrote later that they were totally separate entities from himself.

Beginning writing with pencil and paper, Marion now uses a home computer. She holds one or two sessions a week, of about an hour each, does them very early in the morning and preceded by fifteen minutes of meditation. She is forty-eight years of age, was born in England, is a professional woman and the mother of two grown sons. She has always been psychic.

Of women connecting with their spirit guides, Lynn talks to her guide Gunther through automatic writing and the ouija board, as well as through direct telepathy. Pam makes her requests to her guide Anthony or St. Anthony, by writing them in her journal. She also contacted D'Ar through automatic writing:

I have a feeling that D'Ar/D'Aris is a female higher spirit guide. It isn't anything that's been conveyed to me . . . just a feeling. Here's some of what I channeled the first time D'Ar came through. I was writing in a notebook about the thoughts and feelings I'd experienced earlier in the evening after hearing a particularly inspired speaker . . . *I* wrote, after I'd lighted my white candle and Silver Lotus incense stick, ' . . . there was an abundance of spiritual contact there. Near the end of his talk, there was an infusion of *light*—I was mesmerized by it! It is meant to be a sign to me . . . to carry on in a more public way, the message I've been privileged to hear.'

When the writing started to change . . . my thinking process was more of a listening to a voice coming in my right ear . . . ' In a sense, it has always been your quest but you have not been prepared, until now. We feel that you have begun the path as an initiate; you certainly have succumbed to each and every trial of that which strengthens the metal of the spiritual novitiate. Thus, you have begun a quest, have you not? The quest for greater spiritual openness—and we are at the doors of the further vision—as you are at the door on the other side. The door is not a door in the sense that you know doors—I use that term as you can relate to 'doors.' Such is the path, such is the search—the process—it only becomes more clear, within the realms of your soul; you see, I know you understand this as you have been watched and protected and, rather helped along, *through* these portals and are certainly ready to continue in more influential ways. It is our hope, as a unity of high evolved beings, that you will be a vanguard to the cause—You are so much a cause person, and it gives us pleasure to be able to utilize that part of your personality. Fortunately, the beautiful gains in the Program will temper this and will meet your requirements beautifully, also. We are pleased that you have stepped forward. You want to help and learn and are going out of your way to do this! So pleased. We send love, but you *know* this, tap into it, it's there for you. It's all waiting for you. Blessings from your D'Ar, your friend, teacher and guide.'

A very few women writing to me mentioned seance work, and Pam was one of them:

> My grandmother and I were very close; she's come to me twice through mediums. The first woman asked if the name 'Edith' meant anything to me . . . that was my grandmother's name. She was right on about everything, it was great! This past February, the psychic told me that my mother's mother was watching over me, 'showering me with light and good wishes,' also that she was very proud of me.

Pam wears her grandmother's locket, containing an 1853 dime, as a link to her.

Lola describes holding seances as a child, and perhaps is an untapped resource as a medium today:

> At a very early age, about ten or eleven years old, I remember holding seances, lighted candles and all in a large walk-in closet I had in my bedroom. I knew nothing about these things at that time, of course. In looking back now, even I find it strange how or why I intuitively felt to do this.

Psychic Janet Roman, who sent me newspaper articles published by that name, is the only woman writing to me who described holding public seances:

> I was afraid to attend my first seance. I didn't know what to expect. Are they real? Or just a magic trick? How does one explain these phenomena? . . . I wonder how many people would believe a miracle if they saw one? . . . Yet as I travel through the country people come and tell me of things they experienced of this unexplained happening.
>
> When a seance is announced, we do it more on a last minute basis at any location and sometimes we've had fifty people squeeze into one hotel room, sometimes it's in whoever's house is available, and once in a car!
>
> These are stories that happened in a local restaurant after it was closed.
>
> People were invited spontaneously and I ask them nothing about who they are. They are only to give me a name of who they wish to call. I want no other information. I don't want to know how the person was related, or age, or how they died, or anything. All I want is the name.
>
> In the course of the seance, anyone in the room is invited to tell or relate any experience of communication they may 'feel' or experience.
>
> The first name called was a male. I immediately saw a man (I described him), and he was being attacked by a tiger. He was screaming, the tiger looked like it was killing him. I looked up at the woman to ask if that had any meaning for her. With tears in her eyes, she said it was her father and he died because he worked in a zoo and was killed by a tiger!
>
> Then through a telepathy, or something I can't explain, he gave me a message for his daughter. I relayed it and she verified facts I said that only her father would have known . . .
>
> A couple called down a name. I saw a young man, age sixteen to eighteen, red hair, white teeshirt, all details matched to the kid holding a cigar and walking on a railroad track.
>
> The couple said it was the exact description of a younger brother who had

died on the railroad track and always smoked cigars! . . . He was sorry he died and he was sorry he was reckless. He never expected or heard the train. He told more details to me through a form of telepathy. All the details were confirmed. Oh, by the way, I said, there's a big red shepherd dog with him.

The couple looked amazed. They said that was his dog who died six months before he did!

I am still amazed about these experiences. These are two of over a hundred experiences I've had. I taped almost all the seances, as I don't expect anyone to really believe these, but they happened.

Women who are seance mediums still exist, despite the decline in popularity and study of mediumship and spiritism since after World War I in the United States and Europe. In South America and Mexico, however, the combination of Catholicism with African Voudoun or Macumbe and with Native American religions still practice seances and spirit possession. The following comes from Florinda Donner's novel, *The Witch's Dream*, (New York, Pocket Books, 1985):

> Mercedes Peralta was the last one to come in. She removed the candle from the ledge and distributed the hand-rolled cigars. 'Don't talk to anyone before or after the seance,' she whispered in my ear as she held the flickering flame to my cigar. 'No one else besides Leon Chirino knows you are a medium. Mediums are vulnerable.'
>
> She sat down opposite me. I closed my eyes and puffed skillfully, as I had done countless times in Dona Mercedes patio. I became so engrossed in that act that I lost track of time. A soft moan arose from the smoky darkness. I opened my eyes and saw a woman materialize in the middle of the circle of chairs, a hazy figure. Slowly, a reddish light spread all over her until she seemed to be aglow . . .
>
> Wondering whether I was going through one of the inexplicable visions I had had in the patio, I clutched the mercury jar in my hands and rose from my chair. I stood transfixed as the woman became transparent. I found nothing frightening about her transparency; I simply accepted that it was possible to see through her.
>
> Without any warning the woman collapsed in a dark heap on the ground. The light inside her seemed to have been turned off. I was totally reassured that she was not an apparition when she took out a handkerchief and blew her nose.
>
> Exhausted, I sank into my chair. Leon Chirino, sitting on my left, nudged me with his elbow, gesturing me to keep my attention on the center of the room. There, in the circle of chairs, where the transparent woman had been, stood an old, foreign-looking woman. She stared at me, her blue eyes wide open, frightened, bewildered. Her head jerked back, then forward, and before I could make any sense of the vision, it faded. Not suddenly but slowly, it floated about.
>
> It was so quiet in the room that for an instant I thought everyone had gone. On the sly, I glanced around me. All I saw was the glow of cigars. They couldn't

possibly be smoking the same cigars Dona Mercedes had distributed, I thought. I
had finished mine a long time ago . . . Someone placed a hand on my shoulder.

'Dona Mercedes!' I exclaimed, recognizing her touch . . . I looked up, but she
was not there. I was alone in the room. Everyone else had left. Frightened, I
stood up and ran towards the door, only to be stopped by Leon Chirino.

'Frida Herzog's spirit roams around here,' he said. 'She died on the steps of
this hill.'[34]

In this book, an American woman, a student, goes to Dona Mercedes
in Venezuela to learn psychic healing. During her apprenticeship, she
dis-covers her abilities as a medium.

Discussing mediumship, ouija boards, automatic writing, seances
and channeling raises the question inevitably of "what is death, if Be-
ings from the other side exist to talk about it?" Women have lives and
past lives, and there must be something in between the ending of one
existence and the beginning of the next life. If women have had multiple past (or simultaneous) lives, they must have also have had multiple deaths and multiple experiences of dying and being born. Virtually
all nonpatriarchal religions and cultures believe in reincarnation and
in discarnate spirits, with only Judaism and Christianity rejecting
these tenants. Both held them initially in their beginnings. In women's
spirituality, the concepts of karma and reincarnation are accepted
readily, and mediumship is an increasing phenomenon. The next
chapter, the final chapter of *Stroking the Python: Women's Psychic Lives*,
takes a theosophical and women's spirituality look at death and dying—
some of it from women who have been there.

# FOOTNOTES

1. Jane Roberts, *The Seth Material*, p. 252.

2. *Ibid.*, p. 38-39. Also in Jane Roberts, *The Coming of Seth*, p. 31-32.

3. *Ibid.*, p. 39.

4. *Ibid.*, p. 40.

5. Jane Roberts, *The Coming of Seth*, p. 2-3.

6. *Ibid.*, p. 3. Description and how-to for the ouija board comes primarily from this source.

7. *Ibid.*, p. 6.

8. David C. Knight, *The ESP Reader*, p. 258.

9. *Ibid.*

10. Sandra J. Stevens, *Being Alive Is Being Psychic*, p. 7.

11. *Ibid.*, p. 7-8.

12. *Ibid.*, p. 9.

13. Jane Roberts, *The Coming of Seth*, p. 7-9. Also in Jane Roberts, *The Seth Material*, p. 14-19.

14. Cobra, "Channeling Interview with Gail Fairfield," in *Goddess Rising*, Issue 15, Winter Solstice, 1986, p. 3 and 6.

15. David C. Knight, *The ESP Reader*, p. 259-260.

16. *Ibid.*, p. 262-263.

17. *Ibid.*, p. 301.

18. Enid Hoffman, *Develop Your Psychic Skills*, p. 78-79.

19. David C. Knight, *The ESP Reader*, p. 302.

20. Enid Hoffman, *Develop Your Psychic Skills*, p. 77.

21. Jane Roberts, *The Coming of Seth*, p. 25.

22. *Ibid.*, p. 27.

23. Stewart Edward White, "The Development of Betty: From the Whiskey Glass on the Ouija Board to Trance Voice," in David C. Knight, *The ESP Reader*, p. 294.

24. *Ibid.*, p. 294-295.

25. Melita Denning and Osborne Phillips, *The Llewellyn Practical Guide to the Development of Psychic Powers*, p. 142-155. Description of seances is from this source.

26. *Ibid.* Turning the seance into a wiccan ritual is my own idea.

27. Aspecting is a form of spirit possession being used by some women's spirituality circles. I thank Amber K. for telling me about it.

28. Material on the women mediums is found in David C. Knight, *The ESP Reader*, in Parts Two and Four. Biographies and writings by a number of interesting women is included.

29. *Ibid.*, p. 105. These biographies are all from *The ESP Reader*.

30. *Ibid.*

31. *Ibid.*, p. 156.

32. *Ibid.*, p. 173.

33. *Ibid.*, p. 177.

34. Florinda Donner, *The Witch's Dream*, (New York, Pocket Books, 1985), p. 166-167.

# Chapter Thirteen

# The Transpersonal Point: Death and Beyond

# Near Death Experiences

*Very early, before history as we know it, we retained the ability to keep in touch with other realities, other dimensions, other worlds. Through a series of events and misjudgments and misunderstandings, we have arrived at the present level of unawareness, in which our inner knowingness is blocked off to one degree or another. As a result, most beings on this plane of existence are convinced that this is the only world there is. They may have some religious-based sense of 'life after death,' but for the most part they think they are their bodies, whereas, they are separate entities who live throughout eternity, experiencing, growing and constantly changing, developing, creating worlds and dimensions of their own.*[1]

During the process of writing this book, my grandmother, who I have always felt close to, has been dying. Less than two weeks ago, she made the transition, on a Full Moon in June. Anna Backman was a warrior and an Amazon. She came to this country from Roumania at eleven years old, leaving home at nine in the protection of her older sister, Bessie, who was only eleven herself. It took them two years to reach New York, but they survived, and my grandmother Anna was always a survivor and a fighter. I have pictures of her in the twenties as a teenager with her friends, a piecework seamstress in the sweatshops by day and a flapper by night. In the early days of the unions she was a worker and a steward for the International Ladies Garment Workers Union, and a leader in many strikes for higher wages and better working conditions for women. In Pittsburgh she continued union organizing, raised two daughters, and often supported her family alone.

When it was unheard of for women of different races to mix socially, my grandmother had as many Black friends as she did White ones, as many non-Jewish friends as Jewish. She loved all women

319

equally, and "everyone alike" was her motto. After my grandfather died in 1972, my grandmother continued a highly active life. She moved to a senior citizen's building where she unofficially supervised the kitchen, worked there off the record for years, and was known as the Pearl Mesta of the complex. After my grandfather died she had a heart attack, a broken heart, but wasn't ready to leave this plane until a few months ago.

Operated on for cancer, and seeing it as the end of her strength, health, mobility and independence, my grandmother decided to die. She gave up, totally quit, and became angry about it. She intermittently stopped speaking to her daughters who tried to interest her in life, quit going outdoors or getting dressed in the morning, even when she still was strong enough. She wasn't leaving her apartment, and told me repeatedly that she wouldn't die in a nursing home. I was with her every night until she died. When she became too weak to care for herself, she fell and was put in the hospital. "I'm not leaving here," she said, "I'm not going to the home."

Until then, I had seen her aura as a halo of light, not a wide one, but an aura of light blue. Now her aura became a dark band, almost like an inverted negative. As she deteriorated physically, she entered periods when she wasn't there, when she talked to others who were not in the linear world. I couldn't understand her words, but there was definitely a dialog. The evening I came to her hospital room and couldn't find an aura at all, I knew she would die on the Full Moon. In the week remaining, she had lucid periods, but spent more and more time in the spirit world.

The Full Moon was a Thursday, and around two A.M., I woke suddenly, fully awake with a start of fear. The feeling was of great fear first, but the fear became surprise and then I felt myself relax. Tensions had been high the last few weeks, watching my grandmother leaving, but now it all released and it felt good. I knew she had died, and sent a blessing. My aunt called me with the news when it was day. My first feelings were of relief that it was over, she had suffered badly at the end. My grandmother wanted to die, had worked at it for several months, and now that fight was over. I would miss her, Goddess knows how much, but I was glad that she was free.

At the funeral, my family's reactions upset me more than the death itself. There was my sister crying, who had never visited, taken care of, or talked with my grandmother when she was alive. There was my mother, commenting about my clothes, and my father who was angry at what my grandmother had "put your mother through," but who had never participated, either. My grandmother had seen him too clearly for them to be friends. I didn't feel safe enough there to cry. When they opened the coffin, my grandmother's body was surrounded by an aura of clear/rainbow light, bright and positive, and reaching several feet beyond her. I sent my silent blessing, "You know what you're doing, Bubi. Go ahead." Her presence was not there for the burial; she had gone beyond. If anyone in my life has supported and influenced who I am today, it was Anna Backman. We will meet again.

In women's spirituality, the concept of past lives is a strong one, the idea of reincarnation, and death as the passage to another dimension, another plane of existence. Women read about past life regression work, experience spontaneous flashes of their own past lives, talk about soul mates and karma, and some do past life regressions of their own. More and more in women's spirituality, women are connecting with their spirit guides, and some are dis-covering mediumship—either their own or others', through readings, workshops, video tapes. Each regression, out of body experience or contact with a discarnate entity opens up more information and more questions. Spirit guides and controls discuss their own past lives and where and how they knew the living Be-ings they protect. In seances, women ask for messages from those gone beyond, and they receive messages and information too personal to deny or invalidate. With information from the ouija board, channeling, automatic writing, seances and past life regression, and information about "all time is now" and "all space is here," women's inquiries turn to the subject of death.

What is death, if women have had many lives and many deaths and rebirths? What is death, if by using motor automatisms or mediumship the dead can speak and offer information that sounds more like beginnings than endings? What is death, if the dead protect and help the living? And what is life, if living separates Be-ings from each other and changes reality to something limited, narrow and restricting? If consciousness and Be-ing continues after women leave the earth plane, where is it that they go, and what is it like to be there? If women are all a part of Goddess, and spirit guides and discarnate entities speak as frequently as they do of oneness, then how does Goddess figure in death and the death state? There are lots of questions, and only the beginning of answers.

The answers start with the transpersonal point, the chakra or energy center that's located beyond the physical in women's unseen bodies. The transpersonal point is defined as Goddess, the world beyond; it's the matriarchal, clairvoyant, stroking the python reality begun. There are no physical attributes for this chakra, no spinal cord, gland or organ coordinates. The color is clear/rainbow/white, the combination of all the chakra colors blended in light. (Black is the combination of all the chakra colors blended in matter, and at the other end of the spectrum is the Earth.) All colors blended together are colorless, as all sounds blended together are no physical sound— or all sound, the music of the spheres.

If the crown chakra is women's connection with Goddess and with other realms and dimensions, then the transpersonal point is these other dimensions themselves, and Goddess herself. Crown chakra psychic skills are learning awareness and connection with other realities, other dimensions, other levels of existence. The transpersonal point *is* these other levels, the deeper understanding and oneness of the universe, of life, death and Goddess. Where the root chakra is birth and incarnation, the transpersonal point is her opposite, death and what happens between death and rebirth. Before the womb and the root chakra comes the crossing over into death and the time spent beyond. After her connection with other-level Be-ings is woman's becoming of those discarnate Be-ings herself. Her birth, lives and past lives follow.

Death essentially is the separation of woman's physical self from her unseen psychic bodies. Some women make the separation/transition gradually, spending time in the spirit world before the break, and some make it quickly and often with bewilderment afterwards. In either case, the silver cord that connects the physical dense body to the rest of her self releases. The physical is left behind, and the etheric double, the astral/emotional, mental and spiritual bodies—what is called the soul—go on to the next level of existence. There is a loss at death of about three quarters of an ounce in physical weight, and this is believed to be the weight and mass of the unseen bodies. Women watching actual deaths have observed the separation, with the psychic bodies rising like a mist from the physical at the time of death. Women who have been pronounced dead and then revived describe a process that begins like astral projection and/or the crossing into past lives in past life regression work, then goes further. In numerous accounts, women describe this process and their descriptions all agree.

First is the loosing of the silver cord, observable at times by living women watching someone die, the separation of the unseen bodies from physical dense matter. Eileen Garrett describes this:

> The first time I saw the vital synthetic essence leave the body was at the death of a cousin, in Ireland, when I was a little girl. She was sleeping and my aunt left me with her, to watch, with instructions to call her if Ann waked or stirred . . .
>
> Ann finally stirred, in a kind of spasm, then lay quiet again . . . I became aware of a dim mist that was exuded from her body, weaving intricately within itself in a rhythm that was without agitation, tension, strain or pressure. Fascinated, I watched the faint, small cloud move off into space. (When the aunt returned a moment later, she found that Ann was dead).
>
> Looking back at the incident, I have realized that in my childish ignorance I actually did not know in any way that my cousin had died. But in psychic perceptiveness—which was the level at which I most truly lived in those years—I had intimately attended at the vital event.
>
> Later when my two sons died within a few months of each other, I was again aware of the withdrawal of that essence which is the sum of the synthetic human individuation. The dim misty cloud spiralled out from those small bodies as I held them in my arms, and moved away; and I followed the dim vitalities out and out into endless distances, till the throbbing in my head broke in upon the focus of my concentration.[2]

There are numerous similar descriptions, made by women who could not have known each other or compared stories. One more is by Louisa May Alcott, in the real life event of her sister's death that was described so movingly in *Little Women*:

> The sister of Louisa M. Alcott was in extremis. Around her bed were three persons, Louisa M. Alcott, the family physician, and the dying girl's mother.
>
> Death duly occurred. The doctor made the routine examination and picked up his bag. However, the group remained for a moment longer at the bedside. As they watched, a dim and faintly glowing mist arose from the body, swiftly coalesced, and floated away.
>
> Miss Alcott said: 'Mother's eyes followed mine and when I said, What did you see? She described the same light mist.'
>
> The doctor also said that he had seen the dimly luminescent mist. He could offer no explanation, saying only that there was a world-old belief that something left the body at the moment of death.[3]

This something is present for animals as well as humans. After her aunt had punished her for knowing about Aunt Leon's death (see Chapter Nine), Eileen Garrett, in a child's rage and frustration, drowned the ducklings that were her aunt's prize.

> I looked at the ducks lying limp on the grass beside me and almost hoped they might still be alive. But at this moment something really startling did begin to happen. The ducks were quiet but there was a movement going on all around them. I saw, curling up from each little body a grey smoke-like substance, rising in spiral form. This fluid stuff began to move and curl as it arose and gradually I saw it take on a new shape as it moved away from the bodies of these little dead

> ducks. Fear had now given way to amazement in the face of this spectacle. I was
> joyful because I knew in that moment that the ducks were 'coming alive' again. I
> had forgotten about their dead bodies lying limp below and waited, with tense
> expectancy, to see them take on new shape and run away . . .

After a very disturbed period, she came to this realization:

> Then, all of a sudden came a terrible revulsion against myself for all this killing
> that I had done. The startling truth now came to me in a flash . . . I had killed
> nothing at all, but only had changed its form. . . . I became sick from that time
> on, at the thought of the creatures that died. Anger shook me when I thought of
> those who killed any living thing . . . I wept bitterly for those ducklings which I
> had drowned.[4]

Eileen Garrett's concept of death as a change of form, her ability to see
it psychically, and her revulsion at killing are common reactions to
clairvoyant, stroking the python women. The knowledge was repeated
in her lifetime, in her other experiences with death.

R. DeWitt Miller takes information about death from four sources:
from the observations of psychics watching the death process (above);
from statements given by people at the point of death; from information derived through mediums; and from accounts by people who
have had near death experiences, who have been pronounced dead
and then were revived. Accounts by a wide variety of witnesses in
each category verify and confirm each other. In the case of observations by people on their deathbeds, the consensus of witnesses is
that the dying are not alone, but have dialog with others, relatives
gone before, ancestors, or spirit guides. My grandmother conversed
with others in the last days of her life, though I could not follow the
conversations. At times near the end, she awoke and continued the
conversations, no longer focused on the living beside her.

Are these the hallucinations that orthodox medicine says they
are? I don't believe so. There are accounts of the dying speaking with
others that they did not know had died, as well as with relatives and
friends long gone. A woman dying after childbirth made these comments, witnessed by the hospital matron:

> She said, 'Don't hide it; it's so beautiful.' Then turning away from him (her hus-
> band) towards me (the matron) . . . she said, 'Why there's Vidal,' referring to a
> sister of whose death three weeks previously she had not been told . . . [5]

A doctor gave this account; the woman survived:

> 'I had a patient,' the doctor wrote, 'who was just having a stroke, sit up in bed
> and call out to five people, women she saw at the foot of her bed. I took the list of
> names. When she got better, I asked her who these people were. She said, 'Why
> they are all dead. They are my relatives.' '[6]

This is also the place in the death process where living relatives have been known to see the presence of dying loved ones, dying or newly dead. A number of these experiences are given later.

Another way of gaining information about death is through discarnate spirits communicating through mediums, in seances, automatic writing, or through the ouija board. The purpose of much of the spiritualist movement was to go beyond death, receiving connection with lost relatives as a proof that there is something after dying. Gladys Osborne Leonard channeled this communication from a discarnate woman, name not given, to her still incarnate brother:

> Before finally leaving earth I seemed to be dreaming, and yet it was not wholly a dream. It seemed as if I had come here before the final separation from my physical body. I was only partially conscious towards the last, only half within my body; for my soul was already freeing itself. Nor did it seem wholly strange to me when I found myself here. I must have frequently come during sleep; for I could now remember that I had been here previously.[7]

Information channeled through Gladys Osborne Leonard is summarized as follows. Through Feda, she connected many people to their discarnate loved ones in seances over several decades. The quote is a composite of dozens of similar experiences:

> On awakening from unconsciousness I felt free from pain, quite strong, and full of gladness. It was a great relief to know that death was past. My new-found happiness was increased by the sight of old friends who gathered around and who gave me welcome. I then wished to return to see those left behind; after some little time I was able to do this.[8]

Accounts of these spirits' returns, in dreams, thought-form projections and manifestings have been given throughout this book, and more continue in this chapter. There is speculation as to how these apparitions and manifestings occur, but to anyone who has ever seen one, there can be no doubt that they do occur. Remember also, on the subject of mediums channeling Be-ings who have died, the stories of Seth, Gay Bonner, Patience Worth, Nadal and Siran, and other discarnate entities and controls. The concept is verified by a number of diverse women's experiences.

It is in the category of near death experiences, the stories of women who have died, been pronounced clinically dead, and then revived to life again, that the process of death and dying comes the clearest. Several books of such experiences are in print, with testimonies from a wide range of people and circumstances. The stories of what they saw and felt are strikingly similar. They are essentially stories of astral projections, except that they go further. Since these women returned to the earth plane, it is probable that the process continues further than they witnessed. Elements of the stories, the tunnel and the light particularly, are also present in past life regression experiences.

Raymond Moody, Jr, MD, interviewed a hundred and fifty people who had experienced death and been revived. All had been pronounced clinically dead, and all described the following process encapsulated in this summary. I have changed the pronouns to "she," but otherwise quote directly from Moody's book, *Life After Life*, (New York, Bantam Books, 1975).

> A woman is dying and, as she reaches the point of greatest physical distress, she hears herself pronounced dead by her doctor. She begins to hear an uncomfortable noise, a loud ringing or buzzing, and at the same time feels herself moving very rapidly through a long dark tunnel. After this, she suddenly finds herself outside of her own physical body, but still in the immediate physical environment, and she sees her own body from a distance, as though she is a spectator. She watches the resuscitation attempt from this unusual vantage point and is in a state of emotional upheaval.
>
> After a while, she collects herself and becomes more accustomed to her odd condition. She notices that she still has a 'body,' but one of a very different nature and with very different powers from the physical body she has left behind. Soon other things begin to happen. Others come to meet and help her. She glimpses the spirits of relatives and friends who have already died, and a loving, warm spirit of a kind she has never encountered before—a being of light—appears before her. This being asks her a question, nonverbally, to make her evaluate her life and helps her along by showing her a panoramic, instantaneous playback of the major events in her life. At some point she finds herself approaching some sort of barrier or border, apparently representing the limit between earthly life and the next life. Yet, she finds that she must go back to the earth, that the time for her death has not yet come. At this point she resists, for by now she is taken up with her experiences in the afterlife and does not want to return. She is overwhelmed by intense feelings of joy, love and peace. Despite her attitude, though, she somehow reunites with her physical body and lives.
>
> Later she tries to tell others, but she has trouble doing so. In the first place, she can find no human words adequate to describe these unearthly episodes. She also finds that others scoff, so she stops telling other people. Still, the experience affects her life profoundly, especially her views about death and its relationship to life.[9]

Much of this sounds like an astral projection experience, but carried further than most astral projections. The separation from the body, ringing or buzzing sound, and long tunnel, the ability to look back at the physical body without great concern for it and without feeling pain, are all astral projection experiences. Where the woman projecting, however, travels to a place on the planet (or in past life regressions to another lifetime), the woman in a near death experience travels beyond the linear dimension. Her spirit guides, as relatives or friends gone before, arrive to greet, teach and protect her, and to take her further. She reviews her life, approaches a bridge or border, then is told she must return. Crossing that border is apparently the separation point between life and death. No one interviewed wanted to return. In astral projection or regression, the woman remains on the planet, and in projection any thought of her physical body brings her back to it. This is not true in a near death experience. Her inability to make others believe her experience later is perhaps a built-in safeguard, to prevent the incarnate from seeking death prematurely.

Here is a woman's description of the process. She had hemorrhaged in childbirth and nearly died:

> It was immediately after delivery that I had a severe hemorrhage and the doctor had a difficult time controlling it. I was aware of what was happening as, having been a nurse myself, I realized the danger. At this time, I lost consciousness, and heard an annoying buzzing, ringing sound. The next thing I knew it seemed as if I were on a ship or a small vessel sailing to the other side of a large body of water. On the distant shore, I could see all of my loved ones who had died—my mother, my father, my sister, and others. I could see them, could see their faces, just as they were when I knew them on earth. They seemed to be beckoning me to come on over, and all the while I was saying, 'No, no, I'm not ready to join you. I don't want to die. I'm not ready to go.'
>
> Now, this was the strangest experience because all this time I could see all the doctors and nurses, too, as they worked on my body, but it seemed as if I were a spectator rather than that person—that body—they were working on. I was trying so hard to get through to my doctor, 'I'm not going to die,' but no one could hear me. Everything—the doctors, the nurses, the delivery room, the ship, the water and the far shore—was just sort of a conglomerate. It was all together, as if one scene were superimposed right on top of the other.
>
> Finally, the ship almost reached the far shore, but just before it did, it turned around and started back. I did finally get through to my doctor, and I was saying, 'I'm not going to die.' It was at this point, I guess, that I came around, and the doctor explained what had happened, that I had had a post-partum hemorrhage, and that they had nearly lost me, but that I was going to be all right.[10]

Virginia Randall was a nurse whose patient had a similar experience. The girl, Dorothy (no last name given), had been in an iron lung recovering from polio. She died and was revived, and told the following:

> . . . a wonderful floating feeling. I could walk again, my muscles could do what I wanted them to do, and I felt completely happy—no pain, no restrictions, all light and gay. I was so pleased to leave my worn out shell and be free. A bright light attracted my attention and I moved toward it. As I slowly approached it, I found myself in a new world.
>
> A soft diffused light—not like harsh sunlight—glowed and everything was joyful. Gorgeous flowers perfumed the air, multi-colored birds sang, the grass

was green and there were butterflies. Soothing, minor chord music came from an unseen orchestra, and all the people I saw were smiling and happy looking.

It was as though I thought myself someplace, and lo! There I was! I remembered my dead grandmother and then I was with her, and my aunts, and my dog and several friends whom I had missed so much since they died. It was the most exciting reunion, yet they seemed to expect me. My arrival seemed part of a plan.

Then very suddenly a light appeared—a great Golden Glory that was so dazzling I couldn't look at it. We all hid our faces and from out of the music swelling from the light came a wonderful voice, the sweetest I have ever heard. The voice spoke to me:

'No, Dorothy, I am sorry but it is not time yet. You have more to do down there.'

An interesting corollary to this case is the statement by Nurse Randall that the night before her patient's crisis she was writing a notation at home when a peculiar sensation crept over her hand and arm. Her fingers seemed possessed by some strange force as they wrote words which were not in her mind. The words were:

'Dorothy is here with us but will return.'[11]

Women recognize the last part of this as automatic writing.

A feature of past life regression work (and astral projection) is the black tunnel and buzzing sound, both described in near death experiences. They happen before arriving in the consciousness of a past life event. One more near death experience describes the dark tunnel, with comments explaining what's happening. Ruby Staley describes her grandmother's near death experience, as her grandmother described it to her after:

My grandmother said she felt she was walking through a black railway tunnel (= the 'double' was being released from the body, during which neither the 'double' nor the body was available as an instrument of consciousness). She came out into a glorious light, a green road with banks of arum lilies on either side . . . At the end of the road she saw her (deceased) mother, who called her to 'come along!' She went in. The road seemed like velvet (= 'paradise' conditions, corresponding to the soul body).

Suddenly she heard her husband cry, 'Annie, don't leave me yet; wait until I'm ready!' She turned and saw my (physically embodied) grandfather in the mouth of the tunnel. She went towards him and . . . went back into the tunnel (= her 'double' re-entered her body). She lived to be ninety and my grandfather ninety-one. She was sure that if she had gone on to meet her own mother she would have died.[12]

The tunnel is the separation of the unseen bodies from the dense physical level, a period when consciousness is not yet transferred. The place of crossing the bridge, gate, water or barrier, is called the "second death," the severing of the silver cord, from which time return to the earth plane is no longer possible.

In death, the separation process goes beyond the experience of near death. The silver cord severs and consciousness does not return to the physical body. Theosophists describe a series of levels, or Devachans, that the freed soul passes through, one after the other, and the shedding first of the etheric double, then the astral and mental bodies, until all experience is consolidated and carried on in the causal or spiritual body. From this soul essence reincarnation eventually occurs, with the building of new psychic bodies and entrance into a new physical body.

Some cases of past life regression have described and recorded the several worlds the soul passes through after death, and they are described in *The Tibetan Book of the Dead*, an ancient text on the nature of death and living. Four worlds are described, correspondences to the astral, mental and spiritual bodies. At the "second death," the bridge, the etheric double is shed, and the emotional/astral and mental bodies are shed in the next two worlds. Past life researcher Frederic Lenz, working from *The Tibetan Book of the Dead* and personal accounts, calls the four levels the vital, mental, psychic and soul worlds.[13]

In the vital world, a place of hallucination and chaos follows crossing the bridge and also precedes rebirth. Crookall, the astral projection expert, suggests that this period is the crossing itself, and happens "so swiftly that no impression of unreality is retained by the working brain."[14] Those who experience this world in past life regressions describe it as violent and tormented, sounding much like the Greek Hades or Christian Hell. Other sources state that you get what you ask for after death—women expecting fire and brimstone get it for awhile, and are not satisfied until they do; women expecting the Happy Valley get that instead. Some of those experiencing this level connected their presence there to negative actions in their lives that they felt needed punishing. They would not have felt comfortable without their expectations being met. When a soul leaves the vital world, she leaves behind her astral/emotional body; then she moves to the next level, the mental world.

A place of ideas and knowledge, the mental world is described as where ideas in their germanal form on Earth derive from. Descriptions of it include a clarity unknown on Earth, and "carrier beings" (spirit guides) who help transmit new ideas to those on the earth plane working to manifest or dis-cover them. Women involved with ideas and knowledge in life spend more time at this level than women who have had less interest in this direction. The mental world is described as a positive place, an exciting and positive experience, and when a soul leaves it she leaves her mental body behind.

From the mental world, what remains is the causal, soul or spiritual body, the spirit essence of woman's Being. Each progressing world is decribed as more positive and less like the earth plane, also less easy to describe. The psychic world is filled with music and pastoral settings, as well as luminous be-ings, descriptions of which occur in the near death experiences. It sounds very much like Gladys Osborne Leonard's Happy Valley, or the patriarchal concept of heaven. Joan describes her experience with the psychic world, derived through past life regression work:

> I felt that all my life I had been dressed in a costume but I didn't know it. One day the costume fell away and I saw what I really had been all along. I was not what I thought I was. All my life I had thought of myself as a person, as a body. I thought to myself, 'I am so and so, a woman, a mother, a secretary, and things like that. When I went into this world I realized that all along I was not those things. I was a soul, not a body. I couldn't die; I couldn't be born, I lived forever . . . It was like waking up after having amnesia.[15]

Beautiful Be-ings inhabit the psychic world: angels, helpers and spirit guides. This is the place of reunion with relatives, ancestors and friends who have gone before. Be-ings are described as made of light, but still recognizable outside of the bodies they wore on Earth. From here there is movement to the soul world, the last of the four worlds the discarnate Be-ing travels through.

The soul world is coming home. It's composed of divisions and subworlds, including worlds of the fine arts, and souls rest at their own levels within it. Souls with fewer incarnations stop at a level different from those more experienced. Advanced souls travel through all the levels, while newer ones reach only as far as their experience allows. This is the time of rest and regeneration, of assimilation of learning and experience, before rebirth. Joan, connecting with this world in her past life regression work, describes it:

> I found myself in a vast place. I felt as though I had come home. I had no apprehensions, fears or worries. I no longer remembered my former life on earth. Nothing existed for me but a quiet fulfillment. I was not conscious of time in the usual sense; everything seemed timeless. I felt as if I had always been there. It was similar to the feeling I have when I wake from a dream that has seemed very real, only to discover that it wasn't real but only a dream . . . My former life on earth had been a passing dream which I had now awakened from.
>
> I did not have the sense that I was moving in space. Everything was conscious and pure awareness; there were no dimensions there. I moved through thousands of levels. On each level different souls were resting before being born again . . . Finally I reached a level that I was comfortable on. I stayed there. I

sensed that there were many levels above the one I had stopped at and that souls that were more advanced than I would go there.[16]

Alice describes an art world, one of the divisions of the soul world:

> There is a constant activity in these worlds of art, but it is a joyous activity . . . In these worlds it is all a play of light. One experiences sound as a form of light, and if music is played, there is a corresponding display of light related to the tonalities that are sounded. The same is true of perfumes and flowers and so forth. And since there isn't the heaviness and obstructiveness of the physical mind to contend with, intention is brought to fruition very quickly, and creative people, of course, have a time of tremendous joy. Painters can paint anything in the time it takes to snap your fingers. Composers can compose just like that. They create endlessly here, with a freedom they would never find when they were on earth. And their creations are so much more beautiful. Instead of having the usual number of colors in the physical spectrum, an artist has many more colors that exist in these worlds but not on earth. The same is true of musical tones, and so on. I visited several of these worlds and observed many souls creating there. I also had the feeling that there were many more of these art worlds that I did not see.[17]

With these worlds in mind, Iris Belhayes, deriving her work from contact with spirit guides, describes the stages of the death process, the progression from death to the soul world. She calls the soul world "Home," the place from which spirit guides communicate to the living, the place to which all return after death. Home is a period of rest, reflection, assimilation and evaluation before the trauma of rebirth. Her term for Goddess is All There Is, and she sees Home (the soul world) as a state of energy or a state of mind.

> All that exists is spirit, and that includes all matter, energy, space and time, all dimensions and all creation in All There Is. Now, when we look at the Reality of a Home Universe, we are looking at a point of view—a state of mind. We are looking at Real Reality. It is the same, family to family. When we return to our Home Universe, we are actually returning to a state of mind—a state in which we and the rest of our spirit family share realities and viewpoints of Life upon which we have agreed.[18]

Souls expand in awareness through the experience of their lives, but each has perfect oneness and awareness from the beginning. Women are complete and are a part of Goddess/All There Is. In leaving Home, incarnating, the soul suspends a portion of its knowing in order to be able to experience incarnation fully and learn from other viewpoints. The soul must be part of the linear world for awhile, going beyond it into matriarchal consciousness as far as she can.

In the death process, from the time of leaving the body until the time of reincarnation, Belhayes outlines five steps. They are: 1) Leaving the body; 2) Communication and influence of relatives; 3) Decompression; 4) Reorientation; and 5) Life Evaluation.[19]

In stage one, leaving the body, the woman dies as a choice, though not always a conscious one. She decides to leave, but not always how it'll happen. When she has separated her consciousness from her physical body, she feels good, and usually has no wish to return. In the case of a near death experience, the woman's time to die has not yet come, and she does not choose it. She is helped back to her physical body. When it is time for death, her guides are there, helping her through any confusion, and seeing her through the worlds, including the vital world, safely.

Stage two is communication and influence of relatives. After separating from her body, the woman's consciousness can hover around it for a few days, and is often present at the funeral. The spirit tries to communicate with and comfort those left behind. Relatives' grief holds her close to the earth plane for awhile, making it harder for her to progress through the worlds, and to leave the vicinity of her home or physical body. Negative thought-forms involved with family matters and relationships can create the "hells" of the vital world. In some cases, souls are trapped between the earth plane and the spirit worlds, the cause of some apparitions. In cases of violent or sudden death, these apparitions of trapped souls are more common. Sending love and release to the dead helps prevent them from staying on the earth plane and being trapped in this way, and helps them through the transition period between death and Home (the soul world). Contact with the dead through psychic means or mediums for the first six months is not recommended, unless the discarnate spirit chooses to give communication herself.

The third stage is decompression, the period of movement through the worlds. This is a gradual reawakening to the soul world, and what Iris Belhayes calls Real Reality—the matriarchal stroking the python consciousness of other dimensions, but from the other side. In this period, the woman may move through a hallucinatory after-death state (the vital world) where she experiences what she *thinks* after-death should be. She has to act out this thought-form before her spirit guides can lead her from it. There are teachers, helpers, ancestors, and guides to bring a woman through the decompression process and help her through the worlds. A woman aware in life of the worlds and the Real Reality of death has a faster and easier time at this transition than someone who has not been reminded of it since her last death and reincarnation.

Stage four, reorientation, is a re-cognition and return to Goddess, a return to the soul world, or Home. This is a birth and an awakening, a re-membering of all the soul has forgotten in her process of reincarnation into a body. This is oneness, the self as a part of Goddess and Goddess within all Be-ing. Transcendence experiences on the earth plane are a beginning of this awareness, what women are at least partially able to reach while still incarnated. Transcendence experiences are a glimpse, and Home is the Real Reality. It is also a thought-form and a state of mind. In this reorientation stage, women reconnect with their spirit families, some of which have and will reincarnate with them again and again.

The final stage, stage five, is life evaluation, where the soul looks back at the learnings of her just-ended life, and evaluates her gains. She decides her growth, how far her goals were accomplished, examines her mistakes, and determines where to go from there. She shares her learning with the members of her spirit family and makes the choices for her next life. She may remain in the soul world for a longer or shorter period of time before reincarnating. She may act as a spirit guide to someone else. When she is ready, she works with others of her family to plan her rebirth. There are times when a soul does not return through the worlds, but reincarnates in a new body immediately, as well as times when a soul chooses to undergo only one incarnation and returns to the soul world for good. Suicide is a form of death much frowned upon, and suicides go through a longer process of decompression, with a faster return to the earth plane to complete their interrupted learnings.

Helen Wambach did reincarnation meditations with 750 people,[20] asking them about rebirth. She asked them if they had chosen to be born, did they have help choosing, did they know either of their parents before being born in this life, how they felt about being born in this life and time, did they choose their sex, and did they know their purpose for reincarnating in this lifetime. She asked her subjects about relationships, and asked them about their awareness in the womb, their feelings during the birth process, and their feelings right after being born. Giving the suggestion that they'd experience without feeling pain, she brought them through past lives, death, the after-life and rebirth before bringing them out of trance. She gave them questionnaires to fill out immediately about their pre-birth experiences. Her findings are significant for a study of death and beyond.

After experiencing past lives and their deaths in them, 90% of Wambach's students reported death as a pleasant experience, and

81% said they had chosen to be reborn. Only 28%, however, said they had re-entered life enthusiastically.[21] Subjects were reborn with their consent but with reluctance (67%), and virtually everyone of them experienced the help of guides in the decision. The following responses were typical:

> Yes, I chose to be born, but very reluctantly. There were several others around me when I was deciding and they seemed to be just like me. They said they would be around to help me in the coming lifetime. When you asked about the prospect of being born, I did not want to leave the beautiful garden and my friends there. (Case A-489).

And,

> When you asked if I chose to be born, I felt I didn't really choose, but I was prompted to by a mother figure. I clung to her in the clouds and I hesitated being born. My feelings about the prospect of living and the coming lifetime were that I knew I needed to find my other half and unity. I seemed to be a little girl before I was born with long hair. (Case A-207).[22]

And just one more:

> Yes, I chose to be born. There was a group of us, and they were advising me, and we were planning to go together. I felt regret about leaving where I was, and a sense of dedication for the plan to work with others. (Case A-307).[23]

Fifty per cent of the subjects reported having more than one guide or counselor in the decision to be born, but almost all mentioned at least one guide or counselor. Only .01% saw their guide as the male god, and most saw them as equals and friends, occasionally as ancestors.[24]

When asked about the time period, the twentieth century as their time to incarnate, 41% had no choice or preference about the time to be reborn in. Of those who had a preference, 51% chose this time period for its spiritual growth opportunities.[25] Four per cent chose both the twentieth century and to be female in it, because of the opportunities for women's growth and freedom in this century. The 48% of Helen Wambach's subjects that were female had definitely chosen to be female. A third of these chose it to be able to bear children, but there were other reasons:

> I chose to be a woman because female is more loving, expressive, in touch with self. I feel the female part of myself is better able to reflect this. (Case A-384).
> I chose to be a female because it is a better channel for creative love. (Case A-45).
> I chose to be a woman because a man cannot give as fully as a woman. (Case A-11).
> I came as a woman in the twentieth century to find the potential of the female for spiritual and sexual growth. This time frame allows more freedom for a

woman to experience life today. (Case A-385).[26]

On the question of why they had been reincarnated, most gave purposes of learning to relate to others and learning to love.[27] Twenty eight per cent felt they had come here to teach unity and oneness, and 27% to grow spiritually. Eighteen per cent gave their purpose as working out issues with others they had known in past lives. Of the 750 subjects, 87% said that they had known others in this life before and that their relationships with them were karmic ones.

> I knew from past lives my mother, two friends, and my youngest brother. My mother was my servant, and my father was a lover in past lives. The rest I knew, but not how I knew them. I chose to be a girl because my mother needed a girl. (Case A-508).
>
> My mother was a mother of mine in a past life and also a child of mine in a past life. My children told me they wanted to be my children before I was born, and I knew them not only from past lives, but from the between-life period. (Case A-381).
>
> I noticed a strong physical energy in my heart when you asked about whether I knew my mother, and I had a strong impression she was my sister in a past life. (Case A-91).[28]

Resolving relationships and reuniting with others appears to be a major purpose in reincarnation. Women knew their mothers and other significant people in past lives in various roles, and also in the between-life state. Jane Roberts and Seth comment that three major roles are important for every entity to experience and they reincarnate to fill these roles. The roles are mother, father and child.[29]

In the birth process itself, most subjects were aware of their mothers' feelings while they were in the womb, but 89% did not join with the fetus until near the time of birth, at least after the sixth month, or were in and out of awareness with the fetus. Thirty three per cent did not enter the fetus until just before or during the birth itself. With the between-life state seen as pleasant and most subjects entering incarnation only reluctantly, most souls remained discarnate for as long as possible. Yet 86% were aware of their mother's emotions and thoughts at the time:

> When you asked about my attachment to the fetus, I was outside waiting for it to be ready for birth, so that I could enter. When you asked about the feelings of my mother, I became aware that she was nervous and not too happy about the birth. (Case A-525).
>
> I was not completely attached to the fetus, and I was able to be, and to move, as before I entered the fetus. I only came when it was ready to be born. I was aware of my mother's emotion. She was afraid and I also became aware of the doctor and the nurses and aware of the delivery room. (Case A-246).
>
> When you asked about attachment to the fetus, I had none. It seems that I just

observed it. I was aware of the emotions of my mother. I was being counseled up to the time I entered the body. (Case A-123)

When you asked about the attachment to the fetus, it felt like I was floating above the delivery table until the birth. I was attached by a cord. But I was aware that my mother was very loving and eager to receive me. (Case A-224).[30]

After experiencing their past life deaths and the soul world, incarnation is reluctant and birth is not met with joy. Though the suggestion was given that no pain be felt, Helen Wambach's subjects experienced a high degree of sadness—at being born, at reincarnating, at leaving the spirit world. There were reports of aloneness, alienation and of feeling cut off from Home. There were also strong physical and sensory impressions, overwhelming ones:

Many subjects reported that the onrush of physical sensations on emerging from the birth canal was disturbing and very unpleasant. Apparently the soul exists in a quite different environment in the between-life state. The physical senses bring so much vivid input that the soul feels almost 'drowned' in light, cold air, sounds. Surprising to me was the frequent report that the soul of the newborn infant feels cut off, diminished, alone compared to the between-life state. To be alive in a body is to be alone and unconnected.[31]

Here are some responses to birth and leaving the soul world, leaving Home:

The birth-canal experience for me was impatience, a realization that tolerance would be a major stumbling block for me in this life. As soon as I was born I felt intense cold and bright light. I was afraid of the prospects ahead of me. I felt that the doctors and nurses in attendance were impersonal and cold. They lacked compassion for my mother's fear and pain. I recall being very upset by this lack of feeling of those in attendance. I hovered over my mother throughout this ordeal. (Case A-485).

People were impersonal. I think to myself, 'This is going to be a lonely trip.' I think I must have rushed into this life. (Case A-406).

When you asked about the birth-canal experience, I had a feeling of fighting, like I hadn't argued or put up a fight until the actual experience, because I kept hoping it wouldn't happen. My impressions after birth were that I was in a vast area, and I felt lost and very cold. (Case A-457).

My birth-canal experience was unpleasant, and the feelings were strong that I wished I weren't being born. I wanted to change my mind. My sensory impressions after I was born were of confusion and sadness and the lack of warmth around me. My mother seemed very sad and my father felt guilty. The whole feeling of birth seemed to be an annoying, unpleasant 'trip' to accomplish something in this lifetime. I felt an urgency. (Case A-408).[32]

The consensus of this study is that death is far more pleasant, and more desirable, than the birth process. Ninety per cent of the subjects saw death as pleasant, but only 28% wanted to be reborn. They saw rebirth as something necessary, and chose to do it, and had guides or counselors to help them along the way. Reincarnating subjects chose their parents and their sex, and knew their purpose for coming here. That purpose was generally seen as for learning, and for many it was to work out issues of love and relationship with Be-ings they had known before. Eighty five per cent had known people from this life in other lives, and many could describe the relationships, which were varied. In the fetus, most Be-ings remained outside for as long as possible, or were in and out, some not joining with the body until just before birth. None found the birth process pleasant. All found it traumatic, and their entrance into life problematic, alienated and sad.

Wambach's information clearly backs up the material about death and the death state. Death is a positive state, and the between life state is positive, a going Home to one's spirit family for a time of peace and rest. The vital world, the one negative aspect of the death process, seems to be a state of mind created by the entity herself, and is there for the purpose of working through negative thought-forms, for ending them. The information presented by discarnate or near death sources contradicts what women have been told about death, whatever religion they were raised with. Says Iris Belhayes, women's connection with this information was not meant to have been lost.

Denying the information of the matriarchal reality (Iris Belhayes' Real Reality)—spirit guides, discarnate channelings, near death witnesses, and what women say before they die about their experience— denies the reality of death as something very different from the end of all things that Judaism call it, or the hellfire and punishment of other religions. Perhaps it's that people are easier to control when taught to be "good" in this life for fear of death and after. Women's spirituality wants to know more, and is composed of women who live by choice and free will, rather than by rule books and male dictates. Sources state that knowing the truth about death makes the process when the time comes less confusing. In this chapter, I have outlined the process and compared it with the other side, the more celebrated process of birth.

Women wrote to me about their near death experiences, their witnessing of deaths and their experiences with apparitions at the time of death and after. Other apparition experiences are found in the chapters on manifesting and astral projection, and elsewhere. How ghosts manifest was discussed in these chapters, but in this one the emphasis is on the death experience. Near death occurrences were separated from astral projections, to appear in this chapter.

Gloria's story was the most detailed. It happened because of a drug overdose, an accidental one on a vacation trip. She was in intense pain, outdoors and wrapped in a sleeping bag, when she nearly died:

> I settled down on the bag. I drew myself up in the fetal position to relieve the stomach cramps. My head was ringing. My throat felt like there was a tight rope around it. I could hardly swallow.
>
> I was amazed at how bright and clearly I could see everything around me, though there was only starlight now. I could see almost every detail of the rocks, trees, and the stream flowing next to the road.
>
> The pain kept increasing. After a while, all there is is pain and your mind. I remember my mind thinking, 'No, I don't want to feel this pain any longer.' This continued for several minutes.
>
> I took a deep breath. There was no pain. I breathed again, it felt better than any breath I could remember. I stretched and there was no pain. I felt wonderful.
>
> I looked around. I was above the tree, the tree I was lying under. There was our car and the road! I calmly looked around. I knew I wasn't in my body. I could see me and the sleeping bag about twenty-five feet below.
>
> I was rising higher, so I rotated around. I was looking at everything I could see. The air I breathed entered every pore. I was light. I looked at the sky and I knew more than I had known in my body. Looking down at the ground and the surrounding forest, I knew where every animal sat. My senses were keener than I had ever known.
>
> Looking down at what I thought to be a stream, I could see there was another fork. At this point, there were two rivers rushing down the canyon. I felt such a kinship with the trees, the water. I knew it all in a new way.
>
> There was a bright, misty area to the east of me. The closer I came to the lighted mist, the more I remembered. I had a new awareness of who I was, a whole order in which I belonged, everything belonged.
>
> I was drawn to the light. Adjectives like: calming, loving, knowing, remembering sequenced themselves. I felt a feeling of coming home, like waking from a dream I'd thought was real. I remembered this is how it felt before I began this life.
>
> Now, perhaps 150 feet above the ground, I felt a feeling of coming together. I was a part of a whole that knew itself. There within the misty tunnel I ascended till I came to a presence. I saw no body, my memory expected no body but the presence was a male, or I should correct this by adding, it was an authoritative lower volumed and toned voice—'Go no further.' I thought for a moment and knew I could go on anyway. His words were advice, not orders.
>
> Though I love my three children very much and consider myself a devoted mother, at that moment I felt no remorse about leaving them, nor my husband or any relative. I knew they were on earth experiencing the lessons of life and they would be okay.
>
> The Personality I was speaking with interrupted my thoughts with his, by saying, 'You need to return for his sake,' and my eyes focused on my husband.
>
> There was a questioning thought in my mind. I understood the spirit entity would not lie. As I thought, 'Maybe he's right,' my spirit immediately started

down. I was being drawn back. I turned around like I was going to lie down. I put on my body. My legs entered first and then my trunk. I felt like I had to bend my shoulders forward to fit inside at chest and neck level and my head. I felt the pain again. I stumbled doubled over to the car.

The guys had fallen asleep. I woke them and made them take me to the emergency room. I was found to have a normally lethal level of strychnine in my body. The ER had several reports of similar cases earlier that evening. Later I was told that six people died that weekend from a bad party drug made locally.

After I recovered, I insisted on going back to the spot. I waded across the stream and made my way through the evergreen forest on the other side. I found a second stream about 75 feet in. There I sat and laughed and cried.

I tried to explain that I had left my body, possibly died. It was taken lightly by my companions. I told of the stream and all I could remember. The things I felt and knew while in the light were hard to remember after re-entering my body.

This proved to me that I remembered correctly. It was okay that my husband didn't believe me. While in this body we are ignorant. I could remember only that I knew so very much more in the light. There was personal proof to me that there is life after death. We are not our bodies. When we die, we lose nothing important. I was very surprised by the distant, lack of interest toward even loved ones left on earth. It wasn't a heartless distance but one of confidence. I knew they were okay. Life looked like a series of experiences, lessons of interaction, and once born, we are each okay and up to the lessons.

Compare this with the composite near death experience earlier in this chapter.

Leonie has this account:

I had become extremely ill while in France, and ended up in a German hospital. Later I learned that I was comatose for periods of time during those weeks. All I knew then was that, sometimes, I became one with a warm white light, just as, when I was a child, I had felt complete harmony with plants and animals. While I was a part of that light, all was peaceful and I could feel no pain (a feature of my illness was intense physical pain). When I 'returned' to the physical plane, the pain returned. I decided at some point, while in the white light, that I would accept the pain and learn about it. That is when I 'returned' for good, became interested in yoga and meditation, and eventually began to understand many of the experiences that I couldn't before.

Chris had this near death experience, again caused by an overdose of drugs:

It happened in the early 70's, when the flower child thing had degenerated and bad drugs were becoming widespread. I took something that was supposed to be THC and it turned out to be PCP, and I'd taken way too much. I sat there realizing what had happened. By that time it was well into my bloodstream and I was really kicking myself mentally for doing such a stupid thing. I knew I'd OD'd and I went out pretty fast. My main concern was for my parents, the pain they'd have if I died this way. I was full of regret to die in such a stupid, meaningless way and threw all my energy into a prayer to whatever spirits might hear, that I be allowed to survive this accident, spare my parents the mess it would involve, and go on with my life.

Pretty soon I left my body behind and went somewhere with a lot of rooms, each one with something beautiful in it, but I didn't belong in any of them. (I know this sounds like a 'trip,' but let me say I was very experienced with psychedelics. I'd been tripping for years by then and this was definitely a different order of experience from that. I could tell the difference, just as I knew it was PCP and that I'd had too much. But you'd have to take my word for it).

Then I stumbled into a room that had two beings in it. They were like spirits, like the 'imaginary playmate' I'd had as a child. I think I thought that's who it was, in fact. They seemed female somehow, and were laughing together in sort of a silvery way.

When they realized I was there they said, 'Who's this? How did you get here?' They treated me as adults would a small child who was lost. I spilled out my tale of woe to them and they quite kindly took me in hand, after talking it over between themselves briefly. They told me not to worry, they'd take care of it. I thought they meant they'd help my parents out, but they sort of flew me back to my body, showed me where it was, and told me I'd be okay, then left before I could thank them.

I came out of it quite sober and feeling fine, with no ill effects. The people I was with said I'd just been sitting there cross-legged for about a half hour, and couldn't believe I'd come out of it so fast, as the other guy who took it was out for hours. It turned out he'd taken less than I had—he'd tricked me—and he was twice my size.

Catharine had this dream of death and after. Like other psychic experiences, it's remained vivid over years, an experience asking for comprehension and learning.

When I was in eighth grade I had a dream that is vivid to this day. In this dream I was in a car with three friends (Bonnie, Dianne and Lynn). We were playing a game with another carload of people. The object was to get as close as possible to 'the edge.' (The edge of the pavement was a downhill fall into the Ramapo River). Well, our car went over the edge and sunk to the bottom of the river. We all sat there deciding what to do. I started rolling down the window and water started coming in. My friends started yelling at me, 'What are you doing, are you crazy?' I said we'd run out of air if we stayed there. We had to swim to the surface. They said we should wait for someone to save us.

They stayed and I swam. I made it to the surface and saw tons of people at the river bank pointing to the place the car sunk. There were police and ambulances, etc. I tried to get their attention but no one seemed to see me. I swam to the shore and climbed out. I went up in the crowd and tried to tell people where my friends were. No one paid any attention to me. I ran across the street to a phone booth but couldn't get anyone.

Next, I wandered into a building and was told I had to get my robe. I tried to tell them about my friends but no one would listen to me. They just told me to go in the other room and get my robe. I then went in another room which was filled with church pews and people wearing gold robes (they looked like my school's choir robes). All of a sudden I saw Dianne, Lynn and Bonnie sitting there, in robes. I ran over to them saying, 'God, I'm so glad to see you. I didn't think you'd make it.' Then they told me, 'We didn't make it, neither did you.'

That ended that dream. I'd interpret it as we all died, but we all lived on—it made no difference—we all still possessed consciousness of being . . . I don't know if this stuff is significant to you, but it has been very meaningful to me. Recently I had a friend catch me off guard. We were at the airport waiting for her flight home and she confessed to me that she was afraid of dying. I almost laughed—I said, 'You're afraid of death? There's no such thing.' The words just popped out of my mouth without me knowing they were coming.

Women recovering from near death experiences, physical ones or in dreams, lose their fear of dying, and express it that way.

Sharon also had a near death dream:

I stood in total darkness, so dark I could not see my hand in front of me. In the distance, I noticed a triangular-shaped white light and began walking toward it, feeling the ground beneath my bare feet and a robe around my ankles. As I approached the light, I saw everything around me illuminated by the rays. I felt the warmth, the love, the total acceptance. I reached the barrier of black, shining marble-type rocks that prevented me from going into the light. I felt that this was HOME and I wanted to go HOME! I struggled to pull myself up over the rocks, but the struggle was in vain. I could go no further. I began to cry because the feeling of not being able to cross over, to go home, was devastating.

Telepathically, the light told me, 'You will see when you are ready to see.' My pleas changed nothing. I was not going to be allowed to enter through the triangular-shaped opening. I knew that on the other side of the white light was bigger than the entire universe. I knew I had been there before. I knew I would return there. I tried with all I had to climb the rocks, just to see into the light. I lost my grip on the slick rocks. There was nothing below but darkness, nothing to put my feet onto and my feet dangled in the air. I panicked.

The light said, 'You lack focus and concentration. You must learn to concentrate fully upon what you desire. Visualize a foundation for your feet and you shall have it. You will not fall.' I tried to see a foundation, but none appeared. 'You must learn to concentrate first and all else will come easily.'

I awoke from this 'dream,' and as I write this, I feel all the knowledge of this message. And I am painfully aware that I still have not learned how to do what the light said. I still feel as if I have no foundation. I feel extreme frustration as I write this because I have not learned the art of focus and concentration or visualization. I still feel lost groping in the darkness. Even as I did as a child!

The triangle shape or delta has always been a Goddess symbol and a womb symbol. The barrier and the light are typical of near death experiences.

In one more near death experience, Susan Sheppard writes:

My own paternal grandmother was eighty-nine years old when she died. I happened to look a great deal like her. Grandma was extremely agile and mentally sharp well up until her death. Her agility proved to be the very reason Grandma died at such an 'early age' (her family usually lived well into their nineties). Since Grandma was only 4'10" tall, she climbed upon a box to get a stone bowl off the top of her cupboard. She slipped and pulled a heavy cupboard full of dishes down on top of her. It bruised her heart and broke four ribs.

Grandma survived and was taken to the hospital. When she got home, I went to visit her. She said, 'You know, Susie, I think I must be crazy.' I answered, 'Why, Grandma?' she began her story. 'When I was in the emergency room, I could feel myself slip out of my body. I could see the doctors working on me from 'way up high' near the ceiling. I could hear them saying they didn't think I was going to make it—but kept pushing down on my chest to bring me back. The next thing I knew, I was flying up through a big tube. There were beautiful lights at the top. As I got near the lights, these people were talking to me saying, 'Not now, Grandma. It's not time for you. Go back. Go back.' They were real nice to me so I didn't want to come back down so soon.

'Then the next thing I knew, I was back on the hospital cart—alive. I had made it. But, I was sad because I wanted to go back where it was light and happy.' Then I said, 'You're not crazy, Grandma. You're just like me. We are the same,' (indicating my psychic gifts).

Grandma changed worlds about a month later. A strange event happened. I woke up in the middle of the night with the sensation that 'someone' or 'something' was frantically trying to invade my body. The spirit seemed to want to 'step back in.' Not knowing Grandma had passed on, I opened my eyes in terror. There was little Grandma in her calico dress looking so perplexed. I knew instantly that Grandma thought my body was hers! (Remember, I look almost exactly like her). Poor thing was confused and didn't realize she had passed over. The next morning Mother called to tell me that Grandma had died during the night.

Women's words and actions as they enter death offer further information. Susan also sent me this story:

Isabelle is a beautiful sixty-five year old friend who has an interest in the psychic field. When she was five, her young mother died of scarlet fever. She had been sick for several weeks before she finally passed over.

One day during the long illness, Isabelle's mother seemed to improve. She sat up in bed and talked with relatives well into the evening who had come to visit earlier in the day. Suddenly, a very dreamy expression crossed her face. She jolted upright and said, 'Oh look at the beautiful lights! Can't you see them?' Everything in the room appeared perfectly normal to the rest of the family. So, her mother then said, 'Turn off the lamp so you can see them better! The lights are so beautiful.'

They turned out the light and there was silence. When her family turned the lamp back on, Isabelle's mother was dead.

### And this from Freya:

This last August my ninety-eight year old mother was in the nursing home. On a Thursday night I had a dream (I rarely remembered a dream) that my maternal grandfather came to me. He didn't say a word, he just hugged me. He died in 1933. He never hugged me in his life.

The next day the nursing home called and said that mother had a cold. I called my brothers and my children. We stayed with her, she got weaker and weaker. She had been blind for several years. Just before she died she tried to say something. She opened her eyes and I *know* she saw me. I believe she tried to tell me her father was there.

Freya's mother was guided through the death process by her father who'd gone before. Winston was guided by Sylvia, and Mimi writes of their passings, a story of after death manifesting and apparitions.

Oh yes, I believe in life after death. Here is proof. In 1977 my sister and her husband lived on the north side of Chicago. Sylvia and Robert. My sister would always read in bed and of course smoke. One night she fell asleep and started a fire which in a few minutes raged out of control . . . Her husband was at work at the time. He had been a fireman in Chicago for many years and now retired . . . For six weeks Sylvia lingered with lung problems from the smoke. Then one day he came home to find her dead. He said she looked so peaceful with a smile on her face. Her death proved to be a worry to him, since most of their important papers were not up to date to effectively transfer insurance and property. Many papers needed proof of relationship and signature . . .

One day while reading the paper in his favorite chair, Sylvia came through the house from the back door. She stood in front of him and was talking to him. He watched her dumbfounded but did not understand a word she was saying. He was very anxious over this visit and came to see me, since I am interested in ghosts and had a few experiences. He wanted me to reach her. He believed she was giving him information on the missing papers and I could find out. I explained to him that I never try to reach deceased persons, they come to me with messages for loved ones.

About three weeks later, she appeared to him again, exactly as before. But this time she took him by the hand and led him into the bedroom. He followed without effort, then stood in front of the dresser knowing she wanted him to open it, which he did. He started to unfold the night clothing in it and out fell a large envelope of the papers he was looking for. He said he almost fainted from the excitement.

In a few days she made an appearance to me. I was looking out the window, and there before me appeared a beautiful park, actually a park similar to one she had across the street of one of her homes on the north side of Chicago. I saw her sitting on a white bench under a huge shade tree. I walked over and sat with her. We talked pleasantly as any time in her life. Then she stood up and looked behind her. I saw the two roads she did and I asked where she was going. She only said, 'I'll take this one' and left me as if she knew where she had to go. I only wondered.

A few weeks later she appeared again and pulled on my shirt while I was working in the kitchen. Surprised to see her, I said, 'Hi Syl, how are you?' She said, 'Fine, but I came to see Winston' (Mimi's brother) . . . Then she went into the bedroom and after a few seconds looked at me with a smile and left. She did this twice more in the next few weeks. My brother was quite ill, he had had a serious stroke and lost his speech which therapy could not correct. However, these visits amused me and I looked forward to them. I never told my brother about Syl, he would only laugh as he did with all the stories I told him about my visits with ghosts.

Then in February of 1982, my brother died of another stroke . . . Winston was not a peaceful ghost, he refused to accept the fact that he was dead. When he was laid out in the funeral parlor, I awoke in the middle of the night and saw him there floating at the ceiling. He was calling me to help him get out. He was in a frenzy and so was I . . . Two days later at the cemetery, he did the same thing. He appeared very excited and agitated again telling me to take him home. I almost cried, and looked at all the people at the grave, wondering if any of them could see and feel what I did.

It was three days later that he found his way home ... This experience so unnerved me I wondered how to handle it. Remembering Syl and the times she came in to look for him, I simply said, 'I'm sorry Winston, but you are dead now' ... He looked at me in disbelief and I added, 'Sylvia was here looking for you, do you think you could find her?' ... With a big smile on his face he looked out the window at the sky ... I saw him go right through the window to look for Sylvia. He seemed to know just where to look.

Three weeks later they appeared to me with amazing brightness. They were near the ceiling smiling and holding hands. He was saying, 'Look, I found her, I found her,' and she was saying, 'Look, he found me, he found me.' I was just stunned and had to smile at the happy ending to this difficult death. They just retreated backward out of the room to 'over there'—wherever that is.

Remember Mimi's stories of Lady—dead and alive?! She, Sharon and Susan are gifted with the ability to see discarnate entities. Sharon didn't see her great aunt's ghost, but saw other manifestings of her death and presence:

A great aunt of mine was dying in the hospital ... During the night, a living room lamp turned itself on and startled both my husband and myself. He went to the living room with me following close behind. We both stood there looking around, when suddenly the lamp switched itself off. My husband examined the lamp. There seemed to be no defects in the wiring and the lamp worked fine. This lamp turned itself on and off a couple times more just before my great aunt died. It has not done this since that one night.

In another manifestation at the time of death, Freya sent this one:

My mother and my paternal grandmother were very very close. My mother was awakened at two a.m., and saw my grandmother standing at the foot of her bed. She said, 'Gertrude, I came to tell thee goodbye. I am leaving.' Mother wakened my father and told him, 'Mother just died.' The clock chimed two and my father told her it was a dream. In the morning, my uncle phoned. He told my father, 'Mother died this morning at two a.m.'

So many women sent me accounts of ghosts that early on, I had to put in my ads for psychic experiences, "no more ghosts." If I hadn't, there would have been far less written to me about other psychic stroking the python phenomena. But no book of psychic experiences is complete without a haunted house, so here is one from Linda:

It just so happened that my best friend, who was a year older than I, also had an interest in psychic phenomena. When I got to meet her grandmother and great-grandmother, two absolutely wonderful ladies, my friend told me that she grew up in her grandmother's house with her mother, two younger brothers and sister, and as years went by, her grandfather's ghost! She told me they had seen him at the foot of the stairs in the front hallway, and in the master bedroom near the top of the stairs. There was always the 'cold spot' in this room, which is a sort of trademark to every haunted house ...

One time, when my friend was in the master bedroom with her younger sister, it was at night, and my friend felt something cold brush past her, and then they saw the draperies at the nearby window stand straight out when the window was closed. There was a feeling in the room that so terrified the girls they immediately rushed out to tell their mother.

Then, another night my friend had to go into the room again, . . . and she happened to sit in the old, wooden rocking chair that had belonged to her grandfather. She felt a cold chill on her arms and then a feeling as if she was sitting in his lap, and he was giving her a hug. But, she reported, this did not feel like a friendly embrace! She was afraid the 'arms' would crush her and no matter how she tried, for a few moments she could not move. She of course, was frightened out of her wits. Then her sister came in, and she was able to stand, and rushed from the room.

Mimi's technique for dealing with Winston might have stood in good stead here. Remember free choice and free will, and refuse any entity not wanted. If this was a trapped entity, perhaps he only needed to be informed of his death, and his spirit guides invoked to help him move on.

Pam from Idaho writes about a rebirthing experience, and verifies with it some of Helen Wambach's work:

While doing some things with a friend who's a clinical therapist, we tried a rebirthing session for me. I was not conscious, but able to tell him many things going on inside and outside of my mother while in the process of my imminent birth. The several odd notes about this is that I was blinded by three white lights while still in my mother, that I did not tell my mother about the rebirthing session, and my mother never spoke about my birth, except that it was difficult and we were both very sick. This fall (October, 1986), she related to my sister about having an out of body experience during the birth (something she's never talked about before), along with several other similarities with the rebirthing session, including the three blinding lights. My sister then related the highlights to mom about the session I'd had.

In one final commentary, Kathleen writes about herself as a "walk-in," a woman who chose to die, giving her body to another entity while still on the earth plane. Kathy "died," and Zuleika entered her body and took over her life. The exchange was done entirely by free choice. In her story, she speaks of herself as Zuleika, and Kathy as someone gone.

Kathy began to have the 'feeling' that she would not live past thirty-eight years. As the time came closer, she began to talk to her family a bit about out-of-body experience, death survival and other things she had either experienced or had come to believe in. This was an attempt to prepare the family. You can imagine their reaction. She also began to speak of 'something she had to do, but could still back out of if she wanted to' . . . Although she never brought this knowledge to a completely conscious level, she talked of leaving often . . .

I will try to keep the events of the next few weeks in order, and try for a minimum of confusion . . . Around 7:00 p.m. (July 9, 1984), Kathy, having laid down for a nap before the night shift she worked, said, 'Take me, this time I'm not scared.' (The exchange had been attempted one time before, but when she felt herself leave the body she became scared and the exchange was postponed until she was ready). Kathy turned on her side into her usual sleep position. Then she felt someone take her arm and lift her out of her body. This time there was no fear, only a feeling of peace and warmth. The last memory I maintain is behind what felt to be about two feet above her body. Then suddenly the alarm was going off and I was awakening.

I stretched and thought how good it felt to stretch. Then I got up and went to the bathroom and found I was very clumsy. But finally I left home for work, and had trouble driving the car. I could not judge distance nor steer properly. But I made the one-half mile drive with no major problems. I just fussed at myself (still thinking of myself as Kathy) for the klutz act. At work I found that I could not remember, without really thinking about it, even the most routine of chores. The next day, on a Tuesday, I started to fix my dinner and found the thought of flesh foods nauseating me. I had always been a meat lover. Over the next two days, until my nine-day vacation started, I became more and more upset over small things I could not understand.

She was drawn to a metaphysical meeting, dis-covered it to be about walk-ins, and finding others, learned some of the things Kathy/ Zuleika needed to know. At the meeting Garyn channeled Dover, an entity that answered her questions for over two hours. Kathy/Zuleika began to believe that she was a walk-in. A few days later, when a friend came to call, he reported seeing both entities:

Finally he asked, 'Are you doing this to me?'
'Doing what?'
'Making me see things.'
'What things?'
'I see two of you.'
'Two of me?'

'Yes, but you're not the same, your expression and eyes are different. You're there (pointing) and Kathy is beside you.'

I realized that the wave-like feeling I was experiencing must be from this. But still I couldn't quite believe him. I asked if he was telling the truth. He assured me that he was. After awhile, he said, 'She's going away,' and I felt the wave-like motion slow and stop. Then he told me she was gone.

There was a period of readjustment and past life memories.

After several months I remembered the exchange when I went for hypnosis. At the time of the exchange there were about a dozen 'helpers.' We were sur-rounding the bed, with me at the foot. When Kathy was outside her body, I was told to enter and her silver cord was disconnected and mine connected. The faces of the helpers were all very bright, and seemed to light the entire room. When I was in the body, I heard someone say, 'It's 7:12.'

Kathy had been unhappy in her life, and had asked for the exchange. Are there more versions of death that women generally know about? I hesitated to include this experience, but it opens too many doors to refuse. Emphasis is given that the exchange was made with the full consent of both Be-ings, and with spirit help and approval.

There is no how-to for this chapter on death and beyond, except to suggest that women live their lives fully and well, and grow in their awareness of the limitless possibilities of matriarchal/clairvoyant reality. Women only begin at their skins, and much more of the life force is unseen than is seen. A woman who has read this book has information to start from, beginning understandings of her psychic stroking the python power. She re-cognizes women's power as creation Goddesses, creators of their lives and true realities. She re-gains Goddess and Goddess within for herself.

Women who have contributed to this book—and women who haven't—have stories to tell, things to teach the rest of us. Women are all psychic and they are learning about it. May their stories told and written open the psychic world, the Goddess' richness of women's Be-ing, for the good of all.

# FOOTNOTES

1. Iris Belhayes, *Spirit Guides: We Are Not Alone,* (San Diego, ACS Publishing, Inc., 1985), p. 1.

2. Quoted by R. DeWitt Miller, "This Thing Called Dying—And Sudden Death," in David C. Knight, *The ESP Reader,* p. 477-778.

3. *Ibid.,* p. 477.

4. Eileen Garrett, "My Life As A Search for the Meaning of Mediumship," in David C. Knight, *The ESP Reader,* p. 202-203.

5. R. DeWitt Miller, "This Thing Called Dying—And Sudden Death," in *The ESP Reader,* p. 476.

6. *Ibid.*

7. *Ibid.,* p. 486-487.

8. *Ibid.,* p. 488.

9. Raymond A. Moody, Jr., MD, *Life After Life,* (New York, Bantam Books, 1975), p. 21-23.

10. *Ibid.,* p. 74.

11. R. DeWitt Miller, "This Thing Called Dying—And Sudden Death," in David C. Knight, *The ESP Reader,* p. 482-483.

12. Robert Crookall, *Casebook of Astral Projection, 546-746,* pp. 33.

13. Frederick Lenz, Ph.D., *Lifetimes: True Accounts of Reincarnation,* (New York, Fawcett Crest Books, 1979), p. 106 ff. Material on the four worlds is from Lenz.

14. Robert Crookall, *Casebook of Astral Projection, 545-746,* p. 123.

15. Frederick Lenz, *Lifetimes: True Accounts of Reincarnation,* p. 112.

16. *Ibid.,* p. 115-116.

17. *Ibid.,* p. 117-118.

18. Iris Belhayes, *Spirit Guides: We Are Not Alone,* p. 115.

19. *Ibid.,* p. 116-120.

20. Helen Wambach, *Life Before Life,* (New York, Bantam Books, 1979). Material on rebirth is from her study.

21. *Ibid.,* p. 41-42.

22. *Ibid.,* p. 77-78.

23. *Ibid.*, p. 51.

24. *Ibid.*, p. 62-63

25. *Ibid.*, p. 64 and 68.

26. *Ibid.*, p. 77-78.

27. *Ibid.*, p. 84, 88-91.

28. *Ibid.*, p. 93.

29. Jane Roberts, *The Seth Material*, p. 155.

30. Helen Wambach, *Life Before Life*, p. 99-101.

31. *Ibid.*, p. 123.

32. *Ibid.*, p. 124-127.

# Endplate

Awareness becomes concerned with stimuli that occur in a nonsensory field. I have an inner feeling of participating in a very unified way with what I observe—by which I mean that I have no sense of any subjective-objective dualism, no sense of I and any other, but a close association with, an immersion in, the phenomena. The "phenomena" are therefore not phenomenal while they are in process; it is only after the event that the conscious mind, seeking to understand the experience in its own analytical way, divides up the unity which, after all, is the nature of the supersensory event.

—*Eileen Garrett**

*Eileen Garret, in Lawrence LeShan, *The Medium, the Mystic, and the Physicist*, p. 81.

# BOOKS BY THE CROSSING PRESS

OTHER BOOKS BY DIANE STEIN

## All Women Are Healers: A Comprehensive Guide to Natural Healing

Stein's bestselling book on natural healing for women teaches women to take control of their bodies and lives and offers a wealth of information on various healing methods including Reiki, Reflexology, Polarity Balancing, and Homeopathy.

$14.95 • Paper • ISBN 0-89594-409-X

## Casting the Circle: A Women's Book of Ritual

A comprehensive guide including twenty-three full ritual outlines for the waxing, full and waning moons, the eight Sabbats, and rites of passage.

$14.95 • Paper • ISBN 0-89594-411-1

## Essential Reiki: A Complete Guide to an Ancient Healing Art

This bestseller includes the history of Reiki, hand positions, giving treatments, and the initiations. While no book can replace directly received attunements, Essential Reiki provides everything else that the practitioner and teacher of this system needs, including all three degrees of Reiki, most of it in print for the first time.

$18.95 • Paper • ISBN 0-89594-736-6

## The Goddess Celebrates: An Anthology of Women's Rituals

"... this collection will stimulate discussion among readers interested in women's spirituality."—Booklist

$14.95 • Paper • ISBN 0-89594-460-X

## Healing with Flower and Gemstone Essences

Instructions for choosing and using flowers and gems are combined with descriptions of their effect on emotional balance. Includes instructions for making flower essences and for matching essences to hara line chakras for maximum benefit.

$14.95 • Paper • ISBN 0-89594-856-7

## Healing with Gemstones and Crystals

More than 200 gemstones and their healing properties are listed. Details on how to choose and use the Earth's precious gems are supplemented by explanations of the significance of this type of healing.

$14.95 • Paper • ISBN 0-89594-831-1

## The Holistic Puppy: How to Have a Happy, Healthy Dog

Diane Stein shares her experience and gives useful information about choosing a dog and bringing it home, behavior training, handling and grooming, nutrition, and solving the dog's emotional problems.

$14.95 • Paper • ISBN 0-89594-946-6

# BOOKS BY THE CROSSING PRESS

### Natural Healing for Dogs and Cats

This invaluable resource tells how to use nutrition, minerals, massage, herbs, homeopathy, acupuncture, acupressure, flower essences, and psychic healing for optimal health.

$16.95 • Paper • ISBN 0-89594-614-9

### The Natural Remedy Book for Dogs & Cats

"An informative guide to the use of nutrition, vitamins, massage, herbs, and homeopathy to support your pet's health and vitality. Sure to be effective in reducing veterinary costs, while enhancing your relationship with your furry loved one."—NAPRA Trade Journal

$16.95 • Paper • ISBN 0-89594-686-6

### The Natural Remedy Book for Women

This bestselling, self-help guide to holistic health care includes information on ten different natural healing methods. Remedies from all ten methods are given for fifty common health problems.

$16.95 • Paper • ISBN 0-89594-525-8

### On Grief and Dying: Understanding the Soul's Journey

Weaving together a variety of resources from the Goddess movement, psychic techniques, and the traditions of Buddhism and Greek mythology, Stein leads the reader toward loving acceptance, affirmation and hope.

$15.00 • Hardcover • ISBN 0-89594-830-3

### Prophetic Visions of the Future

We all want to know what will happen to the earth and to those who come after us, our children and our grandchildren. Diane, seeking an answer, has gone to women visionaries and seers: women who channel the future and those who bring it to life in their writings: Sally Miller Gearhart, Sheri Tepper, and Marge Piercy.

$16.95 • Paper • ISBN 1-58091-046-7

### Psychic Healing with Spirit Guides & Angels

A guide to hands-on and psychic healing, this comprehensive book presents a complete program of soul development for self-healing, healing with others, and Earth healing. Advanced skills include healing karma and past lives, soul retrieval, releasing spirit attachments, and understanding and aiding the death process.

$18.95 • Paper • ISBN 0-89594-807-9

### We are the Angels: Healing Your Past, Present, and Future with the Lords of Karma

Stein masterfully presents a detailed understanding of karma and the process of healing karmic patterns. She introduces the Lords of Karma, the supreme karmic record keepers able to grant requests for changed or released karma to those who ask for it.

$16.95 • Paper • ISBN 0-89594-878-8

# BOOKS BY THE CROSSING PRESS

## A Woman's I Ching

A feminist interpretation of the popular ancient text for divining the character of events. Stein's version reclaims the feminine, or yin, content of the ancient work and removes all oppressive language and imagery.

$16.95 • Paper • ISBN 0-89594-857-5

### VIDEOS BY DIANE STEIN

## Diane Stein's Essential Reiki Workshop

Secrets of the Reiki Masters revealed for the first time on video.

$99.50 • 4 video cassettes • ISBN 0-89594-930-X

## The Lords of Karma & Energy Balancing: A Workshop with Diane Stein

We are introduced to The Lords of Karma, the supreme keepers of the Akashic Records, who are able to grant our requests. Diane also presents information on how to clarify and align our energetic selves through energy balancing.

$22.95 • 1 video cassette • ISBN 0-89594-977-6

### RELATED BOOKS BY THE CROSSING PRESS

## Channeling for Everyone: A Safe Step-by-Step Guide to Developing Your Intuition and Psychic Awareness

By Tony Neate

This is a clear, concise guide to developing our subtler levels of consciousness. It provides us with safe, step-by-step exercises to prepare for and begin to practice channeling, allowing wider states of consciousness to become part of our everyday lives.

$12.95 • Paper • ISBN 0-89594-922-9

## Dreams and Visions: Language of the Spirit

By Margaret M. Bowater

Dreams and Visions is an easy-to-follow, practical, and inspirational guide that provides a background to the nature and range of dreams and reveals the power of dream interpretation.

$14.95 • Paper • ISBN 0-89594-966-0

## FutureTelling: A Complete Guide to Divination

By Patricia Telesco

This cross-cultural encyclopedia of divination practices gives over 250 entries, from simple signs and omens of traditional folk magic to complex rituals of oracular consultation.

$16.95 • Paper • ISBN 0-89594-872-9

# BOOKS BY THE CROSSING PRESS

### Ghosts, Spirits and Hauntings
By Patricia Telesco

Ghosts, specters, phantoms, shades, spooks, or wraiths—no matter what the name, Patricia Telesco will help you identify and cope with their presence.

$10.95 • Paper • ISBN 0-89594-871-0

### The Language of Dreams
By Patricia Telesco

Patricia Telesco outlines a creative, interactive approach to understanding the dream symbols of our inner life. Interpretations of more than 800 dream symbols incorporate multi-cultural elements with psychological, religious, folk, and historical meanings.

$16.95 • Paper • ISBN 0-89594-836-2

### Mother Wit: A Guide to Healing and Psychic Development
By Diane Mariechild

"It is a joy to find this material from occult traditions and Eastern religions adapted by her woman-identified consciousness to the needs of women today."-Womanspirit

$14.95 • Paper • ISBN 0-89594-358-1

### Pocket Guide to Visualization
By Helen Graham

Visualization is imagining; producing mental images that come to mind as pictures we can see. These pictures can help you relax, assess and manage stress, improve self-awareness, alleviate disease and manage pain.

$6.95 • Paper • ISBN 0-89594-885-0

### Recurring Dreams: A Journey to Wholeness
By Kathleen Sullivan

Are you troubled by a dream that repeats its message again and again, sometimes over a period of years? What is the dream trying to tell you? Kathleen Sullivan shows you ways to transform your life through exploring your dreams.

$16.95 • Paper • ISBN 0-89594-892-3

### A Wisewoman's Guide to Spells, Rituals and Goddess Lore
By Elizabeth Brooke

A remarkable compendium of magical lore, psychic skills and women's mysteries.

$12.95 • Paper • ISBN 0-89594-779-X

To receive a current catalog from The Crossing Press
please call toll-free, 800-777-1048.
Visit our Web site: **www.crossingpress.com**